Globalization and Transformations of Social Inequality

T0348066

Routledge Advances in Sociology

For a full list of titles in this series, please visit www.routledge.com

Globalization and Transformations of Social Inequality

Edited by
Ulrike Schuerkens

Routledge
Taylor & Francis Group
New York   London

First published 2010
by Routledge
711 Third Avenue, New York, NY 10017

Simultaneously published in the UK
by Routledge
2 Park Square, Milton Park, Abingdon, Oxon OX14 4RN

Routledge is an imprint of the Taylor & Francis Group, an informa business

First issued in paperback 2012

Typeset in Sabon by IBT Global.

Library of Congress Cataloging-in-Publication Data

Globalization and transformations of social inequality / edited by Ulrike Schuerkens.
— 1st ed.
  p. cm. — (Routledge advances in sociology ; 53)
  Includes bibliographical references and index.
  1. Globalization—Social aspects—Case studies. 2. Equality—Case studies.
I. Schuerkens, Ulrike.
  HN18.3.G556 2010
  305—dc22
  2009052035

ISBN13: 978-0-415-87482-3 (hbk)
ISBN13: 978-0-203-84925-5 (ebk)
ISBN13: 978-0-415-81064-7 (pbk)

Contents

PART I
Theoretical and Empirical Introduction: Globalization
and Transformations of Social Inequality

PART II
Changing Dimensions of Social Inequality in a Global World

Tables

Figures

Preface

Ulrike Schuerkens

Globalization and Transformations of Social Inequality assembles some of the most interesting contributions to the Research Committee 09 "Social Transformations and Sociology of Development" of the International Sociological Association presented in sessions organized by the editor at the First ISA Forum of Sociology: *Sociological Research and Public Debate*, Barcelona, Spain, in September 2008. Colleagues and PhD students of the editor at the École des Hautes Études en Sciences Sociales, Paris, and at other universities wrote the other articles.

This collection offers analytical and comparative insights at the world level, with regard to current social inequality, as well as an assessment of the overall social globalization phenomenon in the global world. The introductory chapter discusses the notion of *social inequality*—a notion, which proves to be important in the contemporary global context, where economic, social, and cultural inequalities are widespread. This chapter also reviews from a critical comparative perspective how different regions have dealt with social inequality and whether globalization has played a role in terms of the distinction of different world regions between the *old* bi-polar world order and the *new* center, semi-periphery, and periphery status. This book seeks to assess the overall situation in the world, looking at the world as a socio-economic system where some countries act as winners, others as losers, and some as both winners and losers of socio-economic globalization. The authors also tentatively offer some predictions for future developments of their research topic.

The overall aim of the book is to provide a comprehensive overview of transformations of social inequality in a global world. It is worth noting that while this collection of articles is comprehensive in its coverage of political practices regarding inequality and in its geographical coverage (all major world regions are included), it is also theoretically informed. Hence, additional theoretical or empirical research questions are raised by single authors for further study but are not discussed in the single chapters mainly for reasons of space. The volume aims to become a specialized monograph developing new advances in the field of globalization studies. We hope that the book will help academic readers, policy-makers, and the larger public to better understand current transformations of social inequality and social processes affecting all countries in the world.

The studies in this book refer to socio-cultural anthropology and sociology of inequality. They contribute to an understanding of social processes that are most often lived without grasping their real meanings. The book challenges localized cultural anthropology and shows that some current global processes have caused similarities across the world. What we can find is a world that has changed some of its local socio-political practices on a global scale. The studies show that the neo-liberal credo of the last 30 years had repercussions all over the world and not only in the *core* Western countries. Similarities and differences of this intertwining of local and global elements are shown. It is argued that a sort of *global modernity* is in the making even if differences based on local socio-cultural life-worlds continue to exist.

My special thanks for the support of this publication go to Nina Bandelj, the current co-chair of RC 09 "Social Transformations and Sociology of Development," whose sympathetic support and assistance during the preparation of the book contributed to a great extent to its successful completion, and to three anonymous reviewers, who helped with their comments to clarify the argument.

Part I

Theoretical and Empirical Introduction

Globalization and Transformations of Social Inequality

1 Introduction

Theoretical and Empirical Introduction: Globalization and Transformations of Social Inequality

Ulrike Schuerkens

During the past several years, a number of publications have discussed the link between globalization and inequality. According to these scholars, there seems to be a relative consensus that within-nation inequality has increased almost everywhere in the last 20 years. According to Milanovic and Dollar international inequality has decreased since the end of the 1970s if one includes China and India (Held and Kaya 2007: 5–6). If one excludes China and India, the tendency is that international income inequality has increased, because of the fact that the high impact of China and India with more than one fifth of the world population can change this relation. Nevertheless, global income inequality between nations is very high today according to the Gini index: around 62 to 66 (Held and Kaya 2007: 5). The gap between the richest and the poorest has been very high since the 1980s. According to Held and Kaya (6): "the world Gini coefficient is at a level (. . .) that now exceeds all but two (Namibia and Lesotho) of the most unequal countries by several points." Such a high-income Gini within nations should mean for individual countries that governments would find it too destabilizing, as populations may protest. Yet, on an international level, there are rarely social movements to be expected. Instead, on the top level, elites react currently to this high Gini by trying to change global governance in international institutions (e.g., Doha Development Round or the G20), and on the bottom level, political groups influenced by fundamentalist movements attack tourists, expatriates, and symbols of globalization.

In addition, wage inequality has increased in the global era so that from 1981, at the beginning of neo-liberal globalization, we can find that inequality within countries rose "as a global pattern" (Galbraith 2008). As a result, in some countries, public policy tackled the distribution of income and wealth so that extreme poverty could sometimes be removed. Wade (2007) mentions one of the suggested reasons for this policy: "Inequality not only spurs social troubles but it is also likely to be bad for the economy" (7). If one considers that the poor actually suffer from health problems, lack of education, lack of participation in decision-making, in short, they lack life-chances, it may thus be appropriate to consider policies at global, national, and local levels and no longer to defend the neo-liberal credo that the market alone should determine income and wealth. This book develops these theoretical and empirical links by presenting research on transformations of social inequality in a global era and by questioning the supposed positive influence of the market on social inequality.

The different chapters tackle topics that contribute to transformations of social inequality in our global world. They show that there are multiple possibilities actually used by politicians, and linked to important social and economic structures of the global era that contribute to these changes. Most of the chapters demonstrate that individual countries, political elites, and civil society possess instruments and can use policies to criticize and change social inequalities that may be judged unjustified and that disadvantage particular groups. The focus on these instruments influencing inequality, such as labor unions, social policy measures, migrants' remittances, urban governance, etc. permits us to underline that there are numerous mechanisms to change unequal situations and that concrete outcomes depend on power relations in a particular state and are thus eminently political decisions. The global financial crisis of 2008–09 made obvious the importance and necessity of political actors in the post-neo-liberal economy. Even banks and enterprises that some months ago would have excluded political interventions in what they called the *free market* have defended the position that the market alone cannot—and perhaps never could—regulate in a satisfying manner groups and their divergent interests. The state and political elites accountable to their electorates have thus set in motion activities as responsible actors that defend the interests of the citizens of their country. In this sense, this crisis seems to be an opportunity for the future of our global world insofar as new–old actors have reappeared who try to readjust their respective tasks and their contributions to the creative becoming of our global world.

In fact, there are two theoretical approaches to inequality. *Individualists* favor rational choice theory and empirical research on inequality and are linked to a measurement camp consisting in governments and international organizations such as the World Bank and the International Monetary Fund. Politicians can also often be located in this field. Most of the literature on poverty was for the last 30 years characterized by this approach that changed only some ten years ago to include other, more qualitative, poverty indicators.

On the other side, sociologists, political economists, and some social anthropologists can be found who favor a structural approach. Often, their findings are supported by non-governmental organizations, civil society, trade unions, and left political parties. These *structuralists* argue that one should not only look for obvious empirical findings on inequality, but research should focus on social structures that trigger unequal relations. Thus, measurements *and* dynamic societal fields that distribute life-chances in an unequal manner are to be looked at. Structuralists underline that poverty results from an unfair distribution of resources and not only from a lack of resources. According to them, inequality can be found in the fields of class, gender, race, ethnicity, caste, etc. This approach has focused on socioeconomic processes that have maintained and reproduced the particular structural aspects of inequality.

In order to give some figures, the United Nations Development Program (2005: 55) assessed data from 73 countries and "estimated that 53 countries (containing 80 percent of the world's population) experienced rising inequality. A narrowing of inequality occurred in only nine countries (containing 4 percent of the world's population)" (3). The UNDP had already found in 2003 (282–285) that "the world's three most egalitarian countries (with scores under 25 [Gini, US]) are Japan, Denmark, and Hungary. The most unequal (with scores over 60) are Brazil, Nicaragua, Botswana, Swaziland, Central African Republic, and Sierra Leone. In egalitarian Japan, the poorest 20 percent of the population receive 10.6 percent of income, while the richest 20 percent receive 35.7 percent. This contrasts with Brazil and Botswana where the poorest 20 percent receive just over two percent and the richest 20 percent account for over 70 percent of income (UNDP 2005: 56)." (3)

Regarding absolute poverty, one can find that the number of people living on less than $1 a day in the world declined since 1980 by 375 million people (Dollar 2007: 74). According to Chen and Ravallion (2004), this ratio diminished from 40.4 percent of the population in developing countries in 1981, to 21.1 percent in 2001. The authors continue: "(T)he decline in $2 a day poverty incidence was not as great, from 66.7 percent to 52.9 percent, over the same period" (81). Indeed, about half of the world's population has to make a living with less than US$ 2 a day. In Sub-Saharan Africa, the number of the very poor increased from 164 million to 316 million (about 47 percent of the population) (Dollar 2007: 84). Two thirds of the very poor continue to live in Asia. Nevertheless, the ongoing economic growth in this continent may change the picture so that poverty may be increasingly concentrated in the African continent. According to the director of the International Labor Organization, Juan Somavia, the number of people all over the world who gain less than US$ 1 a day, may increase by 40 million due to the current crises; the number of the "working poor" with US$ 2 a day, who were at the end of 2007 about 1.3 billion people, may even increase by 100 million people (*Frankfurter Allgemeine Zeitung*, October 21, 2008). One year later, the vice-president of the World Bank, Yifu Lin announced the number of 1.4 billion people living on less than US$ 1.25 a day (*Figaro*, October 20, 2009). Almost half of the world population—over 3 billion people—lives today (2009) on less than US$ 2.50 a day.[1]

Regarding wealth and according to Neederveen Pieterse (2004: 4): "The richest 20 percent of the world's population accounted for 70 percent of income in 1960. By 1991 this share increased to 85 percent. Meanwhile the bottom 20 percent declined from 2.3 percent to 1.4 percent. The ratio between the richest and poorest increased from 30:1 to 60:1 (Pieterse 2004:

61). By the end of the millennium, the wealthiest 5 percent of the world's population earned 114 times as much as the poorest 5 percent and the top 1 percent earned the equivalent of the bottom 57 percent (UNDP 2003: 39). The 200 largest US fortunes exceeded the income of 43 percent of the world's population, or the entire wealth of over a billion Chinese." This unequal distribution of wealth may generate an understanding that there is something wrong with the neo-liberal agreement on the economy. The idea of this book stems from these findings.

To introduce an understanding of *longue durée* (Braudel) social inequality, some short remarks on the historical becoming of global social inequality may be of interest. According to Milanovic, who studied long-run historical income statistics, international inequality was rising between 1820 and 1870 (Milanovic 2007: 29). Inequality was also on the rise from 1870 to 1913, although the inter-war period from 1913 to 1938 saw a decline, perhaps stabilization. From 1938 to 1952, inequality rose again. The reason for this was that some rich countries (US, Australia, Argentina, and New Zealand) improved their particular development but most of the rest lost out. Inequality among nations measured by the Gini remained from 1952 to 1978 at the same level. This period corresponded for the richer countries to the Golden Age of economic improvement and for the less developed countries to policies of import substitution and a strong role of the state. Starting around the end of the 1970s, neo-liberal policy led to a sharp increase of inequality. The Thatcher and Reagan rules in Great Britain and the US were at the origin of this trend that has continued ever since, including the recent financial crisis.

Considering current regional inequality, one finds China and India pulled ahead, South America declined, and Africa's situation still worsened. It seems even that we can begin to speak of an "Africanization of poverty," as Milanovic wrote (2007: 33). Another interesting figure is that the share of the total global income received by the 5 percent (10 percent) of the wealthiest people in the world represents 33 percent (50 percent); for the bottom 5 percent (10 percent), this share means 0.2 percent (0.7 percent) of the global income received by the poorest people in the world (Milanovic 2007: 39). These figures show the very unequal distribution of global income in our world currently.

Another possibility to measure inequality is to evoke the position of people from different countries in the global income distribution. According to Milanovic, "the poorest Frenchmen are actually richer than 72 percent of people in the world" (41). And he continues: "Even the richest 5 percent of people in rural India are poorer than the poorest 5 percent of people in France" (41). In policy terms, transfers from the rich countries to the poor countries should thus reach the poor if one considers the relative importance of this link.

The question if global inequality matters has been widely discussed. There are commentators who put forward that the idea is too abstract and that there is no world government interested in a decline of inequality. Yet, if one considers that globalization increases people's knowledge of each other and lets them discover income differences, e.g., in television entertainment and during holidays, one can argue that global inequality matters. As September 11th has shown, poverty and inequality elsewhere affect people in the North more than some decades ago. With high global inequality levels, the richer world may choose the solution of becoming a fortress and closing its borders to the poor. But as European and US migration policies have shown, this is almost impossible in the face of illegal migrants arriving at the seaside of the Mediterranean countries or at the deserts of Mexico. Thus, global financial transfers, and not only remittances sent by migrants, may be necessary in order to create a global safety net similar to that built on a national level by Western European countries confronted with internal socio-economic inequality at the beginning of the twentieth century. Yet, the financial crisis of the second half of 2008 and the first half of 2009 may change the development policy of the geographic North and the richer countries as the new programs of high financial assistance to the banks decided by Western governments in order to limit the negative outcomes of the crisis on financial institutions and the economy may mean that global assistance programs from the North to the South will be reduced.

POLICY AND INEQUALITY

Liberals still consider inequality as a necessary condition in an economy based on a market where competitiveness, innovation, and effort seem to depend on income inequality. According to them, public policy should not worry insofar as income inequality seems to be a result of processes linked to the market. As long as the liberal order isn't threatened by popular movements, inequality doesn't matter according to liberals. But this argument can be challenged as the following findings demonstrate.

The consequences of income inequality on other variables outlined by extensive research are clear. According to Wade (2007: 115), "higher income inequality within countries goes with: (1) higher poverty (. . .); (2) higher unemployment; (3) higher crime; (4) lower average health; (5) weaker property rights; (6) more skewed access to public services (. . .); and (7) slower transitions to democratic regimes, and more fragile democracies."

According to this scholar, the possible impact of "inequality at the national level supports the normative conclusion that income inequality above moderate levels should be reduced via public policy" (118). What is interesting here is that Wade suggests that "economic growth during the 1990s—and presumably the 1980s as well—has benefited mainly two categories of people: those in the upper half of the income distribution of the high-income states, and those who have made it into the swelling ranks of China's middle class" (124). According to Wade, those who are responsible for the perpetuation of the neo-liberal economic model belong to the upper-strata groups who live in the high-income states. Yet, a change has recently been introduced insofar as Northern governments consider that state actions in the economy are necessary in order to avoid financial crashes. For the time being, it is still too early to have an idea about the outcomes of these policies on inequality. There are voices in the current crisis who think that inequality may even sharpen on a global level and inside nations as people lose jobs and incomes. The authors of the different chapters will discuss possible and probable effects of these crises on the particular phenomena they study.

In the face of the existing global inequality structure, one has to ask the following question: What is the acceptable degree of inequality? According to Wade, it "should be one which gives sufficient income incentive to take sufficient risk to generate sufficient economic growth to provide sufficient opportunities for the poorer to become less poor. But not so much difference in income outcomes that the rich can translate their income differential into a political oligarchy which sets rules that continuously fortify these differentials and keeps social mobility at low levels" (126). But it is obvious that these redistributive priorities suggested by Wade are not easily brought onto the political agenda and that there are some difficulties in fixing the actual thresholds in societies worldwide.

If one argues about inequality in political terms, one should also mention the view of the Commission for Africa (2005: 7) that "described the contrast between the world's wealthy and the conditions of the poor in Africa as 'the greatest scandal of our age'" (Greig *et al.* 2007: 1). The arguments of this edited collection are similar to Amartya Sen's research underlining that development should envision individual human advancement rather than national economic development. For Sen, development concerns people who are able to raise their *capabilities* so that they achieve a functioning they value (1999). According to him, unequal social relations contribute to the marginalization of the poor and their social and political subordination. More powerful actors often block their advancement, people who favor their own privileged children so that the poor can never compete with them as neo-liberal economists try to promise us.

The author of these lines agrees with Sen that there is a huge difference between poverty as a lack of resources for the poorest, and poverty as the result of unequal social relations. If policy tries to change these relations with redistributive measures, the latter would mean a more equal society for all. The authors of the chapters in the third part of the book show which sort of actions governments and civil societies have implemented in different societies in order to redistribute economic resources and social and political power to poorer people. It becomes obvious that the discussed changes have been implemented at local, national, and international levels in order to reduce poverty and to promote social justice in our interconnected world. People have learned to use their agency and one cannot continue to speak only of the influential structural constraints of globalization.

The Millennium Development Goals (MDGs) illustrate that ignoring the fate of the poor is not morally acceptable. As the very unequal distribution of wealth in the world lets us presume, it is difficult to believe that humanity does not possess the means necessary to challenge global inequality. Ramonet (2004: 127) gives an interesting argument in this sense: meeting the basic annual needs of the poorest in the world corresponds to the costs of Europe's consumption of perfume! Moreover, the recent financial crisis has been accompanied by voices that have underlined that the amount of the US$ 750 billion program in the US would be sufficient to reach the Millennium Development Goal aimed at eradicating extreme poverty in the world by 2015.

INSTITUTIONS OF INTERNATIONAL GOVERNANCE

The current international system based on democracy and the market needs effective institutions that create opportunities for the poor, improve their conditions, and protect them against the negative outcomes of globalization in an interdependent world. This would mean that states cooperate more and better and develop mechanisms for collaboration on national policy topics. The multilateral institutions, such as the United Nations system, could then improve their governance structure as well, as recent discussions on challenging issues have already shown (Doha Round, G20, and the IMF). International governance will necessarily play an important role in determining whether globalization will benefit people and nations or not. Global governance may challenge new democracies, fragile states, and institutions with feeble civil societies and their smaller possibilities for citizen participation and interest expression. But it cannot be assumed that globalization is neutral: it is a political phenomenon as the empirical outcomes of inequality situations described in this volume show and only efficient political measures will assure that globalization is at the service of the peoples of the world. Contemporary religious fundamentalism in Asia and North Africa draws on the support of the losers of globalization, on those who have been excluded from the benefits of globalization. Strikes, bombs, and attacks against symbols of globalization show that life has become more insecure for many, so that there may be very few alternatives to some of the political measures on social inequality outlined in this book.

The different chapters show that quite a lot of instruments exist at the level of states or regions but that international instruments are still at their beginning. On a global level, instruments to decrease the high international income Gini coefficient are lacking if one excludes, on the one side, migrants' remittances and their impact on the development of poorer countries and, on the other, the increasing number of informal jobs in developing countries and part-time jobs in the developed world, both linked to precarious life-chances in the global post-neo-liberal economy. Transfer measures concerning wealth are existent in most countries via taxes; in others, such as the US, wealthy people may contribute to philanthropic activities by the use of foundations or directly. International governance structures in the International Monetary Fund and the World Bank are much biased and influenced by the powerful countries of the world, such as the G8. The recent financial crisis that exposed the interconnectedness of the world has triggered another understanding of necessary international governance structures in which countries such as China, South Korea, South Africa, and Brazil are asked to contribute to international measures destined for financial institutions, a participation that shows some consideration for their economic and financial power in a world that no longer allows the West to exclude them from the construction of global policies initiated by the powerful nations of the world.

The recent financial crisis has shown that the state and political elites accountable to their electorates have started again to act as responsible actors that defend the interests of the citizens of their countries or their wider political union, such as the EU. The meaning of political actions has changed during the financial crisis of Fall 2008: social phenomena, such as inequality, that were to be regulated by the market, according to the understanding of parts of global elites, have become again elements that political actors are charged to consider in policy programs. Even if the outcomes on social inequality of the financial losses at stock exchanges are such that the richer groups have lost huge amounts and parts of the poorer groups struggle to survive after the loss of houses or jobs, one might be optimistic insofar as political actors begin to re-define financial activities. This means that (1) the high amount of salaries of top executives in banks and enterprises is considered to be a problem, and (2) the ethical responsibility of bank managers in the credit market is challenged, insofar as credit policies are defined only by possible gains rather than including the particular financial situation of individual human beings, so that huge losses are avoided, such as those sustained by poor and middle class families in the US who bought houses under credit conditions that they were incapable of honoring. The public discussion of these topics in 2009 has shown that global elites may still be inclined to decide in their own favor, but political groups defending middle classes and poorer groups have started to influence this debate and have begun to triumph with electoral successes (e.g., Japan and Greece).

SOME TOPICS ADDRESSED IN THIS VOLUME

In this part of the introduction, several topics are discussed that are not always tackled in the different chapters of the book but that need to be included in a volume studying globalization and transformations of social inequality.

Globalization—especially in its non-economic appearance—became an object of anthropological and sociological fascination when market accomplishment came to dominate socio-economic thought during the 1980s and 1990s. As Anna Tsing comments, "globalism is multi(-)referential: part corporate hype and capitalist regulatory agenda; part cultural excitement, part social commentary and protest" (2000: 322). Often, social anthropologists discussing globalization have been able to show how subaltern groups "creatively resist, appropriat(e), or reinterpret some apparently homogenizing influence imposed from above (e.g., advertising, soap operas, forms of labor discipline, political ideologies, etc." (Graeber 2002: 1223). Social anthropology should thus have much to contribute to the debate about global social inequality that inspires social movements, popular campaigns, and imaginings that are central to an understanding of globalization, social change, and development. By the late twentieth century and the beginning of the twenty-first century, cultural anthropologists and sociologists began to focus more on how their methodological approaches might limit an understanding of globalization (e.g., the chapter on mobilities in this volume). Anthropologists' and sociologists' political roles in states or multilateral organizations have similarly received only cursory attention (but see Davis 1999).

Whether globalization is new or not is the subject of much debate. Deregulated global financial markets, declining transport and communications costs, and increasingly important multilateral institutions triggered major changes during the 1980s and 1990s (McMichael 2000). It is most useful to view the world economy as characterized by a renewed era of globalization since the 1980s (see Schuerkens 2008). This has captivated much scholarly imagination. Economic neo-liberalism as a particular form of globalization was celebrated until the global financial crisis that began in the US in 2007. Today, social anthropologists and sociologists can again help explain the difficulties and shortcomings linked to the once favored neo-liberal economic model. The crisis made clear that there are doubts on the reproduction of this model and the idea that there is something inevitable about it. Current processes and policies in different world regions that challenge the reach of economic neo-liberalism can once again be analyzed and may suggest different results than the sharp economic inequalities that characterize the actual world situation. The political and social processes in different world regions that are described in this volume testify that there are various methods to tackle social inequality. Economic globalization has fueled social movements (more in Latin America than in Africa). The earlier political focus on topics such as race, gender, and identity has broadened to include labor rights, corporate power, and justice. The case studies in this volume show that there are dynamic ongoing processes that challenge globalization by illustrating, more than irrational anti-global protests do, possible developments and alternative scenarios. These struggles to preserve and extend various rights prove that they are part of the broader global justice movement. The chapters on China, Nicaragua, and Argentina show that broader movements against neo-liberal globalization have begun to gain momentum. Social anthropology and sociology can thus embrace new research agendas centered on activist networks and social movements inside socio-economic globalization. The recent global crisis has furthermore shown that interventionist state policies are needed not only in the financial realm but in welfare regimes, too. Some chapters in this volume (on Brazil and China) show that government spending on redistributive programs compensate for market-generated inequalities (Garrett 2003). Other chapters demonstrate that in less wealthy countries (Romania), labor that is less qualified and poorly organized decides to migrate to richer nations, so that the consequences of neo-liberal policies are counterbalanced by the remittances of migrants that influence social inequalities and widespread poverty. The chapters on Nicaragua and China show that alternative development strategies are possible that create larger structural changes to developments that economic globalization may generate. Such findings confirm the existing national differences in economic globalization processes that sometimes are presumed to be inexorably homogenizing. One can no longer speak of the tendency that the cultural tends to differentiation and the economic to homogenization (see, e.g., Schuerkens 2004 and 2008).

New debates about alternatives to the neo-liberal globalization have expanded not only since the beginning of the financial crisis in 2007 but even before, as the chapters on China and Nicaragua demonstrate. Voices defending globalization, such as Jagdish Bhagwati (2004), who has underlined that globalization needs suitable governance and institutional reforms, have been reappearing in the realm of the financial crisis. The question whether economic globalization improves or undermines labor standards, gender equality, and social inequality in general continues to be passionately debated. New is that the defenders of economic globalization are now forced to accept state interventions and even asked for them in the years 2008 and 2009, so that imaginative new analytical changes have begun to influence the current era of economic post-neo-liberalism.

Wage Gap, Social Mobility, and Wealth Inequality

The wage gap for 27 countries, where data exists, shows that Brazil, China, India, and the US have the highest wage dispersion; the lowest occurred in Belgium and the Nordic countries (ILO 2008: 12). Regarding inequality and social mobility, education is one of the factors that permit richer families to maintain their status so that segregation between income groups exists and low-income households are often confined to a given income strata even across different generations (23). As financial globalization triggered worldwide financial crises since the early 1990s, low-income households have been particularly affected by unemployment during or after these crises. Wealth inequality is even higher than income inequality as measured by the global Gini coefficient that stands at 89.2 (44) much higher than the income Gini coefficient. To give some figures of the wealth Gini in some countries (2000): US 80.1, Brazil 78.3, Mexico 74.8, Nigeria 73.5, France 73.0, Germany 67.1, India 66.9, China 55.0, and Japan 54.7 (Davies *et al.* 2008, quoted in ILO 2008: 59).

Labor Institutions and Employment Patterns

Over the past decades, there has been an important decline in unionization caused by rising casual forms of labor, such as informal labor, half-time jobs, and precarious jobs. From the 1990s onwards, the capacity of labor institutions to reduce inequality diminished (ILO 2008: 72), even if their redistributive role continued at a reduced manner with the exception of Latin America, as the chapter on Argentina in this volume shows. Non-standard employment has increased in the majority of countries: in high-income countries, part-time and temporary employment is rising; in Africa, Asia, and Latin America informal employment is more widespread. The remuneration of these jobs is most often less than that of standard jobs. In Latin America and India, informal and casual workers earn on average 45 percent less than regular employees (115). Among women in high-income countries, part-time employment is also widespread. During the last decades, companies needed to respond to rapid changes in face of high competition so that they were reluctant to recruit full-time employees. In 2006, informal employment in Latin America represented over half of total employment (120). In Africa, most of the jobs have been insecure, poorly paid, and lack social security benefits.

Taxes and Social Transfers

Inequality can be addressed by a combination of social services, social transfers, and taxation. Yet, exempt the Nordic countries, redistribution in developed economies has failed to stop the rising income inequality. According to data based on the Luxembourg Income Study, "since the 1980s, the Gini coefficient on final income has risen almost as much as that on market income" (ILO 2008: 136). According to Mahler and Jesuit (2006: 491), transfers contribute to 75 percent of total fiscal distribution in OECD countries, compared to only 25 percent from direct taxes. Later chapters of this volume show the important role that social policy measures play regarding inequality (e.g., China, Brazil, Nicaragua). However, there still exists research desiderata and much more research has to be done on the impact of transfers and taxes in additional countries of the world. As such, these three country studies show that the implanted policy measures are linked to a historical and cultural framework that is very different from that of other countries.

Gender

In most regions of the world, opportunities for women in paid employment have risen, although with important regional variations. Often, this female workforce earns less than its male counterpart, a fact that suggests the existence of discrimination in remuneration. Historically, *female* jobs have been undervalued so that the promotion of gender equality in the world of work still requires policies that understand and address female family responsibilities and women's desire to remain in the labor market. Nevertheless, there are positive outcomes: the last 20 years have seen higher female shares in public offices in countries of the geographic South and North. However, in some regions, women have continued to represent a high share of non-employed persons: in the Middle East, North Africa, and Asia.

Socio-political Transformations and Inequality

Most of the chapters in this volume underline that the economic system (e.g., labor and incomes) creates societal dynamics and contributes to the explanation of societal transformations. The authors share the opinion that there is nothing natural about the development of neo-liberal economies. Instead, the chapters in this book show that political elites together with economic, cultural, and social elites try to shape the becoming and future of our global world. These elites cannot act alone: they have to respond to social, political, economic, and cultural processes that middle classes and poorer groups influence and challenge. Conflicts between groups may thus trigger societal developments that shape the future not only of social inequality but also of the global social, economic, and political system.

I would like to tackle here a further point, i.e., the challenge that cultural anthropologists and sociologists face in putting their knowledge to work. This permits me to re-discuss the larger disciplinary imperative to re-define the role of these disciplines in the public sphere. While analyzing transformation processes, sociologists and cultural anthropologists have the possibility to contribute to political projects implanted by economic, social, political, and cultural elites that may influence the needs of the poor (Escobar 1995 and 1997). Since the mid-1970s, as development agencies became interested in working with poorer groups and addressed cultural and social changes, social anthropologists and sociologists got more opportunities to contribute to development outcomes. United Nations agencies hired social scientists practicing development anthropology and sociology, and attracted individuals who believed they could help to reduce the negative impacts of policies with which they disagreed. This means that these professionals translate and mediate their knowledge in public arenas and that their activities imply moral involvement in critical current topics. Decades ago, this attitude had been advocated by Boas and Mead, and in the 1990s by Michael Horowitz (1994), Gow (2002), Bennett (1996), or the sociologist Norman Long (2001).

The polarization between theory and applied research that is found in Western academic institutions does not apply to all regions of the world, covered in this volume by researchers who are finalizing their PhD theses or are already established social scientists. These scholars are actively engaged in policy debates on the topic they are studying while respecting the methodological rules of their disciplines. They are concerned with the poor and contribute to an increased visibility of them. This attention should then permit an increased visibility of disciplines such as sociology and socioeconomic and cultural anthropology in the political debate. These scholars' visions constitute systems of power and control but also means of transforming the conditions under which individuals live (Escobar 1995: 155–156). The different chapters of the book uncover development practices that display wide variations regarding inequality in a neo-liberal and post-neo-liberal economy. The authors testify for complex realities that arise from both center and margin, from global, transnational, and local processes. They are not blind to the ambiguities of their own research on power and inequality. Doing so should improve the effectiveness of their message that advocates for the poor in situations of inequality. Insofar they are articulating a powerful message for sociology and cultural anthropology as a whole (see Escobar 1997: 498).

One may wonder how aware these scholars are of the consequences of their research on the groups or situations they study. Investigations on social transformations can challenge the inequalities of the current world order, which means, at the beginning of the twenty-first century and after the financial crisis, of post-neo-liberal globalization. The world's *historical* and not *natural* character incites these cultural anthropologists and sociologists to engage with the given order. The authors of this volume explicitly question their relationship to global institutions and critically historicize the present situation. The sociology and cultural anthropology presented in this volume do not celebrate the neo-liberal state and its management of the poor. The authors of the different chapters are scrutinizing discourses and institutional practices that may restrain economic neo-liberalism and social inequality. They are no longer captives of modes of analysis in which power situations are not critically examined. Insofar their knowledge represents power, power to suggest other solutions, to criticize morally unacceptable ways of functioning. These scholars explore "the spaces between what we know and what can be done with that knowledge" (Chambers 1987: 322). They are trained to present empirical complexity. Their knowledge cannot easily be translated into policies and programs; yet, their findings are crucial. Let us hope that this book contributes to diminishing levels of poverty and inequality in the future, a target that the MDGs of the United Nations have already launched some years ago at the beginning of the second millennium.

AN OVERVIEW OF THE DIFFERENT CHAPTERS OF THE BOOK

The case study approach used in this volume is advantageous in that the experience of each country serves as a source of policy recommendations for use in cross-country comparisons. In this part of the introduction, I outline the findings and some outcomes of the chapters that may ask, on the one hand, for further research, and, on the other, for possible political measures on the future alleviation of social inequality in our global world.

In the second part of this book, different chapters tackle problems that are still under-researched in the study of transformations of social inequalities and discuss results of case studies on transnational social inequality, financial transfers of migrants, benchmarking at universities, and women and globalization. In the third part, several chapters discuss current policy measures in different countries and regions of the world that may influence or have already influenced patterns of global social inequality in various and challenging ways. The fourth part presents case studies in different regions on the world that discuss the link of globalization and social inequality for the last 30 years.

The book begins with empirical studies on transformations of social inequality in the era of globalization. The first chapter argues in favor of an extension of sociological approaches on social inequality insofar as spatial positions and mobilities are increasingly important aspects of social inequalities. The findings of K. Manderscheid suggest "significant interconnections of the ability to move, the location of residence, and social positions." Similar to researchers working in the field of transnational studies, the author claims "that the national-territorial framing of inequalities is no longer adequate." Mainstream class analysis needs, according to her, an extension in order to include physically and virtually mobile actors and their power to move. Manderscheid underlines the findings of recent research that "there seems to be an increasing polarization between space-autonomous global elites, social groups forced to move (from migrants and refugees to the corporate and academic middle class members), and place bound, cut off, and marginalized social groups." She argues that "(t)he mobilities turn contains a critique of sociology having overly focused upon ongoing geographically propinquitous communities based on more or less face-to-face interactions and co-presence." As the recent rise of transnational research has shown, there is a growing interdependence of social actors across national boundaries so that theoretical approaches and empirical studies based on the nation-state are increasingly challenged. When one considers that in late modernity commuters form the majority of the labor force and that, for instance, in Germany, 54 percent of the active population are either mobile or have got a mobile partner (Ruppenthal and Lück 2009: 2), the influence of mobilities on financial situations becomes obvious. In fact, among mobile people, 70 percent think that their mobility influences positively their careers or their possible salaries (4).

The second chapter in the second part focuses on transnational migrations and their link to national inequality in the country of origin, Romania. The authors find that "(h)igh unemployment ratios and lack of employment opportunities determined significant flows of external migration." Romanians "choose to move to more developed countries in order to increase standards of living for them and their families." These migrants send remittances to their families at home in order to alleviate poverty or to invest in education, real estate, or business. The authors base their study on the 2007 national household survey. As in other countries and regions, remittances have become a very important external financial source added to foreign direct investments. So far, research on the link between remittances and inequality had not yielded clear answers. Remittances seem to have reduced or even increased inequality depending on local historical situations. Jones (1998) has shown that these divergent findings are influenced by different stages of migration. The authors' result in this volume confirms these hypotheses: Romanian migrant households are located among the poorer population strata so that remittances change the level of income distribution in Romania within and between urban and rural areas. The authors find that households and not the single migrant decide to send their migrants abroad aiming at maximizing incomes so that, in the long run, migration leads to a reduction of inequality at the urban–rural scale.

The third chapter of this part written by S. Melo also focuses on transnational phenomena, and, in particular, on "the development of quality education by encouraging cooperation between (EU) Member States." As the EU target is to become "the most competitive and dynamic knowledge-based economy in the world," the education and training systems need to adapt to an improved employment level. Melo uses the technique of benchmarking that helps her "to understand *how* competitors achieve their position and how they develop their products and services." In the EU context, this means making "comparisons of the performance of states in measurable targets (benchmarks) (. . .) based upon a neo-liberal conception of education as a *measurable* key factor." In fact, there are "three strategic objectives for education adopted by the European Council—to improve the quality and effectiveness of education; to facilitate access to education; and to open up European education and training systems to the world." However, Melo warns that "benchmarking information might influence the choice of candidates for a job according to the national territory where they have obtained their academic qualifications." If candidates can compete in monetary terms among educational possibilities in different nation-states, social inequalities would be perpetuated and the outcomes for the European societies would not necessarily be positive. In fact, EU Member States have not got the same conditions to become "best performers." Depending on historical, economical, and political conditions, educational outcomes are different in the EU Member States. Benchmarking stimulates thus competition between them. This technique may then increase social inequalities within the EU region, so that it can become better to acquire qualifications in best performing countries than elsewhere.

In the chapter from Ilse Lenz the conclusions are only understandable if we consider the diminishing gender gaps on different indexes in the world over the last years. *The Global Gender Gap Report 2009* informs us that "the 134 countries covered in the *Report*, representing over 90% of the world's population, have closed over 90% of the gap on health outcomes between women and men and almost 93% of the gap on educational attainment. However, the gap between women and men on economic participation and political empowerment remains wide: only 60% of the economic outcomes gap and only 17% of the political outcomes gap has been closed" (Hausmann *et al.* 2009: 7 and 17). Yet, the report underlines that "there are still significant gaps in the job opportunities for women and in the wages paid to women compared with their male counterparts, and these gaps are even larger in most developing countries" (24). One of the most important statements of the report is that "on the whole the world has made progress on closing gender gaps" (25). Yet, "(n)o country in the world has achieved gender equality. The three highest-ranking countries—Iceland, Finland and Norway—have closed a little over 80% of their gender gaps, while the lowest ranking country—Yemen—has closed only around 46% of its gender gap" (26).

Based on these accomplishments, Ilse Lenz focuses on transformations in gender relations in the newly industrializing countries of East Asia over the last 20 years. Linked to the economic transformations in this region, she finds that women have been introduced in the labor market by market-driven industrialization. Often, their jobs have a semiskilled or irregular character; but women are still burdened with unpaid care work. Lenz's chapter focuses on the differences in the countries of the region according to labor market integration, education, and family changes. Insofar her chapter focuses on aspects that are still under-researched and that lead us a step further than the gender gap debate of the last decades. Her chapter underlines some aspects of "the coming challenges for gender policies and welfare development in NICs." In this sense, the chapter is also interesting for other world regions, as the developments in East Asia may be aspects of the future of other areas, even if Lenz rightly underlines that the gender situation is rather different in East Asia from that in Sub-Saharan Africa with many women working in agriculture or in the informal sector.

Part III of the book addresses social policy initiatives regarding inequality in different countries. The chapter by T. Muhr focuses on the ALBA initiative in Nicaragua that constitutes a powerful counter-hegemonic initiative in Latin America and the Caribbean region. This movement is based on a moral legitimacy that challenges global capitalism. The social dimension of ALBA, quite unknown outside the Hispanophone world, is opposed to the increased social injustice that has characterized global capitalism for the past two decades. ALBA's principal criteria are solidarity, cooperation, and the rejection of capitalist profit making. Instead, direct and participatory democracy is promoted inside the region. The foundation of the Bank of the South is designed to look for financial independence from the international financial institutions and a "broad-based consensus on non-neo-liberal integration among the progressive LAC governments," as Muhr underlines in this chapter. One of the presented initiatives is based on oil shipments that led to, e.g., a considerable diminution of bus fares in Managua. Another major project that is described has concerned the health sector, "in which Cuba and Venezuela committed themselves to undertake ophthalmological operations on six million low-income citizens from the entire region." As Muhr writes, this project permits that "patients are flown to Cuba and Venezuela for operations, free-of-charge surgery and post-surgery treatment [that] include travel, visa, accommodation, food, and medicine, as well as accompaniment by a family member in ten percent of the cases." An interesting factor is that the project is based on "the principle of political, ethnic, and religious neutrality." A further project has led to the declaration of Nicaragua being illiteracy-free in 2009.

ALBA as a "transnational bottom-up construction" has thus got a key influence in combating social inequality and contributes to the creation of a politically integrated region that is characterized by social, economic, and political rules that are absent in large parts of the geographic South. So far, increasing pressure from the US and the European Union (EU) and the global financial crisis of 2007–09 have not slowed down the dynamics of the ALBA initiative in Latin America.

The second chapter in this part presents a classical social policy issue in one of the Latin American countries, which are all characterized by high rates of social inequality. Ivo and Landiado tackle the main features of social policies implemented in Brazil from 1990 to 2007. The neo-liberal approach favored in the country focuses on the principle of compensation that diagnoses material deprivation to be handled by market exchanges and not by generalized solidarity. The social and political measures to be taken are conceived as a concession of the state to needy individuals in case the state can "allocate resources to social programs." The authors of the chapter consider thus "that the social has switched from the field of distribution to that of a management of poverty," or better, from "an understanding of social protection as a generalized national solidarity" to a "selective assistance to individuals." In this sense, individual actors become responsible for overcoming poverty situations.

What is interesting in Brazil is the exclusion from welfare measures of the state of groups that work in the informal sector of the economy. However, in 2006, 57 percent of the economically active population made up this part of the Brazilian society. The national system of social security does not reach all citizens but only the smaller part of society. Therefore, income transfer programs have been introduced (the Family Sponsoring Program and the Program of Continued Assistance) that reduce, for instance, family needs, but that "are not long-term strategies aiming at decreasing inequality." A division of "citizenry into two blocks [can be discovered, US]: those who have rights based on labor corporative organizations protected by the State and those who are clients of contingent and compensatory social policies promoted by the State." However, these latter policies "have promoted income distribution from the waged strata to the poor strata of society" and *not* from the better-off groups, so that Brazil continues to display high rates of social inequality.

The third chapter in the third part tackles the social movements requesting a reduction of social inequality in Argentina. In 1992, the Central of the Argentine Workers (CTA) concluded that "the old type of unionism ended up representing only a minority of workers in the formal sector," according to A. Serdar, so the CTA suggested "a new model of unionism in which workers of the formal and informal sectors, unemployed and retired workers, as well as territorial organizations could come together." In 1996, the CTA was formally established as a labor peak confederation that struggled against the government and its policies. In 1994 and 2000, this movement had organized protest marches to address unemployment and poverty. Furthermore, the movement supported the creation of a larger union—FRENAPO—that defined unemployment as an overexploitation of the labor force and a measure of social discipline. Yet, the election of Nestor Kirchner as president of Argentina in 2003 and the labor-friendly policies of his government demobilized the social protests from the previous period. The integrity of the movement was furthermore divided "by revealing the limits of the alliance of different working class segments." The Argentine economy slowly recovered and unemployment decreased so that the challenge to unite the *working class* disappeared. Finally, as Serdar shows, a traditional union, such as the CGT could re-emerge and the number of union-led conflicts could exceed again other types of differences. The unionized sectors have thus benefited from neo-liberal reforms and were able to use their existing collective bargaining power. Serdar underlines: "Unemployment and the number of people living under the poverty line gradually declined" with the consolidation of Kirchner's political project. This chapter shows thus the dependence of union-led movements on local historical and political conditions.

Part IV of the book illustrates how actual inequality systems in different parts of the world function and underlines some future prospects of social inequality. The part begins with an analyzis of inequality measures in China. As A. Monteil writes: "Thirty years of economic reforms and opening-up resulted in a rise of global-living standards in China, but also in a steady increase of social inequalities." In her contribution to this volume, she focuses on the new phenomenon of urban poverty, linked to the rise of unemployment. The Chinese government has become aware of this problem and has launched two sets of measures: the revival of residents' committees and the enacting of measures targeting jobless urbanites by grassroots institutions. The new poverty phenomena cover various situations characterized by vulnerability, such as former employees of the public sector, rural migrants, and peasants deprived from land.

In China, Monteil writes, laid-off workers not only lost their salary but further social benefits, such as housing, schooling, and medical protection. As a response to this problem, the government has created the status of *xiagang* that has given laid-off workers of the public sector certain rights: a monthly minimum allowance, social security rights, and free training and employment services. Another category, rural migrants, that has been forced into informal jobs has often not been included in the calculation of the Gini index of Chinese towns that is characterized by lower levels than other Asian countries. As Monteil shows, rising urbanization and industrialization have created this group: rural residents who have lost their land with the growth of the cities or the development of the traffic infrastructure. Often, they are not fully integrated in the urban social welfare system but have the right to obtain a financial compensation, sometimes accompanied by job services. There is a last category: young urban intellectuals who returned from re-education camps and could not find adequate jobs in the towns so that they decided to rely on self-employment.

The community projects in the urban centers are driven by the idea to reinforce the Party's legitimacy among these different vulnerable categories and to strengthen social links in neighborhoods so that "human-centered policies" can be implanted. The residents' committees not only suggest help in difficult situations (e.g., looking for jobs or housing) but they also distribute financial allocations. They have a social role as they are in charge of introducing new social norms among the vulnerable: individual responsibility, self-help, and *civilized* behavior (e.g., discussions and not disputes). However, as Monteil underlines, "community informal politics and practices contribute to reinforce the existing segmented social order," but they also "contribute to avoid the emergence of a social problem." In fact, community workers and their different tasks prevent the vulnerable from falling into poverty and social exclusion. The implementation of these social policies depends on grassroots organizations that "contribute to reinforce the existing social stratification." Chinese policy can thus be conceived as a successful approach of a socio-political problem by a regime that is still characterized by a one-party state under the leadership of the Chinese Communist Party.

The second chapter, from Nina Bandelj and Matthew Mahutga, analyzes rising income inequality in Central and Eastern Europe. As the authors underline, "social inequality ((. . .) and income inequality (. . .)) was substantially lower during socialism than inequality in other systems at comparable levels of industrial development." Since 1989 and the fall of the Berlin wall, social inequality has increased throughout the region but there are substantial variations in levels of inequality. The authors attempt to explain these differences and the role of globalization in generating them. They find that "there is a clear positive association between income inequality and foreign capital penetration," as there is an "increasing wage inequality between management and labor within the foreign sector." Another finding of the study is "an expanding difference in average income between agricultural and non-agricultural sectors" and thus sector dualism. As some countries of the region are characterized by "a cultural shift from a collectivist to a more individualistic orientation (. . .) the population declines," so the authors conclude "that poor families continue to live in traditional households and have more children so that wealth concentrates in the segment of households with more educated individuals from middle and upper class backgrounds who adopt new forms of living arrangements." The differences in the countries of the region, according to Bandelj and Mahutga, are also linked to the fact that "countries with weak labor market institutions (. . .) have significantly higher income inequality." Another finding is that "countries with more sizable ethnic minority population have significantly higher Gini coefficients than do those with smaller ethnic minority populations." The authors conclude by underlining that the inequality trends they find "are related to social and cultural challenges that accompany the institutionalization of a market-based order" and do not form "by-products of economic development." Political choices of elites have thus been responsible for higher or lower levels of inequality in the region.

The third chapter of this part focuses on social inequality in India. In the colonial period, British India was considered a wealthy region, as it produced one fifth of world income. Yet, at the end of the colonial period, this part had fallen to 4 percent. Heuzé measures inequality according to the availability of food. In 2007, "75 percent of the citizens had a weight inferior to the norm." The official poverty rate is situated in 2009, according to Heuzé, at about 27 percent. The *Dalit* community (16 percent of the Indian population) belongs quite often (except a small elite) to these poor groups and includes poor agricultural workers, casual workers, and service workers. Heuzé considers the year 1991 as a landmark for the liberalization of monetary, commercial, and industrial policies so that India became the world's *office system* with good job opportunities for engineers and executive staff, poorly paid but well-organized jobs for people working in call centers and other kinds of services, and finally, a large group of poor peons, dispatchers, drivers, guards, and cleaners, who can still get better incomes than informal workers in street-vending or home service. We learn that nine out of ten casual workers in the construction industry cannot sustain a family. A worker in the *organized* sector can feed five persons but a worker in the *unorganized* sector can only feed one and a half persons if he lives in the periphery of the metropolitan areas. In the countryside, poverty is widespread so that "a growing group of small farmers had (. . .) to accept wage migrant labor, handicrafts, or home-based-work (. . .) in addition to their agricultural revenue." What can be considered as a *middle class* in India is a group of 18 percent of the Indian population, which is characterized by "different degrees of *Americanization.*" According to Heuzé, caste inequality has much receded as a result of the practice of reservation during the last years. And he continues: "A majority of the *scheduled castes* and *tribes* are still poor. One half of the population living under the poverty line belongs to these groups." Heuzé concludes his chapter by underlining that "(p)resent-day India has become as much unequal as the US, China, or colonial India. There is much more wealth than in the 1980s but it has been concentrated among a few groups."

The fourth and fifth chapters in this part present the debate on the inequality profile in Africa south of the Sahara. Bankole presents his research from Ibadan, Nigeria, where he has studied the empowerment of local entrepreneurs in the formal sector. He argues that "in the precolonial period, there were local entrepreneurs who engaged in peasant production, crafts, and trading." However, "(t)hey could not favorably compete with the colonial-established expatriate trading firms who had superior capital and possessed monopoly control of banking and shipping facilities." In fact, Nigeria happens to be one of the countries with the highest urban unemployment rate in Africa so that the role of local entrepreneurs as possible job creators becomes obvious and consequently the interest of this chapter.

The group that Bankole has studied is composed of very few female entrepreneurs and is characterized by the youthful age of most of the entrepreneurs (48 percent are at age 30 to 39). About 72 percent of them possess Nigeria's higher national diploma or university degrees. These entrepreneurs belong to two categories: the owner-managers (47 percent) and the employee-managers (53 percent). They form a group that is "motivated by personal gains and the need for personal achievement and self-expression" and thus characteristics that are considered as important for success in economic sociology. Bankole mentions a further interesting fact that has already been treated in the first part of this book: "(T)hose that raise their capital from abroad reveal the increasing importance of monetary and non-monetary remittances from abroad." In the last part of his chapter, Bankole discusses economic policy and the question of entrepreneurship within the global economic order. According to him, Nigerian entrepreneurs face problems in the banking sector, as banks are not supporting the promotion of local businesses and utilize high lending rates. One of the most important problems is, as he tells us, the weakness of the Nigerian state and its inability to function as a development state. The author sees thus a dysfunction of the political system that acts "as a major disincentive to local entrepreneurship." As entrepreneurs cannot influence policymaking even when using their associational platforms, their weakness should be explained by unfavorable political conditions and a global economy based on high competition that is barely accessible to Nigerian entrepreneurs. The dependence on the petroleum industry and the neglect of other sectors explain moreover the low competitiveness of local entrepreneurs. It is interesting that Bankole underlines that "the respondents' rational thinking was found to be consistent with the requirements of the overall business environment," a fact that is different from the *Homo africanus* that one can find in the literature on African economic systems (Hugon 2006: 55). Bankole concludes by asking for a "broadening of the space destined to entrepreneurship" in Nigeria, a situation that should be similar in other countries of the region. The insufficient infrastructure that contributes to the high costs of entrepreneurship in Nigeria (difficulties in electricity supply) and the lack of transparency in governance are considered by Bankole as important points to be addressed by political elites.

The last chapter has been written by François-Xavier de Perthuis de Laillevault and the author of this introduction. We discuss poverty in Senegal, first by presenting theoretical approaches, and then by studying the empirical manifestations of poverty. Despite early discussions on poverty, the topic gained ground in international institutions only in the 1990s. The theoretical work of A. Sen influenced the apprehension of poverty, so that the UNDP published in 1997 a Human Development Report on the eradication of poverty. In the eighth plenary meeting of the UN General Assembly in 2000, the declaration of the Millennium Development Goals was adopted by 189 United Member States. The MDGs made poverty alleviation a universal concern to be accepted by civil society.

In Senegal, two approaches have predominated: the utilitarian approach and multidimensional aspects of poverty. However, as the authors underline, the "conceptual discussion of poverty comes to the conclusion that *something is missing*," meaning a monetary threshold that permits characterization of someone as poor or not poor. The discussion on poverty alleviation had begun in Senegal in the 1980s, and in 2002 Senegal adopted policies destined to reduce poverty. This approach was based on the premise "to increase the incomes of the poor through economic growth and to promote trade liberalization." In the 1990s, household surveys had "permitted the identification of population groups most in need according to the monetary approach." An approach based on economic and social manifestations of poverty was included in a survey from 2001 that focused on the wellbeing of each individual and thus included "the individual's subjective relation to his/her economic and social situation."

Surveys from 1994–95 and 2001–02 revealed that the part of households in poverty decreased from 61 to 48 percent, which is rather important for this short duration. In Senegal, poverty is more often a phenomenon of rural areas than urban centers. In the capital Dakar, 17.8 percent of households were poor in 2004. Education is one of the most important factors predicting an absence of poverty: the higher the educational level of the household head is, the lower is the presence of poverty; households whose head has no formal education add up to 80 percent of poor households. Moreover, an activity in the informal sector, comparable to India, is linked to poverty. We could also find an interesting poverty difference between households headed by men or women that we explained as resulting from remittances sent to women by migrant husbands abroad.

An important contribution of the chapter to the literature on poverty is the demonstration of the importance of networks under Senegalese poor that permit them to cope with their difficult situations. People underline that social relationships are important in adaptation strategies and that they help to find material or immaterial opportunities that may ensure the families' daily needs. The chapter shows that the poor in Senegal have agency: they aspire to better lives and work hard to seize opportunities.

CONCLUSION

This introductory chapter has outlined some historical benchmarks of social inequality, major twentieth- and twenty-first-century theoretical debates about social inequality and globalization, and some empirical findings on global and national inequality. The edited collection unites case studies that illustrate empirical situations of inequality under conditions of globalization. It seems to us that in a world where large parts of the population subsist with a small amount of money, the search for alternatives to the harsh realities of the present is timelier than ever.

NOTES

1. Source: http://www.globalissues.org/issue/2/causes-of-poverty, accessed on October 3rd, 2009.

BIBLIOGRAPHY

Bennett, John (1996) "Applied and Action Anthropology: Ideological and Conceptual Aspects," *Current Anthropology*, Supplement 37 (1): 23–53.

Bhagwati, Jagdish (2004) *In Defense of Globalization*. Oxford: Oxford University Press.

Chambers, Erve (1987) "Applied Anthropology in the Post-Vietnam Era: Anticipations and Irony," *Annual Review of Anthropology* 16: 309–337.

Commission for Africa (2005) *Our Common Interest: An Argument*. London and New York: Penguin Books.

Chen, Shaohua and Mertin Ravallion (2004) "How Have the World's Poorest Fared Since the Early 1980s?" *World Bank Research Observer* 19 (2): 141–169.

Cornia, Giovanni Andrea and World Institute for Development Economics Research (2004) *Inequality, Growth, and Poverty in an Era of Liberalization and Globalization*. Oxford and New York: Oxford University Press.

Davies, James B., Susanna Sandström, Anthony Shorrocks, and Edward N. Wolff (2008) *The world distribution of household wealth*. Discussion Paper No.

2008/03 (Helsinki, UNU-WIDER). http://www.wider.unu.edu/publications/working-papers/discussion-papers/2008/en_GB/dp2008–03/, accessed on August 30, 2009.

Davis, Shelton H. (1999) "Bringing Culture into the Development Paradigm: The View from the World Bank," *Development Anthropology* 16 (1–2): 25–31.

Edelman, Marc and Angelique Haugerud (eds) (2006) *The Anthropology of Development and Globalization: From Classical Political Economy to Contemporary Neoliberalism.* Malden, CA, Oxford, UK, Carlton, Victoria: Blackwell.

Escobar, Arturo (1995) *Encountering Development: The Making and Unmaking of the Third World.* Princeton: Princeton University Press.

Escobar, Arturo (1997) "Anthropology and Development," *International Social Science Journal* 49 (154): 497–515.

Firebaugh, Glenn and Brian Goesling (2007) "Globalization and Global Inequalities: Recent Trends," in George Ritzer (ed.) *The Blackwell Companion to Globalization.* Blackwell, 2007, Blackwell Reference Online. http://www.blackwellreference.com/subscriber/tocnode?id=g9781405132749_chunk_g978140513274932, accessed on October 20, 2008.

Frankfurter Allgemeine Zeitung (2008) "Finanzkrise könnte 20 Millionen Jobs kosten," October 21.

Galbraith, James K. (2008) "Inequality and Economic and Political Change," *The University of Texas Inequality Project*, UTIP Working Paper N° 51, http://utip.gov.utexas.edu/papers/Utip_52.pdf, accessed on February 15, 2010.

Garrett, Geoffroy (2003) "Global Markets and National Politics," in David Held and Anthony McGrew (eds) *The Global Transformations Reader.* 2nd ed., 384–402. Cambridge: Polity Press.

Gow, David (2002) "Anthropology and Development: Evil Twin or Moral Narrative?" *Human Organization* 61 (4): 299–313.

Graeber, David (2002) "The Anthropology of Globalization (with Notes on Neomedievalism, and the End of the Chinese Model of the State)," *American Anthropologist* 104 (4): 1222–1227.

Greig, Alastair, David Hulme, and Marc Turner (2007) *Challenging Global Inequality: Development Theory and Practice in the 21st Century.* Houndmills, Basingstoke, Hampshire: Palgrave MacMillan.

Hausmann, Ricardo, Laura D. Tyson, and Saadia Zahidi (2009) *The Global Gender Gap Report.* World Economic Forum: Geneva.

Held, David and Ayse Kaya (eds) (2007) *Global Inequality: Patterns and Explanations.* Cambridge: Polity Press.

Horowitz, Michael (1994) "Development Anthropology in the Mid-1990s," *Development Anthropology Network* 12 (1–2): 1–14.

Hugon, Philippe (2006) *L'économie de l'Afrique.* 5th ed. Paris: La Découverte.

Inglis, David and John Bone (eds) (2006) *Social Stratification: Critical Concepts in Sociology.* London and New York: Routledge.

International Labor Office (2007) *Equality at Work: Tackling the Challenges.* Geneva: ILO. www.ilo.org/wcmsp5/groups/. . ./wcms_082607.pdf, accessed on August 30, 2009.

International Labor Office (2008) *World of Work Report 2008: Income Inequalities in the Age of Financial Globalization.* Geneva: ILO. www.ilo.org/public/english/bureau/inst/. . ./world08.pdf, accessed on August 30, 2009.

International Labor Office (2009) *Global Wage Report 2008/09. Minimum Wages and Collective Bargaining: Towards Policy Coherence.* www.ilo.org/wcmsp5/groups/. . ./wcms_100786.pdf, accessed on August 30, 2009.

Jomo, K. S. and Jacques Baudot (eds) (2007) *Flat World, Big Gaps. Economic Liberalization, Globalization, Poverty and Inequality.* London and New York: Zed Books, Orient Longman, TWN.

Jones, Richard J. (1998) "Remittances and Inequality: A Question of Migration Stage and Geographic Scale," *Economic Geography* 74 (1): 8–25.

Kaplinsky, Raphael (2005) *Globalization, Poverty and Inequality: Between A Rock and A Hard Place*. Cambridge: Polity Press.

Kohl, Richard and Organization for Economic Co-operation and Development. Development Center (2003) *Globalisation, Poverty and Inequality*. Paris: Development Center of the Organization for Economic Co-operation and Development.

Korzeniewicz, Roberto Patricio and Timothy Patrick Moran (2007) "World Inequality in the Twenty-first Century: Patterns and Tendencies," in George Ritzer (ed.) *The Blackwell Companion to Globalization*. Blackwell, Blackwell Reference Online. http://www.blackwellreference.com/subscriber/tocnode?id= g9781405132749_chunk_g978140513274933, accessed on October 30, 2008.

Long, Norman (2001) *Development Sociology: Actor Perspectives*. London and New York: Routledge.

Mahler, Vincent A. and David K. Jesuit (2006) "Fiscal Redistribution in the Developed Countries: New Insights from the Luxembourg Income Study," *Socio-Economic Review* 4 (3): 483–511.

Mahler, Vincent A. and David K. Jesuit (2008) Redistribution Dataset, Version 2, February. http://www.lisproject.org/publications/fiscalredistdata/fiscred.htm, accessed on August 30, 2009.

Mazumdar, Dipak (2008) *Globalization, Labor Markets and Inequality in India*. London and New York: Routledge.

McMichael, Philip (2000) *Development and Social Change: A Global Perspective*. 2nd ed., Thousand Oaks, CA: Pine Forge Press-Sage.

Milanovic, Branko (2005) *Worlds Apart: Measuring International and Global Inequality*. Princeton and Woodstock: Princeton University Press.

Milanovic, Branko (2007) "Global Income Inequality: What it IS and Why it Matters," K. S. Jomo and Jacques Baudot (eds) *Flat World, Big Gaps. Economic Liberalization, Globalization, Poverty & Inequality*, 1–23. London and New York: Orient Longman, Zed Books, Third World Network.

Muchie, Mammo and Xing Li (2006) *Globalization, Inequality, and the Commodification of Life and Well-being*. London: Adonis and Abbey.

Neederveen Pieterse, Jan (2004) *Globalization or Empire?* London and New York: Routledge.

Nissanke, Machiko and Erik Thorbecke (eds) (2007) *The Impact of Globalization on the World's Poor: Transmission Mechanisms*. Basingstoke and New York: Palgrave Macmillan in Association with UNU World Institute for Development Economics Research.

Nissanke, Machiko and World Institute for Development Economics Research (2005) *Channels and Policy Debate in the Globalization-Inequality-Poverty Nexus*. Helsinki: UNU World Institute for Development Economics Research.

OECD (2008) *Growing Unequal? Income Distribution and Poverty in OECD Countries*. www.oecd.org/dataoecd/45/42/41527936.pdf, accessed on August 30, 2009.

Ramonet, Ignacio (2004) "50 années qui ont changé notre monde," Paris, *Le Monde diplomatique*. March.

Ruppenthal, Silvia and Detlev Lück (2009) "Jeder fünfte Erwerbstätige ist aus beruflichen Gründen mobil," *Informationsdienst Soziale Indikatoren* 42: 1–5.

Russel Sage Foundation, Pranab K. Bardan, Samuel Bowles, and Michael Wallerstein (2006) *Globalization and Egalitarian Redistribution*. New York and Princeton: Russell Sage Foundation and Princeton University Press.

Schuerkens, Ulrike (ed.) (2004) *Global Forces and Local Life-Worlds*. London, New Delhi, Thousands Oaks: Sage.

Schuerkens, Ulrike (ed.) (2008) *Globalization and Transformations of Local Socio-Economic Practices*. London and New York: Routledge.

Scrase, Timothy J., Joseph Miles Holden Todd, and Scott Baum (2003) *Globalization, Culture and Inequality in Asia*. Melbourne, Victoria and Abingdon: Trans-Pacific Press.

Sen, Amartya (1999) *Development as Freedom*. Oxford: Oxford University Press.

Smith, Timothy B. (2004) *France in Crisis: Welfare, Inequality, and Globalization Since 1980*. Cambridge and New York: Cambridge University Press.

Tilly, Charles (2005) "Historical Perspectives on Inequality," in Mary Romero and Eric Margolis (eds) *The Blackwell Companion to Social Inequalities*. Blackwell, Blackwell Reference Online. http://www.blackwellreference.com/subscriber/tocnode?id=g9780631231547_chunk_g97806312315476, accessed on October 20, 2008.

Tonkiss, Fran (2006) *Contemporary Economic Sociology: Globalization, Production, Inequality*. London and New York: Routledge.

Tsing, Anna (2000) "The Global Situation," *Cultural Anthropology* 15 (3): 327–360.

Tulchin, Joseph S. and Gary Bland (eds) (2005) *Getting Globalization Right: The Dilemmas of Inequality*. Boulder, Col. and London: Lynne Rienner.

United Nations Development Program (UNDP) (2005) *Human Development Report 2005: International Cooperation at a Crossroad: Aid, Trade and Security in an Unequal World*. New York: Palgrave Macmillan.

United Nations Development Program (UNDP) (2007) *Human Development Report 2007/2008: Fighting Climate Change: Human Solidarity in a Divided World*. New York: Palgrave Macmillan.

Wei, Yehua Dennis (2000) *Regional Development in China: States, Globalization, and Inequality*. London and New York: Routledge.

Wade, Robert H. (2007) "Should We Worry About Income Inequality?" in David Held and Ayse Kaya (eds) *Global Inequality*, 104–131. Cambridge: Polity Press.

Part II

Changing Dimensions of Social Inequality in a Global World

1 Mobilities as Dimensions of Social Inequalities

Katharina Manderscheid

INTRODUCTION

In some visions of globalization, the final stage is pictured as a globally integrated society within instantaneous, completely connected space, where there is no need to travel anywhere anymore. This vision is rooted in an untroubled belief in economic growth and technologically-founded progress and largely ignores the actual power relations creating new exclusions and frictions in the socio-spatial world. Thus, in order to better understand the unequal re-structurings and re-stratifications against the background of processes labeled as globalization, I suggest an extension of the sociological approaches on social inequality.

The argument that I want to make here is twofold. Drawing on the spatial as well as the mobilities turn and in contrast to the dominant quantifying inequality analysis, I see spatial positions and mobilities as increasingly important aspects of social inequalities. With results taken from an ongoing bi-national comparative study of Switzerland and England, I will substantiate this argument, and assess impacts of the different infrastructural and spatial settings of these two countries. The meaning of mobilities as a central pre-condition for social participation will be underlined with empirical findings referring mainly to labor market participation. The findings show significant interconnections of the ability to move, the location of residence, and social positions. Then I emphasize the claim of many scholars that the national-territorial framing of inequalities is no longer adequate against the background of increasing interconnections beyond national borders in all spheres of social life. Yet, the available data is not sufficient to analyze these border-crossing mobilities of people, nor do they account for the various forms of travel and movement. Thus, taking mobilities and space seriously as dimensions of social inequality and studying their impacts on large-scale levels requires adapted data collection and research approaches. Far from an integrated global society in instantaneous spaces, the constitution of spatial borders and the unequal ability to overcome frictions in space by movement requires new theoretical and methodological approaches as well as adequate data collections.

SPATIAL AND MOBILE INEQUALITIES

Social inequalities have been a central issue in sociology from its very beginning. The concept of class resulting from relations of production became the core of these debates (cf. Erikson and Goldthorpe 1992, Grusky 1994, Wright 2000). During the last decades, the academic discussion circled the questions of how to define these classes, how stable they are, whether or not they are still socio-politically relevant categories and whether or not they still have an impact on people's identities and practices (cf. Beck 1986, Bradley 1996, Bourdieu 2001, Savage 2000, Sayer 2005). Whereas large parts of class analysis seem to have been pre-occupied with methodologically sophisticated details of the measurement of social inequalities and social mobility, the questions of why and how these different distributions impact people's everyday lives and how to include other forms of social differentiations into research and theory (such as gender, ethnicity, age, sexual orientation, religion, etc.), with their complex interactions with material inequalities, have drawn attention mainly outside this research strand.

Some broader and more theoretically embedded approaches highlight the multidimensional and relational character of social inequalities. For example Bourdieu (1986, 2000) differentiates between three main social spaces[1] in which chances are defined by the availability of structural resources. These spaces are: the economic space and correspondingly economic capital, the space of qualifications and education, thus cultural capital, as well as the space of social contacts and networks, and thus social capital. The disposition and structure of these capitals define positions within the social space of power relations (Bourdieu 1986). Emphasizing the relationality of stratification, Bourdieu (2001) amongst others argued that the value of resources at stake is highly power infused and largely defined by the dominant classes, yet continuously contested and thus potentially open for change. Similarly, Bradley suggested that we should understand inequalities as multidimensional and relational factors, which

> exist outside us as individuals, they put constraints upon us, they affect our life-chances. (. . .) Class refers to relations arising from the organization of production, distribution and consumption. Gender refers to the varied and complex arrangements between women and men, encompassing the organization of reproduction, the sexual division of labour and cultural definitions of femininity and masculinity. 'Race' and ethnicity refer to arrangements surrounding the possession of territories and processes of migration arising from them. Age refers to the way we organize the progress of individuals and cohorts through the life course. All these lived relations involve differential access to power and resources and are therefore not only aspects of social differentiation but also of social inequality. They merge together to form the complex hierarchies which are characteristic of contemporary societies. (Bradley 1996: 202–203)

As emphasized by approaches informed by post-structuralist and feminist theory, the relations dividing the social along the lines of gender, ethnicity, age, as well as religion, language, sexual orientations, and others, are understood as cutting across and interacting with these vertical differentiations of resource allocation. They are not congruent with material distributions and thus cannot be ignored or simply added as further variables (cf. Bradley 1996, Walby 2001: 123). Prominently, Fraser (2003) suggested a multifaceted theoretical and political approach, in which she differentiates between recognition and redistribution, trying to combine issues of cultural differences with economic issues.

In the aforementioned approaches, social stratification and inequalities are thought to be multifaceted, multidimensional, relational, and constantly contested within social power struggles. Therefore, the spaces in which these struggles take place and differentiations are made, are contingent and change, as the history of claims for cultural recognition of differences and material justice has shown (cf. Fraser 2003). Drawing on these insights, I will flesh out the argument that against the background of various processes of globalization, space, spatial position, and movement have become factors of increasing relevance for social inequalities and stratifications. Although most sociological approaches on stratification and inequality are conceptualized without explicitly considering their social spatialities, class and the connected discourse of the ideal of equal chances are rooted implicitly in a very specific understanding of the social as a territorially bound society (Urry 2000: 9). Thus, mainstream class analysis is embedded in the ideological foundations of the post-war national welfare states of the Western world. This specific socio-economic and spatial configuration of the European nation-states seems to have arisen in the era of policies aiming[2] at leveling out the negative impacts of social and spatial origins by providing public education systems as well as access to transportation and roads. In this light, spatial planning guidelines were aimed at the creation of an isotropic territory as the container of the national society. Thus, as Massey (2005: 64) pointed out, the isomorphism of territory and society, their internal cohesion, and the distinction against the outside, which served as the legitimization of the nation-state, were less the pre-conditions but the products of this socio-spatial formation by means of welfare and planning policies (cf. Taylor 2003). In this sense, Graham and Marvin (2001) have characterized this Western post-war era of increasing wealth, investment in national welfare, and spatial coverage as the "infrastructural ideal." The emergence of the "system of automobility" (Urry 2004) as individualized mass-mobility in the Fordist system also appears paradigmatic for this zenith of national economies and welfare states in first modernity (Beck 1986). The provision of transportation and communication infrastructure in order to level out spatial frictions constitutes thus a dimension of national welfare and equity policy facilitating or impeding access to socially valued goods, activities, and resources that is fostering social integration (Painter 2008: 342). Correspondingly, spatial frictions and differences within the national container were interpreted as leftovers from the past (Massey 2005).

Yet, as has been illustrated with rich examples by Graham and Marvin (2001), as part of the neo-liberal globalization process, this infrastructural ideal of national spatial planning and welfare is on the decline. Although this seems to constitute a general global tendency, these processes differ between countries. They began in Britain, where Margaret Thatcher induced privatization and deregulation in the 1980s, and continued in countries such as Germany, Denmark, or Switzerland. Several processes seem to have been at work, which have been fundamentally changing the spatial structure of the social world and have been dissolving more or less coherent socio-spatial national territories. Within current processes of socio-spatial re-structuring, already connected centers and elites seem to be at the heart of development and investment, whereas peripheries and marginalized groups are increasingly bypassed and ousted (Sassen 2001a, Graham 2001, Graham and Marvin 2001, Castells 2002, Manderscheid and Bergman 2008).

The ongoing changes require considering space and spatial positions in relation to valued places, goods, and people. Space can no longer be simply captured in territorial terms and metric proximities; instead the more dominant spatialities are characterized by links, referred to as flows and networks (Castells 2002) as well as fluids (Mol and Law 1994) and various other topologies (cf. Urry 2000: 32ff.). Analyzing spatialities of social relations highlights that socially valued resources are not equally and ubiquitously available and accessible. Whereas most inequality research conceptualizes power and resources as appropriated capitals and as a more or less personal property, a number of scholars have pointed out that capital as a resource of power should be understood according to its spatio-temporal context (Allen 2003, Manderscheid 2009: 11). In this vein, the specific topologies of economic capital and its global spatialities of flows, the bypassed peripheries of places, as well as the corresponding nodes of global cities have been outlined quite prominently (Sassen 2001a and b, Castells 2002). Less attention has been paid to changing spatialities of other resources, for example, the changing spatialities of education. After decades of national standardization, at present, cultural capital—at least in the Western world—is undergoing processes of international standardization and evaluation, for example, through the Bologna process and the PISA assessment.[3] When one regards the geographies of academic education, there seems to be an emerging (hierarchically organized) networked European social space of university education with strong links to North America and other selected states.[4] Social capital also forms spatialities and is increasingly spatially dispersed, encompassing people at larger distances (cf. Larsen, Axhausen, and Urry 2006, Axhausen 2007):

> [E]xtensive weak ties generate social networks that are sustained through intermittent meetings and communications. Such networks

increasingly spread across the globe and therefore depend upon multiple mobilities for their reproduction. (Urry 2008: 48)

The lengthening of the chains of interdependencies (Elias 2000) and the changing spatialities of resources further suggest a highly increased significance of movement in order to access resources and thus social chances and social integration.

> All societies presuppose multiple mobilities for people to be effective participants. Such access is unequally distributed but the structuring of this inequality depends inter alia on the economics of production and consumption of the objects relevant to mobility, the nature of civil society (. . .), the geographical distribution of people and activities, and the particular mobility-systems in play and their forms of interdependence. (Urry 2008: 16)

Or, as Rammler put it, the process of ongoing differentiation and spatial separation is accompanied by a parallel integration process and by means of institutional, organizational, cultural, and technological bridging of the separation (Rammler 2008: 67). Drawing on these assumptions, the argument I want to emphasize here is that due to processes of socio-spatial lengthening of chains of interdependencies, and the geographical stretching of social relations, in combination with socio-spatial polarizations, spatial positions related to infrastructure and opportunities are increasingly significant in order to get access to activities, goods, and resources (Sheppard 2002). Furthermore, the ability to be physically and virtually mobile, and the power to move other people and goods have become contested resources of social participation (Bauman 2000: 120) and form new patterns of stratification. These patterns of mobile and spatial inequalities do not necessarily follow the known lines of social differentiation and stratification, but seem to interact with them, thus re-articulating some forces, such as patriarchal dependencies, in combination with the privatization of social infrastructures and peripheral locations. Moreover, new inequalities seem to be emerging, which cut across the known ones such as income, education, gender, etc. For example, practices around arranging face-to-face meetings using a combination of technological devices (cf. Shove 2002, Larsen, Axhausen, and Urry 2006, Wajcman 2008) seem to stratify in a new way, differentiating between insiders and outsiders of the technologically mobile world. On a global level, there seems to be an increasing polarization between space-autonomous global elites, combined with social groups forced to move (from migrants and refugees to the corporate and academic middle class members), and place-bound, cut-off, and marginalized social groups (Castells 2002, Weiss 2005). According to Massey's interpretation, these observations are not unintended side products but rather pre-conditions as well as expressions of power relations.

The current world order of capital's (anyway highly unequal) globalisation is as predicated upon holding (some kinds of) labour in place as was early modernity upon slavery. (Massey 2005: 87)

In the following, I will analyze the interrelation of spatial positions, movement, and other dimensions of inequality from a large-scale perspective, focusing mainly on work-related movement and access to means of transportation and the availability of communication devices. The latter are expected to interact with other dimensions of inequality depending on the social and spatial context, which will be studied by comparing quantitative findings for Switzerland and England.

STRUCTURES OF CONNECTIVITY AND UNEQUAL PATTERNS OF MOVEMENT

Patterns of movement emerge at the interface of social and spatial structures, personal resources, life situations, and corresponding perceptions, involving socio-culturally differentiated orientations and competences (Kaufmann, Bergman, and Joye 2004, Jetzkowitz, Schneider and Brunzel 2007). Although, as has been argued elsewhere (Graham and Marvin 2001, Kaufmann 2002, Allen 2003, Urry 2007, Manderscheid 2009), the availability of and metric proximity to infrastructures of connectivity—from roads or public transport to means of virtual mobility such as the Internet or mobile phones—is not sufficient to connect people to the social world of networks, flows, and places[5]; still, the material base of mobilities constitutes a necessary pre-condition for movements to be carried out (cf. Castells 2002). Trying to assess the impact of the decline of the infrastructural ideal and the resulting spatial polarization on another dimension of social inequality, this chapter compares movement patterns in England and in Switzerland. These two countries display similarities as well as differences. Neither has got a welfare system developed as highly as those of Scandinavian States. Whereas the United Kingdom underwent a very early process of economic and political neo-liberal deregulation and privatization during Thatcherism, Switzerland has sustained a very modern standard of public service and provision of infrastructures until the present time. This seems linked to the different economic structures of the two countries, which led (in particular the northern) English cities into deindustrialization during the second half of the twentieth century, whereas Switzerland with its strong financial sector did not have to face similar restructurings. On the other hand, both countries are economically and politically affected by transnational neo-liberal forces, which were argued to increase the importance of spatial positions and the ability to move. Another difference concerns the administrative level; whereas the Swiss political organization is highly decentralized, Britain has got a strong central government. The results presented here attempt to investigate this interweaving of social inequality and mobility, which has so far attracted little attention in theory-informed, large-scale studies.

Data, Variables, and Research Frame

The results presented here are taken from an ongoing study, which in the future will be extended by further cases and methodological approaches. Therefore, the results are still limited in scope. A further limitation is given by the data used. It is very difficult to obtain data sets, which include more than rudimentary indicators of both social and spatial positions and mobilities and which are comparable regarding operationalization. This study uses household panel data, which will allow future analysis of changes over time.

The British Household Panel Survey (BHPS) began in 1991 and is carried out annually. The wave of 2005 used here contained, for the whole of the UK, 8,700 households with 15,600 interviewed individuals, of which the 5,165 living in England and aged between 25 and 65 were selected for the analysis. The Swiss Household Panel (SHP) started in 1999; the British survey inspired it. The wave of 2005 used here contained altogether 16,900 interviewees in 6,800 households, of which 9,535 fulfilled the criteria of being aged 25 to 65 years. In order to validate the findings, when possible, a comparison is made to the results of other transportation studies in both countries, in particular, the National Travel Survey (DfT 2006) and the Transportation Micro-census (BFS and ARE 2007).

Regarding spatial patterns, movement, and social inequalities, there is the problem of linking theoretical approaches to empirical analysis, which is often limited to available indicators, so that they are never able to get 'the whole picture' of the social world. Correspondingly, the theoretical basis outlined above contains more potentialities than are *used* for this empirical analysis, emphasizing the character of the chapter as exploratory and open rather than complete and definitive.

This research uses education, income, and social position as indicators of social inequality. Education is difficult to compare at national levels. The English scale used here consists of five levels, the Swiss one of three, which is in accordance with the standard aggregation of educational levels. Because it indicates social positions as derived from positions in the labor market, the Cambridge Social Interaction Scale (CAMSIS) was chosen. The theoretical foundation of this scale is the idea that differential association is an essential feature of social stratification arrangements. Assuming that acquaintances, friends, and marriage partners will all tend to be chosen much more frequently from within the same group than from without, the CAMSIS approach uses patterns of interaction in order to assess social proximity and distance between different social groups. As a result, CAMSIS conceives stratification as a single continuous scale (Prandy 1990, Bergman, Lambert, Prandy, and Joye 2002). However, this operationalization of stratification (as individual probabilities of marriages/cohabiting in terms of occupational groups) limits the explanatory and theoretical reach of the CAMSIS scale so that it is only used here as one indicator of social inequality amongst others.

Variables on income are another difficult parameter of unequal social position, which involve the problems of different tax deductions and a consideration of household sizes. Moreover, due to the tax sovereignty of Swiss cantons, which permits some cantons to attract foreigners with high income levels,[6] the link between income and other dimensions of social inequality as well as the spatial distribution of income is strongly biased in Switzerland. Both data sets contain the gross annual household income as well as differently equalized income variables. Both are included in the following analysis but it is necessary to be aware of the problems. The analysis uses the variables of gender, household structure, and children living in the household as indicators of further differences and inequality structures.

Regarding space and mobility, the data sets include information about the region or canton of residence and the degree of urbanization of the town or village of residency as derived variables. Furthermore, there is some information whether the interviewee has access within the household to a car or a computer as a means for corporeal or virtual mobility. As one of the most important forms of everyday corporeal movement, travel time to work is included in the data, but the Swiss data give no additional information on the means of traveling. Therefore, the work draws on additional statistical reports in order to analyze commuting.

In the empirical investigation so far, social inequality is defined with an emphasis on the labor market as a powerful mechanism of distributing material conditions and life-chances in exchange for other resources. Yet, in line with earlier claims (that inequalities should be understood as multidimensional and as being reproduced with increasing significance along the lines of mobilities and space, and that mobilities should be understood as consisting of multiple forms of corporeal and virtual movement of oneself, others, goods, and information), employment-induced movement and material inequality represent only one part of the picture. The empirical investigation of other aspects of inequality and movement should be pursued, including those social networks, their spatialities, and corresponding movement.

The Spatial Structure of Switzerland

The spatial pattern in Switzerland is defined by its poly-centric structure but also by the increasing concentration of economic activities in a few large agglomerations, mainly the region of Zurich, the area of Lake Geneva (*Arc Lémanique*) encompassing Geneva and Lausanne, Basel, Bern, and the metropolitan region in Ticino, including Lugano. Apart from Bern, the Swiss metropolitan regions also include bordering foreign regions in France, Italy, and Germany. Yet, the national data set used here does not reflect the linkages with the bordering countries, e.g., the high number of cross-border commuters. The increasing geographical polarization is defined as the concentration of jobs, growth of population, and higher levels of education and income. Moreover, these agglomerations are centers of growing areas of commuting and are linked by roads and a public transportation system so that processes of economic and social concentration are continuously progressing (ARE 2008). Switzerland seems characterized by a high degree of spatial coverage infrastructure and by means of transportation, and therefore by a rather high degree of spatial homogeneity, although the Alpine valleys and the area of the Jura Mountains are situated on the periphery and appear to have less access to the metropolitan areas. Taking the difficult geographic conditions of the mountainous regions into consideration, the spatial coverage achieved seems rather astonishing and is the result of a political achievement. The Swiss public transportation system is administered by the State, although the privatization of the Swiss Federal Railways is continuously discussed.

The Spatial Structure of England

England's spatial structure is shaped by the economic dominance of London and an overall high degree of urbanization, with around 80 percent of the population living in urban areas (Pointer 2005: 46). Outside London, the most populous but not necessarily economically prosperous urban areas in England are: the West Midlands Urban Area, Greater Manchester, the West Yorkshire Urban Area, Tyneside, the Liverpool Urban Area, the Nottingham Urban Area, the Sheffield Urban Area, and the Bristol Urban Area. In these areas, about a third of the UK population lives (Pointer 2005: 46). The north of England underwent large economic restructurings during the last decades. After a long period of internal southward migration, the trend seems to have changed to a northward migration since the beginning of the millennium (Champion 2005: 101).

The public transport system in Britain has been privatized and is profit-oriented, serving market demands rather than understanding transportation as a public good (cf. Graham and Marvin 2001). However, large parts of local public transportation still receive high subsidies from the State. More remote places are not covered by public transportation, whereas almost half of train journeys take place in London and the South East (DfT 2008: 14). In comparison to Switzerland, and due to the island situation, international land traffic and commuting interconnections are less of an issue for England. But as a result of its imperial history, its economy is highly linked to international markets and its population has been, and continues to be, influenced by immigration.

Mapping Social Inequalities

The first analysis being presented here is the spatial distribution of social positions. Although spatially differentiated occupational structures, and changes therein, are somewhat part of the academic common knowledge (Massey 1984, Herod 1997) obtained by international comparisons of states, spatial positions within national territories are seldom included in the analysis of social inequality (Savage 1988). However, the decline of the *infrastructural ideal* as underlying the territorial integration of nation-states is expected to increase spatial differences and also impact on peoples' opportunities. On a European scale, this process has been termed euphemistically as regionalization.

For the following analysis, the CAMSIS, an indicator of social positions, was mapped onto the Swiss and English territories divided into 26 cantons and 17 regions and metropolitan areas respectively. The spatial areas mapped are rather large, so that the differences identified signify major economic-spatial imbalances within the countries. Both countries show spatially differentiated occupational structures, which are reflected in an uneven distribution of spatial positions. Whereas in England, London is the unquestioned center and place of the highest social positions, Switzerland shows a lower degree of socio-spatial inequality, which seems to exist mainly between the urban agglomerations and the rural cantons.

For England, the large dominance of London becomes obvious, which also seems to impact the surrounding region of the South East. As a secondary economic center, the metropolitan area of Greater Manchester shows another significantly above-average score. On the other hand, the metropolitan county of South Yorkshire, which is one of the least prosperous areas in Western Europe and has received funding from the European Regional Development Fund, still shows lower average scores. Furthermore, some of the more rural regions show scores significantly below the national average.

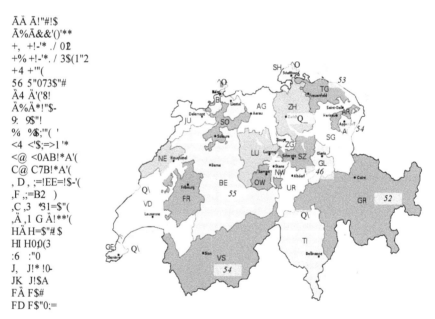

Figure 1.1   CAMSIS Scores in Switzerland (using Swiss Household Panel 2005) across cantons. The figures on the map are cantonal means significantly above or *below* the national mean of 57.

Source: http://commons.wikimedia.org/wiki/Category: Maps_of_Switzerland, accessed on October 14, 2009, GNU FDL and author's calculation.

Figure 1.2   CAMSIS Scores in England (using the British Household Panel 2005) across regions and metropolitan counties. The figures on the map are regional means significantly above or *below* the national mean of 39.

Source: http://commons.wikimedia.org/wiki/Category: Maps_of_the_United_Kingdom, accessed on October 14, 2009, GNU FDL and author's calculation.

For Switzerland, there is a low degree of socio-spatial inequality, which seems to exist between the urban agglomerations and the rural cantons. This ongoing trend has been critically discussed and observed (Kübler 2004 and 2006, Glauser, Jeanneret, and Hotz 2006). Overall, spatial polarization appears here less articulated than in England.

Both countries display significant differences in socio-spatial chances, which seem to go hand in hand with the spatially differentiated economic structure. Yet, this is a very static view of the socio-spatial formation, somehow assuming a congruency of the location of the residence and lived spaces, ignoring the actual movement of people. As an example, movement may overcome geographical frictions related to unequal occupational chances. After the Second World War, with the increase of the means of transportation (in particular the car), the distance between the workplace and the place of residence has increased, so that the lived spatialities of people have expanded.

Availability of Means of Mobility

Because the main means of corporeal mobility is still the car, it is hardly surprising that in both countries more than 90 percent of the interviewees live in households with a car.[7] In both countries, car availability seems highest in family households with children and lowest in one-person households. Yet, car dependency seems to decrease with the degree of urbanity (Table 1.1) and is lower in the centers— London in the case of England and the five agglomerations in Switzerland—where only two thirds of the households have a car. This can be explained partly by the higher percentage of family households living in suburban and rural communities rather than centers; people living in other English city regions outside London have a car available almost as often as the national average. This finding suggests that in London and in the Swiss agglomerations, it is either less convenient or less necessary to have a car, due to a better public transportation system than elsewhere in the respective countries. Interestingly, although in both countries having a car correlates with household income (see also: DfT 2006: 35), people with higher social positions are slightly less

Table 1.1   Availability of a Car by Degree of Urbanization: Switzerland and England

Switzerland (percent)

	Urban	Town or Fringe	Village	Hamlet and Isolated Dwelling
No car	19.60	7.70	3.60	3.60
Car available	80.40	92.30	96.40	96.40
All	100.00	100.00	100.00	100.00
N	2762.00	2963.00	1033.00	2336.00

Pearson's Chi-squared test: X-squared=460.6998, df=3, p<2.2e−16
Cramer V (URBCAR) 0.2250772
tau=−.19

England (percent)

	Urban	Town or Fringe	Village	Hamlet and Isolated Dwelling
No car	10.60	4.90	1.40	0.60
Car available	89.40	95.10	98.60	99.40
All	100.00	100.00	100.00	100.00
N	3696.00	569.00	441.00	178.00

Pearson's Chi-squared test: X-squared=71.5547, df=3, p=1.983e−15
Cramer V (URBCAR) 0.1210406
tau=−.12

Source: *Swiss Household Panel* 2005 and *British Household Panel* 2005.

likely to have a car in Switzerland, but more likely in England. Also, in England the availability of a car correlates with being employed, whereas in Switzerland it seems to be a mere luxury good. This finding seems to indicate that the link between an access to means of movement and economic inequality is in Switzerland only an expression of inequality, but seems to be connected with an access to the labor market in England, and thus contributes to a reproduction of unequal social chances.

The second means of mobility included in this analysis is the availability of a computer[8] in the household as the necessary means to be mobile in the virtual space. In both countries, more than 80 percent of the interviewees have a computer at home; in both countries, a low social position slightly increases the chance of having no computer at home (r = −.15 in England and r = −.16 in Switzerland). Moreover, access to a private computer seems to depend on income and correlates with being in the labor force in England, but this is not the case in Switzerland. Thus, a computer seems to be linked more closely to an access to the job market in England than in Switzerland.

Corporeal Movement

Regarding geographies of inequality, the place of residence is only one node in peoples' lived spatialities, which are fundamentally rooted in movement. The technologically based time-space convergence, and, in particular, the increased availability of cars after the Second World War, allowed for a gradual replacement of irreversible by reversible mobilities (Kaufmann 2002: 24ff.). As an example, the necessity to move caused by job location can more easily be substituted by everyday commuting across longer distances.

Concerning the daily mobility represented by commuting, the data sets contain the time it takes to travel from home to work but no information about the actual distance traveled. According to other sources, in 2005, the average distance between home and workplace is 14 kilometers in England (DfT 2006: 26) and 12 kilometers in Switzerland (BFS and ARE 2007: 45). The findings of this study on the time spent commuting almost match the official sources of 22 minutes per journey in Switzerland (cf. BFS and ARE 2007: 45) and 25 in England (27 in the UK, DfT 2006: 26). This means that the time spent with traveling and the distances between the home and the place of work in the two countries are roughly the same. In England, more than three quarters of the commuting distances are traveled by car (as passenger or driver, DfT 2006: 49), whereas in Switzerland this fact applies only to two thirds (BFS and ARE 2007: 45). Taking all trips and distances into account, official statistics also show the high importance of the car in the UK, where 80 percent of the distances and 64 percent of the trips were carried out by car (as driver or passenger; DfT 2006: 13f) compared to 69 percent of the distances and 37 percent of the trips in Switzerland (BFS and ARE 2007: 38). Correspondingly, in Switzerland, the car seems to have a lower importance as a means of access to employment, which corresponds with the well-developed public transportation system.

A linear regression model (Table 1.2), explaining the length of the commuting time,[9] finds for both countries a shortening influence of the availability of a car, whereas higher education and higher social position tend to go hand in hand with longer commuting times. Furthermore, in both countries women tend to travel shorter for shorter times, and in Switzerland the existence of children in the household further shortens the commuting time (cf. Abraham and Nisic 2007: 79, Næss 2008, cf. Cattan 2008: 87ff.). In the English case, living in London seems to increase the time spent traveling to work.

A second linear regression model (Table 1.3) with social positions as the dependent variable shows once again the importance of spatial positions: in both countries the urban economic centers are important. A major impact on social positions is of course the level of achieved education. In both countries, longer commuting times significantly correlate with higher social positions, a correlation which is slightly stronger for England (r=.20) than for Switzerland (r=.14). Furthermore, in both countries virtual mobility and access to a computer seem to correlate with higher social positions. Whereas in Switzerland the availability of a car is slightly less likely for high social positions, this correlation is the other way round in England and suggests a stronger interaction of private means of mobility and social positions. This finding supports the importance of the well-developed public transportation system in Switzerland as a moderating factor on socio-spatial polarization.

Overall, the results presented here emphasize that spatial positions, access to means of mobilities as well as actual movement are interrelated with labor-induced inequalities such as social position and income (Table 1.4). The spatial infrastructure is seen to have a moderating effect, as the better spatial coverage in Switzerland has reduced the impact of access to individual transportation means and of participation in the labor market. With an increasing spatial polarization between well-connected centers and bypassed regions, accompanied by a decline of social infrastructure, the relational spatial position and the ability to move are expected to have an increasing influence on social participation. "Spatial arrangements are both products and sources of other forms of inequality" (Tickamyer 2000: 806).

However, as was argued earlier, patterns of actual movement are not determined by the available means of movement but emerge at the interface with social structures, a socio-spatial specific *habitus* and corresponding lifestyle orientations, as well as household arrangements (Jetzkowitz, Schneider, and Brunzel 2007: 150ff.).

Table 1.2 Linear Regression Models Explaining the Commuting Time: Switzerland and England

Commuting Time in Switzerland

	Estimate	Std. Error	t value	Pr(>|t|)
(Intercept)	1.719218	0.366393	4.692	2.78e–06 ***
CAR	–0.248514	0.049264	–5.045	4.73e–07 ***
CAMSIS	0.005001	0.001130	4.426	9.83e–06 ***
PC	–0.043209	0.035918	–1.203	0.22904
CENTER: other settlements	–0.007046	0.046177	–0.153	0.87873
EDURED.L	0.202603	0.042624	4.753	2.06e–06 ***
EDURED.Q	0.037590	0.026642	1.411	0.15833
KIDS	–0.099732	0.030929	–3.225	0.00127 **
SEX Female	–0.175563	–0.028707	–6.116	1.04e–09 ***
log(EQINCOME)	0.094991	0.033441	2.841	0.00452 **

Signif. codes: 0 '***' 0.001 '**' 0.01 '*' 0.05 '.' 0.1 ' ' 1
Multiple R-squared: 0.05598, Adjusted R-squared: 0.05407; F-statistic: 29.37 on 9 and 4457 DF, p<2.2e–16

Commuting Time in England

	Estimate	Std. Error	t value	Pr(>|t|)
(Intercept)	3.1737083	0.0673947	47.091	< 2e–16 ***
CAR	–0.0943919	0.0416078	–2.269	0.0234 *
CAMSIS	0.0067832	0.0009679	7.008	3.00e–12 ***
LONDON: Rest of England	–0.3509310	0.0514257	–6.824	1.07e–11 ***
PC	–0.0074451	0.0299333	–0.249	0.8036
EDURED.L	–0.2711515	0.0405281	–6.690	2.66e–11 ***
EDURED.Q	–0.0125792	0.0330248	–0.381	0.7033
EDURED.C	–0.0071794	0.0399730	–0.180	0.8575
EDURED^4	0.0335442	0.0362845	0.924	0.3553
KIDS.L	–0.0413645	0.0230991	–1.791	0.0734 .
SEX Female	–0.2354372	0.0293268	–8.028	1.43e–15 ***
log(EQINCOME)	–0.1343442	0.0536974	–2.502	0.0124 *

Signif. codes: 0 '***' 0.001 '**' 0.01 '*' 0.05 '.' 0.1 ' ' 1
Multiple R-squared: 0.1227, Adjusted R-squared: 0.1194; F-statistic: 36.64 on 11 2881 DF, p<2.2e–16

Linear regression models explaining (log) commuting time (COMTIME) by availability of a car (CAR), social position (CAMSIS), whether the interviewee lives in one of the five Swiss agglomerations (CENTER) or in London (LONDON), availability of a computer at home (PC), highest level of education achieved (EDURED), whether the interviewee lives in a household with children (KIDS), the gender (SEX) and the equalized income (EQINCOME) of the interviewee. The models have a rather poor explanatory power. Source: *Swiss Household Panel* 2005 and *British Household Panel* 2005

Table 1.3 Linear Regression Models Explaining Social Position: CAMSIS Switzerland, CAMSIS England

CAMSIS Switzerland

	Estimate	Std. Error	t value	Pr(>|t|)
Intercept	50.6311	0.9469	53.468	<2e–16 ***
CAR	–1.2487	0.6200	–2.014	0.0440 *
log(COMTIME)	1.1099	0.1877	5.913	3.58e–09 ***
PC	–3.6115	0.4509	–8.009	1.43e–15 ***
CENTER: other settlements	–1.2035	0.5911	–2.036	0.0418 *
EDURED.L	14.5120	0.4985	29.112	<2e–16 ***
EDURED.Q	2.2348	0.3356	6.660	3.04e–11 ***
KIDS	–0.1846	0.3660	–0.504	0.6140
SEX: female	4.2136	0.3633	11.600	<2e–16 ***

Signif. codes: 0 '***' 0.001 '**' 0.01 '*' 0.05 '.' 0.1 ' ' 1
Multiple R-squared: 0.2604, Adjusted R-squared: 0.2592; F-statistic: 217.1 on 8 and 4934 DF, p<2.2e–16

CAMSIS England

	Estimate	Std. Error	t value	Pr(>|t|)
(Intercept)	29.3264	1.6103	18.212	<2e–16 ***
CAR	2.8735	0.7874	3.649	0.000267 ***
log(COMTIME)	2.5275	0.3522	7.177	9.03e–13 ***
LONDON: rest of England	–3.5706	0.9827	–3.634	0.000284 ***
PC	–2.2942	0.5586	–4.107	4.12e–05 ***
EDURED.L	–20.8766	0.6709	–31.119	<2e–16 ***
EDURED.Q	1.3914	0.6298	2.209	0.027225 *
EDURED.C	–1.4736	0.7623	–1.933	0.053314 .
EDURED^4	–1.2149	0.6920	–1.756	0.079256 .
KIDS	–0.6440	0.4048	–1.591	0.111732
SEX female	5.9837	0.5548	10.786	<2e–16 ***

Signif. codes: 0 '***' 0.001 '**' 0.01 '*' 0.05 '.' 0.1 ' ' 1
Multiple R-squared: 0.3549, Adjusted R-squared: 0.3527; F-statistic: 159.1 on 10 and 2891 DF, p <2.2e–16

Linear Regression Models explaining social position (CAMSIS) by the availability of a car (CAR), the time traveling to work (COMTIME), whether the interviewee lives in one of the five Swiss agglomerations (CENTER) or in London (LONDON), the availability of a computer at home (PC), the highest level of education achieved (EDURED), whether the interviewee lives in a household with children (KIDS) and the gender of the interviewee. The models are statistically highly significant, but the English one has a higher explanatory power. (SHP 2005 and BHP 2005)

Table 1.4   Mean Commuting Time by Gender and Household

	Switzerland		England	
	Female	Male	Female	Male
One person in working age	23.2	21.6	28.3	29.1
Single parent	19.6	27.7	23.9	26.3
Couple without children	22.3	24.1	25.0	28.7
Couple with children	17.3	24.1	19.1	27.6
Other	21.7	27.8	28.5	27.7

Source: *Swiss Household Panel* 2005 and *British Household Panel* 2005.

MOBILITIES AS CRUCIAL ELEMENTS OF THE SOCIAL

Looking at the interrelations between (work-related) travel and position in social space on the basis of two representative national data sets has underlined the need to include movement as well as spatial positions in the analysis of social inequality. The spatial and infrastructural setting of one's geographical position appears to impact one's chances in social space. This has been shown by the differences between England and Switzerland as well as the internal differences between urban and rural areas. Furthermore, the need to travel for work purposes also depends on one's social position, as the longer commuting times of people in highly qualified jobs suggest. Processes of specialization and work differentiation which happen in an unequal manner geographically explain this finding.

The so called "mobilities turn" (Cresswel 2006, Urry 2007, Canzler, Kaufmann, and Kesselring 2008) put the dimension of movement as a crucial constitutive part of the social on the research agenda of the social sciences. The central argument of the mobilities paradigm sees "all social relationships as necessitating diverse 'connections' that are more or less 'at distance', more or less fast, more or less intense, and more or less involving physical movement" (Urry 2008: 13). Using the plural, these approaches typically refer to different forms of mobilities and movement,[10] which are normally analyzed separately, e.g., commuting, tourism, and virtual mobility. But only the complex assemblage of these different mobilities contingently builds and maintains social connections, relations, and structures. They should thus be studied in their interrelations. Urry identified five different forms of mobility underlying social life organized across distance, which are: (1) corporeal travel of people for different purposes of everyday life, (2) physical movement of objects to producers, consumers, and retailers, as well as souvenirs and gifts, (3) imaginative travel effected through the images of places and peoples through print and visual media, (4) virtual travel, and (5) communicative travel through person-to-person messages (Urry 2007: 47).

The mobilities turn contains a critique of sociology as having been overly focused on geographically propinquitous communities[11] based on more or less ongoing face-to-face interactions and co-presence (Urry 2008: 13). Furthermore, this turn questions some fundamental assumptions of social theory, amongst others the concept of the social as territorially bound entities, such as national societies, cities, or neighborhoods (Urry 2000: 1–20, Massey 2005: 149–162). These criticized "sedentarist metaphysics" (Cresswell 2006: 26) form the background against which Putnam (1995) identifies mobilities as a threat to social capital defined as engagement in local, closely integrated communities. But this pre-occupation with localized communities has overlooked social relations at a distance, which have gained more importance with the aforementioned processes of lengthening chains of interdependencies. Such distanced social relations constitute increasing normality in all spheres of the social. The larger spatial extension of social relations and the connecting significance of mobilities affect people's lives, but in highly differentiated, stratified, and complex ways. Whereas for some people the availability of means of movement and the resulting chance to move to different locations represent new opportunities and new degrees of freedom, other people are forced to move—be it for ecological, political, or economic reasons—and others are unable to leave their locations. This highlights the need to analyze different forms and means of movement together and within the context of their emergence rather than separately and as isolated phenomena. As an example, the distances traveled by a person may be the result of either forced or voluntary movement and thus corporeal movement cannot be seen as signifying autonomy and power (Sklair 2001, Weiss 2005 and 2008, Kellermann 2006, Beck 2007 and 2008).

In order to analyze different motivations and forms of travel and movement on a large scale, the available data collections require adapting accordingly, accounting better for different forms of mobilities rather than the more static aspects of the social. This means that research should cover various aspects of traveling, including modes of corporeal and virtual traveling, along with their frequencies, reasons, and attitudes. Household panel data surveys extended in this way would then allow carrying out elaborate research on changing patterns over time.[12]

Also at stake, as an increasingly stratified and stratifying force, is not simply the ability to move oneself from one location to another, but the ability and the power to participate in the continuously changing social world by gaining or keeping access to its valued goods, activities, values, symbols, knowledge, etc. (cf. Cass, Shove, and Urry 2005). With his concept of network capital, Urry suggests that we focus on a set of elements, which enable people to sustain social relations by means of mobilities. Network capital comprises then eight elements which "in their combination produce a distinct stratification order that now sits alongside social class, social status and party" (Urry 2007: 197). These eight elements are: (1)

an array of appropriate documents, visas, money; (2) qualifications that enable safe movement; (3) social contacts at a distance offering hospitality and invitations; (4) physical and informational movement capacities; (5) location-free information and contact points such as real or electronic diaries, answer phones, mobile phones, email, etc.; (5) communication devices; (6) appropriate and safe meeting places; (7) access to means of transportation; and (8) time and other resources to manage and coordinate the other seven elements (Urry 2007: 197f.). The network capital approach focuses on the relations between individuals, which results from the proliferation of new mobilities (Urry 2007: 198). Therefore, each of these elements represents a starting point for more detailed further research on their unequal distribution, which should not be analyzed in an isolated manner but in relation to other aspects of mobilities, network capital, and social inequality. As an example, Shove (2002) elaborates on the element of time coordination, highlighting the inherent stratifying force of time-organization skills, which are more and more demanding with a collective socio-temporal order becoming more and more individualized and diverse (Shove 2002: 8). For a broader representative study of network capital, large data sets such as the household panels should consider defining these elements and including them in the standard sets of questions on socio-demographic characteristics asked in every wave. This would allow for a systematic study of network capital as a powerful stratifying force against the backdrop of globalizing processes.

RELATIONAL SPACES OF INEQUALITIES

The theoretical approaches of mobilities and space as well as the findings of the empirical investigation sketched in the last section support an understanding of the social world as being largely rooted in different forms of mobilities, thereby constituting different spaces (Löw 2001, Massey 2005, Sheller, and Urry 2006: 216). Whereas for decades the territorial frame of the nation-state appeared to be the dominant container of social relations, these containers are more and more seen to be leaking (Taylor 2003: 108ff.), due to lengthened border-transgressing chains of interdependencies and their connected movement. Most obviously, economic activities take place on an increasingly transnational scale rather than on a national level. Political, cultural, and social processes also tend to be linked and interconnected increasingly across borders. On the other hand, some social relations seem confined to very limited areas on a sub-national level, constituting disconnected or self-sufficient spaces like various forms of ghettos or islands. Reflecting on these observations, the spatial turn in the social sciences attempts to deconstruct essentialist understandings of the isomorphism of societies and territories (Massey 2005, Painter 2008: 346). By emphasizing the heterogeneity of space-transgressing constitutive relations, trajectories, and movement (Massey 2005, Urry 2000 and 2007), the continuous process of the making of spaces moves into focus. The second aspect of my claim is that we need to include space and mobilities into inequality research as one aspect of globalization, drawing on these assumptions and insights. Therefore, I want to argue in favor of looking for new framings and methods to understand the structure of contemporary inequality relations.

Mobilities as crucial elements of social relations and a corresponding connotation of progress are not new but have been linked to Western capitalist modernity from the very beginning. The co-emergence of capitalism, modernity, and the spatial lengthening of chains of interdependencies with more general, larger socio-spatial formations like internally pacified states has been described by Elias (1999), who coined this development as the process of civilization. In this perspective, the political system of nation-states containing nationally defined societies on a confined territory appears less as the *natural* form of the social but as a historically developed one which has been politically produced, and represents a contingent intermediate stage of an ongoing but not teleological development.

In the literature, there is a debate on the question whether there has been a qualitative increase of global interconnectedness and its linked mobilities (understood as being mainly caused by technological innovations, especially information and communication technologies) or whether this is rather a continuing process (Nowicka 2006: 416ff.). Bauman (2000) argues that there has been a paradigmatic change from *heavy* modernity, the era of territorial conquest, to *light* or *liquid* modernity, where space has been annihilated by time, and has thus become insignificant (Bauman 2000: 10, 118):

> What surely cannot be in doubt is that the world geography of those [economic] relations has been transformed. Global space, as space more generally, is a product of material practices of power. What is at issue is not just openness and closure or the "length" of connections through which we, or finance capital, or whatever (. . .) go about our business. What are at issue are the constantly-being-produced new geometries of power, the shifting geographies of power relations. (Massey 2005: 85).

In order to avoid the trap of assuming some sort of final stage as a totally integrated world of instantaneous space, Urry understands globalization as a series of ongoing global processes, which are incomplete (Urry 2000: 13). Correspondingly, he does not argue that mobilities are new, rather that there is a qualitative change related to:

> the scale of movement around the world, the diversity of mobility systems now in play, the especial significance of the self expanding

automobility system and its awesome risks, the elaborate interconnections of physical movement and communications, the development of
mobility domains that by-pass national societies, the significance of
movement to contemporary governmentality, and an increased importance of multiple mobilities for people's social and emotional lives.
(Urry 2007: 195)

Thus, despite the relevance of nation-states, the increased movement of
goods, information, and people as well as risks and environmental destruction across borders highlight the coexistence and increasing relevance
of other, non-territorial spatialities. Similarly, Beck has argued that the
still-growing interdependence and interconnection of social actors across
national boundaries based on these increased mobilities forms a multidimensional process, which is irreversibly changing the very nature of the
social world. This process has been termed by Beck as "real existing cos-
mopolitanism" or "forced cosmopolitanization" (Beck 2008: 26f.). However, although the significance of the national territorial frame as a center
of these power relations seems to decrease, this does not mean the end of
international differences. Rather, territorial spatial position and citizenship
itself appear to be an increasingly important dimension of inequality. As
Beck (2007: 690) and Weiss (2005) argue, the membership of a nation-
state remains an important aspect of the access to chances and resources.
For example, access to welfare, health, education systems, and everything
that involves border-crossing is facilitated or constrained by citizenship.
Correspondingly, the concept of network capital contains the aspects of
appropriate documents rendering traveling easy or difficult. Moreover, as
I have shown on the basis of comparing data from two countries, national
transportation systems can moderate or accentuate the impact of one's geographical position in relation to other locations.

Thus, in order to analyze inequalities, it seems necessary not only to
focus on the national spatial framework but also on further spatial frames
and geographies of these lived inequality relations linked to empirical analysis. This refers to several levels of socio-spatial inequality research. The
inclusion of space and mobilities into inequality research should try to re-
construct the spaces that people as well as goods and other resources create
with their movement rather than simply to assume congruency of space and
the social by using pre-defined territories as frames of analysis. This also
applies to the construction of inequality measures like the CAMSIS scale,
which assumes national societies as frames of social interactions. The network capital of people or social groups together with their trajectories in
different spaces, the unequal chances of participating in the different social
fields, and the ways by which they are reproduced need to be analyzed.
The overlapping, interrelations, and separations within these social spaces
can move into the focus of analysis, indicating socio-spatial and powerful, as well as disconnected and powerless, "positionalities" (cf. Sheppard

2002). The national frame of my own research constitutes the largely administrative political and territorial geography of inequalities and the specific landscape shaped by national spatial planning policies. However, this national territory is crisscrossed by further relational spaces made by the movement of goods, information, risks, and people following different logics and forces (Painter 2008). Studying the spatial figurations of Switzerland emphasizes that the border-transgressing movement of daily commuters, migrants, international capital, knowledge, etc. are crucial, and form strongly stratified parts of the picture. For England, the history of being at the center of an Empire, with its resulting immigration patterns as well as an internationalized economy along with the particular relations to the European Union, seem to constitute relevant elements of different spatial extensions. Furthermore, spatial planning policies (as well as many other areas of politics) are increasingly ruled by the European Union, accounting for new spatial relations and aiming at European spatial cohesion (cf. Peters 2003, Richardson 2006). These movement-based spaces, their creation, and their impact are to be analyzed in future research.

Understanding social inequality as multidimensional and spatial asks the question of the relevance of these different dimensions for people's lives and identities. The history of social movement indicates that these dimensions are constituted through broader cultural movements of recognition and are subject to change (Fraser 2003). Similarly, Bourdieu (2001) understood the social world as consisting of social spaces in which significant differences are the object of ongoing power struggles. The relations of these spaces are contested. This means that the significance and experience of the dimensions of social inequality for people and social groups within their specific context should also be included in mobile and spatial approaches to inequalities.

However, studying inequalities in the context of these changing and mobile frames is linked to several problems. For example, how are inequalities defined, for whom, and involving which geography? Neither the national society nor the global stratified society appear to be sufficient reference points.[13] In contrast to the construction of an objective viewpoint outside the social, from where social classes are constructed, the actor's perspective allows for a better understanding of the social construction, framing, and legitimization of inequalities. This involves further challenges for data collections, definitions, and sampling frames.

Yet, in order to understand the contingent and contested construction and significance of identities and inequalities centered in these reference frames, more mobile and spatially informed research and data sources are needed. The mobilities turns as well as multidimensional inequality approaches in social theory offer some fundamental concepts accessible to integration and definition. More systematic, large-scale research and adequate data sets, which contain information about peoples' trajectories, movements, and spaces are still missing. Moreover, the largely a-spatial approach of quantifying statistical analysis in sociology should be extended to more spatial methods of analysis and visualization. Thus, the goal of a corresponding re-conceptualization of inequality research could involve the development of interdisciplinary approaches and new methods adequate in addressing mobility.

NOTES

1. Bourdieu uses space in a metaphorical sense.
2. At least on the forefront, these aims served as legitimization and kept up the liberal ideal of equal chances, and social justice, education, welfare, and spatial policies pursued these goals. Critical sociological theory has long since unveiled that these policies also worked as subtle mechanisms to reproduce inequalities and power (cf. Bourdieu 1983 and 2001, Kreckel 1992, Vester 2004).
3. The Bologna process aims at the creation of a European higher education area by standardizing academic degrees and introducing quality assurance standards. PISA refers to the Program for International Student Assessment, a triennial test of 15-year-old school-children's scholastic performance, and is coordinated by the Organization for Economic Cooperation and Development (OECD).
4. One of these phenomena is the case of the highly standardized MBA, an internationally accredited and internationally recognized degree in business administration, forming a hierarchical networked space of business schools.
5. But, as highlighted prominently by Kaufmann (2002: 61), although in general there seems to be an increase of "connexity," "motility" as the potential to be mobile consists of "access to different forms and degrees of mobility, competence to recognize and make use of access, and appropriation of a particular choice" (Kaufmann, Bergman, and Joye 2004: 750).
6. For example Michael Schumacher, who is thought to be one of the richest people in Switzerland.
7. This finding is similar to that of the National Travel Survey 2005 (DfT 2006: 8) and the Swiss Transport Micro-census 2005 (BFS and ARE 2007: 26).
8. Unfortunately, for Switzerland there is no information about Internet access.
9. In order to balance out the skewness, the logarithm of the variable *commuting time* was included into the model.
10. In the literature, the terms *mobility* and *movement* are used largely interchangeably. *Mobility* still refers more to the "social processes around movement" (Drewes Nielsen 2005: 53) thus denoting "the socially produced motion" (Cresswell 2006: 3), whereas *movement* focuses more on the "act of displacement (. . .) between locations" (Cresswell 2006: 2f.). The use of these terms in this chapter follows this terminology without emphasizing or elaborating on their different focus.
11. Sociology has taken geographical proximity as the pre-condition for social interaction and overlooked interaction and social relations at a distance, which happen to be rather paradigmatic for modern societies (Urry 2000).
12. The official sources such as the National Travel Survey in the UK use sample data rather than panel data. In Switzerland, the Federal Office of Statistics was able to use census data, which are difficult to access and not available for most countries.
13. Yet, as has been suggested here, the national frame and national citizenship remain a stratifying force. Further, as Sklair (2001: 10ff.) argued, a transnational capitalist class can be identified within a global system, actually acting like a class in some spheres. Thus, both reference frames are necessary but not sufficient by themselves.

BIBLIOGRAPHY

Abraham, M. and N. Nisic (2007) "Regionale Bindung, räumliche Mobilität und Arbeitsmarkt—Analysen für die Schweiz und Deutschland" *Schweizerische Zeitschrift für Soziologie* 33 (1): 69–88.

Allen, J. (2003) *Lost Geographies of Power*. Malden: Blackwell Publishing.

ARE (2008) "Monitoring urbaner Raum Schweiz," *Themenkreis B4: Verkehr im Schweizer Städtesystem*. Bundesamt für Raumentwicklung.

Axhausen, K. W. (2007) "Activity Spaces, Biographies, Social Networks and their Welfare Gains and Externalities: Some Hypotheses and Empirical Results," *Mobilities* 2 (1): 15–36.

Bauman, Z. (2000) *Liquid Modernity*. Cambridge: Polity Press.

Beck, U. (1986) *Risikogesellschaft. Auf dem Weg in eine andere Moderne*, Frankfurt a.M.: Suhrkamp.

Beck, U. (2007) "Beyond Class and Nation. Reframing Social Inequalities in a Globalizing World," *The British Journal of Sociology* 58 (4): 679–705.

Beck, U. (2008) "Mobility and the Cosmopolitan Perspective," in W. Canzler, V. Kaufmann, and S. Kesselring (eds) *Tracing Mobilities. Towards a Cosmopolitan Perspective*, 25–35. Aldershot: Ashgate.

Bergman, M. M., P. Lambert, K. Prandy, and D. Joye (2002) "Theorization, Construction, and Validation of a Social Stratification Scale. Cambridge Social Interaction and Stratification Scale (CAMSIS) for Switzerland," *Swiss Journal of Sociology* 28 (1): 7–25.

BFS and ARE (2007) *Mobilität in der Schweiz. Ergebnisse des Mikrozensus 2005 zum Verkehrsverhalten*. Bundesamt für Statistik, Bundesamt für Bauwesen und Raumordnung, Neuchâtel, Bern.

Bourdieu, P. (1986) "The (three) Forms of Capital," in J. G. Richardson (ed.) *Handbook of Theory and Research in the Sociology of Education*, 241–258. New York and London: Greenwood Press.

Bourdieu, P. (2000) *Distinction. A Social Critique of the Judgment of Taste*, Cambridge, Mass.: Harvard University Press.

Bradley, H. (1996) *Fractured Identities. Changing Patterns of Inequality*. Oxford and Cambridge: Polity Press.

Canzler, W., V. Kaufmann, and S. Kesselring (eds) (2008) *Tracing Mobilities. Towards a Cosmopolitan Perspective*. Aldershot: Ashgate.

Cass, N., E. Shove, and J. Urry (2005) "Social Exclusion, Mobility and Access," *Sociological Review* 53 (3): 539–555.

Castells, M. (2002 [1996]) "The Space of Flows," in I. Susser (ed.) *The Castells Reader on Cities and Social Theory*, 45–63. Oxford: Blackwell Publishers.

Cattan, N. (2008) "Gendering Mobility: Insights into the Construction of Spatial Concepts," in T. P. Uteng, and T. Cresswell (eds) *Gendered Mobilities*, 83–97. Aldershot: Ashgate.

Champion, T. (2005) "Population Movement within the UK," in National Statistics (ed.) *Focus on People and Migration*. Office for National Statistics: London, 91–114.

Cresswell, T. (2006) *On the Move: Mobility in the Modern Western World*. New York and London: Routledge.

DfT (2000) *Social Exclusion and the Provision and Availability of Public Transport Report*. London, Department for Transport.

DfT (2006) *Transport Statistics Bulletin: National Travel Survey 2005*. London, Department for Transport.

DfT (2008) *National Rail Travel Survey. Final 2008 Report. Final Results of Rail Travel across Great Britain*. London, Department for Transport in Association with Transport Scotland.

Elias, N. (2000 [1939]) *The Civilizing Process: Sociogenetic and Psychogentic Investigation*. Oxford: Blackwell Publishers.
Erikson, R. and J. H. Goldthorpe (1992) *The Constant Flux. A Study of Class Mobility in Industrial Societies*. Oxford: Clarendon Press.
Fraser, N. (2003) "Soziale Gerechtigkeit im Zeitalter der Identitätspolitik. Umverteilung, Anerkennung und Beteiligung," in N. Fraser and A. Honneth (eds) *Umverteilung oder Anerkennung? Eine politisch-philosophische Kontroverse*, 13–128. Frankfurt a.M.: Suhrkamp.
Frello, B. (2008) "Towards a Discursive Analytics of Movement: On the Making and Unmaking of Movement as an Object of Knowledge," *Mobilities* 3 (1): 25–50.
Glauser, P., B. Jeanneret, and M.-C. Hotz (2006) *Regionale Disparitäten in der Schweiz. Teilbericht 1: Analyse regionaler Disparitäten*. Zürich, Bundesamt für Statistik (BFS), Sektion Räumliche Analysen (RA), Abteilung Raumwirtschaft und Nachhaltige Entwicklung (RW).
Graham, S. (2001) "The City as Sociotechnical Process. Networked Mobilities and Urban Social Inequalities," *City* 5 (3): 339–349.
Graham, S. and S. Marvin (2001) *Splintering Urbanism. Networked Infrastructures, Technological Mobilities and the Urban Condition*. London and New York: Routledge.
Grusky, D. B. (ed.) (1994) *Social Stratification. Class, Race, and Gender in Sociological Perspective*, Boulder, San Francisco, Oxford: Westview Press.
Harley, J. B. (2002) "Deconstructing the Map," in M. J. Dear and S. Flusty (eds) *The Spaces of Postmodernity. Readings in Human Geography*, 277–289. Oxford, Malden: Blackwell Publishing.
Harvey, D. (1990) *The Condition of Postmodernity. An Enquiry into the Origins of Cultural Change*. London: Blackwell Publishers.
Healey, P. (2004) "The Treatment of Space and Place in the New Strategic Spatial Planning in Europe," *International Journal of Urban and Regional Research* 28 (1): 45–67.
Herod, A. (1997) "From a Geography of Labor to a Labor Geography: Labor's Spatial Fix and the Geography of Capitalism," *Antipode* 2 (1): 1–31.
Holden, E. (2007) *Achieving Sustainable Mobility. Everyday and Leisure-time Travel in the EU*. Aldershot: Ashgate.
Janelle, D. G. (1968) "Central Place Development in a Time-Space Framework," *Professional Geographer* 20 (1): 5–10.
Jetzkowitz, J., J. Schneider, and S. Brunzel (2007) "Suburbanisation, Mobility and the 'Good Life in the Country': A Lifestyle Approach to the Sociology of Urban Sprawl in Germany," *Sociologia Ruralis* 47 (2): 148–171.
Jiron, P. M. (2007) "Unraveling Invisible Inequalities in the City through Urban Daily Mobility. The Case of Santiago de Chile," *Schweizerische Zeitschrift für Soziologie* 33 (1): 45–68.
Kaufmann, V. (2002) *Re-thinking Mobility. Contemporary Sociology*. Hampshire: Ashgate.
Kaufmann, V., M. M. Bergman, and D. Joye (2004) "Motility. Mobility as Capital," *International Journal of Urban and Regional Research* 28 (4): 745–756.
Kellerman, A. (2006) *Personal Mobilities*. London and New York: Routledge.
Kreckel, R. (1992) *Politische Soziologie der sozialen Ungleichheit*. Frankfurt a.M.: Campus.
Kübler, D. (2006) "Wider eine Drei-Klassen-Schweiz. Drei Szenarien für das verstädterte Land und was daraus zu folgern ist," *Neue Züricher Zeitung*. (March 15th)
Kübler, D. (2004) "Städte und Agglomerationen in der Schweiz: eine Herausforderung für Politik und Institutionen," in C. Suter, I. Renschler, and D. Joye (eds) *Sozialbericht 2004*, 112–133. Reihe Gesellschaft Schweiz Zürich: Seismo.

Larsen, J., K. W. Axhausen, and J. Urry (2006) "Geographies of Social Networks: Meetings, Travel and Communications," *Mobilities* 1 (2): 261–283.

Lash, S. and J. Urry (1994) *Economies of Signs and Space*. London, Thousands Oaks, Delhi: Sage.

Lechte, J. (1995) "(Not) Belonging in Postmodern Space," in S. Watson and K. Gibson (eds) *Postmodern cities and spaces*, 99–111. Oxford: Blackwell Publishers.

Löw, M. (2001) *Raumsoziologie*. Frankfurt a.M.: Suhrkamp.

Lyotard, J.-F. (1984) *The Postmodern Condition: A Report on Knowledge*. Manchester: Manchester University Press.

Manderscheid, K. (2007) "Urbanität im 21. Jahrhundert—Verfall oder Chance einer Lebensform? Eine soziologische Kontextualisierung," in D. Baum (ed) *Die Stadt in der Sozialen Arbeit. Ein Handbuch für soziale und planende Berufe*, 52–70. Wiesbaden: VS Verlag für Sozialwissenschaften.

Manderscheid, K. (2009) "Integrating Space and Mobilities into the Analysis of Social Inequality," *Distinktion* 18: 7–27.

Manderscheid, K. and M. M. Bergman (2008) "Spatial Patterns and Social Inequalitiy in Switzerland—Modern or Postmodern?" in G. Pflieger, L. Pattaroni, C. Jemelin, and V. Kaufmann (eds) *The Social Fabric of the Networked City*, 41–65. London and New York: Routledge.

Marx, K. (1973 [1861]) *Grundrisse. Outlines of the Critique of Political Economy*, Harmondsworth: Penguin.

Massey, D. (1984) *Spatial Divisions of Labour*. London: Macmillan.

Massey, D. (2005) *For Space*. London, Thousand Oaks, New Delhi: Sage.

Mol, A. and J. Law (1994) "Regions, Networks and Fluids: Anaemia and Social Topology," *Social Studies of Science* 24 (4): 641–671.

Næss, P. (2008) "Gender Differences in the Influences of Urban Structure on Daily Travel," in T. P. Uteng and T. Cresswell (eds) *Gendered Mobilities*, 173–192. Aldershot: Ashgate.

Nassehi, A. (1995) "Der Fremde als Vertrauter. Soziologische Beobachtungen zur Konstruktion von Identitäten und Differenzen," *Kölner Zeitschrift für Soziologie und Sozialpsychologie* 47 (3): 443–463.

Nowicka, M. (2006) "Mobility, Space and Social Structuration in the Second Modernity and Beyond," *Mobilities* 1 (3): 411–435.

Painter, J. (2008) "Cartographic Anxiety and the Search for Regionality," *Environment and Planning A* 40 (2): 342–361.

Peters, D. (2003) "Cohesion, Polycentricity, Missing Links and Bottlenecks: Conflicting Spatial Storylines for Pan-European Transport Investments," *European Planning Studies* 11 (3): 317–339.

Pointer, G. (2005) "The UK's Major Urban Areas," in National Statistics (ed.) *Focus On People and Migration*. London: Office for National Statistics.

Prandy, K. (1990) "The revised Cambridge Scale of Occupations," *Sociology* 24 (4): 629–655.

Putnam, R. D. (1995) "Bowling Alone: America's Declining Social Capital," *Journal of Democracy* 6 (1): 65–78.

Rammler, S. (2008) "The *Wahlverwandtschaft* of Modernity and Mobility," in W. Canzler, V. Kaufmann, and S. Kesselring (eds) *Tracing Mobilities. Towards a Cosmopolitan Perspective*, 57–75. Aldershot: Ashgate.

Richardson, T. (2006) "The Thin Simplification of European Space: Dangerous Calculations?" *Comparative European Politics* 4 (1): 203–217.

Richardson, T. and O. B. Jensen (2008) "How Mobility Systems Produce Inequality: Making Mobile Subject Types on the Bangkok Sky Train," *Built Environment* 34 (2): 218–231.

Sassen, S. (2001a) *The Global City*. Princeton: Princeton University Press.

Sassen, S. (2001b) "Spatialities and Temporalities of the Global. Elements for a Theorization," in A. Appadurai (ed.) *Globalization*, 260–278. Durham and London: Duke University Press.

Savage, M. (1988) "The Missing Link? The Relationship between Spatial Mobility and Social Mobility," *The British Journal of Sociology* 39 (4): 554–577.

Savage, M. (2000) *Class Analysis and Social Transformation*. Buckingham, Philadelphia: Open University Press.

Sayer, A. (2005) *The Moral Significance of Class*. Cambridge: Cambridge University Press.

Sheller, M. and J. Urry (2006) "The New Mobilities Paradigm," *Environment and Planning A* 38 (2): 207–226.

Sheppard, E. (2002) "The Spaces and Times of Globalization: Place, Scale, Networks, and Positionality," *Economic Geography* 78 (3): 307–330.

Shove, E. (2002) *Rushing around: Coordination, Mobility and Inequality*. Published by the Department of Sociology, Lancaster University, Lancaster LA1 4YN, UK. http://www.comp.lancs.ac.uk/sociology/papers/Shove-Rushing-Around.pdf, accessed on July 20, 2009.

Simmel, G. (1950 [1908]) "The Stranger," in K. Wolff (ed.) *The Sociology of Georg Simmel*. New York: Free Press, 402–408.

Simmel, G. (1950 [1903]) "The Metropolis and Mental Life," in K. Wolff (ed.) *The Sociology of Georg Simmel*, 409–424. New York: Free Press.

Sklair, L. (2001) *The Transnational Capitalist Class*. Oxford: Blackwell Publishing.

Taylor, P. J. (2003) "The State as Container: Territoriality in the Modern World-System," in N. Brenner, B. Jessop, M. Jones, and G. MacLeod (eds) *State/Space. A Reader*, 101–113. Malden, Oxford: Blackwell Publishing.

Tickamyer, A. R. (2000) "Space Matters! Spatial Inequality in Future Sociology," *Contemporary Sociology* 29 (6): 805–813.

Urry, J. (2000) *Sociology beyond Societies*. London and New York: Routledge.

Urry, J. (2007) *Mobilities*. Cambridge: Polity Press.

Urry, J. (2008) "Moving on the Mobility Turn," in W. Canzler, V. Kaufmann, and S. Kesselring (eds) *Tracing Mobilities. Towards a Cosmopolitan Perspective*, 13–23. Aldershot: Ashgate.

Vester, M. (2004) "Die Illusion der Bildungsexpansion. Bildungsöffnungen und soziale Segregation in der Bundesrepublik Deutschland," in B. Krais, and S. Engler (eds) *Das kulturelle Kapital und die Macht der Klassenstrukturen*, 13–54. Weinheim: Juventa.

Wajcman, J. (2008) "Life in the Fast Lane? Towards a Sociology of Technology and Time," *The British Journal of Sociology* 59 (1): 59–77.

Walby, S. (2000) "Analyzing Social Inequality in the Twenty-First Century. Globalization and Modernity Restructure Inequality," *Contemporary Sociology* 29 (6): 813–818.

Walby, S. (2001) "From Community to Coalition: The Politics of Recognition as the Handmaiden of the Politics of Redistribution," *Theory, Culture and Society* 18 (2–3): 113–135.

Weiss, A. (2005) "The Transnationalization of Social Inequality: Conceptualizing Social Positions on a World Scale," *Current Sociology* 53 (4): 707–728.

Weiss, A. (2008) "Raumrelationen als zentraler Aspekt weltweiter Ungleichheiten," in H. Bude and A. Willisch (eds) *Exklusion. Die Debatte über die "Überflüssigen,"* 225–245. Frankfurt a.M.: Suhrkamp.

Wright, E. O. (2000) *Class Counts*. Cambridge: Cambridge University Press.

2 Impact of Remittances on Income Inequalities in Romania

Ana Maria Zamfir, Cristina Mocanu,
Eva Militaru, and Speranta Pirciog

INTRODUCTION

Transition form plan to market brought massive lay offs and cut real wages and living standards for most of the people in Romania. High unemployment rates and lack of employment opportunities determined significant flows of external migration. After the first years of transition, emigration was slowly replaced by temporary migration abroad as a new form of external migration emerged: circulatory migration. Internal migration has remained rather low as it implies high costs and poor returns. During the last decade, as the Romanian economy started to grow, prices of real estate, including rentals, skyrocketed especially in several emerging urban areas. In the same time, wages displayed a moderate increase so that not many people could afford to migrate from rural to urban localities. Therefore, year by year, workers, with or without their families, temporary or even definitely, chose to move to more developed countries in order to increase standards of living for themselves and their families.

Nowadays, Romania has realized nine consecutive years of economic growth and has joined the European Union. However, the economic gap between Romania and Western countries still remains significant and pushes Romanians to migrate in order to look for employment abroad using well-developed migration paths and networks of migrants. Poverty and vulnerability, lack of employment opportunities at the local level, or poor prospects of personal achievement motivate Romanians to leave their home communities and families in order to work abroad. Most of them send remittances to their families at home in order to help them to cope with poverty or financial constraints or simply to invest in long-lasting estates, education, or small-scale businesses. Although there are important public debates on the mixed outcomes of remittances, research studying migration issues continues to cope with lack of reliable official data.

In this chapter, our aim is to assess the impact of migration and remittances on interhousehold income inequalities. We build our analysis on data on incomes and remittances from a 2007 national household survey. In order to validate our findings, two different methods of impact assessment are employed: one in which remittances are considered as an *exogenous transfer* of the migrant households and another in which remittances are treated as a *substitute income* of home earnings. On the one hand, income inequalities are estimated in the presence and absence of remittances as they are considered independently from home earnings. Therefore, in order to assess the impact of remittances, observed inequalities as they result for household incomes including remittances are compared to those characterizing the income distribution without remittances. On the other hand, observed inequalities are compared to a counterfactual scenario in the absence of migration and remittances. For this, we estimate a simulated income of migrant households in order to project the income distribution in the absence of migration. As migrant households are systematically different from non-migrant households, we reduce the selection bias by taking into account both observed and unobserved factors linked to the decision to migrate. We assess thus the impact of remittances by comparing observed income inequalities to those from the simulated counterfactual scenario. As we aim to investigate the impact of remittances on inequalities at the national level, as well as in between and within urban and rural areas, interhousehold income inequalities are measured by estimating the Theil index T, which is a well-known measure of inequality with the possibility of decomposition by subgroups.

Thus, the first part of this chapter analyzes main evolutions of migration flows from Romania during the transition period and in recent years in order to set a background for the understanding of the outcomes of migration on the Romanian social structure. The following parts present the theoretical framework and the methodological approach, whereas the last section is dedicated to the main findings.

RECENT HISTORY OF EXTERNAL MIGRATION

After 1989, both the amplitude and the causes of emigration changed. After the end of communism, and linked to the instability of the political regime, emigration peaked at 100,000 Romanians in 1990. Emigration followed then a constantly decreasing trend that reached about 11,000 emigrants in 2005. The transition period also brought changes to the key drivers of emigration as economic motivation became more and more important (Fig. 2.1). Another phenomenon emerged: irregular migration with the purposes of working abroad. Beginning in the mid-nineties, apace with the constant decline of legal emigration, irregular migration gained ground and became the most important component of Romanian migration, boosted by the new visa-free regime in the European Union (Militaru, Mocanu, and Zamfir 2007).

Official statistics failed in measuring temporary migration so that most estimates have been established by data provided by several household surveys. According to a recent Open Society Foundation study, more than one third of Romanian households had at least one migrant member during 1990–2006 (Sandu 2006). Three stages of migration can be identified and are described by Sandu (2006), as follows:

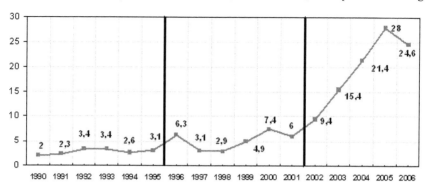

Figure 2.1 Migration for Employment Abroad—Rate at 1,000 Inhabitants, 1990–2006.

Source: Temporary Living Abroad: Economic Migration of Romanians: 1990–2006, Open Society Foundation 2006: 27.

The first stage of migration from Romania was circumscribed to the period 1990 to 1995, being characterized by an emigration rate of 3 per 1,000 people. The most important destinations were Israel, Turkey, Italy, Hungary, and Germany: "This was the period of a first exploration of Europe by the Romanians in search of work, of a better living," as Sandu argued (2006: 14). Men represent the overwhelming majority of these "adventurers" looking at exploring the worldwide opportunities during their migration. Most of them were married, aged 30 to 54 years, with a medium education (vocational or high school), who most often originated from the urban areas.

The second stage, between 1996 and 2001, was characterized by emigration rates of 7 per 1,000 people, with Spain, the USA, and Canada as the main countries of destination. Even if being a man remained a prerequisite for migration abroad, the share of women looking for employment abroad started to rise during this phase of migration. Rural areas gained ground, on a parity with urban areas in their importance as pools for economic migration. The profile of migrants changed, as the share of not-married men and women, and the number of migrants with a secondary education, increased. The share of youth aged 15–29 years rose during this stage and the following one, both for rural and urban areas.

The last stage of migration was boosted by the removal of the Schengen Visa and covered the period from 2001 to 2006. Emigration rates rose to 28 per 1,000 people in 2005, and the main destinations were Italy, Spain, Germany, Hungary, and Israel. "Following the access granted within the Schengen area, in January 2002, the process intensified. Working abroad becomes a mass phenomenon, with a temporary emigration rate between 10% and 28%" (Sandu 2006: 14). According to the same estimations, for this time period, women represented 45 percent of the total number of migrants.

Progressively, as migration networks and other information sources have developed the phenomenon, migration has become more and more hetero-geneic, comprising rather diverse population segments.

Strongly connected to the increasing flows of migration for working abroad, remittances have become the second largest external financial source after foreign direct investment, according to the estimations of the National Bank of Romania (Copaciu and Răcaru 2006). Remittances were estimated at US$ 1.753 billion in 2004 and rose to US$ 4.440 billion in 2005, when they actually accounted for approximately 4.5 percent of GDP (Copaciu and Răcaru 2006). Consumption has become the most important utilization of remittances, accounting for 65 percent of them, whereas only 35 percent are used for investments and savings (Liviu Voinea, Group of Applied Economics 2006).[1]

THEORETICAL BACKGROUND

A variety of theories and models have been developed in order to explain international migration and its outcomes. There has been considerable the-oretical and empirical research on the impact of the movement of people on social and economic structures, both in countries of origin and destination. Migration theories conceptualize the causes and effects of movements by using a wide range of concepts, assumptions, and levels of analysis.

From a macro-perspective, neoclassical economics considers that dif-ferentials in wages and employment opportunities are the most important determinants of labor migration (Lewis 1954, Ranis and Fei 1961, Todaro 1976, Borjas 1989). Mismatches between the demand for and the supply of labor force in different countries and development gaps cause movements of workers that are followed by flows of capital investment that may in the long run reduce disparities. From a micro-perspective, individuals act as ratio-nal actors and decide to migrate due to cost-benefit calculations that make them anticipate net positive returns from migration (Todaro 1976). Accord-ing to this point of view, people migrate wherever the expected net returns are higher and, thus, the size of expected net returns determines the size of migration flows.

More recently, theories of migration have shifted the focus from the individual to the household that represents a more appropriate unit of analysis. This approach considers that when sending one or more family members to work abroad, families/households can maximize their income while minimizing risks and constraints of the local market (Stark 1984, Taylor 1986). Moreover, workers comparing incomes decide to migrate as a response to their feelings of relative deprivation (Stark and Bloom 1985). They migrate in order to change their status within their reference group or to change their reference group. Therefore, communities characterized by higher inequality are likely to display a higher propensity to migration.

However, the migrant takes migration decisions together with his/her family members as they commit themselves to share both costs and returns of migration. Remittances represent one important part of this arrangement between migrants and their families (Stark and Bloom 1985). Moreover, new economics of migration theorize a potential indirect effect of migration and remittances on other sources of income in the migrant-sending households, with a focus on the participation in the labor market of the remaining members of the family.

Nevertheless, important steps have been made in order to reunite different perspectives into a coherent approach that could offer a proper background of analysis for migration research. Migration decisions are taken by family members within their households, considering socioeconomic conditions at the local level. Moreover, features of the local context are influenced by national and international policies which need to be understood in a historical perspective (Massey 1990).

Migration and Inequality

A number of studies have examined the linkages between migration and inequalities, both in the countries of origin and destination. However, the impact of migration on sending communities/countries is still a subject of considerable debate. Although many analysts agree that remittances represent a path of income redistribution among countries, they fail to agree on their outcomes on families, localities, and urban-rural areas (Jones 1998). Findings from other studies investigating the impact of migration and remittances on economic inequalities are rather mixed as some of them find positive and others negative results. Thus, Stark, Taylor, and Yitzhaki (1986) showed that remittances reduce income inequalities in northern Mexico. More recently, Brown and Jimenez (2007) found positive effects of migration income and remittances on poverty alleviation and income inequality in Fiji and Tonga. On the other hand, analyzing income distribution in Vietnam, Cuong (2008) discovered that although foreign remittances have decreased poverty while increasing household income and consumption, they also increased inequality, albeit at a small magnitude. Pernia (2008) found that international remittances raise average incomes for all income groups in the Philippines, but more so for richer households than for the poorer ones. Therefore, these remittances cause an increase in the level of income inequalities.

Many analysts show that a selective process determines the access to remittances for different groups of people, a fact that changes the interfamilial inequality in different ways. As Jones (1998) pointed out, structuralists believe that migrants come from the higher strata of the social structure, creating a *migrant elite* and increasing inequality (McArthur 1979), whereas functionalists consider that migrants originate in the lower strata, producing inequality reduction in the localities of origin (Taylor 1986).

In this context, Jones (1998) has developed a spatio-temporal perspective on remittances and inequality, showing that these divergent conclusions are linked to a couple of factors: the variations of the unit of analysis and different stages of migration characterizing inequality. Thus, different regions can experience the beginning period, an intermediate, or advanced stage of their migration history. This theory explains changes in the selectivity process and, subsequently, in inequality across various migration stages. At the beginning of the migration history (in the so-called *innovator stage*), only individuals from the richer households can afford the costs of migration, determining an increase of income inequalities at the local level. In the next stage (*early adopter stage*), due to communication and networks that decrease the costs of migration, a larger segment of individuals has access to migration and remittances, generating a decline of income inequalities. In places with long migration history (*late adopter stage*), migrants compose an above-average income class apart from poor households with no migration experiences that makes localities display rather high levels of income inequalities. However, analyses made at a different scale show that inequality between urban and rural areas declines during the last two stages of migration (Jones 1998). Thus, "migration stage and spatial scale are controls on the relationship between migrant selectivity, remittances, and inequality." (Jones 1998: 12)

METHODOLOGY

In order to decide whether migration is beneficial to inequality reduction, we need to compare income distribution including migration and remittances to income distribution in the absence of migration. The latter variable, incomes of migrants in the absence of migration, cannot be observed. Therefore, the methodology that we use in the present chapter is based on the estimation of incomes of migrant households as if migration had not occurred, according to two approaches. First, remittances are treated as exogenous transfers and the income of migrant households in the absence of remittances is obtained by the observed household income excluding remittances. Second, a counterfactual scenario is obtained by estimating the household income of migrant households if they had not migrated, on the basis of non-migrant households using econometric models.

The Theil inequality index for both estimated income distributions, as well as the observed situation are then computed. Then we compare the values of the index in three situations: observed, observed without remittances, and counterfactual without remittances.

As the first method of estimating the income of migrants in the absence of remittances—by subtracting remittances from the observed income—is a very intuitive one, our attention will be focused on the second method, that of constructing a counterfactual scenario for migrant households.

We shall obtain our counterfactual scenario in two steps: (1) we estimate a model of household earnings based on the observed situation but taking into account only non-migrant households, and (2), we predict the income of migrant households in the absence of migration on the basis of the estimated model.

Because migrant and non-migrant households are not randomly selected from the general population, it is very difficult to obtain an appropriate comparison group of non-migrants. Therefore, the direct estimation of the income of migrant households could be biased and corrections of a selective bias are needed in order to get consistent estimates. To correct the selective bias, we use a standard selection model and the two-step Heckman procedure[2]:

$$P_i^* = \alpha Z_i + \varepsilon_i, \quad P_i = 1 \Leftrightarrow P_i^* > 0; P_i = 0 \Leftrightarrow P_i^* \leq 0 \tag{1}$$

$$\log y_{0i} = \beta_0 X_i + \mu_{0i} \text{ observed for } P_i = 0 \tag{2}$$

where P_i is a dummy variable for migration, being equal to 0 for non-migrant households and equal to 1 for migrant households; α is the vector of coefficients for the independent variables Z_i; P_i^* is a non-observed continuous latent variable that will be estimated using a Probit model on Z_i, which is a vector of independent variables of participation in the migration process; $\log y_{0i}$ is the dependent log income for non-migrant households; X_i is a vector of independent variables influencing income; μ_i and ε_i are unobserved error terms following a normal distribution.

First, we estimate a Probit equation for the decision of the household to participate in migration (1). On the basis of the estimated coefficients, we compute the Inverse Mills Ratio (λ) that measures the expected value of the contribution of unobserved characteristics to the decision to participate in migration, conditional on the observed participation in migration:

$$\hat{\lambda}_i = E(\varepsilon_i / P_i) = \begin{cases} -\phi(\hat{\alpha} Z_i)/(1 - \Phi(\hat{\alpha} Z)_i, \text{ for } P_i = 0 \\ \phi(\hat{\alpha} Z_i)/\Phi(\hat{\lambda} Z_i), \text{ for } P = 1_i \end{cases} \tag{3}$$

where φ is the density function for the standard normal distribution and Φ is the standard normal cumulative density function, whereas $\hat{a}$ is the estimated value for α in equation (1).

The computed lambda for non-migrant households ($P_i=0$) is used as a variable in the equation that models the household earnings of non participants in migration. So the equation (2) becomes:

$$\log y_{0i} = \beta X_i + \gamma \hat{\lambda}_i + \mu_i, \text{ for } P_i = 0 \tag{4}$$

where $E(\mu_{0i}/P_i)=0$, $\text{VAR}(\mu_{0i}/P_i) = \sigma_0^2$

Using the estimated parameters from equation (4), we can predict the counterfactual household income of migrant households if they had not migrated:

$$\log \hat{y}_{0i} = \hat{\beta} \, X_i + \hat{\gamma} \, \hat{\lambda}_i + \hat{\mu}_i, \text{ for } P_i = 1 \tag{5}$$

In order to have a full distribution of the counterfactual income, unobserved terms for migrant households have to be generated:

$$\hat{\mu}_{0i} = \hat{\sigma} \, \Phi^{-1}(r)$$

where $\hat{\sigma}_0$ is the estimated standard error of μ_{0i} for non-migrant households, r is a random number between 0 and 1, and Φ^{-1} is the inverse of the cumulative density function.

Having got the counterfactual income distribution for migrant households in the non-migration scenario, we can estimate the inequality of income distribution in both situations: observed and counterfactual. We can also compare the distribution of the observed income with the distribution of the observed income without remittances. Consequently, our results show the extent to which inequality changes in the *counterfactual–observed* and *observed without remittances–observed* comparisons, thus suggesting the impact that different approaches may have on the results of our study. It is also important to note that the counterfactual approach does not take into account the possible effects of migration on features of local labor markets.

As mentioned above, we use the Theil index T for income inequality measurement, our choice being mainly motivated by its property of being additively decomposable (the total inequality can be considered being the sum of between-group and within-group inequality), which permits us to study the changes that migration induces in income inequality within and between urban and rural areas. Moreover, the Theil index satisfies several desirable properties of inequality indices, such as mean independence (or income-zero-homogeneity), the principle of population replication (or population-size independence), and the Pigou-Dalton principle of transfers (Bourguignon 1979, Shorrocks 1980).

The formula that we use for the Theil index T is[3]:

$$T_T = \frac{1}{N} \sum_{i=1}^{N} \frac{y_i}{\bar{y}} \ln\left(\frac{y_i}{\bar{y}}\right)$$

where y_i is the per capita household income, $\bar{y}$ is the mean income, and N is the number of observations.

The values of the Theil index T range between 0 (if everyone has the same income) and $\ln N$ (if one person has the total income).

To determine the per capita household income, we use the household income adjusted by an adult equivalent scale based on two parameters:

the priority assigned to the needs of children (0.5 of those of an adult) and the technical assumptions about economies of scale in consumption (0.90). The formula that we use in order to determine the number of adult equivalents in a household is the following:[4]

$$AE = (A + 0.5C)^{0.9},$$

where A is the number of adults in a household and C is the number of children under 15 years.

As already mentioned, the Theil index T will be decomposed by rural and urban areas in order to capture the contribution of each group to inequality, as well as to study the changes in inequality both within and between groups. The decomposition formula that we use is:

$$T_T = \sum_{i=1}^{m} s_i T_{T_i} + \sum_{i=1}^{m} s_i \ln \frac{\overline{y_i}}{y},$$

where s_i is the income share of group i in the total income, T_{T_i} is the Theil index T for the group i, and $\overline{y}_i$ is the average income in group i.

Data

We base our analyses on data collected in a national representative survey carried out in October 2007 on 1,086 households. The survey sample was a random one, stratified by historical/cultural regions, areas of residence, and type and size of localities. In order to investigate external migration, the data gathered in a national survey in the origin country can provide reliable and valuable information on the profile of migrant households. However, they are limited by the fact that any such household survey misses one important category: households with one migrant member or households with all members migrated temporarily abroad. Results can thus easily under-estimate the extent of migrations, but they are adequate to assess the impact of remittances on income inequalities.

Table 2.1 Investigated Households by Area of Residence and Participation in Migration

	Non-migrant households	Migrant households	Share of migrant households in %	Total
Urban	576	42	6.8	618
Rural	412	56	12.0	468
Total	988	98	9.1	1086

MAIN FINDINGS

Of the investigated households 9.1 percent have migrants among their members (migrant households), whereas 90.9 percent of them do not (non-migrant households). (Table 2.1) More migrant households are located in rural areas (12.0 percent of the investigated rural households) than in urban ones (6.2 percent of the investigated urban households). Table 2.2 shows that migrant households are located mostly among households from the lower strata of the income distribution (poor and lower middle strata households). This is a first indicator of the fact that remittances may reduce income inequalities at the national level.

Most migrant households from rural areas come from the poor and lower middle strata of the per capita income distribution, whereas in urban areas they are overrepresented among households from poor, lower middle, and middle strata groups. It seems that remittances are mostly channeled towards the lower strata of the population, especially in rural areas. This could influence not only income distribution within urban and rural areas, but also inequality between them.

Following the methodology discussed earlier we estimate a simulated income that the migrant households would have earned if they were not participating in migration. We make this estimation based on the

Table 2.2   Households Distribution by Area of Residence (in percent), Per Capita Income,* and Participation in Migration

Area of residence	Strata based on per capita income*	Non-migrant households	Migrant households	Total
Rural	Poor	31.3	35.0	31.7
	Lower middle	23.4	35.0	24.6
	Middle	21.5	7.5	20.1
	Higher middle	11.4	15.0	11.8
	Rich	12.3	7.5	11.8
	Total	100.0	100.0	100.0
Urban	Poor	9.5	13.8	9.8
	Lower middle	17.9	20.7	18.1
	Middle	16.8	20.7	17.0
	Higher middle	28.3	20.7	27.9
	Rich	27.4	24.1	27.2
	Total	100.0	100.0	100.0

*adjusted by adult-equivalent scale

regression of the observed income of non-migrant households. But as migrant households are not uniformly and randomly distributed among the investigated population, we take into account observed and unobserved factors linked to participation in migration.

So, the Probit model explaining participation of households in migration shows that two main factors influence the dependent variable: the history of migration and the human capital of the households. Table 2.3 shows the Probit equation coefficient estimates for the dependent variable: household participation in migration.

The results of the Probit model show that the probability of participating in migration increases with the household size and with the migration experience of the household members. Better education is associated with a smaller probability to migrate, and the same is true in households where salary is the main income source. Moreover, the number of dependent household members (children and elderly) is negatively associated with the migration decision. Therefore, we can say that our findings may be explained by theories of the new economics of migration, which treat migration decisions at the household level as being driven by the goal of minimizing risks at household level (Stark and Bloom 1984).

Moreover, we estimate the Inverse Mills Ratio based on the Probit approximation. The Inverse Mills Ratio measures the expected value of the contribution of unobserved characteristics to the decision to participate in

Table 2.3   Estimation of the Participation in Migration—Probit Equation (Dependent Variable = 1 if the Household Participates in Migration)

Variable	Estimates	t-statistics
Dummy for migration experience of household	1.875*	13.294
Number of household members with tertiary education	-0.387*	-2.920
Dummy for salary of the main income source	-0.469*	-3.244
Number of dependent household members (under 15 and over 60 years)	-0.239*	-3.279
Number of household members	0.232*	4.621
Constant	-2.209*	-12.182
S.E. of regression	0.230	
Log likelihood	-204.181	
Goodness-of-Fit Pearson Test	1056.593 (Prob. 0.838)	
Prediction evaluation percentage correct	92.97	
Dependent = 0 (non-migrant household) percentage correct	97.10	
Dependent = 1 (migrant households) percentage correct	55.45	

Note: *significant at 1 percent.

migration, conditional on the observed participation in migration. It was included as an independent variable in the income estimation equation for non-migrant households. Thus, the selection bias was corrected. Using the Probit model as the selection equation, we estimate the income equation of the non-migrant households. The estimations of this model are shown in Table 2.4.

The results of the log income regression model for non-migrant households suggest that the household size and the number of employees in the household have a positive impact on the level of income. Positive income returns to education (variable: average years of education for the household members aged 15 and over) can also be identified. Households where expenditures are mainly based on salary earnings are not only less likely to migrate, but also have a higher level of income. As we had expected, income levels in urban areas were significantly higher than in rural ones. Whereas the number of children and young people in the household affects income negatively because these people are often still in schools or at universities and do not earn any income, the number of dependents that includes children and elderly, has a positive impact on income, probably because the latter category benefits from pensions.

The fact that the coefficient of the Inverse Mills Ratio is negative indicates that the unobserved factors that make participation in migration more likely tend to be associated with lower income levels. Having estimated the

Table 2.4 Estimation of the Income Equation for Non-migrant Households (Method: OLS, Dependent Variable: Log Income)

Variable	Estimates	t-statistics
Number of household members	0.189*	5.273
Number of employees in the household	0.162*	3.456
Average years of education for the household members aged 15 and over	0.125*	14.333
Dummy for household in urban area	0.239*	4.334
Dummy for salary of the main income source	0.364*	4.391
Number of children (under 15 years)	-0.281*	-5.330
Number of dependents	0.154*	3.964
Number of young people in the household (15-25 years)	-0.140*	-2.682
Inverse Mills Ratio	-0.311**	-2.080
Constant	4.386*	41.125
R Square	0.504	
F-statistics	652.023 (Prob. 0.05)	

Note: *significant at 1 percent, **significant at 5 percent.

coefficients of the income equation of non-migrant households, we can now estimate the counterfactual income without migration and remittances for migrant households, as described in detail in the methodological section. We can go further with our analysis and reach the core of it by computing the inequality Theil index for the income distribution of households in three different scenarios: observed with remittances, counterfactual without migration, and observed without remittances.

Table 2.5 clearly shows that remittances determine income inequality reduction at the national level (all groups). Thus, the distribution of income with remittances (as it was collected in the survey) displays the lowest level of Theil index T (0.2588). Therefore, the observed situation presents the lowest level of inequality, whereas both observed income without remittances and counterfactual income in the absence of migration are characterized by higher inequalities (0.2657 for the first and 0.2715 for the second). Furthermore, one has to notice that the highest level of Theil index T emerges from the counterfactual scenario. However, both approaches indicate that migration and, subsequently, remittances determine a reduction of interhousehold income inequalities at the national level.

Decomposing Theil index T by areas, we find that remittances are conducive to the reduction of inequalities, both between as well as within urban and rural areas. First of all, Theil index T is lower for the observed income with remittances and higher for the income without remittances and the counterfactual scenario, for both urban and rural areas. Remittances have thus a positive impact on inequalities at the level of both urban and rural zones. Second, by decomposing Theil index T, we see that remittances determine the reduction of inequalities within groups, as well as

Table 2.5   Inequality Decomposition by Area of Residence—Theil Index T

Area of residence	Observed income with remittances	Counterfactual income without migration	Observed income without remittances
Urban	0.2033 (50.82%)	0.2104 (50.47%)	0.2088 (51.03%)
Rural	0.2911 (39.74%)	0.3065 (39.35%)	0.2980 (39.32%)
All groups	0.2588	0.2715	0.2657
Within groups	0.2344 (90.56%)	0.2439 (89.82%)	0.2401 (90.35%)
Between groups	0.0244 (9.44%)	0.0276 (10.18%)	0.0256 (9.65%)

Note: The contributions to inequality at the national level are given in brackets.

between groups. The results of both employed methods are consistent and indicate a decline of the level of Theil index T in the presence of remittances for both parts of the index: the within component, as well as the between one. Yet, the counterfactual scenario registers the highest level of inequalities in between and within urban and rural areas. In fact, it displays the highest contribution of the between component to inequality. Following both methods of impact assessment, we find that remittances determine a decline of inequalities between and within urban and rural areas, as well as reducing the contribution of the between component to the total amount of inequalities.

CONCLUSION

This chapter addresses the question on how migration and remittances impact interhouseholds income inequalities in Romania. This initiative is very important and new for Romania. After validating our results via two different methodological approaches, some important conclusions have emerged:

1. Migrant households are located mostly in the lower strata of the income distribution, which means that remittances are channeled to the poorer households, especially in rural areas. This leads to significant changes in the level of income distribution in Romania.
2. The probability of participation in migration increases with the household size and with past experiences of migration of the household members, whereas it decreases with a higher number of members with tertiary education and of dependents (children and elderly). Households with salaries that are their main source of income are also associated with a lower probability of migration. Our findings are consistent with the theories of the new economics of migration that underline that migration decisions are taken at the level of the household and that households decide to send their members to work abroad in order to maximize incomes and minimize risks and constrains.
3. Following two different methods, we have found that remittances reduce inter-household income inequalities at the national level. They also determine a decline of inequalities both within and between urban and rural areas, and they reduce the contribution of the between component to the total level of inequality.
4. Considering Romania's recent history of migration (Sandu 2006), our results that indicate a positive impact of remittances at the level of urban–rural inequalities confirm Jones's spatio-temporal perspective (1998) as he theorizes that longer migration experience results in inequality reduction at the urban–rural scale.

When it comes to the impact of transnational migrations on development and globalization, we have to consider migrants as actors of change. Local and national development depends on how remittances are spent and/or invested by migrants' households. A large majority of migrants' households spend remittances for consumption, survival, or the acquisition of durables.[5] Thus, one can find big houses and expensive cars in Romania, but no decent roads or other modern infrastructures in communities with high migration outflows. Although migration for employment helps large groups out of the poverty trap, the social participation and social cohesion of these communities continue to be seriously affected. Migration transforms the age structure of the population or even produces a depopulation of areas. In some communities, the massive migration of young and middle-aged people leaves behind the elderly and the children, who are vulnerable to social risks, especially in rural areas where the access to public goods and services is lower and traditional intergenerational mechanisms are important. Therefore, communities with a high share of inactive populations display a lower capacity to organize themselves and to pursue their interests. Moreover, when returning home, some migrants experience difficulties with their social reintegration.

We must also point out that there are migrants coming back from abroad with new skills and high motivation, representing interesting inputs to the Romanian economy. There are also migrants who return home with some financial capital and start their own businesses, thus stimulating community development and the local business environment. But their numbers are still rather low.

Moreover, highly educated actors represent a quarter of emigrants with a permanent change of their legal residence what means a loss for Romania in terms of human capital.[6] But there is some empirical evidence that lots of youngsters drop out of school and migrate looking for employment abroad through networks involving friends, neighbors, and acquaintances. Their migration affects thus their educational level and reduces their potential for future educational development.

When the global financial crisis emerged in Fall 2008, a return of Romanian migrants from Spain and Italy was expected, but there is no notable empirical evidence so far to support this projection. A decline of the inflows of remittances has also been expected due to the recession in the construction and industry sectors in the most important destination countries of Romanian migrants. There is some casual evidence indicating a reduction of these transfers.[7] Furthermore, it has been expected that the traditional destination countries of Romanian migrants, such as Spain, Italy, and France will adjust their labor markets and migration policies in order to discourage migrant workers and protect their native populations. However, it is too soon to make estimations on how these adaptations will impact on income inequalities in Romania. So far, we can conclude by underlying the mixed *blessing* of globalization and migration for Romania's development.

NOTES

1. http://www.euractiv.ro/content/section%7creadStory/stID_22/pT_dosare/ pID_258/, accessed on May 10, 2009.
2. See Zhu and Luo (2008).
3. http://economicsbulletin.vanderbilt.edu/2008/volume15/EB-07O10036A. pdf, accessed on May 20, 2009.
4. Romania: Poverty Assessment, World Bank 2003.
5. See also Sandu 2009: 136-140.
6. Militaru, Mocanu, and Zamfir 2007: 104–107.
7. UNICEF and World Bank 2009: 6.

BIBLIOGRAPHY

Akita, Takahiro, Rizal Affandi Lukman, and Yukino Yamada (1999) "Inequality in the Distribution of Household Expenditures in Indonesia: A Theil Decomposition Analysis," *The Developing Economies* 37 (2): 197–221.

Alderson, Arthur S. and François Nielsen (2002) "Globalisation and the Great U-turn: Income Inequality Trends in 16 OECD Countries," *The American Journal of Sociology* 107 (5): 1244–1299.

Borjas, George J. (1989) "Economic Theory and International Migration," *International Migration Review* 23 (3): 457–485.

Brown, Richard P.C. and Eliana Jimenez (2007) *Estimating the Net Effects of Migration and Remittances on Poverty and Inequality. Comparison of Fiji and Tonga.* World Institute for Development Economics Research. http://www. wider.unu.edu/publications/working-papers/research-papers/2007/en_GB/ rp2007-23/, accessed on April 15, 2009.

Copaciu, Mihai and Irina Răcaru (2006) *Romania's External Balance— Qualitative and Quantitative Approaches.* Occasional Papers, no. 18, National Bank of Romania, www.bnro.ro, accessed on September 14, 2008.

Cuong, Nguyen (2008) "Do Foreign Remittances Matter to Poverty and Inequality? Evidence from Vietnam," *Economics Bulletin* 15 (1): 1–11.

Davies, James B. and Ian Wooton (1992) "Income Inequality and International Migration," *The Economic Journal* 102 (413): 789–802.

Giles, Margaret J. (2001) *Heckman's Methodology for Correcting Selectivity Bias: An Application to Road Crash Costs.* School of Finance and Business Economics. Working Paper Series, Working Paper 01.11.

Jones, Richard C. (1998) "Remittances and Inequality: A Question of Migration Stage and Geographic Scale," *Economic Geography* 74 (1): 8–25.

Lewis, W. Arthur (1954) "Economic Development with Unlimited Supplies of Labour," *The Manchester School of Economic and Social Studies* 22 (2): 139–191. http://www.unc.edu/~wwolford/Geography160/368lewistable.pdf, accessed on May 18, 2009.

Massey, Douglas S. (1990) "Social Structure, Household Strategies and the Cumulative Causation of Migration," *Population Index* 56 (1): 13–26.

Massey, Douglas S. (ed.) (1993). "Theories of International Migration: a Review and Appraisal," *Population and Development Review* 19 (3): 431–466.

McArthur, H. J. (1979) "The Effects of Overseas Work on Return Migrants and their Home Communities: A Philippine case," *Papers in Anthropology* 20 (1): 85–104.

Metro Media Transilvania and Romanian Agency for Governmental Strategies (2007) *Romanians in Italy: Social Conditions, Values and Expectations.* http:// www.publicinfo.ro/library/sc/cri.pdf, accessed on April 18, 2009.

Metro Media Transilvania and Romanian Agency for Governmental Strategies. (2008) *Romanians in Spain: Social Conditions, Values and Expectations,* http://www.publicinfo.ro/library/sc/comunitatea_romaneasca_in_spania.pdf, accessed on April 18, 2009.

Militaru, Eva, Cristina Mocanu, and Ana Maria Zamfir (2007) "Tackling Migration for Employment in an Emergent, Medium-sized Open Market Economy," in *National Human Development Report Romania 2007: Making EU Accession Work for All.* Bucharest, UNDP, 97–144. http://www.undp.ro/download/files/publications/NHDR%202007%20EN.pdf, accessed on May 3, 2009.

Murphy, Rachel (2000) "Migration and Inter-household Inequality: Observations from Wanzai County, Jiangxi," *The China Quarterly* 164: 965–982.

Oberai, Amarjit S. and H. K. Manmohan Singh (1980) "Migration, Remittances and Rural Development: Findings of a Case Study in the Indian Punjab," *International Labour Review* 119 (2): 229–241.

Pernia, Ernesto M. (2008) *Migration, Remittances, Poverty and Inequality. The Philippines.* http://www.econ.upd.edu.ph/respub/dp/pdf/DP2008-01.pdf, accessed on April 5, 2009.

Ranis, Gustav and John Fei (1961) "A Theory of Economic Development," *American Economic Review* 51 (4): 533–565.

Sandu, Dumitru (2006) *Temporary Living Abroad: Economic Migration of Romanians: 1990–2006.* Open Society Foundation, www.osf.ro, accessed on April 5, 2009.

Sandu, Dumitru (coord.) (2009) *Comunitati Romanesti in Spania,* Open Society Foundation, www.osf.ro, accessed on June 10, 2009.

Stark, Oded, J. Edward Taylor, and Shlomo Yitzhaki (1986) "Remittances and Inequality," *Economic Journal* 96 (383): 722–740.

Stark, Oded and David E. Bloom (1985) "The New Economics of Labour Migration," *The American Economic Review* 75 (2): 173–178.

Stark, Oded and J. Edward Taylor (1989) "Relative Deprivation and International Migration," *Demography* 26 (1): 1–14.

Stark, Oded (1984) "Migration Decision Making: A Review Article" *Journal of Development Economics* 14 (1): 251–259.

Taylor, J. Edward (1986) "Differential Migration, Networks, Information and Risks" in Oded Stark (ed.) *Research in Human Capital and Development* 147–171. Greenwich, Conn.: JAI Press.

Taylor, J. Edward (1992) "Remittances and Inequality Reconsidered: Direct, Indirect and Intertemporal Effects," *Journal of Policy Modeling* 14 (2): 187–208.

Taylor, J. Edward, Jorge Mora, Richard Adams, and Alejandro Lopez-Feldman (2005) *"Remittances, Inequality and Poverty: Evidence from Rural Mexico,"* Department of Agricultural and Resource Economics, University of California, Davis, Working Paper No. 05-003. http://arelibrary.ucdavis.edu/working_papers/files/05-003.pdf accessed on May 15, 2009.

Todaro, Michael P. (1976) *Internal Migration in Developing Countries.* Geneva: International Labor Office.

Vella, Francis (1998) "Estimating Models with Sample Selection Bias: A Survey," *Journal of Human Resources* 33 (1): 127–169.

UNICEF and World Bank (2009) *Romania: Rapid Assessment of the Impact of Economic Crisis on Poverty.* http://www.unicef.org/romania/Crisis_Impact_UNICEF_WB.pdf, accessed on June 10, 2009.

World Bank (2003) *Romania: Poverty Assessment. http://*siteresources.worldbank.org/INTROMANIA/Resources/PovertyAssessment_Eng.pdf, accessed on May 9, 2009.

Zhu, Nong and Xubei Luo (2008) *The Impact of Remittances on Rural Poverty and Inequality in China.* World Bank Working Paper. http://www-wds.world-bank.org/external/default/WDSContentServer/WDSP/IB/2008/05/28/0001583 49_20080528140510/Rendered/PDF/wps4637.pdf, accessed on May 20, 2009.

3 Creating *Best Performing* Nations in Education

The Case of the European Union's Use of Benchmarking

Susana Melo

INTRODUCTION

The Treaty on the European Union, signed in Maastricht by foreign and finance ministers of Member States in 1992, contains a number of provisions on education based upon the principle of non-interference in the content and organization of the Member States' education and training systems. In Article 126 of the Treaty, the European Union's sphere of action in this policy area is restricted to "contribute to the development of quality education by encouraging co-operation between Member States and, if necessary, by supporting and supplementing their action" (Paragraph 1). This legal basis continues to prevent the European Union (EU) from a more direct intervention in national education systems. Until 2000, the EU's educational work was very much focused on the development of higher educational programs under the SOCRATES framework, of which the ERASMUS student mobility program is the best known (Keeling 2006). However, in March 2000, the European Commission secured support to expand its involvement in educational issues as the Heads of States agreed on an overall strategy in the Lisbon European Council meeting (henceforth, the Lisbon Agenda) for the following ten years aimed at achieving the new goal of the EU: "(T)o become the most competitive and dynamic knowledge-based economy in the world, capable of sustainable economic growth with more and better jobs and greater social cohesion" (European Council 2000: Paragraph 5). According to the Lisbon Agenda, "Europe's education and training systems need to adapt both to the demands of the knowledge society and to the need for an improved level and quality of employment" (Paragraph 25). Based on this conclusion, EU-level common action, in order to *modernize* the education systems of the Member States, was regarded as a key priority. Therefore, the European Council, at its Stockholm meeting in 2001, adopted concrete objectives for education systems and, in 2002, approved a work program on the follow-up of these objectives, which was understood to be a means to the development of a coherent and comprehensive strategy in education and training (European

Commission 2002a: 6). The work program determines that the organization of follow-up activities is to be done according to the Open Method of Co-ordination (OMC) predicaments.

The main procedures of the OMC are: the definition of guidelines to be translated into national policy, combined with periodic monitoring, evaluation, and peer review (European Council 2000: Paragraph 37). There is no formal attempt to control outcomes, so that it is a method without legal norms, obligations, or sanctions. Thus, it is adequate for a policy area like education because it does not raise questions of legitimacy. The coordination process is determined by the use of benchmarking, structured as a mutual learning instrument that emphasizes Member States' competence, the voluntary alignment of policies, and the identification of *good practices* from which lessons may be drawn. Benchmarking is in its origin a technique of comparative quantitative analysis used in business as a management tool in order to understand *how* competitors achieve their position and how they develop their products and services (Spendolini 1992: 13). It often involves comparisons between the internal practices and processes of different firms in order to identify *best practices* (Arrowsmith, Sisson, and Marginson 2004: 312). When transferred to the context of the EU, benchmarking consists of comparisons of the performance of states in measurable targets (benchmarks) that underpin common policies in a specific area. It also includes comparisons between the EU and other countries, such as Japan and the United States (US). And, it certainly serves other purposes than the improvement of business processes in order to gain a better position in the marketplace.

This chapter looks at how the EU uses benchmarking to steer its educational policies and asks the following question: what purposes does benchmarking serve, and what are the implications of using this mechanism? To examine the first question, I draw upon a theoretical approach to governance and suggest that because Member States agreed to have their educational policies monitored through benchmarking, they have not only transferred sovereignty for the task of setting goals for their education systems, but also delegated normative power to the EU. Although, formally, Member States remain responsible for their education systems, they are now under pressure to develop policies according to the EU standards and their efforts subject to assessment as good or bad according to how well they achieve supranational goals. Then I analyze empirically the second question. The analysis builds on documentary data in the form of policy texts (for example, political speeches, reports, communications, and so on) from the EU, which were published in the public domain from 2000 to 2008. In particular, I focus on the way in which education has been framed in the EU discourse of a knowledge-based economy, the relationship between the concrete educational objectives, and the benchmarks selected to follow-up on Member States' achievement of them, and the way in which the EU reports the progress made. I argue that the use of benchmarking has contradictory effects:

on the one hand, it creates an understanding of the European region united against competitors such as Japan or the US; on the other, it sets out competition between Member States on unequal terms because the comparative analyses that are carried out understate contextual specificities. I conclude that one of the social consequences of putting into effect a positional competition of nations in the domain of education is the increase in the number of students moving across educational spaces within the EU area in order to get *better* certificates. This type of mobility may stimulate the emergence of a form of social inequality that derives from differences in individual economic power to afford academic studies abroad.

BENCHMARKING AND THE GOVERNANCE OF EUROPEAN EDUCATION

The term governance is employed across disciplines, including international relations (global governance), development policy (good governance), European studies (multilevel governance), finance and management (corporate governance), and at many levels of public policy (e.g., educational governance) (Walters 2004: 28). The different contexts of the use of governance presuppose different meanings. In this chapter, I understand governance to be a language that can capture key aspects of ongoing changes in the forms of government (31). I draw specifically upon Dale's (2005: 129) definition of governance as the "co-ordination of the co-ordination of the work of governing." This concept rests upon two assumptions: first, the work of governing can be divided into different activities; second, not all these activities need to be performed or coordinated by the state. Dale suggests that, in the case of education, the activities of governing may be divided into funding, provision, ownership, and regulation, and are undertaken by agencies, such as the household, the community, or the market, either separately or in combination with the state as well as by the state. The main point is that a focus on governance entails the recognition that, methodologically, it is crucial to go beyond the nation-state/education dichotomy in order to explain how education is conceived and delivered today (Dale and Robertson 2007: 6). The state is not the sole actor playing a role in it. Moreover, not each educational task needs to be located within the national territory. Indeed, the activities of governing education and their coordination can be found at distinct scales—local, national, regional, or global. The EU's involvement in education is an illustration of how certain activities (e.g., the provision and funding of higher education mobility programs) are undertaken by an entity other than the state. From this point of view, the EU is not considered to be an extension of particular national interests. The focus is rather on what is done at the EU-level that may contribute to the governance of education in European societies. When looking at the case of the EU's use of benchmarking, an important question concerns the functions this mechanism may have in the development of educational tasks.

Benchmarking can be used in various forms and can be applied to very distinct organizational contexts (Kyrö 2003). Nonetheless, some continuities in the way in which it is applied can be identified: it is a process that includes target setting, some form of measurement to coordinate and evaluate progress, and an identification by the comparison of *best practice* as the recommended means to achieve targets (Sisson, Arrowsmith, and Marginson 2002: 8). These core procedures entail several purposes when they are applied to monitor the progress EU Member States make in the area of education. First, benchmarking enables the EU to identify desirable, common goals for all education systems within the EU area, no matter their diversity. This activity can be described to be indirectly regulatory—or normative: Member States transfer to the EU level the task of defining priorities that will constitute a framework for their national public policies (Borrás and Jacobsson 2004: 197) and legislative initiatives, and will place in the hands of the EU the power to determine what *proper* outcomes of education can be imagined (Dale 2005: 119). In other words, EU benchmarks function as standards in education. Second, benchmarking is a mechanism that minimizes the coordination of the alignment of Member States with European educational policies to the monitoring of measurable and comparable results. All effects of educational policies and processes that cannot be translated into numbers are not taken into account in the follow-up of the implementation of the EU's strategy. To be sure, the use of benchmarking permits a reduction of complexity in the analysis of changes that have eventually been introduced at the national level in light of the EU objectives. Such reduction facilitates the regular preparation of reports within a short period of time (every two years) and creates a dynamic and fast progress. However, the question is raised to what extent the results analyzed reflect an accurate and meaningful degree of achievement of the EU goals. Third, benchmarking information legitimates the EU's authority to formulate recommendations and required solutions, to praise or criticize the performance of Member States, and to expand the scope of its educational work.[1] This is a basis for putting forward a vision of what education should be and should do for societies.

Finally, the EU's use of benchmarking is accompanied by the suggestion that in order to attain the established targets, Member States whose results are not good can *learn* from the practices of others that figure as being the *best performers*. In spite of it being a good means of "spreading best practice" (European Council 2002: 5), there are no noticeable efforts at the EU-level to coordinate *learning* activities. This apparent absence of interest in taking advantage of benchmarking as a learning instrument is not particular to the EU. According to the scientific literature on the application of benchmarking techniques, it is a commonly found shortcoming. Arrowsmith, Sisson, and Marginson (2004: 312) point out that because of the technical and practical difficulties of benchmarking, the definition of *best practice* is problematic and even when *best practices* are identified, their transference rarely occurs because of contextual particularities. Therefore, the comparisons made in order to identify *best practices* could be understood as being pointless; but they have consequences. Sisson, Arrowsmith, and Marginson (2002: 16) write:

> Instead of being about learning and continuous improvement (. . .) benchmarking tends to be concerned exclusively with quantitative measures (. . .) instead of being a force for change, benchmarking can amount to little more than a lemming-like copying of (yesterday's) best practice (. . .) The playing of catch-up benchmarking encourages can put a stop to serious analysis of problems and/or experimentation with their solutions.

In the context of the EU, beside the lack of depth in the examination of the reasons why some Member States achieve results closer than others to the fixed targets, there are further important consequences I will explore below.

EDUCATION AS A MEASURABLE FACTOR FOR ECONOMIC GROWTH

The EU's selection of a quantitative comparative method to implement and monitor its educational policies is not a unique or isolated phenomenon. Other international organizations, such as the Organization for Economic Co-operation and Development (OECD), UNESCO, and the World Bank have adopted similar mechanisms of governance[2] to disseminate their educational policy agendas. Indeed, it acts at present as part of a global effort to improve internationally comparable statistics on education in which the EU participates. Such effort is in direct relation to a global consensus in education policy, based upon a neo-liberal conception of education as a *measurable* key factor in the successful implementation of the knowledge-based economy (Henry *et al.* 2001). The EU educational strategy contains a vision of what is necessary to change in education systems in order to achieve the global competitiveness goal of the Lisbon Agenda, which is, in broad terms, in accordance with the model of economic development promoted by the OECD and the World Bank (see Robertson 2005). In this section, I will examine the relationship between the core ideas of this model and the EU objectives for education on which the establishment of the five benchmarks in education was based.

The following excerpt illustrates the main point made in the argumentation that permits a common educational strategy in all EU Member States:

> (C)ompetitive advantage is increasingly dependent on investment in human capital. Knowledge and competences are, therefore, also a powerful engine for economic growth. Given the current uncertain economic climate, investing in people becomes all the more important. (European Commission 2001a: 6)

The often-cited relationship between economic growth and *investment in people* draws upon a renewed human capital theory in which education is regarded as being a form of human capital investment that is directly related to the generation of the prosperity of nations (Henry *et al.* 2001: 60). This view entails assumptions (such as the larger the number of inhabitants highly qualified, the wealthier is the country) that emphasize the economic dimension of education, which tends to downplay the significant although *immeasurable* benefits education may confer to both individuals and societies. It is an approach, however, that is often oblivious to ideas of education for personal betterment, empowerment, or intellectual growth. On the one hand, it focuses on the contribution of education to the needs of the labor market. On the other, it advocates that education is an individual good and a source of individual economic benefits, and therefore its users should pay for it. Thus, it reduces equity considerations to an understanding of education as a public service to which everybody should have access, but where not everybody should benefit from it for free. These fundamental aspects help to further understand what the three strategic objectives for education adopted by the European Council—to improve the quality and effectiveness of education, to facilitate access to education, and to open up European education and training systems to the world—(7) entail.

The *quality* and *effectiveness* of education is very much dependent on its ability to generate learning outcomes suitable to the needs of the EU labor market. If this objective is achieved, not only will the economy have the adequate knowledge available for its growth but more EU citizens will have a higher level of employability (and a higher potential as consumers fuelling the economic cycle). The following quote illustrates this idea:

> In economic terms, the employability and adaptability of citizens is vital for Europe to maintain its commitment to becoming the most competitive and dynamic knowledge-based society in the world. Labour shortages and competence gaps risk limiting the capacity of the European Union for further growth, at any point in the economic cycle. (European Commission 2001a: 7)

The reference to the "adaptability of citizens" leads to the second objective concerning access to education. The *Action Plan for Skills and Mobility* (European Commission 2002b) describes in detail the envisaged *adaptable* EU citizen. Citizens are meant to be adaptable in two ways: (1) they are keen to change their workplace on a regular basis as well as to move away from one location to another according to where job opportunities exist or where they are better; (2) throughout their lives, they update their skills and competences in accordance with the requirements of work. The latter idea is underlined in the argument that education systems should be restructured in order to facilitate access to education for all. It is the basis for the EU promotion of a lifelong learning culture in Europe. According to the European Commission, the notion of *lifelong learning* is to be understood as:

(A)ll learning activity undertaken throughout life, with the aim of improving knowledge, skills and competences within a personal, civic, social and/or employment-related perspective. (European Commission 2001a: 9)

And one of the challenges of its implementation is to determine:

(H)ow to match learning opportunities to learners' needs and interests and how to facilitate access by developing the supply side to enable learning by anyone, anywhere, at any time. (Ibid: 4)

From this viewpoint, "education for all" means education for all ages, and "facilitate" entails an effort to satisfy any demands for learning made by all sorts of individuals and organizations. The change from a traditional education system to a lifelong learning system is considered as being done better in partnership with all relevant actors in and outside formal institutions. Thus, it is important to achieve the third objective of opening up education systems. The openness of an education system is determined by the number of links with businesses and employers in order to "increase their understanding of the needs of employers and thus to increase the employability of learners." (European Commission 2001b: 5)

The understanding that education is to be conceived and delivered on the basis of the involvement of various actors under-pins a re-positioning of the state as one among other sources of funding for education institutions, i.e., a governance approach. This is important to note. When the EU refers to "investment in human capital," there is not the political expectation that the state will be the only *investor*. However, the EU discourse on this topic is ambivalent with respect to how much the state should *invest* or if it should do so at all. The Lisbon Agenda states that there is the need for "a substantial annual increase in per capita investment in human resources" (European Council 2000: Paragraph 26), but it does not make explicit who is responsible for such increase, or what "human resources" refer to. Later, as opposed to the other benchmarks in education set at the EU-level, Member States are invited to communicate to the European Council and Commission the benchmarks they set themselves in this respect (European Commission 2002a: 4). Moreover, it is mentioned that public expenditure on education is regarded as a positive factor of differentiation among the EU competitors:

European citizens have greater expectations of the state than their equivalents in Asia or America. The **public sector tends to play a big role, either through regulation or government spending, in the organisation and financing of national systems.** In addition, all Member States have played a strong role in the delivery of **high quality services of general interest** which have been a key feature of economic and social development. (Highlighted in the original) (European Commission 2005: 4)

But it is also stated that the increase in public expenditure "needs strong institutional commitment, coordination and partnership with all relevant stakeholders" (European Council 2008: 7). Furthermore, and in line with the new theory of human capital, students are identified as one of those *stakeholders* who are expected to contribute to the funding of their education systems:

> In order to bring about a more equitable balance between the costs funded by individuals and society and the benefits accrued by each, and *to contribute to providing universities with the extra funding* they need, many countries are turning to the main direct beneficiaries of higher education, *the students, to invest in their own futures by paying tuition fees*. (my italics) (European Commission 2006a: 7–8)

The lack of clarity in the common action to be undertaken by all Member States in this respect highlights some tensions found in the EU's case for *investment in people*. There is a tension between the articulation of the argument that lifelong learning is an answer to issues of social inequality and the role of coordinator and partner the state plays in funding education. It is obvious that both employer and employees may benefit from continuously updating of skills and competences, and, within the logic of the renewed human capital theory, the argument that they could finance that learning makes sense. However, the question arises in the case of individuals who are unemployed or working under poor conditions: could they be expected to afford their continuous education and training in order to increase their level of employability? Who would *invest* in these people? Other tensions are found between the governance approach underpinning the discourse of public expenditure on education and the methodological approach applied to follow-up on progress towards the achievement of the educational objectives: the EU process of benchmarking puts the idea that states are the sole actors responsible for the work of governing education to the fore, as if the successful achievement of the fixed EU targets would not depend on the agreement of other actors and the work carried out at a local level (schools, higher education institutions, training agencies, etc.).

THE FIVE BENCHMARKS IN EDUCATION AND THEIR IMPLICATIONS

Progress towards the three strategic objectives for education systems is to be observed through five benchmarks, defined as "concrete targets" that should be attained by 2010 (European Commission 2002a: 3). These targets are grouped into the following areas: Early School Leavers; Key Competencies; Completion of Upper Secondary Education; Graduates in Mathematics, Science, and Technology; and Participation in Lifelong Learning. Since 2002, when they were first proposed, there have been changes both in the formulation of the benchmarks and in the quantified reference values. The following two examples testify for these changes:

- Member States should at least halve the rate of early school leavers, with reference to the rate recorded in the year 2000, in order to achieve an EU-average rate of 10% or less. (European Commission 2002a: 3)

  By 2010, an EU average rate of no more than 10% early school leavers should be achieved. (European Commission 2006b: 59)

- Key competencies: the percentage of low-achieving 15-year-olds in reading and mathematical and scientific literacy will be at least halved in each Member State. (European Commission 2002a: 3)

  Therefore, by 2010, the percentage of low-achieving 15-year-olds in reading literacy in the European Union should have decreased by at least 20% compared to the year 2000. (European Council 2003: 3)

In both examples, the focus has shifted from what Member States should achieve to the EU envisaged totals. In the second example on Key Competencies, the benchmark became a less ambitious target. These changes signal difficulties in stabilizing the standard criteria. Moreover, none of the five selected benchmarks looks at the objective of opening up education systems. Four out of five targets refer to the *effectiveness* of education. The remaining benchmark takes into account the implementation of lifelong learning. It determines that the EU average level of participation in lifelong learning should be at least 12.5 percent of the adult working age population (between 25 and 65 years old). Thus, it poorly relates to the above-cited definition of lifelong learning as being learning for *all* ages. In fact, in technical terms, the validity of these EU-comparable measurements is open to discussion. They would be valid if they measured what they were intended to measure: how a new political strategy has developed into concrete results and how the results are closer to the pre-decided targets. The comparisons carried out within the EU process of benchmarking depend on data available in 2000 as a reference level to recognize progress. Therefore, they do not necessarily reflect the consequences deriving from new policies launched in 2000, but rather the improvement of what had already been implemented before 2000.

Nonetheless, there is no doubt that the five benchmarks frame areas of intervention. The benchmark on Graduates in Mathematics, Science, and Technology is the one that best illustrates the role benchmarks play in defining what is regarded as important to invest in. The decision of measuring the number of graduates in these disciplines highlights their relevance to an economy that is believed to be significantly dependent on scientific innovation and technological advancement (European Commission 2000). In order to achieve this EU target, one of the consequences at the national level might be to prioritize funding to the development and expansion of these disciplines as a means of attracting more students and thus create an understanding of other areas of knowledge, such as humanities, as being less important in *modern* societies. Other examples are the benchmarks on Early School Leavers and Completion of Upper Secondary Education, which underline that the achievement of a higher level of education by the younger generation should be pursued. However, they are designed to indicate the number of those enrolled in the national education systems, and not the quality of their learning. They do not take into account the distribution of the student population in different educational pathways. This information would be important to an understanding of the educational level (and social opportunities) achieved in each country, because post-compulsory vocational training courses, for example, differ from secondary education designed for students who intend to attend university. Because that kind of information is absent, the result seems rather to encourage a focus on raising the numbers by keeping young people in the education system no matter what kind of education they have access to. In conclusion, benchmarks are a way through which the EU might draw attention to particular issues that put an emphasis on quantified changes rather than on qualitative improvements. This fact has consequences for the idea of education.

THE COMPARISONS OF PERFORMANCE IN EDUCATION

To date, three follow-up progress reports based upon benchmarking information have been issued (European Council 2004, 2006, 2008a). These reports contain collective recommendations based upon the EU average for each benchmark; they compare the EU totals with Japanese and US totals; and they identify not only the three *best performing* countries in education and training, but also on some occasions name countries that are *good* or *not so good* in certain areas. The reports are accompanied by the presentation of the comparable results in tables and graphs. In the tables, the results of Member States are detailed in alphabetical order, so that there is no explicit ranking of *performers*. This option suggests an implicit politics of convergence where emphasizing differences is not desirable (Wallace 2001: 588). Despite this, there are comparisons that specifically highlight divergent behavior:

> Total public expenditure on education as a percentage of GDP increased in the EU between 2000 (4.7%) and 2003 (5.2%), but then decreased to 5.1% in 2004. Levels of expenditure continue to show huge variations between countries (between 3.3% of GDP in Romania and 8.5% in Denmark). (European Council 2008b: 7)
> The share of young people (aged 20–24) who have completed upper-secondary education has only slightly improved since 2000. There was

thus little progress in achieving the benchmark (. . .). However, some countries with a relatively low share, notably Portugal and Malta, have made considerable progress in the recent past. It should also be noted that many of the new Member States already perform above the benchmark set for 2010 and that four of them, the Czech Republic, Poland, Slovenia and Slovakia, and in addition Norway and Croatia, already have shares of 90% and above. (European Council 2008b: 29)

As mentioned above, public expenditure on education has not been clearly set as a EU-level benchmark. Nevertheless, the reports contain information on the levels of expenditure, as the first excerpt illustrates. It is obvious from these excerpts that the comparative analysis of results is decontextualized. The contrast between Romania's level of public expenditure and Denmark's level is noted, but there is not any reference to background differences in the financial capacity of the two states. Because contextual specificities are not taken into account, the analysis yields the misleading idea of equal background circumstances for the achievement of the same goals. It also stimulates a competitive outlook in a region where economic development is still significantly uneven.

In the second excerpt, Norway and Croatia are mentioned. These countries are not EU members, and their inclusion suggests that the EU is not only interested in collecting data about them, but also in conveying the idea that they are aligned with the EU policies. In the tables, beside Norway, other non-EU countries, such as Turkey or Iceland, are included as well. This fact raises the question of what results count for the calculation of the overall EU averages, which serve to evaluate the EU's competitive position with respect to Japan and the US in the following way:

> The European Union must catch up with its main competitors (. . .). As regards performance in the knowledge-based economy, the EU also lags behind the US but is ahead of Japan. Things did improve in the second half of the 1990s, but the EU needs to step up its efforts to be in position to close the gap with the US by 2010. (European Council 2004: 6)

Rosamond (2002: 157) claims that the EU constructs an imaginary "European economic self" and attempts to deepen the integration process in particular policy directions together with the expansion of its own policy competence by insisting on the idea of European competitiveness. Considering that the above statement is made in a report on education, this construction of the European economic self implies two fundamental things. First, it offers a view of the value of education as being exclusively economical. Second, whereas it creates the idea of a united group against *others*, it represents the EU as an entity that has as much authority in the area of education as the two sovereign states have. Furthermore, the selection of Japan and the US as the competitors with whom the EU compares itself indicates that the defined criteria for measuring the achievement of the European goals coincide with statistical information collected about these two countries. Such coincidence not only reinforces the idea that the EU educational strategy reflects a global consensus in education, as previously mentioned, but also evidences the existence of cooperation between the EU and other international organizations in terms of data collection and exchange. The following excerpt signals this situation:

> (T)he Commission in close co-operation with Member States identified EU data needs on adult skills (. . .). At present it is examined, if these data needs could be covered by a survey focused on adult skills measurement which is under preparation by OECD, or if a new EU survey needs to be developed. (European Commission 2006b: 49)

According to Grek (2009: 32), the alliance between the EU and OECD is indeed strong and the OECD collects more than 50 percent of the data for the EU's benchmarking reports on the implementation of the Lisbon Agenda. This situation can be clearly observed with respect to the benchmark in the area of Key Competencies, which looks specifically at the achievement in reading literacy of 15-year-olds. This indicator is the same as the reading literacy indicator the OECD Program for International Student Assessment (PISA) examined in 2000, 2003, and 2006. PISA is a joint study of the OECD member countries that has been conducted not only in the US and Japan, but also in all EU Member States with the exception of Cyprus and Malta. The PISA survey data on reading literacy constitute the data on which the EU bases its analysis in the follow-up reports every two years. It is reasonable that the EU attempts to optimize resources and avoid the duplication of data collection, but it should be noted that Member States agreed to provide data to the EU on the defined educational benchmarks on a voluntary basis (European Commission 2002a). Bearing this in mind, it becomes obvious that the voluntary principle is overlooked. In cooperation with the OECD, the EU does not always depend on the collaboration of Member States or on the capacity to gather the necessary information for the coordination of its policies. Apart from the OECD, the EU indicates its concern with the development of cooperation with other international organizations involved in educational work, such as UNESCO, in order to attain better coherence in data collection (European Council 2005: 2). The issue of data under-pins the global interdependency of the EU benchmarking exercises in education. Moreover, the pursuit of data coherence may be interpreted to be important for the EU concerning its proposal for European strategies, that are evidence-based responses to global competitiveness in education. In any case, the data sources the EU uses in its monitoring and evaluation processes signal an informal *functional expansion* of the EU in a policy area where supranational actions are legally limited (Borrás and Jacobsson 2004: 201).

THE CONTRADICTORY EFFECTS OF
THE USE OF BENCHMARKING

The creation of understandings on the value of education credentials, based on performance evaluations of education institutions, has been a common practice in the UK since the Thatcher reforms. As a consequence, education institutions started struggling for prestige in detriment of quality; the gap between elite institutions—which get more public funding—and others has become wider so that social stratification has increased (Apple 2001, Brown 2008). The EU benchmarking in education may introduce a similar problematic at a different scale. It puts forward the idea that in some countries education is *better* than in others and, consequently, it promotes an understanding of the quality of diplomas according to the national territory where they are obtained. On the one hand, it motivates Member States to compete for a better position in benchmarking evaluations at the cost of a focus on the quality of the education actually delivered. As it has been observed in the previous section, the selected benchmarks stimulate a kind of educational work aimed to increase numerical outputs that do not necessarily indicate qualitative improvement. This competition makes it difficult to reconcile the vision of a European educational space united by common educational strategic objectives and the ambition of individual countries to become *best performers*. Another contradiction is related to job opportunities and student mobility. Considering that the EU area is not only a common market in terms of goods but also in terms of labor, benchmarking information might influence the choice of candidates for a job according to the national territory where they have obtained their academic qualifications. For instance, if an employer is aware of Nordic countries being among the *best performers* in education, graduates from the respective countries may be preferred in the labor market despite candidates possibly holding similar levels of academic qualifications and previous work experience from other countries. Once the EU names *best performing* countries, it may indirectly contribute to student academic mobility for the purposes of acquiring valuable credentials. This possible effect contradicts the rationales underlying the EU student mobility programs, which have prioritized academic mobility as an educational means to create European consciousness and enable students to acquire language mastery and intercultural competence (Papatsiba 2005: 174). Taking into account that many households cannot afford the cost of studies abroad, there will be students who can obtain credentials in top-rated nations—a European elite—and those who cannot. The latter will be in competitive disadvantage in the labor market. Educational competitiveness, when based upon how much individuals can pay for their certificates, is prone to perpetuate social inequalities and may generate more social loss than profit in European societies.

CONCLUSION

The EU's use of benchmarking to monitor and evaluate the progress that Member States make in the achievement of their common educational objectives illustrates how, despite its legal limits, the EU can play an indirect role in the conception, organization, and content of national education systems. Benchmarking is a way through which the EU determines particular political directions that underpin a neo-liberal global approach to investment in human capital as a crucial factor for economic growth. This is an instrumental approach to education which is focused on the global competitive advantage of having education systems that are able to continuously generate the kind of labor force the labor market needs. It is thus a mechanism of coordination of educational policies that urges Member States not only to adopt EU-level fixed targets, but also the political ideologies they entail.

In spite of the potential that comparable measurements of performance in education may have in terms of facilitating the political and ideological alignment of Member States, the process of benchmarking has various shortcomings in the context of the EU. First, the relationship between the selected five benchmarks in education and the EU educational strategy objectives is not easily perceptible. Second, the comparisons made are based upon the erroneous assumption that all EU members have equal conditions to achieve the position of *best performer*, that is, no contextual specificities are taken into account. Third, the identification of *best performers*, although justified to be a way in which Member States can learn from each other, does not lead to actual consequences in terms of collective initiatives to change education systems according to *best practices*. Finally, the benchmarking reports underscore unresolved tensions: whereas they are intended to promote the development of educational work in accordance with common goals, they stimulate competition within the Union; although they are supposed to determine progress made towards objectives that are presented as being EU objectives, they bear obvious similarities to other international organizations' agendas and governance mechanisms; and despite the fact that they are aimed to facilitate the improvement of the quality of education, they also motivate a national competition to increase numbers so that a better positioning in the two-yearly benchmarking reports may be noted.

Above all, the EU benchmarking in education seems to function as the definition of measurable standards to identify where, in the European region, there is better convergence of policies aimed at *growing* the knowledge-based economy. However, these standards also serve the purpose of qualifying educational provision. Indeed, they imply the creation of an understanding of the value of educational credentials according to the national territory where they are obtained, which may result in an increase of social inequalities within the EU area. These inequalities would derive from individual differences in economic capacity to fund studies in *best performing* countries in education in order to acquire qualifications that, in the common EU labor market, may be viewed as being *better* than others obtained elsewhere.

NOTES

1. In the detailed work program (European Council 2002), the three strategic objectives are broken down into thirteen objectives and 42 key issues reflecting the wide spectrum of areas related to education and training. These objectives and issues constitute the basis for the formulation of indicators and benchmarks. The number of benchmarks has not increased since 2003, but with respect to indicators, in 2006, the Commission had already defined 29 indicators in areas such as language skills, learning to learn skills, or teachers' training.
2. See Henry *et al.* (2001) and Grek (2009) for empirical studies on the work the OECD has developed on indicators of performance in education since the 1990s.

BIBLIOGRAPHY

Apple, W. M. (2001) "Comparing Neo-liberal Projects and Inequality in Education," *Comparative Education* 37 (4): 409–423.
Arrowsmith, J., K. Sisson, and P. Marginson (2004) "What Can 'Benchmarking' Offer the Open Method of Co-ordination?" *Journal of European Public Policy* 11 (2): 311–328.
Borrás, S. and K. Jacobsson (2004) "The Open Method of Co-ordination and New Governance Patterns in the EU," *Journal of European Public Policy* 11 (2): 185–208.
Brown, R. (2008) "Higher Education and the Market," *Perspectives* 12: 78–83.
Dale, R. (2005) "Globalisation, Knowledge Economy and Comparative Education," *Comparative Education* 41 (2): 117–149.
Dale, R. and S. Robertson (2007). "Beyond Methodological 'Isms' in Comparative Education in an Era of Globalisation," Bristol, Center for Globalisation, Education and Societies. http://www.bris.ac.uk/education/people/academicStaff/edslr/publications/14ird, accessed on August 17, 2008.
European Commission (2000) *Innovation in a Knowledge-Driven Economy*, (September), Communication, COM (2000) 567 final. http://eur-lex.europa.eu/LexUriServ/LexUriServ.do?uri=COM:2000:0567:FIN:EN:PDF, accessed on June 16, 2009.
European Commission (2001a) *Making the European Area of Lifelong Learning a Reality*, (November), Communication, COM (2001) 678. http://eur-lex.europa.eu/LexUriServ/LexUriServ.do?uri=COM:2001:0678:FIN:EN:PDF, accessed on June 16, 2009.
European Commission (2001b) *The Concrete Objectives of Education Systems*, (January), Report, COM (2001) 59 final. http://ec.europa.eu/education/policies/2010/doc/concrete-future-objectives_en.pdf, accessed on June 16, 2009.
European Commission (2002a) *European Benchmarks in Education and Training: Follow-up to the Lisbon European Council*, (November), Communication, COM (2002) 629 final. http://ec.europa.eu/education/policies/2010/doc/bench_ed_trai_en.pdf, accessed on June 16, 2009.

European Commission (2002b) *Commission's Action Plan for Skills and Mobility*, (February), Communication, COM (2002) 72 final. http://eur-lex.europa. eu/LexUriServ/LexUriServ.do?uri=COM:2002:0072:FIN:EN:PDF, accessed on June 16, 2009.

European Commission (2005) *European Values in the Globalised World. Contribution of the Commission to the October Meeting of Heads of State and Government*, (October), Communication, COM (2005) 525 final. http:// ec.europa.eu/growthandjobs/pdf/COM2005_525_en.pdf, accessed on June 16, 2009.

European Commission (2006a) *Efficiency and Equity in European Education and Training Systems*, (September), Communication, COM (2006) 481 final. http:// ec.europa.eu/education/policies/2010/doc/comm481_en.pdf, accessed on June 16, 2009.

European Commission (2006b) *Progress Towards the Lisbon Objectives in Education and Training. Report Based on Indicators and Benchmarks*, (May), Staff Working Paper, SEC (2006) 639. http://ec.europa.eu/education/policies/2010/ doc/progressreport06.pdf, accessed on June 16, 2009.

European Council (2000) *Presidency Conclusion: Lisbon European Council 23th and 24th March.* http://www.europarl.europa.eu/summits/previous.htm, accessed on June 7, 2007.

European Council (2001) *Report from the Education Council to the European Council on the Concrete Future Objectives of Education and Training Systems*, (February), Outcome of Proceedings, 5980/01 EDUC 23. http://ec.europa.eu/ education/policies/2010/doc/rep_fut_obj_en.pdf, accessed on June 16, 2009.

European Council (2002) "Detailed Work Programme on the Follow-up of the Objectives of Education and Training Systems in Europe," *Official Journal of the European Communities* 2002/C 142/01, 14–06–2002. http://eur-lex. europa.eu/LexUriServ/LexUriServ.do?uri=OJ:C:2002:142:0001:0022:EN:PD F, accessed on June 16, 2009.

European Council (2003) *Council Conclusions on Reference Levels of European Average Performance in Education and Training (Benchmarks)*, (May), Outcome of Proceedings, 8981/03 EDUC 83. http://ec.europa.eu/education/ policies/2010/doc/after-council-meeting_en.pdf, accessed on June 16, 2009.

European Council (2004) "Education and Training 2010: The Success of the Lisbon Strategy Hinges on Urgent Reforms. Joint Interim Report of the Council and the Commission on the Implementation of the Detailed Work Programme on the Follow-up of the Objectives of Education and Training Systems in Europe," *Official Journal of the European Union*, 2004/C 104/01, 30–04–2004. http:// eur-lex.europa.eu/LexUriServ/LexUriServ.do?uri=OJ:C:2004:104:0001:0019: EN:PDF, accessed on June 16, 2009.

European Council (2005) "Council Conclusions of 24 May 2005 on New Indicators in Education and Training," *Official Journal of the European Union*, 2005/C 141/04, 10–06–2005. http://eur-lex.europa.eu/LexUriServ/LexUriServ. do?uri=OJ:C:2005:141:0007:0008:EN:PDF, accessed on June 16, 2009.

European Council (2006) "Modernising Education and Training: A Vital Contribution to Prosperity and Social Cohesion in Europe. 2006 Joint Interim Report of the Council and the Commission on Progress under the Education and Training 2010 Work Programme," *Official Journal of the European Union*, 2006/C 79/01, 01–04–2006. http://eur-lex.europa.eu/LexUriServ/LexUriServ.do?uri=OJ:C:2006 :079:0001:0019:EN:PDF, accessed on June 16, 2009.

European Council (2008a) "2008 Joint Interim Report of the Council and the Commission on the Implementation of the Education and Training 2010 Work Programme Delivering Lifelong Learning for Knowledge, Creativity and Innovation," *Official Journal of the European Union*, C 86/1, 05–04–2008. http://

eur-lex.europa.eu/LexUriServ/LexUriServ.do?uri=OJ:C:2008:086:0001:0031: EN:PDF, accessed on June 16, 2009.

European Council (2008b) *Joint Progress Report of the Council and the Commission on the Implementation of the Education and Training 2010. Work Programme—Delivering Lifelong Learning for Knowledge, Creativity and Innovation*, (January), Draft, 5585/08 EDUC 24 SOC 46. http://ec.europa.eu/education/pdf/doc66_en.pdf, accessed on June 16, 2009.

European Union (1992) "Treaty on the European Union". *Official Journal of the European Communities*, C 191, July 29. http://eur-lex.europa.eu/en/treaties/dat/11992M/htm/11992M.html, accessed on May 10, 2009.

Grek, S. (2009) "Governing by Numbers: The PISA 'Effect' in Europe," *Journal of Educational Policy* 24 (1): 23–37.

Henry, M., B. Lingard, F. Rizvi, and S. Taylor (2001) *The OECD, Globalisation and Education Policy*. Oxford: Pergamon.

Keeling, R. (2006) "The Bologna Process and the Lisbon Research Agenda: The European Commission's Expanding Role in Higher Education Discourse," *European Journal of Education* 41 (2): 203–223.

Kyrö, P. (2003) "Revising the Concept and Forms of Benchmarking," *Benchmarking: An International Journal* 10 (3): 210–225.

Papatsiba, V. (2006) "Mapping the European Union Agenda in Education and Training Policy," *Comparative Education* 42 (1): 93–111.

Roberston, S. L. (2005) "Re-imagining and Rescripting the Future of Education," *Comparative Education* 41 (2): 151–170.

Rosamond, B. (2002) "Imagining the European Economy: "Competitiveness" and the Social Construction of 'Europe' as an Economic Space," *New Political Economy* 7 (2): 157–177.

Sisson, K., J. Arrowsmith, and P. Marginson (2002) *All Benchmarkers now? Benchmarking and the 'Europeanisation' of Industrial Relations*. Working Paper 41/02, "One Europe or Several Programmes," Brighton, University of Sussex.

Spendolini, M. J. (1992) *The Benchmarking Book*. New York: AMACOM, American Management Association.

Wallace, H. (2001) "The Changing Politics and the European Union: An Overview," *Journal of Common Market Studies* 39 (4): 581–94.

Walters, W. (2004) "Some Notes on Governance," *Studies in Political Economy* 73 (Spring/Summer): 27–46.

4 Gender, Inequality, and Globalization

Ilse Lenz

THE CHANGING FACE OF GLOBALIZATION AND GENDER IN NEWLY INDUSTRIALIZED COUNTRIES

Globalization has influenced gender relations in multiple ways. Its dynamics increased after 1990. Whereas at the beginning, research focused on the negative impacts (i.a. Mies 1986, Wichterich 1998, Young 1998), now after 20 years, it seems an adequate moment to reflect the comprehensive and deep socio-economic changes in gender relations induced by globalization. Globalization must be related to modernization, because it interworks and intercuts with internal modernization as the debates on "glocalization" have shown.[1]

Globalization has impacted world regions and the local cultures they contain very differently, according to their position in the international power structure. For example, gender relations in poor agrarian regions in Sub-Saharan Africa are in fact very different from those in newly industrialized countries (NICs) in East Asia. Therefore, changes in gender relations must be contextualized according to the local socio-cultural context. In this chapter, I will focus on newly industrialized East Asian countries.[2]

In NICs, a rapid and basic transformation of gender relations resulted from the interworking of globalization and modernization. In short, this transformation can be seen as selective incorporation into *and* exclusion from the public spheres of work, politics, and civil society along the lines of gender, class, and ethnicity. Gender relations have changed, as currently some women as well as most men are integrated into the public spheres of work, politics, and civil society (whereas most women are still assigned to carry out unpaid care work in the home; cf. Lenz, Ullrich, Fersch 2007). Because this process was based on the emerging labor markets in export-oriented industrialization in NICs, the public integration of women can be seen as market-driven economic integration of women into the labor force while unpaid work for social reproduction was not re-distributed and was even increased due to economic re-structuring. Thus, the situation has become very different from the former hegemonial exclusion of most women outside of these public spheres. These processes of selective incorporation and exclusion have created new chances as well as deep tensions and contradictions. As the following example illustrates, class and ethnicity are important factors in shaping these different developments.

In economic globalization, for example, large groups of women have entered the labor market. Most often, these women entered paid work in semiskilled/non-skilled or irregular jobs at lower wages in the service sector or in manufacturing while still burdened with unpaid care work for the family. These women have become part of the working class as housewives as well as wage workers. But some educated women have moved up into middle-range jobs or management positions where they have joined the emerging middle class as employees or housewives (Lenz 2002). Whereas these women are still responsible for unpaid care work, they often employ domestic servants for a low wage, thus delegating a large part of care work to them. In many cases, these servants are migrants from less economically developed countries and regions, who leave their own children with relatives when entering the global care chain (Hochschild and Ehrenreich 2003, Ochiai and Molony 2008). These migrants are often informally or even illegally employed, and thus possess few rights at their work place. Although women have entered the labor market, their chances are unevenly allocated in the context of class and ethnicity, as this example of social differences among women from different geographic regions illustrates. The extensive literature on gender inequality in globalization has highlighted the importance of two perspectives: (a) the interrelations of wage work and unpaid care work in analyzing gender inequality at work and (b) the interactions of gender and other forms of inequality, such as class, world region, situation of migration, and ethnicity.

The industrial rise of large world regions, in particular China and India, brought up the issue of structural changes in globalization. According to some theorists, globalization has changed during the last 30 years and is now moving to a second stage (Pieterse Nederveen 2008). These assessments are based on an underlying deep-going power shift in economy and politics. Whereas the late 1990s were characterized by the unilateralism of the US and the West, in the new millennium global power relations are shifting towards a multipolar fragile balance including China, Brazil, India, and Russia.

Jan Pieterse Nederveen sums up the evidence in several fields:

In trade, South–South and East–South trade has increased, and regional and interregional groupings, such as Mercosur in Latin America and ASEAN in Asia, have become more important. China has established a free trade zone with the ASEAN countries. The United Nations Conference on Trade and Development (UNCTAD) actually perceives a "new geography of trade" that Pieterse Nederveen describes as follows:

> The new axis stretches from the manufacturing might and emerging middle classes of China, and from the software powerhouse of India in the south, to the mineral riches of South Africa, a beachhead to the

rest of the African continent, and across the Indian and Pacific oceans to South America which is oil-rich and mineral- and agriculture-laden. (Pieterse Nederveen 2008: 708)

The export-oriented world market–driven industrializations of China and India have led this development towards a multipolar trade. China's share of world exports has more than doubled since 1998: from less than 4 percent to just over 8 percent in 2006. Due to her positive export balance, China has become a major financial power, in particular, in respect of the foreign debt of the US. In the field of finance, the core financial regulation institutions, such as the IMF and the World Bank, have lost some weight and have become more fragile. According to Pieterse Nederveen, the US can still claim political and military "hegemony" (Pieterse Nederveen 2008: 711). Whereas the US government under President Bush relied on unilateralism and was reluctant in issues of human and women's rights, the US government under President Obama has returned to and intensified the mixed uni- and multipolar approach of the 1990s to cooperative security. Thus, developments in trade, finance, and political hegemony point towards a "next round" of globalization. Whether "its axis is turning slowly like an oil tanker from North–South to East–South" as Pieterse Nederveen has predicted (2008: 707) is not yet obvious. Several scenarios can be projected from the North–East over the South to the South–East. In fact, global power relations have become more multipolar and have displayed an open character as the recent changes in the IMF governance structure that increase the role of China and India (2009) have demonstrated.

Under these circumstances, the NICs will still intensify their international weight. Their gender relations may even influence those existing in other world regions. This is a further argument for a separate analysis of gender questions according to the local context in order to overcome the long-lasting image of the "third world woman." But these developments also beg the question, can global gender equality still be understood adequately with models that assume the superiority of the "West" and see it as the only hegemonic power (cf. Mohanty 2003)? The feminist critique has incorporated parts of such dualistic models. Certainly, this was important regarding the global power relations in the 1970s and contributed to creating multicentered global feminisms that raised their own voices and demands originating in their socio-cultural context (Connell 2009). But these critiques have also tended to consolidate dualistic worldviews, confronting and locking the "West" and other regions in a schematic dualism while neglecting to look at new powers, such as China. Whereas Western hegemony is still strong, the "blind spot" of this dualism appears in its neglect of the shift of global power relations and gender relations in the "next round" of globalization.

Globalization is shifting to new economic and political power relationships, as argued earlier. Therefore, an integrated perspective is highly relevant that combines the view on the global reconfiguration of economic, social, and political relations with their concomitant gender transformations. This chapter argues that globalization influences gender inequality in a contradictory and complex way. It starts from the hypothesis that globalization has contributed to a market-driven economic integration of women into the labor force of NICs in East Asia and Latin America while unpaid work for social reproduction was not redistributed and even increased due to economic restructuring. I will give an overview on these changes by looking at labor market integration, education, and family changes. Globalization has in that sense promoted a polarization among women according to class and ethnicity.

Whereas economic globalization contributed to inclusion and polarization, political globalization established norms of gender equality at the national and global levels. In particular, the UN Decade for Women provided chances for reform-oriented states and international civil society, e.g., feminist networks, and established global norms of equality. Whereas globalization has been a period of deregulation in formal male-centered work, some soft forms of regulation with an egalitarian orientation have been achieved in the field of gender.

In the final part of this chapter, consequences for research on evolving gender policies in NICs will be considered. In particular, the debate on comparative gender welfare regimes will contribute to this examination. Whereas this debate has been expanded in the context of European industrialization and path development, it may also be fruitful for other world regions.

GENDER INEQUALITY IN ECONOMIC GLOBALIZATION AND WORK

Globalization has been understood as a set of interrelated processes in economic, political, social, and cultural fields (Lenz 2007). I will start discussing some gender issues of economic globalization. The ascending power of financial capital, an acceleration of foreign direct investment (FDI), high enterprise mobility, offshore production on a global scale, and the rise of transnational corporations (TNCs) have characterized this process (cf. Lenz 2000 and 2002). According to the annual survey of the UNCTAD,[3] FDI has been increasing in the long run. It has been mainly directed to developed countries, and, most often, it also originated there.

But since the 1990s, NICs have grown as important sources of FDI, which they have re-directed to highly developed countries as well as to developing countries. One important reason is the outward expansion of Asian TNCs from China, India, and South Korea. South–South investment from East Asia, in particular state and semiprivate investment from China in the extracting and mining industries in developing countries, especially in Africa and Latin America, is another important cause.[4] Some NICs such as China, Brazil, India, South Korea, and their leading TNCs have entered the global economic game on their own: they develop North–South as well as South–South cooperation. They have brought in their own strategies and varieties of capitalism with their related gender arrangements.

TNCs as specific forms of internationalized economic organizations have shown up as main global actors. They emerged with spectacular dynamism over the last 40 years. Their numbers grew rapidly from 7,000 in 1969 to some 40,000 parent firms with 250,000 foreign affiliates in 1994 and doubled again up to 79,000 TNCs and their 790,000 foreign affiliates in 2007 (UNCTAD 1995: xx and 2008: xvi). In 2007, the added value (gross product) of foreign affiliates worldwide represented an impressive estimated 11 percent share of global GDP. The number of employees rose to some 82 million persons (UNCTAD 2008: xvi). Whereas this trend expresses a rising importance of employment in global firms, the 82 million persons in quantitative terms are not dominant when compared to the about three billion persons employed at the global level.[5] Yet, since the 1990s, the importance of TNCs in newly industrializing East Asian and Latin American countries has increased (UNCTAD 2008: xvi).

Nevertheless, the qualitative aspects of FDIs and TNCs are important, because they have shaped gendered work organizations and the culture of organizations. As pioneers of industrialization, TNCs have spread their gendered work organizations and gender culture to offshore manufacturing in NICs. In textiles, electronics, or food processing, as well as in semiskilled service jobs (for example, tourism), TNCs have established and deepened the gender segmentation of jobs by assigning low-skilled jobs without any possibility of upward mobility to young unmarried women with some basic education (cf. Wichterich 2009). In other industries, such as car assemblies, men were recruited into unskilled jobs. This recruitment gave them access to some on-the-job-training and some mobility, and into skilled jobs such as foremen or technicians (Anker 1998, Lenz 2002, Carr and Chen 2004). Thus, in many world regions,[6] TNCs have promoted and rationalized a deep-going gender segmentation of working conditions and training that had not been known in a systematic manner in local industries.

Industrial TNCs do not only use low-paid industrial female labor, but also exploit women in informal home work in subcontracting relations that are frequently gendered. Workers in home work are formally self-employed, even if they have worked for the same company for a long time period. Furthermore, these workers are often supposed to be housewives, and, thus, to be economically covered by their husbands or their families, even if they are the principal earners or head of households (Carr and Chen 2004).

Whereas employment and labor market integration of women in NICs have rapidly increased, working conditions have been characterized by low gender-discriminatory wages and long hours. These conditions provide no long-term perspective for an independent individual existence based on one's own work, neither for the women alone, nor for their families or their children (cf. Wichterich 2009).

POLITICAL GLOBALIZATION AND REGULATION FOR EQUALITY

Political globalization has been characterized, on the one hand, by the increasing importance of global supranational organizations like the EU and other regional political associations, such as ASEAN, and, on the other, by NGOs and global civil society. The global multilevel system has evolved in such a way that supranational organizations, states, and NGOs negotiate norms and rules in global governance structures. In particular, NGOs move between the different levels of the multilevel system of the UN, regional political associations, states, and the local level, aiming at mobilizing for their goals. The emerging global gender regime is thus a very interesting example of political globalization.

The UN Decade for Women and its world conferences, in particular the Fourth World Conference on Women held in Beijing in 1995, formed the core of this process of global governance. The UN institutions and processes offered a rapidly expanding structure of international opportunity for women's movements all over the world (United Nations 1995, Wichterich 1998). They provided an arena as well as a framework for debates and the establishment of universal norms on gender equality (UN 1995). The UN is the legitimate, central institution that is appropriate to establish universal norms, as it constitutes the international community of nations. Gender perspectives had also been integrated into the UN social conferences of the 1990s.

During the UN Decades for Women from 1975 to the present, global feminist networks emerged in an unprecedented scope (Meyer and Prügl 1999, Wichterich 1996 and 2001). These networks discussed the different issues that they brought from local and national contexts to global developments. They had to learn how to find a common language while respecting cultural differences between them. But they also had to confront inequalities in global women's movements like the higher access of Western networks to ressources and to recognise and negotiate these hierarchies even if they could not overcome them in the global inequal context. Thus learning through *conflicts in sisterhood*, they could initiate political problem definition with a multifocal set of issues and could play a proactive role in global agenda setting. In these processes, they had to find convergent concepts in which their differences could be respected. For example, women's movements from different socio-cultural backgrounds came to share concepts such as equality in work, struggling against violence against women, or women's empowerment on a global level; but they associated these topics with different meanings and developed different strategies to realize these concepts in their various local contexts (Meyer and Prügl 1999, UN 1995). The *women's/human rights approach* proved very productive in bridging differences and developing convergent strategies for women's movements in the South, the East, and the West. This approach could also be translated into global discourses on human rights and social issues. Thus, global feminist and transnational networks and women's movements could influence UN processes around the Decades for Women and the UN social conferences—from the Rio Conference on ecology in 1992 to the World Social Summit in 1996—as well as put pressure on national governments.

Three documents are particularly pertinent for the topic of gender inequality:

1. The United Nations General Assembly adopted the Convention for the Elimination of all Forms of Discrimination against Women in 1979 (CEDAW 1979). It aimed to overcome the first fragmentary UN approaches after 1945 against *sex discrimination* by providing an integrated framework to abolish all forms of discrimination. It had the legal status of an international law for the states that had ratified it and that were a broad majority of UN member states (but not the US). In article 2 of CEDAW, states pledged to prohibit all forms of discrimination against women and to take appropriate measures to eliminate discrimination against women by any person, organization, or enterprise. Article 11 contained a specific commitment for eliminating all forms of discrimination in employment, including the right to work and equality in recruitment, training, promotion, wages, and benefits (CEDAW 1979, Zwingel 2005).

2. The UN Women's Conference in Mexico in 1975 and the UN world action plan of 1980 had committed governments to establish women's divisions or focal points in central governments. Women's political mechanisms—women's offices or ministries, equal opportunity departments, etc.—were enlarged or established in the subsequent national negotiations on UN gender norms. Their tasks included the implementation of these norms (Unifem 2000: 37–61). Since the beginning of the Decade for Women (1975–85), these norms and institutions contributed to an expansion of the political opportunity structure, as *femocrats*[7] were established in states and supranational bodies in order to develop potential allies.

3. The Fourth UN World Conference on Women in Beijing 1995 came up with a Declaration and Platform for Action (United Nations 1995) that established basic norms and steps for gender equality in a process of international negotiations between governments and feminists from very different regions and approaches. The central principle of gender mainstreaming has been fundamental in the change of organizations and enterprises; it has been incorporated in the EU Treaty of Amsterdam (1997) and in gender policies of national states, such as Sweden or South Africa. The Platform for Action from 1995 had included broader goals of empowerment and autonomy, e.g., the body and sexuality, equality in work, education, development, peace and non-violence in public as well as in personal relationships, and political participation. It can be seen as a charter for global gender democracy.

The momentum and political innovation of the UN Decades has receded since the Beijing Conference in 1995. The follow-up process of the 2000 conference in New York was characterized by an inward concentration on the bureaucratic and *femocrat* institutions of the UN and member states, by a decline of feminist mobilization, and the involvement of strong counter-movements.

But there was an agreement on the main goals and norms of CEDAW and the Beijing Platform for Action by most governments of the world. They had also established women's offices or divisions in governments that had the purpose to promote and monitor the adequate application and implementation at the local and national levels. These women's offices in the administrations had developed co-operations with local women's movements who negotiate with them in critical conflict partnerships. Recent studies have shown that local activists engage in the translation and application of norms of equality and nonviolence (Merry 2006, Siebert 2009). By these activities, they bring these norms (such as better education for girls and ending domestic violence) into everyday life in the local communities. Local and national movements are thus decisive.

In East Asian NICs, states have participated in and supported the UN process of establishing gender norms of equality. The transformation of gender relations that will be described in the next part of this chapter, was influenced by the neo-liberal economic globalization process and by political processes linked to the emerging gender equality regime.

GENDER TRANSFORMATIONS IN EAST ASIAN NICS

Export-oriented industrialization was most marked in East Asia and in some Latin American and Caribbean countries. In East Asian NICs, since the 1960s, a fundamental transformation of gender relations evolved under the interrelated influences of globalization and modernization. Some East Asian authors call this interrelated process "compressed modernity" as these societies evolved at a rapid pace while confronted with and working with globalization (Chang 1999, Ochiai and Molony 2008). In East Asian developing countries, in the 1960s, women worked most often in agriculture. Their level of education was considerably lower than men's and women were a small minority in political decision-making (except in China). In Table 4.1, key data for this transformation in East Asian NICs have been compiled showing the changes from 2000 to 2007.

One important trend is the seminal decline of the birthrate in China (1.7 in 2007), South Korea (1.3 in 2007) and in Taiwan (1.1 in 2007). Some scholars, such as S. Huntington (1996), have considered these countries as the core of the "Neo-Confucian belt;" their "cultural otherness" was supposed to grow from their family system and was characterized by

Table 4.1 The Transformation of Gender Relations in Newly Industrializing Countries in East Asia

	Total Fertility Rate (Births per Women)			Male Labor Force Participation (Percent of Female Population Aged 15–64)			Female Labor Force Participation (Percent of Female Population Aged 15–64)			Ratio of Female to Male Enrollment in Tertiary Education			Proportion of Seats Held by Women in National Parliament		
	2000	2004	2007	2000	2004	2007	2000	2004	2007	2000	2004	2007	2000	2004	2007
China	1.7	1.7	1.7	87.6	85.8	85.1	79.3	77.9	77.1	..	97.8	97.8	22.0	20.0	20.3
Indonesia	2.4	2.3	2.2	87.0	87.6	88.5	52.3	51.7	51.7	76.5	79.4	78.9	8.0	8.0	11.3
Japan	1.4	1.3	1.3	85.3	84.5	84.2	59.6	60.3	61.0	85.4	88.7	87.9	5.0	7.0	9.4
South Korea	1.5	1.2	1.3	75.9	76.7	76.3	52.1	53.8	53.8	58.5	62.9	65.2	4.0	6.0	13.4
Malaysia	3.0	2.7	2.6	83.2	83.1	82.7	46.6	46.7	47.3	106.1	126.1	129.4	10.0	11.0	9.1
Philippines	3.6	3.4	3.2	82.8	83.5	82.2	49.9	51.2	51.2	129.5	127.5	124.1	12.0	18.0	22.4
Taiwan	1.7	1.2	1.1	..	..	..	..	..	..	..	..	..	..	..	..
Thailand	1.9	1.8	1.9	85.0	85.5	85.0	70.5	70.5	70.1	119.8	118.2	123.2	6.0	9.0	8.7
Vietnam	2.4	2.2	2.1	81.7	81.4	80.8	75.9	75.2	74.5	72.5	..	..	26.0	27.0	25.8

Compiled from the World Bank gender stats files. Cf. http://web.worldbank.org/WBSITE/EXTERNAL/TOPICS/EXTGENDER/EXTANATOOLS/EXT-STATINDDATA/EXTGENDERSTATS/0,,contentMDK:21442585~menuPK:4851736~pagePK:64168445~piPK:64168309~theSitePK:3237336,00.html, accessed on August 14, 2009.

a "family first outlook." According to Orientalist descriptions, the neo-patriarchal family is more important then individual fulfillment. The development of the one-child or two-children family shows that these totalizing culturalist approaches were not sensitive to the internal modernization of these societies.

In the People's Republic of China, the enforced population and child reduction policy played an important role as well as the high rate of women's full-time employment. But in South Korea and Taiwan, the decline of the birthrate was caused by other reasons, presumably women's high labor market integration and the individualization trend of the last decades (Hong 2006).

The birthrate is rapidly falling in Indonesia (2.2 in 2007), Thailand (1.9 in 2007), and Vietnam (2.1 in 2007). It is moving to a threshold of 2.0 or below. The birthrate in Malaysia and the Philippines is somewhat higher, but is also diminishing. The reasons for these diverging levels can be found in the socio-cultural contexts of each nation and cannot be generalized. What can be summarized, however, are deep-going demographic changes influencing gender relations and the importance of the family. One negative generalization may be appropriate: the myths of the traditional roles of Asian women *living for the family* and the Asian extended family as the lodestar of the group life are becoming shadows of the past as families are changing and more and more women are included in the labor market. The demographic change is indicative of new family forms and somewhat individualizing life-patterns. The emphasis here is on *new* family forms: the importance of the family is eminent in new re-organized forms (as public childcare) that relate to the labor market, the state, and civil society. For example, grandparents will bring children to the *Kindergarten* while the mothers do shift work (Ochiai and Molony 2008). But these modernizing gender relations are not simply dictated by traditional family roles. Rather, new balances have to be found and gender relations will have to be negotiated in the modernizing and globalizing context.

A second important trend is the high to medium labor market integration of women resulting from export-oriented industrialization. Female labor force participation is highest (although slightly receding) in the People's Republic of China (77.1 percent in 2007). This high level of female employment is due to several reasons: it reflects the socialist ideology, the chosen development path of export-oriented industrialization, and the reliance on women's wage work in export-oriented manufacturing such as electronics, textiles, etc. Female employment has crossed 70 percent in socialist Vietnam (74.5 percent in 2007) and Thailand (70.1 percent in 2007) with a traditionally high share in agriculture and export-oriented industrialization. In South Korea with its rapid industrialization and compressed modernization (Chang 1999), more than 50 percent of women are engaged in wage work as well as in the Philippines. In Indonesia and Malaysia, female employment in agriculture was high in the past and has been promoted by export-oriented industrialization.

In times of technological upgrading and innovation in globalization, labor-intensive low-paid female jobs may be replaced by male skilled work (Carr and Chen 2004). Car factories and steel mills may follow the electronic assembly lines. From a perspective of international equality, this technological advancement and fuller industrial profile are desirable. Yet, women should not become the dismissed foot soldiers of national industrialization after having given their energy, and often having risked their health. Therefore, vocational training and desegmentation of the labor market are urgent issues. They may be promoted by the demographic change that calls for a more comprehensive employment strategy of women in skilled and longtime jobs.

An international research group has compared the changes of family size, mother's life-patterns, and female employment in East Asia (Ochiai and Molony 2008). These scholars found three types of female life-courses. The first type is a continuously high labor market participation of women throughout their productive years: this type is characteristic for the People's Republic of China and Thailand. In China, after the socialist revolution, women were mobilized out of the household and its separate spheres. The couple carries out childcare with a marked involvement of fathers, while grandparents and public institutions support the couple. Women see full and lifelong employment as a right that has been guaranteed by the state ideology of equality. But this right is undermined by new ideologies of gender difference, that emphasize women's role as mothers, and by working in export-oriented global industries especially in South China (Wichterich 2009).

In Thailand, however, high female employment was supported by women's public role in agriculture, the bilateral kinship system trends, and a high recognition of women's (especially daughters) strong economic and social contributions. But due to the lack of public childcare, women come under pressure when they have children: caring by grandparents and other relatives cannot fully compensate for that (Ochiai and Molony 2008: 32–40).

The second type of country are societies such as Singapore and Taiwan where women's participation rates are very high in their youth but slowly decline from their thirties onwards. Women stay in the labor market after the birth of children while childcare is largely entrusted to relatives (e.g., grandparents and siblings). But many mothers withdraw when the children are school age and concentrate on their education, an activity that they consider as being a mother's responsibility (Ochiai and Molony 2008: 41–48).

The third type of country is, for example, South Korea, where women show a high labor market participation in their youth, then withdraw with the birth of children, and finally re-enter the labor market in their middle age, often in flexible or irregular employments; this trend results in the typical M-shaped female labor force participation by age. This M-curve pattern was a new development as women used to be active in wage work either throughout their life or after completing childrearing until the 1970s. Better-qualified women are actually often confronted with discriminating working conditions for women as well as with increasing demands for their children's education. Therefore, some women withdraw from the labor market and concentrate on their children (Ochiai and Molony 2008: 48–52). These research results show marked differences in the life-courses of women from wage work to childcaring. The emergence of NICs in the process of globalization has thus led to different types of gender welfare regimes.

Female general education levels have progressed rapidly and it maybe assumed that the knowledge fundamental for more equal vocational training already exists. The gender gap between men and women in tertiary education has nearly closed in the People's Republic of China whereas it is greatest in South Korea (65.2 percent in 2007). A reverse gender gap with more women than men in tertiary education has developed in Malaysia, Thailand, and the Philippines while the reasons remained unclear.

Increasing political participation of women is an important part of gender transformations. Politics have ceased to be a male monopoly and women have at least gained a political voice. Their descriptive representation (i.e., the share of women) is highest in the Philippines with its democratic transition and its strong women's movements, as well as in socialist China and Vietnam with their state ideology of equality. In Indonesia and Thailand, the share of women has slowly increased due to mobilizations and democratization. In South Korea, the women's movement made spectacular campaigns to increase the rate of women in government and parliament, which doubled from 2004 to 2007. The reasons for this increase of political voice are manifold and cannot be summarized here. But it can be assumed that international norms such as the CEDAW and the Beijing world action platform played an important role as did women's movements and gender politicians who used national and global norms to introduce political changes.

The gender transformations in East Asian NICs can be summed up as changes in demography and family, as high to medium labor market integration of women, as an educational advance for women, and as increasing political participation. Yet, no comparative data could be found on the inequalities according to gender, class, and ethnicity. One has then to ask the question, what do these gender transformations mean for gender policies?

GENDER WELFARE REGIMES—A USEFUL CONCEPT FOR THE GENDER TRANSFORMATION IN EAST ASIAN NICS?

In East Asian NICs, the development of welfare systems has been put on the political agenda. South Korea has been developing its welfare system since the late 1980s (Peng 2004). In the People's Republic of China, urgent social problems of social displacement, the one child family, and the elderly in rapid economic modernization and globalization call for new welfare approaches and social security.

Thus, it is very important to reflect on gender inequality in welfare state development and to look for useful egalitarian concepts. The debate on gender welfare regimes provides pertinent approaches for this issue (cf. Orloff 1993 and 2005, Pascall and Lewis 2004, Peng 2004, Osawa 2007a and b, Ochiai 2009). This discussion started from the feminist critique of Gøsta Esping-Andersen's comparative typology of welfare states (Esping-Andersen 1990 and 2002).[9]

Esping-Andersen built his typology on the concept that individual welfare relies on three pillars:

- The state that provides access to financial transfers and services;
- The market (mainly the labor market) that provides access to income;
- The family that provides access to unpaid care for children, the sick, and elderly persons (2002).

Furthermore, as Mari Osawa and Emiko Ochiai have noted, the community or civil society with its non-profit organizations has provided a fourth important pillar of welfare in paid and unpaid care for children, the sick, and elderly persons. Linking these main providers of welfare—state, market, family, and civil society—in a parallelogram, a "care diamond" (Ochiaia 2009) can be drawn with these institutions at its corners.

Esping-Andersen's typology of the welfare regime relies on the main mechanism of providing welfare: whether by the state or the market, as in liberal welfare states. The state can either work according to the principle of universal equality including gender (Nordic social-democratic welfare states) or according to negotiations between state, employers, and trade unions (corporate welfare state). The second important mechanism is whether care work is assigned to the family (*familialization*) in the form of unpaid work and is done by the housewife/mother or whether the state or civil society supports it (*defamilialization*). The labor market participation of women is highest in social-democratic welfare states where the state provides basic security and public care by a strategy of *defamilialization*. Liberal welfare states where women have to look for market-driven solutions for childcare are in second place in female labor market participation. Corporate welfare states that rely on male breadwinners and on the *familialization* of care work by housewives have both the lowest female labor market participation and the lowest birthrates.

Feminists criticized Esping-Andersen for largely ignoring gender and because of his tendency to equalize gender with family (Orloff 2005, Betzelt 2007). Instead, feminists developed several concepts of gender welfare regimes. The appeal of the concept of gender welfare regimes is that it allows a combination of cultural and institutional factors as well as long-term studies based on path dependency that influence gender relations. Following the definition of Heather MacRae:

"Gender regime" refers to a set of norms, values, policies, principles and laws that inform and influence gender relations in a given polity

(...) A gender regime is constructed and supported by a wide range of policy issues and influenced by various structures and agents, each of whom is in turn influenced by its own historical context and path. (MacRae 2006: 524–525)

Jane Lewis (Pascall and Lewis 2004) has rooted her concept of gender welfare regimes in the forms of compatibility between wage work and care work. The breadwinner/housewife model stands for conservative gender regimes (Germany and Japan) where social security systems (unemployment and health) and wage/bonus are linked to male breadwinners, whereas the reproduction work of care for children and elderly persons is assigned to the unpaid work of housewives. In the dual earner model in Scandinavian countries, two earners and two carers (mother and father) support the family with an equal involvement in wage and care work. They are taxed as two individuals and they have individual social security entitlements (individual unemployment, health insurance, and pension rights). They can profit from parents leave for fathers or mothers that is often higher than one single leave) and from well-established public services for care (*Kindergarten*, care for the elderly, etc.) (Pascall and Lewis 2004, Betzelt 2007).

Ann Orloff (1993 and 2005) linked the gender welfare regime debate to the concept of citizenship that denotes the social, economic, and political rights persons can have access to as members of their nation. She paid attention to the incomplete access of women to economic citizenship (wage work and unpaid work) and to political citizenship. Women have been considered mothers and thus have mainly been assigned to unpaid care work and housework. Therefore, according to Orloff (1993, 2005), gender policies should be assessed by the following questions:

- How far do they support women's right to work?
- How far do they support their capacity to form an autonomous household?

In a wider comparative perspective, Mari Osawa proposed the concept of the livelihood security system (2007b) that can be applied to developing countries. She defines it as the articulation of the governmental social safety net with non-governmental institutions such as the family, the enterprise, and not-for-profit enterprises. Social safety nets encompass: (1) governmental programs such as social security (comprised of social insurance and public assistance) and the tax system that is also referred to as income transfer system; (2) social services such as childcare, education, health care, nursing, employment policies, and labor market regulations.

Her main types of livelihood security systems are: (1) the male breadwinner model, (2) the dual earner model, and (3) the market-oriented model as in liberal welfare states (Osawa 2007a and 2007b).

Ito Peng has questioned the applicability of the comparative welfare state models (and by implication the gender welfare regimes) to East Asia because they were developed in the European context (Peng 2004). Some other approaches have pointed to the Confucian tradition and the strong labor market dualism in East Asian countries (Holliday 2000, Peng 2004: 391). They have a certain flavor of "welfare orientalism" (Osawa 2007: 48) or culturalism in broadly referring to an "East Asian Confucianism" which is actually being eroded or changed by current welfare reforms such as the introduction of public care for children and the elderly. Some new approaches (cf. Osawa 2004, Uzuhashi, Totani, and Kimura 2009) emphasize the developmental character of East Asian emerging welfare states. The state is a main actor in planning and regulating export-oriented development and does not simply follow the market. Whereas developmental states like Korea or Taiwan in East Asia were characterized as authoritarian dictatorships in the 1960s and 1970s, from the 1980s the democratic transitions led to welfare developments with some exchange with civil society i.a. women's groups (ibid.).

Based on empirical research on social networks caring for children and the elderly, Emiko Ochiai suggests the fallacies of simple categories such as the "Asian model" or "familialism" (2009). She is able to show that the patterns of "care diamonds" in East Asia are quite different according to the society and the type of care, and that they change over time. The Chinese socialist regime shows a move towards a community care organization for the elderly rather than a state organization. In Singapore, *developmentalism* is wedded with strong liberalism, whereas Korea and Taiwan, according to Ochiai, have "familistic regimes" with elements of liberalism and community.

Path development has also been quite different: the developmental, market-oriented, socialist gender regime in the People's Republic of China relied on export-oriented industrialization based on cooperation of Chinese management with foreign investors. This fact promoted large female non-skilled and skilled industrial employment. Yet, economic capitalist freedom is combined with dictatorial political control from the Communist Party that claims a monopoly on political leadership. The Communist Party and the semi-official Chinese Women's Federation propagate the ideology of public gender equality. In analyzing women workers' resistance to these working conditions, Christa Wichterich showed that working women in export industries were able to fight and negotiate for better wages, more stable working conditions, and some basic work rights (2009), whereas the trade unions affiliated to the state system remained rather inactive or controlled women workers.

In the last decades, the recourse to Confucianism as well as the propagation of a soft and nurturing female sexual role in commercial media and science have both tried to popularize gender differences and tend to delegitimize equality. The gender regime in China combines high economic activity by women (and a certain access to management and skilled work) with moderate political participation (about 20 percent of seats in representative bodies). Since the Chinese Women's Federation engaged in discussing women's problems in economic and political change, there is also a critical discourse on inequality and gender that is supported by the cooperation with gender studies.

In the developmental gender regime in the (post-)authoritarian East Asian states such as South Korea or Taiwan, the democratic transitions of the 1980s and 1990s were based on democratic and feminist forces. Export-oriented state-coordinated economic development was based on women's low-wage labor in manufacturing. While female economic activity grew in the "tiger states," labor market gender segmentation was deeply entrenched. But the feminist mobilization of women resulted in an increasing political participation that in South Korea was doubled from 6 percent (2004) in parliament to 13 percent in 2005 (Hong 2006).

This short overview suggests that the notion of a gender welfare regime can prove to be a useful category of analysis for gender transformations in East Asian NICs. This category can help to understand the changing gender inequality in globalization and compressed modernization. Thus, it can contribute to an understanding of the coming challenges of gender policies and welfare developments in newly industrializing countries. But the time has not yet come to establish an adequate typology. We need more empirical research on social policy development and more theoretical debates about adequate concepts that avoid falling in the traps of welfare Orientalism or self-orientalization and can combine path-development, cultural, and institutional factors.

CONCLUSION

Looking at the transformation of gender relations, this chapter has argued that globalization must be related to modernization and that it has impacted world regions and the local cultures they contain very differently, according to their position in the international power structure. The chapter considered the impact of economic and political globalization: economic globalization promoted a market-driven integration of working class and rural women into export-oriented industries while some women could reach qualified middle-range jobs in global corporations. In political globalization, soft forms of regulation for equality could be established.

Looking at the gender transformation in East Asian societies helped to concretize this global perspective. These developments can be summed up as changes in demography and family, as high to medium labor market integration of women, as an educational advance for women, and as increasing political participation. Thus, new gender orders are emerging under the double influences of globalization and modernization that bring new challenges for gender and equality policies. It was argued that in the case of NICs, inequality at work, in the family, and in politics could be successfully analyzed with the concept of gender welfare regimes. It is important to see the dynamics of inequality in globalization and to develop concepts that reflect the concurring gender transformations.

NOTES

1. The concept of *modernization* has been revitalized by the discussions on multiple modernities (S. Eisenstadt), reflexive modernization (Ulrich Beck), and compressed modernity (Chang 2009). In East Asia, the interrelations between modernization and globalization are intensely debated currently. My use of the concept of modernization draws on these debates that have grappled with the problems of the modernization debates of the 1960s and 1970s and developed new perspectives.
2. I will mainly consider NICs in East Asia according to my own research focus.
3. UNCTAD (United Nations Conference on Trade and Development). Its annual publication *World Investment Report* gives an overview of FDI flows and TNCs (as well as some data on the 100 largest TNCs respectively) in developed and developing countries, whereas the OECD concentrates on OECD members and the ILO on national employment data.
4. Global FDI inflows came up to $1.833 billion in 2007. Reinvested earnings accounted for about 30 percent of total FDI inflows as a result of the increased profits of foreign affiliates, particularly in developing countries. FDI inflows into developed countries reached $1.248 billion (68 percent of all FDI). The United States maintained its position as the largest recipient country, followed by the United Kingdom, France, Canada, and the Netherlands. The European Union (EU) was the largest host region, attracting almost two thirds of total FDI inflows into developed countries. In developing countries, FDI inflows reached $500 billion (27.3 percent of all FDI, the rest went to post-socialist transition countries). Among developing and transition economies, the three largest recipients were China, Hong Kong (China), and the Russian Federation (cf. UNCTAD 2008: xv). At the same time, however, developing countries continued to increase their importance as sources of FDI, with outflows rising to a new record level of $253 billion (12.8 percent of all out-flowing FDI) (cf. UNCTAD 2008: 253–255). While this is a rather low share, the amount has risen remarkably from the early 1980s (about 5 percent from 1980 to 1984) and the early 1990s (10 percent from 1990 to 1994) (cf. UNCTAD 1995: xxvii).
5. This estimate is from ILO (2009): *Global Employment Trends/January 2009*: 12.
6. It is interesting that in TNCs in China, gender relations seem to be more varied and women can get access to vocational and technical training in some industries (Guthrie 2006, Lüthje 2007).
7. Members of the government and the administration who support gender equality have been called *femocrats* in the gender policy debate.
8. The data have been put together from the World Bank gender stats files. While they are rather broad, they give a comparative view on East Asian NICs. Unfortunately, these data give no information on class or ethnicity.

Japan has been inserted to provide a comparison to post-industrial East Asian society.
9. As this volume does not address specialists of the welfare state, I shortly introduce Esping-Andersen's approach.

BIBLIOGRAPHY

Anker, Richard (1998) *Gender and Jobs. Sex Segregation of Occupations in the World*. Geneva: International Labor Office.

Asian Center for Women's Studies (2005) *Women's Studies in Asia Series*. Seoul: Ewha Womans University Press.

Aulenbacher, Brigitte, Maria Funder, Heike Jacobsen, and Susanne Völker (eds) (2007) *Arbeit und Geschlecht im Umbruch der modernen Gesellschaft. Forschung im Dialog*. Wiesbaden: VS Verlag für Sozialwissenschaften.

Betzelt, Sigrid (2007) *"Gender Regimes": Ein ertragreiches Konzept für die komparative Forschung. Literaturstudie*. Göttingen: SOEB Arbeitspapier. 2007–1.

Beck, Ulrich (1986) *Risikogesellschaft*. Frankfurt a.M.: Suhrkamp.

Carr, Marilyn and Marta Chen (2004) "Globalization, Social Exclusion and Gender," *International Labour Review* 143 (1–2): 129–160.

CEDAW (Comvention on the Elimination of All Forms of Discrimination Against Women) (1979) http://www.un.org/womenwatch/daw/cedaw/, accessed on February 28, 2010.

Chang, Kyung-Sup (1999) "Compressed Modernity and its Discontents. South Korean Society in Transition," *Economy and Society* 28 (1): 30–55.

Chang, Kyung-Sup (2010) *South Korea Under Compressed Modernity*. (Routledge Advances in Korean Studies), London: Routledge.

Connell, Raewyn (2009) *Short Introduction. Gender*. Cambridge: Polity Press.

Eisenstadt, Shmuel N. (2003) *Comparative Civilizations and Multiple Modernities*. Leiden: Brill.

Esping-Andersen, Gøsta (1990) *The Three Worlds of Welfare Capitalism*. Cambridge: Polity Press.

Esping-Andersen, Gøsta (ed.) (2002) *Why We Need a New Welfare State*. Oxford: Oxford University Press.

Gottfried, Heidi, Mari Osawa, Karen Shire, and Sylvia Walby (eds) (2007) *Gendering the Knowledge Economy: Comparative Perspectives*. Basingstoke, Hampshire: Palgrave Macmillan.

Guthrie, Doug (2006) *China and Globalization: The Social, Economic and Political Transformation of Chinese Society*. London and New York: Routledge.

Hochschild, Arlie and Barbara Ehrenreich (eds) (2003) *Global Woman. Nannies, Maids, and Sex Workers in the New Economy*. New York: Metropolitan Press.

Holliday, Ian (2000) "Productivist Welfare Capitalism: Social Policy in East Asia," *Political Studies* 48 (4): 706–723.

Hong, Mihee (2006) *Der Wandel des Geschlechterverhältnisses und die Frauenbewegung in Südkorea*. PhD Bochum. http://www-brs.ub.ruhr-uni-bochum.de/netahtml/HSS/Diss/HongMihee/diss.pdf, accessed on November 14, 2009.

Huntington, Samuel (1996) *The Clash of Civilizations and the Remaking of World Order*. New York: Simon and Schuster.

International Labor Office (2009) *Global Employment Trends/January 2009*. Geneva: ILO.

Lee, Ching Kwan (1998) *Gender and the South China Miracle*. Berkeley and Los Angeles: University of California Press.

Lenz, Ilse (2002) *Geschlechtsspezifische Auswirkungen der Globalisierung in den Bereichen Global Governance, Arbeitsmärkte und Ressourcen.* Gutachten für die Enquête-Kommission "Globalisierung der Weltwirtschaft—Herausforderungen und Antworten". Berlin, Germany.

Lenz, Ilse (2007) "Globalization, Varieties of Gender Regimes, and Regulations for Gender Equality at Work," in Heidi Gottfried, Mari Osawa, Karen Shire, and Sylvia Walby (eds) *Gendering the Knowledge Economy: Comparative Perspectives*, 110–140. Wiesbaden: VS Verlag für Sozialwissenschaften.

Lenz, Ilse, Charlotte Ullrich, and Barbara Fersch (eds) (2007) *Gender Orders Unbound? Globalisation, Restructuring, Reciprocity.* Leverkusen: Verlag Barbara Budrich.

Lenz, Ilse (2008) "Transnational Social Movement Networks and Transnational Public Spaces: Glocalizing Gender Justice," in Ludger Pries (ed.) *Rethinking Transnationalism. The Meso-link of Organisations*, 104–126. London and New York: Routledge.

Lüthje, Boy (2007) "'Desorganisierter Despotismus'. Globale Produktion, soziale Diskriminierung und Arbeitsbeziehungen in der Elektronikindustrie in China," in Brigitte Aulenbacher, Maria Funder, Heike Jacobsen, and Susanne Völker (eds) *Arbeit und Geschlecht im Umbruch der modernen Gesellschaft. Forschung im Dialog*, 201–217. Wiesbaden: VS Verlag für Sozialwissenschaften.

MacRae, Heather (2006) "Rescaling Gender Relations: The Influence of European Directives on the German Gender Regime," *Social Politics* 13 (3): 522–550.

Merry, Sally Engle (2006) *Human Rights and Gender Violence. Translating International Law into Local Justice.* Chicago: University of Chicago Press.

Meyer, Mary and Elisabeth Prügl (1999) *Gender Politics in Global Governance.* Lanham: Rowman and Littlefield.

Mies, Maria (1986) *Patriarchat und Kapital. Frauen in der internationalen Arbeitsteilung.* Zürich: Rotpunkt.

Moghadam, Valentine (2005) *Globalizing Women. Transnational Feminist Networks.* Baltimore: Johns Hopkins University Press.

Mohanty, Chandra Talpade (2003) "Under Western Eyes Revisited: Feminist Solidarity through Anti-capitalist Struggles," *Signs* 28 (2): 499–537.

Nederveen Pieterse, Jan (2008) "Globalization the Next Round. Sociological Perspectives," *Futures* 40 (8): 707–720.

Ochiai, Emiko (2009) "Care Diamonds and Welfare Regimes in East and South-East Asian Societies: Bridging Family and Welfare Sociology," *International Journal of Japanese Sociology* 18(1): 60–78.

Ochiai, Emiko and Barbara Molony (2008) *Asia's New Mothers. Crafting Gender Roles and Childcare Networks in East and Southeast Asian Societies.* Folkestone: Global Oriental.

Orloff, Ann (1993) "Gender and the Social Rights of Citizenship: The Comparative Analysis of Gender Relations and Welfare State," *American Sociological Review* 58 (3): 303–328.

Orloff, Ann (2005) "Social Provisions and Regulation: Theories of States, Social Policies and Modernity," in Julia Adams, Elisabeth Clemens, and Ann Orloff (eds) *Remaking Modernity: Politics, History and Siociology*, 190–224. Durham, NC: Duke University Press.

Osawa, Mari (ed.) (2004) *Ajia shokoku no fukushi senryaku.* (Welfare Strategies in Asian countries) Tokyo: Minerba shoten.

Osawa, Mari (2007a) *Gendai Nihon no seisan Hosho shisutemu.* (The Welfare System in Present Japan) Tokyo: Iwanami.

Osawa, Mari (2007b) "The Livelihood Security System and Social Exclusion: The Male Breadwinner Model revisited," in Ilse Lenz, Charlotte Ullrich, and

Barbara Fersch (eds) *Gender Orders Unbound? Globalisation, Restructuring, Reciprocity,* 277–302. Leverkusen: Verlag Barbara Budrich.

Pascall, Gillian and Jane Lewis (2004) "Emerging Gender Regimes and Policies for Gender Equality in a Wider Europe," *Journal of Social Policy* 33 (3): 373–394.

Peng, Ito (2004) "Postindustrial Pressures, Political Regime Shifts, and Social Policy Reform in Japan and South Korea," *Journal of East Asian Studies* 4 (3): 389–425.

Pietilä, Hilkka (2007) *The Unfinished Story of Women and the United Nations.* United Nations. Non-Governmental Liaison Service (UN-NGLS). Geneva. http://www.un-ngls.org/pdf/UnfinishedStory.pdf, accessed on November 14, 2009.

Pries, Ludger (ed.) (2008) *Rethinking Transnationalism. The Meso-link of Organisations.* London and New York: Routledge.

Pries, Ludger (2008) *Die Transnationalisierung der sozialen Welt. Sozialräume jenseits von Nationalgesellschaften.* Frankfurt a. M.: Suhrkamp.

Siebert, Christina (2009) *Frauenbewegungen und Frauenrechte in der Globalisierung* Diploma thesis, Ruhr University Bochum (Germany).

United Nations (1995) *Report on the Fourth World Conference on Women (Beijing, 4–15 September 1995).* A/CONF.177/20.

UNCTAD (1995, 2008) *World Investment Report.* New York, Geneva: UNCTAD.

Unifem (2000) *Progress of the World's Women 2000.* New York: Unifem.

Uzuhashi, Takafumi, Hiroyuki Totani, and Kimura Harumi (2009) *Higashi Ajia no shakai hosho. Nihon–Kankoku–Taiwan no genjô to kadai.* (Social Security in East Asia. The Situation and Issues in Japan–South Korea–Taiwan). Tokyo: Nakanish shuppan.

Wichterich, Christa (1998) *Die globalisierte Frau—Berichte aus der Zukunft der Ungleichheit.* Reinbek: rororo.

Wichterich, Christa (2009) "Kämpfe an der Quelle der Wertschöpfungskette in China," in Uwe Hoering, Oliver Pye, Wolfram Schaffar, and Christa Wichterich (eds) *Globalisierung bringt Bewegung. Lokale Kämpfe und transnationale Vernetzungen in Asien,* 120–135. Münster: Westfälisches Dampfboot.

Young, Brigitte (1998) "Genderregime und Staat in der globalen Netzwerkökonomie," *Prokla* 111 (28, 2): 175–199.

Zwingel, Susanne (2005) *How do International Women's Rights Norms Become Effective in Domestic Contexts? An Analysis of the Convention on the Elimination of all Forms of Discrimination against Women (CEDAW).* PhD Ruhr-University Bochum. at www-brs.ub.ruhr-uni-bochum.de/netahtml/HSS/Diss/ZwingelSusanne/diss.pdf, accessed on November 14, 2009.

Part III

Redistributive Mechanisms and Social Policies Tackling Social Inequality

5   Nicaragua

Constructing the Bolivarian Alliance for the Peoples of Our America (ALBA)[1]

Thomas Muhr

INTRODUCTION

Over the past decades, Nicaragua's national development has been subject to recurrent fundamental re-orientations: between 1979 and 1990, after toppling one of the longest-lasting United States (US)-supported dictatorships in the region, the Sandinista National Liberation Front (FSLN or Sandinistas) under President Daniel Ortega attempted to transform the dependent capitalist agro-economy towards a democratic socialism—a prefiguration of contemporary Venezuela's "21st Century Socialism" (Walker 2003, Raby 2006). However, over this period, the national effort to produce substantial change, which included considerable gains in social justice particularly in land redistribution, relative basic food security, free basic health care, and a reduction of illiteracy from over 50 percent to 12 percent (MED 1982), was met by what is widely regarded as Washington's multi-dimensional *war of attrition*. Overt and covert terrorism, justified by the media, provided favorable conditions for US polyarchy promotion which, as the political complement to global neo-liberal economics, has reduced democracy to a choice between competing fractions of a transnational capitalist class (Robinson 1992, 1996, Harris 1998). The FSLN's defeat in the 1990 elections ushered in 16 years of neo-liberal rule, which formally terminated with Ortega's return to the presidency on January 10, 2007. Whereas at the national level, the FSLN constitutes a 38 percent minority government, the party is the strongest political force at the local level: between 2004 and 2008, the FSLN governed in those 87 municipalities (out of 153) where more than three-quarters of Nicaraguans live;[2] in the November 2008/January 2009 municipal elections, the party could still increase its leadership, when it won 109 mayoralties, including the capital Managua.

Within a critical globalization theory framework, this chapter analyzes the emergence of the Bolivarian Alliance for the Peoples of Our America (ALBA) in Nicaragua.[3] Launched by Cuba and Venezuela in 2004, the initiative has been joined by Bolivia (2006), Nicaragua (2007), Dominica (2008), Honduras (2008), Ecuador (2009), St. Vincent and The Grenadines

(2009), and Antigua and Barbuda as full members, whereas Paraguay and Grenada have observer status. In neo-Gramscian terms, ALBA constitutes both an increasingly powerful counter-hegemonic idea and an emergent Latin American and Caribbean (LAC) regionalism that is nourished by a form of moral legitimacy that challenges global capitalism. Under ALBA, the economy should serve the people, rather than vice versa. The purpose of this chapter, however, is not to provide a comprehensive analysis of ALBA. Rather, by drawing on the Nicaraguan case, it aims at exemplifying two aspects: first, the construction of ALBA from the bottom up by a transnational interplay of state and non-state actors; and, second, to show that in contrast to other contemporary regionalisms, the social dimension of ALBA is foundational and assumes a key definitional and integrationist role. I support my claims by analyses of the *ALBA Petroleos de Nicaragua* (ALBANIC) oil supply scheme, the *Yo Sí Puedo!* (I Can Do It!) literacy campaign, and the *Misión Milagro* (Mission Miracle) ophthalmology program. These programs were initiated during a *crisis of governability* in the two years preceding Ortega's re-election in November 2006, which involved the country's full membership in ALBA from January 11, 2007 on. As to date little is known outside the Hispanophone world about the precise contents of ALBA, the final section of the chapter provides an overview of ALBA as national policy under the FSLN administration in the period from January 2007 to July 2009.

ALBA AS A COUNTER-HEGEMONIC REGIONALISM[4]

Based on Antonio Gramsci's concept of hegemony, i.e., rule based on consent rather than on coercion, Robert Cox has argued that hegemony is constructed and reconstructed by the dialectical interaction of forces—material capabilities, ideas, and institutions—which are both products and facilitators of a particular world order (Cox 1996: 97–99, Gill 2008). Although an historical structure, or *historical bloc*, sets a framework that conditions action, successful resistance to a prevailing historical structure can produce a counter-hegemonic rival structure. Neo-liberal, hegemonic globalization, or globalization *from above*, Portuguese sociologist Boaventura de Sousa Santos (2002) has added, is by many people—including its victims—assumed as the only, inevitable form of globalization, or as the "natural order" (Cox 1996: 151). Counter-hegemony, therefore, would "offer new understandings and practices capable of replacing the dominant ones and thus of offering a new common sense" (Santos and Rodríguez-Garavito 2005: 18).

ALBA, as I argue in this chapter, constitutes such an emergent rival structure. Like the resurgence of the Left in the region, ALBA should be understood as an historical phenomenon produced by the contradictions in hegemonic globalization, above all the increased social injustice as the "cumulative result" of the structural reforms of the past two decades (UN 2005). Global inequality means, for instance, that the 40 percent of the world's population who live on less than US$ 2 per day account for 5 percent of global income, whereas the richest 20 percent account for three-quarters (UNDP 2007: 25). It is the latter for whom globalization *works*, whereas the *subaltern rest* are either assigned "'feeder' roles" (as providers of cheap labor or raw materials) (Robinson 2001: 559) or, an estimated 40 percent, are rendered structurally irrelevant both in terms of production and consumption (Castells 2000, Chossudovsky 2002: 89).

In Nicaragua, in the years preceding Ortega's re-election, the neo-liberal regime had accumulated a tremendous social debt that justified speaking of an "economic genocide" (Chossudovsky 2002: 42): from 1990 to 2006, the country dropped from rank 60 to rank 120 in the United Nations Human Development Index (HDI) (UNDP 2000: 18 and 2008). As 80 percent of Nicaraguans subsisted on less than US$ 2 per day, regressive distribution (severe income and consumption inequality) manifested itself in an HDI gap of 87 places between the country's richest and poorest fifths (UNDP 2006: 270, 2007: 239). Because neo-liberal employment creation had concentrated on the exploitative export-processing sector, rather than prioritizing rural development, about one third of Nicaraguans suffered chronic under-nourishment (CENIDH 2006b). Milk, for instance, became a luxury item for the majority as, under a dairy sector controlled by multi- and transnational corporations (MNCs/TNCs), one liter cost between US$ 0.6 and US$ 0.7 in 2006. As elsewhere in Central America, privatization has produced a dysfunctioning public utilities sector charging high consumer rates: for instance, only 17 and 2 percent of Nicaraguans, respectively, have got access to telephone and Internet (UNICEF 2006: 120). While in 2006, the poorest 20 percent of Nicaraguans allocated about 10 percent of their expenses to water, and as 72 percent of the rural populations had no access to drinking water at all (CENIDH 2008), MNCs (e.g., Coca Cola, Parmalat) were tacitly permitted to tap the aquifer and wells (UNDP 2006: 51, CENIDH 2006a). The systematic undermining of the constitutional right to free primary education under World Bank–led privatization diminished average schooling from 8.3 (1990) to 4.6 years at the beginning of the millennium; the extremely poor could expect 1.9 years (MECD 2004, UNESCO 2005). Illiteracy had increased to over 35 percent, and almost two thirds of 13- to 17-year-olds were excluded from secondary education (PREAL 2004).

The Emergence of ALBA

The ALBA challenge consists in the regionalization of Venezuela's endogenous development, or *development from within*, which is rooted in 1980s/1990s neo-structuralist theory that attempted to respond to the shortcomings of structuralist, inward-oriented political economy (import-substitution industrialization), and neo-liberal, export-led economics. In pursuit of a transition to a *21st Century Socialism*, however, Bolivarian endogenous development departs from the original concept as elaborated by Osvaldo Sunkel and his collaborators (1993) in at least three important respects. First, among the ALBA partners, the orthodox economic principle of comparative advantage, which presumes competition through a functioning price mechanism, is superseded by the logic of the *cooperative advantage* (MICE/BANCOEX n.d.). The ALBA principles of solidarity, cooperation, and complementarity reject capitalist profit-making criteria, which are identified as the root causes for the asymmetric relationships within and between countries. By placing human rights and state sovereignty over commercial interests, ALBA counters neo-liberal, deregulatory state reforms and aims at correcting the entrenched injustices by curbing MNC/TNC mono- and oligopolic power, as well as the "pernicious influence" of the international financial institutions (IFIs) (Chávez 2003). Second, rather than individual countries' vertical integration into global capitalism (Fritsch 1993), ALBA means horizontal integration to construct a more democratic multi-polar world order. Third, whereas Sunkel (1993) implicitly presumed liberal representative democracy, Bolivarian endogenous development promotes "revolutionary democracy," which complements the representative model with direct and participatory democracy (Muhr 2008b: 129–175).

ALBA has evolved from the Cuba–Venezuela Integral Cooperation Agreement (2000) and was formalized via the ALBA Integration Agreement (2004), followed by the 2005 Implementation Accord. During Bolivia's accession meeting in Havana in April 2006, ALBA was complemented by President Morales' proposal of bilateral Peoples' Trade Agreements [*Tratados de Comercio entre los Pueblos*] (PTAs), characterized as a *fair trade* alternative to the US-promoted Free Trade Agreements (FTAs). In competing with the hegemonic paradigm on the global, regional, sub-regional, national, and a range of sub-national/local scales, the systematic, inter-scalar de- and re-construction of hegemonic social structures transcends international relations by utilizing a set of transnational mechanisms. This must be highlighted because ALBA is often portrayed as a purely multinational bloc. However, two other integration instruments are used: first, bi-national agreements between Venezuela and most LAC countries, especially Argentina, Brazil, and Ecuador, which are intended to culminate in a collective network; and, second, as the Nicaraguan case exemplifies, direct agreements between ALBA governments and sub-national/local entities (mayoralties, civil organizations) that bypass (adverse) national governments.

ALBA builds on the identification of common interests to construct consensus and strategic alliances for global structural transformation. However, the incipient ALBA regionalism has been paralleled by the construction of the South American Union of Nations (UNASUR) and a *re-vitalization* of the Southern Common Market (MERCOSUR). UNASUR, which was formalized on May 23, 2008, via the South American Union of Nations

Constitutive Treaty, includes all South American countries except French Guiana. MERCOSUR, launched by Argentina, Brazil, Paraguay, and Uruguay in 1991, is currently in the process of enlargement and, possibly, redefinition, as Venezuela joined on July 4, 2006. However, the ratification of Venezuela's full membership by the Brazilian senate and the Paraguayan parliament has been pending, despite the respective presidents' full support of Venezuela.[5] I here restrict myself to two observations: although ALBA appears to compete with UNASUR and MERCOSUR in geo-political terms, only ALBA integrates the entire LAC region; as regards the ideational level, the ALBA principles appear to increasingly shape the other two projects, in which Venezuela has been assuming a leading role. Moreover, the ALBA idea is also globalized through cooperation with non-LAC countries, cities, and communities worldwide. The different processes are not free from contradictions and potentially conflicting interests between individual LAC countries. Background documentation of the UNASUR foundation process points to such conflicts (MICE 2007: 27–37), which involve shifting alliances between different countries on different issues. Brazil, for instance, allied with Colombia and Paraguay in (unsuccessfully) proposing an integration project based on a convergence of existing neo-liberal sub-regional projects, the Andean Community (CAN) and MERCOSUR. Simultaneously, Brazil joined Venezuela, Argentina, and Bolivia in the foundation of the Bank of the South, which, as an UNASUR development bank, is designed to become a cornerstone of an envisaged "new regional financial architecture" to challenge the power of the existing international financial institutions (IFIs)—the World Bank, the International Monetary Fund, and regional development banks, such as the Inter-American Development Bank—and to strengthen the continent's role in the globalized financial and commercial spheres (*Declaración de Quito* 2007).[6] Whereas Brazil may be interested in defending its leadership role on the continent, it would be too simplistic to adopt a *two-lefts-thesis* (which largely builds on a supposed rivalry between Venezuela and Brazil). In this respect, it should be considered that since September 2007, the presidents Luiz Inácio Lula da Silva (Brazil) and Hugo Chávez (Venezuela) have been convening quarterly meetings to discuss integration and multilateral cooperation, in which Presidents Rafael Correa (Ecuador) and Evo Morales (Bolivia) participated for the first time in September 2008.[7] The borders between the different integration projects are fluent, and the emergent common denominator appears to be a broad-based consensus on non-neo-liberal integration among the progressive LAC governments, which seems to support a gradual strengthening of ALBA. The process of regional institution building, to which I draw attention below, supports this notion.

New Regionalism Theory is useful for improving our understanding of ALBA, as it argues that regions are socially constructed, or created, and re-created ("region in the making"), in processes of regionalization that have accompanied globalization. Björn Hettne and Frederik Söderbaum define *regionalization* as "the process whereby a geographical area is transformed from a passive object to an active subject, capable of articulating the transnational interests of the emerging region" (Hettne and Söderbaum 2000: 461). Regional coherence and community is defined by five "levels of regionness":

1. *Regional space*: a region is rooted in territorially bounded space (a geographical unit).
2. *Regional complex*: progressively widening trans-local social relations based on historically derived identities, nevertheless constrained by the nation-state system.
3. *Regional society*: a multidimensional, rule-based pattern of relations involving state and non-state actors (inter- and/or transnational society).
4. *Regional community*: the region becomes an active subject with a distinct identity, which includes the convergence and compatibility of ideas, organizations, and conflict resolution by non-violent means, a transnationalized regional society, social equality mechanisms, and social learning to construct a regional collective identity.
5. *Region state*: a political entity grounded in fundamental values, and cultural and ethnic heterogeneity (plurality). A forced standardization, as in the former Soviet Union, is not viable.

Hettne and Söderbaum (2000: 470) emphasize that despite a certain developmental logic, the five phases of *regionness* are not a series of stages. Especially in the case of ALBA, a sense of urgency has required all levels to occur simultaneously. ALBA's *regional space* is the LAC, defined by the region's peoples' shared territoriality, their historical and cultural roots, as well as their common interests, needs, and potentialities. In an effort of constructing a *regional complex*, the reference made to regional, national, and local resistance heroes in the ALBA declarations suggests an attempt to construct a regional, popular-revolutionary consciousness and identity based on a "collective memory" to counteract the historical monopolization of external relations ("who is friend or foe") by the countries' national elites (cf. Hettne and Söderbaum 2000: 463). As already indicated, the focus of this chapter is the bottom up construction of the *regional society* by a transnational interplay between state and non-state actors along multiple dimensions, which I categorize as *energy*, the *politico-ideological, social, economic-industrial, environmental, cultural, military, financial dimensions, education and knowledge*. Whereas energy integration is the major tool that facilitates ALBA, in stark contrast to traditional regionalisms, such as the European Union (EU), the North American Free Trade Agreement (NAFTA), the Caribbean Community (CARICOM), and MERCOSUR, where the social dimension (welfare) is either non-existent or occurs at the fourth or fifth level of regionness (Hettne 2003), in ALBA the social has taken on a key integrationist role from the outset. The social, however, is not a normative end in itself, but is also a means, given the high degree of inequality in LAC and the necessity to achieve a *regional balance* which, as Hettne (2003: 361) suggests, is indispensable in the long-term transition from a community to a union of nations and, ultimately, to something like a *region-state*. The latter is historically personified in South American liberator Simón Bolivar's vision of a "Grand Homeland" (*Patria Grande*), Cuban José Martí's *Our America*, and Nicaraguan *guerrillero* Augusto César Sandino's *Plan for the Realization of Bolívar's Supreme Dream*. The idea of a unified LAC has literally been translated into strategy since the 5th ALBA Summit (April 28/29, 2007), when the concept of the "grand-national" [*grannacional*] was incorporated in the form of bi- and multi-state "grand-national projects" (GNPs) and "grand-national companies" (GNCs), which are the counter-hegemonic responses to MNCs/TNCs. GNPs orientate their productive dynamics towards goods and services that satisfy human needs within the emergent ALBA market, which is defined as a "fair trade zone". They complement the regional production chains composed of "mixed enterprises" (owned by two states) and "social production enterprises," the latter being considered the economic "vanguard" of 21st Century Socialism as they prioritize non-capitalist forms of socioeconomic organization (Troudi and Monedero 2007).

PETROCARIBE

Increasingly, material capabilities (nationalization and socialization of resources, technology, production) and ideas are complemented by institutions, such as PETROAMERICA, TELESUR, the ALBA Bank, the Bank of the South, the University of the South, and the cultural ALBA Houses—a process that points to the formation of a counter-hegemonic bloc. PETROAMERICA integrates the three sub-regional blocs PETROCARIBE, PETROANDINA, and PETROSUR. Thirteen Caribbean countries—the entire CARICOM, except Barbados and Trinidad/Tobago—signed the PETROCARIBE Energy Cooperation Agreement with Venezuela in 2005 (PETROCARIBE 2005); Haiti, Nicaragua, and Honduras joined in 2007, Guatemala in 2008, and Costa Rica and Panama were in the process of adherence in May 2009.

PETROCARIBE is a mechanism designed for economic, social, and political integration. PDV Caribe S.A., a subsidiary of Venezuela's national oil company PDVSA, operates it. Energy policies comprise oil and its derivatives, gas, electricity, as well as the development of alternative, renewable energies. Priority is given to the countries with the biggest developmental needs. PDV Caribe is in charge of the logistics (distribution, terminals, storage facilities, and refinery capacity) as well as knowledge and technology transfer and exchange. The principle by which this works is for savings to accrue in the participating countries from a low interest rate, long-term financing scheme, as well as from the elimination of intermediaries along the value chain, as participation is restricted to state companies, which are created with Venezuelan assistance where no adequate state infrastructure exists. In fact, in the PETROCARIBE Energy Security Treaty of August 11, 2007, the signatories have explicitly committed themselves to increase their energy infrastructure "as much as possible" in order to "diminish the dependence on the transnational actors" (PETROCARIBE 2007).

Energy savings are paid into the *ALBA Caribe Fund*, a structural convergence fund into which Venezuela made an initial payment of US$ 112 million (PDVSA 2008). These funds are then allocated to economic and social development projects in the respective countries. By mid-2008, the fund had benefited 15.4 million people in ten countries, or one in three inhabitants (PDVSA 2008).[8] Although the PETROCARIBE Agreement does not specify the exact financing mechanism of the fund, it can be assumed to be similar to that of the ALBA Fund, as specified in the ALBA Energy Agreements signed by Bolivia, Haiti, and Nicaragua on April 29, 2007. The basis for payments into the fund is the previously referred to beneficial financing scheme: in the case of ALBA (whose regulations slightly differ from PETROCARIBE), the oil bill is split into two equal shares, of which one half has to be paid within 90 days of delivery, and the rest over a period up to 25 years, including a two-year grace period.[9] Fifty percent of the deferred payments are paid into the ALBA Fund, after incurred costs (operational and financial) have been deducted. The rest has to be paid by the respective partner state enterprise over the stated 25 years. This means that 25 percent of the total oil bill benefit the country and the region in the form of social and infrastructure projects.[10] Put differently, PETROCARIBE has integrated energy security with social security as was, for instance, made explicit with respect to food security in the Final Declaration of the Presidential Summit *Food Sovereignty and Security: Food for Life*, convened in Managua on May 7, 2008. Attended by representatives from 11 LAC countries in response to the global food crisis, this emergency meeting was, in fact, a follow-up to the ALBA Agreement on the *Implementation of Cooperation Programs for Food Sovereignty and Security*, ratified two weeks earlier in Caracas, on April 23, 2008.

From 2004 until the November 2006 elections, Nicaragua experienced an extended structural crisis in the social, political, energetic, environmental, and institutional spheres, which culminated in an "environment of ungovernability" (CENIDH 2006a, Muhr 2008a). In this context, the first ALBA project—the *Yo Sí Puedo* literacy campaign—was launched. The following section illustrates the construction of ALBA in Nicaragua from the municipal and civil societal level upwards with respect to *ALBA Petroleos de Nicaragua* (ALBANIC), *Yo Sí Puedo*, and the *Misión Milagro* ophthalmology program.

CONSTRUCTING ALBA FROM THE BOTTOM UP: THE FIRST YEARS (2005–06)

ALBANIC

Within the context of Nicaragua's unprecedented energy crisis, ALBANIC was founded as a joint venture between the Association of Nicaraguan Town Councils (*Asociación de Municipios de Nicaragua*, AMUNIC) and PETROCARIBE. According to the Hydrocarbon Agreement of April 25, 2006, all Nicaraguan municipalities, irrespective of political representation, should equally benefit. AMUNIC, a not-for-profit civil association formed by all 153 municipalities and then presided over by Managua's FSLN mayor Dionisio Marenco, assumed a key role due to FSLN's strength at the local level. Strategic collective action through AMUNIC was further favored by the fact that a number of non-FSLN mayoralties had also joined the initiative. However, the neo-liberal national government and US-officials construed the initiative as an ideological one and attempted to boycott ALBANIC. This included the forced withdrawal of the liberal mayoralties from the agreement as well as the denial of state infrastructure to store and distribute the Venezuelan oil. Despite logistical problems, oil shipments arrived from October 2006 and immediately effected a 17-percent diminution of bus fares in Managua (CENIDH 2006b). The socio-economic impact cannot be overestimated as, for instance, in the southern department of Río San Juan (RSJ) the production of export and non-traditional crops had stagnated due to the doubling of transportation costs in 2005/2006.

Misión Milagro

Misión Milagro was originally a bilateral health program for poor Venezuelans to undergo complex operations (principally eye, heart, cancer, and orthopaedic surgery) in Cuba, when the Venezuelan state system lacked this capacity. The mission was inter- and transnationalized through the Sandino Commitment [*Compromiso Sandino*], signed in *Ciudad Sandino* (Cuba) on August 21, 2005, in which Cuba and Venezuela committed themselves to undertake ophthalmological operations on six million low-income citizens from the entire region over a period of ten years. In addition to its geopolitical and humanitarian significance, *Misión Milagro* also assumes a cultural-educative role in the process of regionalization, in order to foster transnational contacts to build trust and identity.

In Nicaragua, where the initiative started on March 10, 2006, the first phase was limited to treatments of cataracts and opacity, with the option of including other pathologies, such as astigmatism, retinopathy, and ocular paralysis, at a later stage. Qualification for treatment does not follow any economical investment viability rationale, as there is no age restriction. Whereas a cataract operation in a private clinic in Nicaragua costs close to US$ 2,000[11], *Misión Milagro* patients are flown to Cuba and Venezuela for operations. Free-of-charge surgery and post-surgery treatment include travel, visa, accommodation, food, and medicine, as well as accompaniment by a family member in 10 percent of the cases.

As several local coordinators and Nicaraguan news coverage have confirmed, the mission has observed the principle of political, ethnic, and religious neutrality. In accordance with the ALBA principle of "non-interference in national affairs" (PETROCARIBE Agreement), the 2006 *Compromiso Sandino* Implementation Instruction of the Venezuelan embassy in Managua highlights that the mission "has to be free from any *(political partisan)* contents and incorporate the governments of the countries where Venezuela has diplomatic missions" (emphasis original). Whereas the then right-wing national government cooperated by granting departure tax exemptions, post-surgery treatment, as well as some logistical support, the president of AMUNIC was in charge of the national coordination. *Misión Milagro* offices, which were established in the participating municipalities, have been in direct contact with the Cuban and Venezuelan embassies, and their coordinating commissions have incorporated diverse local organizations and grassroots actors. In San Carlos (RSJ), for example, in 2006, the Catholic Church, *Médicos del Mundo*, the Local System for Integral Health Care (SILAIS), the Communal Development Boards, the Friends of Río San Juan Foundation (FUNDAR), private doctors, the FSLN base structure, and the mayoralty's manager of the mission all cooperated to use scarce resources most efficiently.

Yo Sí Puedo

In early 2005, the Carlos Fonseca Amador Popular Education Association (henceforth: the Foundation) called for international support to alleviate the national education crisis in order to achieve the Millennium Development Goal with respect to literacy. The Cuban government was the only one to respond by providing the innovative *Yo Sí Puedo* method, together with logistical support in the form of the resources for 5,000 *literacy points* (TV sets, video players, sets of videos primers, and facilitator guides). The campaign set out to declare Nicaragua illiteracy-free in 2008 and implementation occurred in several stages: (a) students from three national universities in Managua conducted surveys in the communities, (b) a piloting stage, which was (c) followed by massification (dramatic expansion), which in 2006 included 30,000 learners in 75 municipalities, 11 of which were non-FSLN governed. However, the dependence of the method on energy imposed its limitations, as about 40 percent of

Nicaraguan communities have no electricity—a situation that was aggravated during the energy crisis.

Whereas at the time the Foundation's National Commission was responsible for coordination, training and evaluation, similar to *Misión Milagro,* local NGOs, the Church and the Community Women's Network participated in the campaign in the municipalities. Local actors have considered such grassroots support an expression of democracy and a strong sense of solidarity among Nicaraguans. However, it has also been a necessity given the resource scarcity under which the program has been running, as costs are incurred by training, monitoring, transport of the equipment, and graduation ceremonies. Whereas in 2006, Cuba only provided a total of six consultants, Nicaraguan volunteers were running the campaign. Classes were commonly held in the facilitators' or community leaders' own homes, and occasionally in community centers, or NGO, and ecclesiastical premises. A direct political-partisan character was consciously avoided, which was reflected in the neutrality of the *Yo Sí Puedo* teaching materials and the absence of the FSLN black and red party colors. Nevertheless, as in the cases of ALBANIC and *Misión Milagro*, the then national government assumed an obstructive rather than a constructive role. Despite officially recognizing the initiative, the agreed import tax exemption of the Cuban equipment was delayed, which blocked the start of the campaign for two months. Moreover, the utilization of the educational infrastructure (schools for evening and weekend classes) was denied in many cases by the departmental education authorities.

ALBA AS NATIONAL POLICY: THE FIRST 30 MONTHS

ALBA is an incipient project that has made rapid advance within the few years of its existence. Nevertheless, to date very little is known outside the Hispanophone world about the precise contents of ALBA and why such South-South cooperation has appeared more attractive to the respective countries than conventional international development cooperation. Therefore, this final section outlines the comprehensive cooperation agreements, memoranda, and letters of intent signed by the incoming FSLN administration on and after January 11, 2007. As the regionalization of Venezuela's endogenous development, ALBA epitomizes a holistic approach to development, which in Nicaragua integrates the following sectors: energy, resources, and environment (oil, gas, electricity, renewable energies, water); petro-chemistry; agriculture; industry; finance; health/medicine; food; telecommunications; infrastructure (transport, housing); tourism; education; culture; and sports. Concrete development initiatives in the immediate aftermath of Nicaragua's adherence to the bloc have included Venezuela's unconditional cancellation of a US$ 31.8 million bilateral debt; the development of geo-thermal power; the supply of 1.8 million energy-saving light bulbs free of charge as part of Mission Energy Revolution [*Misión Revolución Energética*]; feasibility studies for two aluminum processing factories and for a tractor assembly plant; training of Nicaraguans in Petrochemicals of Venezuela (PEQUIVEN); the creation of a branch of Venezuela's Economic and Social Development Bank (BANDES), which administers a Cooperation Fund of initially US\$ 20 million, half of which as a grant for social projects, the other half as a loan for productive (agricultural) microcredits and machinery; an increase of Nicaragua's food storage capacity and the setting up of a subsidized food-chain similar to Venezuela's MERCAL; telecommunication centers in marginalized communities for social use; and the offer of 500 undergraduate studentships for Nicaraguans to study in Venezuela. Although many agreements are of an intergovernmental nature, interinstitutional instruments include Nicaragua's peasant umbrella organization *Nicarao Farming Cooperative Enterprise* (NICARAOCOOP, R.L.). Throughout 2006, NICARACOOP had already facilitated the not-for-profit import of urea for Nicaraguan family producers under Venezuela's popular economy scheme *Fertilizers for Life*, which was formalized in January 2007. NICARAOCOOP is also the partner organization in the establishment of an industrial bag factory.

ALBANIC was dissolved on April 26, 2007. Three days later, at the 5th ALBA Summit, Nicaragua signed the ALBA Energy Treaty with Bolivia, Cuba, and Venezuela, as well as the bilateral ALBA Energy Agreement, which increased the maximum supply rate from 10,000 barrels (January 2007) to 27,000 barrels of fuel per day. This amount was further raised to cover the entire national consumption when Nicaragua joined PETROCARIBE on August 11, 2007. A newly created mixed enterprise—ALBA de Nicaragua S.A. (ALBANISA)—is in charge of the imports. The ALBA Energy Treaty has further established the GNC-PETROALBA, a *grandnational* oil company owned by all ALBA countries that guarantees oil supply to all ALBA member states for the next 25 years through shares in Venezuela's Orinoco oil strip. Moreover, the same treaty founded the GNC-Energy for gas, electricity, alternative energies, energy saving, and petrochemicals. At the same summit, 44 long-term GNPs corresponding with the above-stated sectors were approved which, for Nicaragua, included the construction of an oil refinery, a 120-megawatt power plant, and an ALBA House [*Casa del ALBA*]. The ALBA Houses form a regional network of socio-cultural and political centers, with other ones opening in Argentina, Bolivia, Ecuador, Haiti, and other Caribbean countries. Nicaragua joining TELESUR has meant the reactivation of a state TV station that had been closed down since 2002 (CENIDH 2008: 67).

In 2007, according to Nicaragua's Central Bank, the country received a total of US\$ 1,020.3 million in official development assistance (multi- and bi-lateral finance flows to private and public institutions in Nicaragua). Of this, the total ALBA cooperation volume amounted to US\$ 184.9 million. The main areas were oil cooperation, direct foreign investment, and bi-lateral (Venezuela/ALBA-Fund) donations and loans. The donations made up US$ 93 million, excluding the social-humanitarian programs, *Yo Si Puedo* and *Misión Milagro*. This is a considerable share if compared with the US, which, as the largest bi-lateral donor, contributed US$ 40.5 million, and the EU, as the largest multi-lateral donor, US$ 64.7 million (BCN 2008). The ALBA/Venezuela contributions are likely to further increase over the coming years, as three ALBA-Environment GNPs "Integral Management of Hydrographic Basins," "Forest," and "Water and Urban and Rural Clean-up" were endorsed by the ALBA members at a meeting of high level technical commissions in Managua, on May 12–13, 2008, and with Panama as an observer. Respective initiatives approved by Nicaragua refer to cleaning and preserving the San Juan River and improvement of the rural aqueducts and Managua's water and sewer system. The three GNPs are expected to extend over three to ten years with an estimated ALBA Fund budget of US$ 150 million, of which US$ 66 million are to benefit the Nicaraguan projects.[12]

In accordance with the PETROCARIBE Agreement and the ALBA logic, Nicaragua pays in goods and services at fixed rates higher than world market prices. This is referred to as *trade compensation mechanism*. Nicaraguan payments, as established in the respective agreements, have included US$ 0.7 million in livestock, US$ 0.1 million in grain (108 tons of black beans), and US$ 0.4 million in meat (95 metric tons) (PDVSA 2008). In Gramscian terms, it could be argued that in a *war of position*, ALBA's cooperative advantage at the heart of the fair trade economy functions so that exports are diverted to the South that otherwise would have gone to the North at lower world market prices. As regards payment in services, Nicaragua has explored the economic feasibility of studentships for Venezuelans to study in Nicaragua. Moreover, Nicaragua's wealth in expertise regarding fair trade, organic certification, and cooperative organization, which Venezuela lacks, forms part of the payment scheme. Therefore, Nicaragua has committed itself to providing training for Venezuelan cooperative workers in both Nicaragua and Venezuela. Already in 2006, as part of the urea deal, NICARAOCOOP was reported to beengaged in such knowledge transfer to ten Venezuelan endogenous development nuclei (NUDEs), comprising 40 agricultural cooperatives.[13]

Although *Misión Milagro* is now promoted by Nicaragua's Ministry of Health, the municipal coordinating structure has been maintained. In 2007 and 2008, 770 Nicaraguans received eye treatment in Cuba, and 3,021 in Venezuela. Parallel to *Misión Milagro*, *Operación Milagro* [Operation Miracle] has been launched, meaning that Nicaragua has joined those other 15 LAC countries where governmental cooperation with Cuba and Venezuela has facilitated the installation of ophthalmological centers—in the Nicaraguan case, in Managua, as well as in Bluefields and Bilwi in Nicaragua's Autonomous Atlantic Region. Whereas so far the mission has benefited over 1.54 million people in 33 LAC countries since 2004 (plus

11,222 beneficiaries in Angola and Mali), the Nicaraguan centers treated 15,002 patients in 2007, and 22,000 between January and September 2008 (Government of Nicaragua 2009: 33).[14]

As the *Yo Sí Puedo* literacy campaign became government policy in April 2007, since May 1, 2007, Venezuelan specialists have joined the Cuban advisors in supporting the mission: by conducting surveys, establishing literacy points, imparting methodological skills, installing solar panels, diagnosing visual problems among participants and providing spectacles, and by offering specialist workshops for Nicaraguan facilitators on the *Yo Sí Puedo* Sign Language and Braille method.[15] Nevertheless, the participation of the organized society has remained an essential feature of the campaign. Throughout 2008, 27,687 mainly young facilitators educated in all 153 departments (MINED 2009), organized in the Federation of Secondary Students (*Federación de Estudiantes de Secundaria*, FES), the National Union of Students of Nicaragua (*Unión Nacional de Estudiantes de Nicaragua*, UNEN), the Sandinista Youth 19 July (*Juventud Sandinista 19 de Julio*), as well as from the more recently formed Citizen Power grassroots structure.[16]

By mid-2009, *Yo Sí Puedo*, which operates in 28 countries worldwide, had reached over 3.8 million illiterate people in 20 LAC countries, as the method has been adapted to 14 different linguistic and cultural contexts.[17] In Nicaragua, the program was re-launched as the National Literacy Campaign *From Martí to Fidel* on June 23, 2008. One year later, in July 2009, the country was declared illiteracy-free in accordance with the criterion of the United Nations Educational, Scientific, and Cultural Organization (UNESCO) of less than 5 percent illiteracy among the 15- to 65-years age group (UNESCO *et al.* 2009).[18] On the regional scale, the Declaration of Margarita, issued at the 1st Meeting of ALBA Education Ministers on March 13, 2009, has reiterated the importance of *Yo Sí Puedo* and the post-literacy method *Yo Sí Puedo Seguir* [I Can Continue!] as "fundamental tools" in a "politics of inclusion" integral to the "processes of participation and social justice" within ALBA as a "model of integration and instrument of effective liberation" (ALBA 2009: 2–3).

CONCLUSION

This chapter has employed a critical globalization theory framework to analyze ALBA as an emergent regionalism and rival structure to global capitalism. At the heart of ALBA's political project is the construction of a social and popular economy that considers people being more important than profit. The benefit of a globalization theory approach lies in transcending methodological nationalism, which takes the nation-state within an interstate system as the unit of analysis, in order to recognize ALBA as not merely a bloc of (currently) nine nations, but as an integration mechanism that employs transnational processes across different scales. Whereas ALBA consists of multiple, interdependent, simultaneously advanced dimensions, the Nicaraguan case—especially up to 2007—illustrates the transnational bottom–up construction of ALBA and the key role of social development therein.

Put into perspective, the ALBA principles and practices accord with those expressed in a range of United Nations (UN) declarations, above all the 1974 UN Declaration on the Establishment of a New International Economic Order (NIEO), the 1986 UN Declaration on the Right to Development (UNDRD) (see Articles 3, 4, and 7), and the 2002 UN Office of the High Commissioner for Human Rights (UNHCHR) Draft Guidelines on a Human Rights Approach to Poverty Reduction Strategies (especially Articles 220 and 249). Recently, the representative of the UN Food and Agriculture Organization (FAO) in Caracas, Francisco Arias Milla, has stated that the Venezuelan initiatives with respect to food security, which underlie the ALBA food policies, are in line with the FAO recommendations. Milla also pointed to Venezuela as being the Latin American country that most supports food security on the African continent.[19] This points to the broader South–South cooperation dimension of ALBA, as Venezuela extends the ALBA fair trade principles also to developing countries in Africa and Asia, such as Mali, Malawi, and Vietnam.

ALBA appears to be a democratic and participatory project, as this case study has suggested with respect to Nicaragua. The Nicaraguan Human Rights Observatory has highlighted that "in less than a year [the FSLN government, TM] has guaranteed the enjoyment of a series of rights that other governments could not [guarantee, TM] in the past 16 years" (PDDH 2008: 5). This refers particularly to social, economic, cultural, as well as collective rights, which are often a pre-condition for the exercise of civil and political rights, or "freedoms" (Nowak 2003: 23–25). Although presidents and ministers seem to dominate the scene, once ALBA has become national policy, large-scale popular participation is pursued through the *ALBA-Social Movements Council*, which was created at the 5th ALBA Summit in 2007 as a complement to the *ALBA-Presidential Council* and the *ALBA-Ministerial Council*. Because these are truly incipient processes, it is difficult to state whether the democratic claims stand up to scrutiny, and future research on ALBA would be expected to focus on such issues.

As before, in the 1980s, when Nicaragua posed the "threat of the good example," as ex-FSLN Minister of Culture Ernesto Cardenal (LaRamée and Polakoff 1999) expressed Nicaragua's resistance to hegemony at the time, the country as well as its ALBA allies, are under increasing pressure from the US, the EU, and individual European countries. The measures taken by *the North* to undermine the autonomy-seeking efforts include threats to cut official development assistance (ODA) and destabilization through illegally funded subversive civil society organizations in the respective countries (e.g., Golinger 2008, Government of Nicaragua 2009: 48).

Nevertheless, in response to the global economic and financial crisis, and as the dynamics of the UNASUR-Bank of the South project appear to have slowed down in the course of 2008 and early 2009, at the 3rd ALBA-PTA Extraordinary Summit on November 26, 2008, concrete decisions towards the construction of an economic and monetary ALBA zone were taken by ALBA's six full members and Ecuador. According to the respective declaration, greater independence from the world financial markets and the US dollar is sought through the creation of a reserve stabilization fund and a common currency, with the highly symbolic name of *sucre* (ALBA, 2008).[20] Although Venezuela undoubtedly has a leading role in ALBA, and as the resource dependence—above all, oil—of the other members will not disappear, decisive are the ALBA terms and conditions of cooperation. In this respect, the fact that non-radical Left and centrist governments, such as in Dominica and Honduras, as well as Costa Rica, with respect to PETRO-CARIBE, seek cooperation with Venezuela would suggest that countries are not straight-jacketed in ALBA. An indicator for this may also be that Dominica has reserved itself the right of observer status with respect to the common currency zone.

NOTES

1. This chapter is based on over a decade of commitment with Nicaragua and ESRC-funded critical ethnographic PhD and post-doctoral research into aspects of Venezuela's "Bolivarian revolution" and ALBA. Over 14 months of fieldwork were conducted between 2005 and 2009, six weeks of which in Nicaragua in 2006 and 2009. Critical discourse analysis has been used to analyze official documentation, over 300 ALBA-related and UNASUR declarations and agreements from 2000 to 2009, and over 50 semistructured interviews with officials and civil and organized society coordinators, and legal advisors. The author has translated from Spanish into English where necessary.
2. *Revista Envio*, 272, November 2004, http://www.envio.org.ni/articulo/2656, accessed on November 5, 2008.
3. Translated from Spanish, the acronym ALBA means *dawn*. It counter-poses ALCA, the Spanish abbreviation of *Area de Libre Comercio para las América* (Free Trade Area of the Americas, FTAA). Venezuelan President Chávez first coined the term at the Association of Caribbean States Summit in December 2001. *ALBA* initially stood for *Bolivarian Alternative for the Americas*, was reformulated as *Bolivarian Alternative for Our America* (Nicaraguan adhesion documents, January 2007), *Bolivarian Alternative for the Peoples of Our America* (5th ALBA Summit, April 2007), and since the 6th Extraordinary ALBA Summit (June 2009) stands for *Bolivarian Alliance for the Peoples of Our America*.
4. For analytical purposes, it is useful to conceptually distinguish ALBA regionalism from ALBA as a counter-hegemonic globalization project. Nevertheless, both are intertwined.
5. I here ignore other sub-regionalisms, such as the Andean Community (CAN) and the Latin American Integration Association (ALADI), as they are restricted to commercial aspects and appear to be on the decline.

6. Initially referred to as *Development Bank of the South* in a bilateral agreement with Brazil (February 14, 2005), Venezuelan President Chávez proposed (unsuccessfully) the creation of the Bank of the South at the 16th Andean Presidential Council (June 18, 2005). Whereas the project was discussed in a ministerial meeting at the 30th MERCOSUR Summit in Córdoba, Argentina, on July 2006, the proposal regained momentum through a joint declaration by Chávez and the Ecuadorian President Correa (December 21, 2006), an agreement between then–Argentine President Kirchner and Chávez (February 21, 2007), and through a memorandum between Venezuela, Bolivia, and Argentina (March 3, 2007). Subsequently, a number of sub-regional declarations incorporated Brazil, Paraguay, and Uruguay. The Bank was formalized by Argentina, Bolivia, Brazil, Ecuador, Paraguay, Uruguay, and Venezuela via the Foundation Charter of December 12, 2007. The headquarters are in Caracas (Venezuela) and sub-offices exist in Buenos Aires (Argentina) and La Paz (Bolivia). The declared objective is to break with the established financial cycle, where developing countries deposit national savings in banks in the more developed countries of the North, by re-directing and investing them in the LAC region. On May 8, 2009, the seven members agreed to provide the Bank of the South with US$ 7,000 million of initial capital. Although individual shares vary considerably—Argentina, Brazil, and Venezuela have invested US$ 2,000 million each, Ecuador and Uruguay US$ 400 million each, and Bolivia and Paraguay US$ 100 million each—in contrast to the existing voting power in the IMF, it is equally distributed within the Bank of the South.
7. "Chávez, Correa, Morales y Lula apuntan a unir el Atlántico con el Pacífico," Agencia Boliviana de Información, http://abi.bo/index.php?i=noticias_texto_pa leta&j=20080930232236&l=200809300021_Los_presidentes_Ch%E1vez,_ Morales,_Lula_y_Correa_en_la_%22foto_oficial%22_del_encuentro_(ABI) and "Presidentes de Ecuador, Brasil, Bolivia y Venezuela se reunirán este martes en Manaos," Agencia Bolivariana de Noticias, http://www.abn.info.ve/ noticia.php?articulo=151262&lee=16, both accessed on September 30, 2008.
8. For information on specific projects implemented in the various countries, see PDVSA (2008: 32–34).
9. In reaction to the global energy crisis, this ratio was modified at the 5th Extraordinary PETROCARIBE Summit on July 13, 2008: at a world market price from US$ 100.00 to 199.99 per barrel, 40 percent of the bill have to be paid within 90 days; at a price of US$ 200 and more per barrel, only 30 percent have to be immediately paid.
10. PETROCARIBE real supply was 77,000 barrels/day to the member states in the first semester 2008. Between 2005 and mid-2008, the trade volume totaled US$ 4.7 billion, of which US$ 2 billion were financed under particular conditions. During that period, member countries saved an estimated US$ 921 million. US$ 552 million were invested in energy infrastructure, and US$ 106 million were spent on social projects through the ALBA Caribe Fund (PDVSA 2008).
11. Source: http://www.elpueblopresidente.com/ACTUALIDAD/1259.html, accessed on July 10, 2008.
12. Sources: http://www.marena.gob.ni/index.php?option=com_content &task=view&id=339&Itemid=411; http://www.marena.gob.ni/index. php?option=com_content&task=view&id=336&Itemid=411, accessed on July 10, 2008; http://www-ni.laprensa.com.ni/archivo/2008/mayo/14/noti-cias/nacionales/259586.shtml, accessed on July 10, 2008.
13. "Primer cargamento de 10 mil tm de urea a Nicaragua," *Diario Vea* (April 6, 2006: 15).

14. For the regional and global figures, see http://www.cubacoop.com/cubacoop/misionmilagros.htm, accessed on April 27, 2009.
15. Information received in print from the national *Misión Robinson* Coordination, Ministry of Education, Caracas, July 30, 2007.
16. Interview with national *Yo Sí Puedo* coordinator Mario Rivera, "40 Municipios libres de analfabetismo", accessed on July 27, 2008: http://www.elpueblopresidente.com/educacion/100708_minedlibre.html.
17. http://www.cubacoop.com/cubacoop/yosipuedo.htm, accessed on April 27, 2009.
18. See: http://www.cnanicaragua.org.ni/Campana-Nacional-de-Alfabetizacion.html, accessed on April 27, 2009.
19. "Venezuela está tomando iniciativas acertadas," Panorama in http://www.aporrea.org/actualidad/n124182.html, accessed on November 17, 2008.
20. *Sucre* refers to General Antonio José de Sucre (1795–1830), who is praised in South America for inflicting upon the Spanish empire the decisive defeat in the Battle of Ayacucho (1824). The *sucre* was the Ecuadorian currency prior to its substitution by the US dollar in 2000.

BIBLIOGRAPHY

ALBA (2008) *Declaración de la III Cumbre Extraordinaria de Jefes de Estado y de Gobierno de la Alternativa Bolivariana para los Pueblos de Nuestra América—Tratado de Comercio de los Pueblos (ALBA-TCP).* http://www.mre.gov.ve/Noticias/A2008/cumbre_alba/Doc-01.htm, accessed on January 28, 2009.
ALBA (2009) *Declaración de Margarita.* http://www.me.gob.ve/media/eventos/2009/dl_18244_132.pdf, accessed on March 14, 2009.
BCN (Banco Nacional de Nicaragua) (2008) *Informe de cooperación oficial Nicaragua 2007.* http://www.bcn.gob.ni/publicaciones/nicaragua/cooperacion2007.pdf, accessed on November 28, 2008.
Castells, M. (2000) *End of Millennium.* 2nd ed. Oxford: Blackwell.
CENIDH (Centro Nicaraguense de Derechos Humanos (2006a) *Centroamérica 2004–2005: Desde una perspectiva de derechos humanos.* San Salvador: CENIDH.
CENIDH (2006b) *Derechos humanos en Nicaragua 2006.* Managua: CENIDH.
CENIDH (2008) *Derechos humanos en Nicaragua 2007.* Managua: CENIDH.
Chávez, H. R. (2003) *De la integración neoliberal a la alternativa Bolivariana para América Latina. Principios rectores del ALBA.* Intervención en ALADI, Montevideo, August 16, 2003.
Comité para la Anulación de la Deuda del Tercer Mundo (2007) *Declaración de Quito.* http://www.cadtm.org, accessed on September 8, 2007.
Chossudovsky, M. (2002) *Global Brutal. Der entfesselte Welthandel, die Armut, der Krieg.* Frankfurt a.M.: Zweitausendeins. (Extendend and updated translation of *The Globalization of Poverty. Impacts of IMF and World Bank Reforms.* 2nd ed.)
Chossudovsky, M. (2002) *The Globalization of Poverty. Impacts of IMF and World Bank Reforms.* 2nd ed. Penang, Malaysia: Third World Network.
Cox, R. W. (1996) *Approaches to World Order.* Cambridge, UK: Cambridge University Press.
Declaración de Quito (2007) http://www.cadtm.org, accessed on September 8, 2007.
Fritsch, W. (1993) "The New International Setting: Challenges and Opportunities," in O. Sunkel (ed.) *Development from Within,* 317–332. London: Lynne Rienner.

Gill, S. (2008) *Power and Resistance in the New World Order*, 2nd ed. (fully rev. and updated). Houndmills, Basingstoke: Palgrave Macmillan.

Golinger, E. (2008) *Bush vs. Chávez. Washington's War on Venezuela*. New York: Monthly Review Press.

Government of Nicaragua (2009) *Informe anual del presidente de la República 2008*. http://www.enlaceacademico.org/uploads/media/Informe_DOS__2008_01.doc, accessed on April 26, 2009.

Harris, D. J. (ed.) (1998) *Cases and Materials on International Law*, 5th ed. London: Sweet and Maxwell.

Hettne, B. (2003) "Global Market Versus the New Regionalism," in D. Held and A. McGrew (eds) *The Global Transformations Reader*, 359–369. Cambridge, UK: Polity Press.

Hettne, B. and F. Söderbaum (2000) "Theorising the Rise of Regionness," *New Political Economy* 5 (3): 457–473.

LaRamée, P. M. and E. G. Polakoff (1999) "The Evolution of the Popular Organizations in Nicaragua," in G. Prevost and H. E. Vanden (eds) *The Undermining of the Sandinista Revolution*, 141–206. New York: St. Martin's Press.

MED (Ministerio de Educación) (1982) *La educación en tres años de revolución*. Managua: MED.

MECD (Ministerio de Educación, Cultura y Deportes) (2004) *Políticas de educación básica y media*. Managua: MECD.

MICE (Ministerio de Comercio Exterior) (2007) *Memoria y cuenta*. Caracas: MICE.

MICE/BANCOEX (n.d.) *Qué es el ALBA?* http://www.mre.gov.ve/Noticias/A2008/6ALBA-Min/Organigrama1.htm, accessed on June 18, 2008.

MINCI (Ministerio de Comunicación e Información) (2008). *Desarrollo endógeno. Desde adentro, desde la Venezuela profunda*, 2nd ed. Caracas: MINCI. http://www.mct.gob.ve/Vistas/Frontend/documentos/Folleto%20Desarrollo%20Endogeno-2.pdf, accessed on August 24, 2008.

MINCI (2004) *Desarrollo endógeno. Desde adentro, desde la Venezuela profunda*. Caracas: MINCI. http://www.mct.gob.ve/Vistas/Frontend/documentos/Folleto%20Desarrollo%20Endogeno-1.pdf, accessed on August 24, 2008.

MINED (Ministerio de Educación) (2009) *Informe Final. Campaña Nacional de Alfabetización "De Martí a Fidel"*. Managua: MINED.

Muhr, T. (2008a) "Nicaragua Re-visited: From Neoliberal 'Ungovernability' to the Bolivarian Alternative of the Peoples of Our America," *Globalisation, Societies and Education* 6 (2): 147–161.

Muhr, T. (2008b) *Global Counter-Hegemony, Geographies of Regional Development, and Higher Education for all*. Unpublished PhD Thesis, University of Bristol, UK.

Nowak, M. (2003) *Introduction to the International Human Rights Regime*. Leiden and Boston: Brill Academic Publishers.

PDDH (Procuraduria para la Defensa de los Derechos Humanos) (2008) *Informe anual 2007*. http://www.pddh.gob.ni/, accessed on July 10, 2008.

PDVSA (Petróleos de Venezuela Sociedad Anónima) (2008) *Management report PETROCARIBE (1st Semester)*. Caracas: RBV. http://vcumbredepetrocaribe.menpet.gob.ve/interface.sp/database/fichero/publicacion/521/28.PDF, accessed on July 13, 2008.

PETROCARIBE (2005) *Acuerdo de cooperación energética PETROCARIBE*. http://www.pdvsa.com/index.php?tpl=interface.sp/design/biblioteca/readdoc.tpl.html&newsid_obj_id=1349&newsid_temas=111, accessed on April 26, 2009.

PETROCARIBE (2007) "Tratado de seguridad energética PETROCARIBE," in *Gaceta Oficial de la República Bolivariana de Venezuela*, No. 38.861, January 30, 2008.

PREAL (Programa de Promoción de la Reforma Educativa de América Latina y el Caribe (2004) *Informe de progreso educativo de Nicaragua*. Managua: PREAL.

Raby, D. L. (2006) *Democracy and Revolution: Latin America and Socialism Today*. London: Pluto.

Robinson, W. I. (1992) *A Faustian Bargain: US Intervention in the Nicaraguan Elections and American Foreign Policy in the Post-cold War Era*. Boulder: Westview.

Robinson, W. I. (1996) *Promoting Polyarchy: Globalization, US Intervention, and Hegemony*. Cambridge, UK: Cambridge University Press.

Robinson, W. I. (2001) "Transnational Processes, Development Studies and Changing Social Hierarchies in the World System: A Central American Case Study," *Third World Quarterly* 22 (4): 529–563.

Santos, B. d. S. (2002) *Toward a New Legal Common Sense*. London: Butterworth.

Santos, B. d. S. and C. A. Rodríguez-Garavito (eds) (2005) *Law and Globalization From Below*. Cambridge, UK: Cambridge University Press.

Sunkel, O. (ed.) (1993) *Development from Within*. London: Lynne Rienner.

Troudi, H. E. and J. C. Monedero (2007) *Empresas de producción social*. 2nd ed. Caracas: CIM.

UN (2005) *Report on the World Social Situation 2005: The Inequality Predicament*. New York: United Nations.

UNDP (United Nations Development Program) (2000) *El desarollo humano en Nicaragua, 2000*. New York: UNDP.

UNDP (2006) *Human Development Report 2006. Beyond Scarcity: Power, Poverty and the Global Water Crisis*. New York: UNDP.

UNDP (2007) *Human Development Report 2007/2008. Fighting Climate Change: Human Solidarity in a Divided World*. New York: UNDP.

UNDP (2008) *Human Development Indices: A Statistical Update*, http://hdr.undp.org/en/statistics/data/hdi2008/, accessed on April 26, 2008.

UNESCO (2005) *EFA Global Monitoring Report 2005*. Paris: UNESCO.

UNESCO (United Nations Educational, Scientific, and Cultural Organization), OEI (Organización de Estados Iberoamericanos), INIDE (Instituto Nacional de Información de Desarrollo), UNAN-Managua (Universidad Nacional Autónoma de Nicaragua), IDEUCA (Instituto de Educación Universidad Centro-Americana) (2009) *Informe. Comisión Nacional de Verificación: Verificación de la Tasa Nacional de Analfabetismo en Nicaragua 16/06/2009*. Managua: UNESCO-Managua/OEI/INIDE/UNAN/IDEUCA.

UNICEF (2006) *The State of the World's Children 2007*. New York: UNICEF.

Walker, T. W. (2003) *Nicaragua: Living in the Shadow of the Eagle*, 4th ed. Boulder: Westview.

6 The Transformation of the Social Issue

Poverty, Society, and the State[1]

Anete Brito Leal Ivo and
Ruthy Nadia Laniado

INTRODUCTION

This chapter discusses the nature and scope of social policies enforced since the 1990s in Latin America, and more specifically in Brazil. It tackles the impact of these policies on social inclusion and their effects on citizenship in a region where severe social inequalities have been historically persistent.[2]

Social policies are herewith understood as institutional mediations associated with processes linked to social change. They define social bonds as well as the nature of the social contract (the modern relationship between regulation and emancipation), and they design the political relationship between citizenship and the State (Ivo 2001). It must be underlined that social policies are the historical result of the liberal response of the nineteenth century to the Marxist critique of political liberties and a core element of social development. The State implemented social rights and European liberalism institutionalized social and economic conditions in order to assure a minimal standard of living and the enjoyment of a decent life that corresponds to the capacity of wealth accumulation of the nation. These conditions were understood as a fundamental aspect of liberty (Schnapper 2002).

The backbone of modern democracy and civil, political, and social rights is justice as an organizing moral principle of society. Social movements throughout modern history have required democratic changes and justice on three levels: as emancipation (individual dignity), as experience and usufruct (access to social rights and decision-making processes according to pluralist social interests), and as solidarity (strong bonds between individuals and collectivities as well as intergenerational responsibility) (Laniado 2001). However, the actual development of different societies with respect to these three levels of structural arrangement did not result in a balanced relationship between society and the State. Advanced capitalist societies managed to produce a more reasonable equilibrium of these threefold structuring elements. Nevertheless, injustice and inequality are widely spread in most Western societies, and have manifested the unequal development of capitalism and democracy within nations and among nations. Poverty is the most visible expression of this unequal development.

Contemporary collective action has confronted the unbalanced equilibrium of democratic requirements by criticizing inequality and poverty; it has also fought against the primacy of the market over civil society and social justice, and has required that the State's mediating role in social conflicts and social distribution is reinforced. Accordingly, social justice has become the fundamental field of critique and debate on social integration and social inclusion/exclusion in contemporary societies, both in terms of political resistance linked to oppression (minorities, apartheid, national identities, etc.) and in terms of democratic changes and institution building, such as in processes of rebuilding democracy (Milani and Laniado 2006 and Laniado 2008).

In fact, social justice is not only the quantitative distribution of goods, but also a qualitative principle that organizes life in society, that guides social practices, and that consolidates institutions and their role in the democratic order. It is an intellectual and practical principle. Therefore, justice transcends the utilitarian notion of material distribution by expressing, on the one hand, the more comprehensive perception of life-quality and individual dignity, and, on the other, that of the collectivity, which derives from the access to individual and public goods, such as education or retirement benefits (Miller 2001). The field of justice does not describe an external property of the social organization, but it describes the form of the social organization itself. Hence, justice is embedded in each level of the structure of a society; it is expressed according to specific cultural and historical developments that produce the meaning and the relevance of norms and goods that are associated to justice as well as to the mechanisms and procedures for its effective use in a community (Douglas 1995). Thus, social policies are resources of social justice that have emerged from struggles of individuals, groups, and classes for social recognition and social distribution (Fraser 2000).

It is important to analyze social justice and its relations to necessity, equality, and inclusion from three standpoints: (a) the bonds that it establishes in a community, (b) the way institutions impact on individual lives, and, finally, (c) the normative and organizational conditions of producing legal means and public policies that are implemented by the State and its agents. Social policies are an important political fact permitting an understanding of social justice; they are the institutional means that integrate social and civic rights, and guarantee a minimum redistribution standard and dignity according to existing power relations. Actually, social policies inform the dynamics of conflict and social inclusion. Hence, the study of social policies in the context of democratic changes is important in order to understand the quality and extension of these transformations, to see what has been achieved for citizens, and to overcome inequalities that have resulted from historical circumstances.

In this chapter, we focus on Latin American countries, in particular Brazil that displays high levels of social inequalities. In order to understand inequality here, it is important to take into account some aspects of its historical development: (1) the creation of the labor market and informal labor, which resulted from the inclusion/exclusion process among those who have gotten universal social rights and those who have not; (2) the process of democratic transition that occurred in the region throughout the 1980s and 1990s after multiple and lengthy experiences of military dictatorships. This period displayed situations of inequality between the twofold logic of a historical process: first, the return to democracy and an extended development of citizenship, and second, the reformist strategies of the State in order to integrate the region according to the economic principles favored by the Washington Consensus and economic neo-liberalism. The latter re-qualified citizenship rights while reducing the role of the State, which had provided a social protection net, introduced by social rights movements throughout the twentieth century. And third, the institutional framework of neo-liberalism triggered a high concentration of wealth in the upper social strata and in multinational corporations, despite a recent decline in labor income concentration in Brazil. The following data inform on the scope of this issue.

The gross domestic product (GDP) of Brazil was estimated at US$ 1.8 trillion in 2007, which placed the country on the ninth position of the world economic ranking as specified by the International Monetary Fund. Brazil was according to the World Bank the tenth economy of the world for the same period. In addition, economic growth in 2007 was 5.7 percent higher than in 2006 (data of the Brazilian Institute of Geography and Statistics). As for the country's living standard in terms of GDP *per capita,* it was US$ 8,600.00 in 2006. Nevertheless, data of the National Household Survey (PNAD 2007) inform us that the Gini index for labor income distribution was reduced from 0.540 in 2006 to 0.528 in 2007, a considerable reduction which, however, was not enough to change the general income distribution and inequality profile in Brazil because the index only refers to income improvement for the lower strata (through an implementation of social policies and an increase of the purchasing power of the minimum wage).[3]

This chapter will debate some aspects of the dilemmas put forward by these recent changes in Latin America and Brazil, and will focus on the main features of social policies implemented from 1990 to 2007. These changes express a transformation of social rights under the hegemony of neo-liberalism. The focus of liberal arguments is that the present form of social policies aims, on the one hand, at reducing the consequences of the structural adjustments introduced by the strategies of the Washington Consensus, and on the other, at placing social policies outside the configuration of institutional rights and historically developed social protection schemes. Therefore, the neo-liberal approach displaces the principle of social justice from that of a constitutive element of society to a fragmented justice aiming at introducing the principle of compensation; this approach focuses on a material deprivation that is diagnosed and managed by market exchanges, and not by generalized solidarity. This point of view ignores that social justice is also perceived as human dignity, and social status as the position of the individual actor in the national social community. The measures proposed by neo-liberal directives in order to confront deprivation have not been conceived as a collective commitment of society, but as a concession of the State to needy individuals, whenever the macro-economic situation permits the State to allocate resources to social programs (Ivo 2004).

In the case of Brazil, since the 1980s, democratic struggles at different levels have required agendas that challenge poverty. As a result, it is possible to find two parallel meanings for the past decade of State actions on the social issue: (a) to comply with the agenda of international agencies in fighting poverty, and (b) to correspond to a historical compromise with social movements and social classes in order to overcome inequalities in Brazil. Since 2003, the government of Luis Inácio Lula da Silva has described this dual perspective as situated amidst the transformation of social aspects and democratic politics.

This new social policy orientation, triggering unbalanced situations between economic growth and social justice, has come in conflict with the social contract defined in the Constitution of 1988, which has got a universal character. This unbalance has made governability more difficult and has caused a desocialization of the Brazilian society in the sense underlined by Castel (1995), and a depoliticization of the social issue at the level of the State—that is, the market has become hegemonic and has been able to define the links between capital and labor. The result, as we have argued earlier, is that the social has switched from the field of distribution to that of a management of poverty.

THE PARADOX OF DEMOCRATIC TRANSITION IN BRAZIL

During the 1970s and 1980s, the first stage of democratic transition after the military regime was characterized by an increase in civil and political liberties and the return to a lawful State sanctioned by a new Constitution that was approved by the Congress in 1988. Access to universal social rights was given to marginal social actors and different minorities. The mobilization of civil society, social movements, and organized social classes was important in order to produce a new pattern of governance expressed in the new Constitution. Concomitantly to these changes, Latin American societies experienced neo-liberal policies that favored the free market, fiscal reforms, structural adjustments, monetary stability, new mechanisms of decentralization of the State, as well as the privatization of public assets, and a reform of the social security scheme and the labor market system (Barba, Ivo, Valencia, and Ziccardi 2005).

These changes in the economic system and the State characterize the contradiction produced by the transition; they express an ambivalence between the strengthening of civil society, a widespread social mobilization, and, at the same time, the enforcing of new regulatory measures that aimed at decentralizing the State and at decreasing its responsibility for universal social protection. As a consequence, the transformation of the economic production, the deregulation of labor rights and social rights, as well as structural unemployment produced a desocialization of the economy, contrary to the constitutional directives asking for the promotion of equity. The outcomes were new forms of poverty, narrowed social mobilities, and strongly segmented social rights (Lautier 1999).

However, as a counterbalance to the desocialization of the economy, international agencies advocated in most countries new directives to deal with poverty. During the increasing globalization of the economy, a new framework on social issues was established: it was dislocated from the field of universal social protection (which had included rights linked to illness, old age, education, etc.) to the field of civil protection (human rights [gender, ethnicity], access to the consumer market, bank loans and credit possibilities, public security and policing, etc.) combined with a set of selective policies targeted at the poor. In the medium term, the disconnection between social rights and the labor market that resulted from unemployment and employment quality deterioration has produced a *déffiliation*[4] of individuals, in the sense underlined by Castel (1995), from the different spheres of social life, such as labor, family, urban or rural environment.

Targeting the indigent poor[5] and the poor, new policies of social protection have been put forward. These groups do not take part in a national social security system of redistribution and social justice, because these targeted policies are not founded on universal principles of social rights regulated by constitutional law and a comprehensive understanding of citizenship. They are government programs aiming at assisting in poverty situations; they are flexible and dependent on the market and fiscal economic policies. Therefore, these strategies are characterized as compensatory programs of income distribution and do not promote an inclusion into the labor market or opportunities for social mobility; because they are a punctual relief from poverty, they have achieved little impact on intergenerational reciprocity, such as is the case in Western European welfare states.

These arguments explain the dilemma of the re-conversion of the social issue from re-distribution (based on social justice) to that of compensation (to alleviate deprivation caused by poverty). Is there any re-distributive capacity in such policies? Do they imply any political advances in terms of institutionalized welfare? Are they capable of changing the income concentration? These questions are the guideline that permits us to develop the discussion on the transformation of the social issue in terms of poverty, society, and the State.

According to universalistic social policies, the market is the focus of distributive conflicts, so that the State has a decisive role as a mediator and regulator of interests. The targeted social policy approach distances itself from the universalistic approach and advocates the relevance of a strategic management of public expenses related to poverty as the most efficient motor of obtaining equity. This policy is associated to an instrumental and operational perspective, combined with selective decisions on social expenditures (Candia 1998). It is not linked to an understanding of social protection as a generalized national solidarity, instead protection is transformed into selective assistance to individuals: those who deserve it and who will develop specific capabilities. Targeted policy supposes that the poor have to be capable of fighting against poverty and that they (and not society or the State) are largely responsible for overcoming poverty. Therefore, this policy is not based on the principle of institutional responsibility of the State, but introduces the notion of individuals as customers of the goods and services of a society.

The targeted policy standpoint may be questioned by asking how citizens can face problems related to national policies in general, and can face decisions about the allocation of resources to social protection when a fair distribution of wealth is no longer considered a constitutional right, but solely a political decision taken by the government. Following this line of argument, we would like to recall the three core areas of social rights as they were described in the Brazilian Constitution of 1988 (IPEA 2003). First, there are basic rights that are a characteristic element of the State, such as social security. Second, there are rights that are inscribed into constitutional norms, but they are enforced according to structural programs of the government, such as land reforms. Third, there are emergency programs conceived to provide assistance to the most vulnerable segments of society, such as the Family Sponsor Program (*Programa Bolsa Família*), whose implementation and continuity depend on the decisions of the government. The focus on social inclusion expressed by the Brazilian Constitution, and related to the first and second categories of the rights mentioned earlier, has been minimized by the practice of social policies in the last ten years.

However, from the management point of view, these targeted programs were efficient—they increased the number of families served by this form of social assistance from 3.7 million to 11.1 million families (from 2003 to 2006). At the same time, there was an increase in the value of the minimum wage, which resulted in a decrease in the Gini index from 0.583 in 1995 to 0.544 in 2005 (PNAD 2005: 80).

But Theodoro and Delgado (2003) consider this re-distribution strategy as an intensified distributive conflict at the very baseline of social stratification, because it opposes the unprotected poor (excluded from welfare) to the non-poor or to the less poor (included in welfare).

How was it possible to counter the parallel dynamics of democratic achievements (participation and political pluralism) and economic distribution (displacement of social rights and selective compensatory programs)?

How was it possible to merge into one political agenda the struggle against poverty by actors who were otherwise in conflict: those with an historical demand expressed in social movements and class solidarity and those operating the state in its new role in the globalized economy? How did the transition from the universal principle of social policy to the individualistic one encounter political grounds of legitimacy in Brazilian society?

There is more than the transformation process under analysis. There is an ideological and symbolic deconstruction of the national security system propagated by the rhetoric of the national security crisis and the fiscal deficit of the State. This has produced an ambiguous perception of citizenship: those who are included in the security system are referred to as *privileged citizens* who receive more than they deserve from the State budget. Those who do not benefit from social security are presented as victims of the *privileged*. Historically, the development of the national security system has been fragmented; it has only included the formal sector of the labor market: wage workers, corporative organized labor, professionals, and civil servants; more recently, since 1988, rural workers have benefited from the national security system. The other part of Brazilian society, the larger one (approximately 57 percent of the economically active population (2006)), is made up of workers in the informal sector and non-workers; they are hardly entitled to any social protection and any rights.

It is this historical gap between the *haves* and the *have-nots* that is captured by the dominant discourse of the transformation process in Brazil. Workers who are considered as belonging to the *privileged classes* are held responsible for poverty and for the historical inequality in Brazilian society. This means that there has been a displacement of the reasons (insufficiency, deficiency, and fragility) that produced the welfare system in the last century from the field of collective responsibility to that of individual responsibility assigned to those who have been included in welfare provisions. In fact, middle class waged sectors and civil servants have become the *bad guys* of a universal national system of social security that has never reached all citizens.

This conflicting situation has reversed the relationship between binomial rights and obligations: once, these rights made up the core field of reciprocity for citizenship and collective life, and laid the foundations of social justice as a structural element of society. Hence, this reversal is considered a rupture of social bonds that are organized by a social contract and the State in a democracy, a rupture that is expressed by a crisis of legitimacy and civic resistance.

THE *CIRCULARITY* OF THE SOCIAL ISSUE: DISTRIBUTIVE CONFLICT AND THE SEGMENTATION OF SOCIAL PROTECTION

The new social policies are directed at the indigent poor and the poor that are excluded from social protection. The Organic Law of Social Assistance

(Law no. 8.742) of 1993 adopted two sets of guidelines for qualifying the poor and for selecting those entitled to social assistance. The law did not take into account distribution problems related to poverty such as the need for land reform, the restrictive legal requirements to access the national social security system, and structural unemployment among others. On the contrary, this law contributed to the expression of the symbolic and ideological discourse on social protection mentioned earlier, and to the reversing of the historical principle of justice, which declared that social rights related to labor were legitimate. Thus, it diffused the idea of generalized poverty with the purpose of producing tensions and conflicts among different segments: wage labor (those included in social welfare and benefiting from universal social rights), those benefiting from targeted policies (social assistance and social quotas for minorities) and the State. This new scheme can be called a restricted field of distributive conflicts—it has restricted social disputes to wage and labor topics and has excluded the better-off strata of society.

This approach to poverty and inequality as well as to regulation and distribution constitutes a new form of segmentation that has emerged in Brazil and can be classified into five groups according to Lautier's analysis (1999): (a) protected citizens (*the privileged*); (b) individuals protected by the Law of Social Assistance; (c) individuals benefiting from structural programs such as land reforms; (d) individuals benefiting from targeted social programs, and (e) a large sector of the population made up of those who are excluded from social assistance, social protection, and employment and referred to by Lautier as the "no man's land"; these are temporary workers, the unemployed, the self-employed, the handicapped, and poor people who are not poor enough to qualify for assistance.

According to more recent data of the National Household Survey (PNAD 2007), benefits perceived by income transfer programs are as follows: only 54 percent of the 4.122 million indigent poor households have received some sort of benefit; and only 44 percent of the 8.249 million poor households have received some benefits.[6] Two income-transfer programs of different nature can illustrate the segmentation of social assistance referred to earlier: the Program of Continued Assistance (*Benefício de Prestação Continuada—BPC*) is a constitutional right and provides a minimum wage to individuals over 65 years and to handicapped people incapable of working or living by themselves. The Family Sponsor Program (*Programa Bolsa Família—PBF*) is a non-constitutional right; its policy character is that of an income-transfer program for indigent poor or poor families with per capita incomes between R$ 60.00 (US$ 37.72) and R$ 120.00 (US$ 75.45)·. It is important to distinguish the total expenses of each program from the number of beneficiaries. The correlation of the estimated monthly stipends announced in 2008 (*Folha de São Paulo* and Ministry of Social Development 2008) is the following: (a) the Program of Continued Assistance (a constitutional right): R$ 415.00 (US$ 260)/per person (2008 minimum salary value), for a total of 2.8 million beneficiaries with a total budget of R$ 13.9 billion (US$ 8.7 billion); (b) the Family Sponsoring Program (a non-constitutional right): it pays from R$ 18.00 (US$ 11.31) up to R$ 172.00 (US$ 108.14)/per family (according to the number of children up to the age of 17), for a total of 11.1 million families (approximately 51 million people) with a total budget of R$ 10.4 billion (US$ 6.5 billion). Workers in the informal sector with a family income of up to half of the minimum wage are not entitled to one of the income-transfer programs described earlier. This is what Theodoro and Delgado (2003) call a cheap solution found for the social issue: they consider that the Family Program pays much less to a much larger number of beneficiaries. Targeted social programs thus reduce family needs, but are not long-term strategies aimed at decreasing inequality.

The neo-liberal justification of the targeted programs that fight against poverty is to implement an efficient system and to make a rational use of resources by state agents. Moreover, the priority given to these programs, as opposed to the improvement and the expansion of the national security system, characterizes the programs as vulnerable policies exposed to political and budget contingencies, which are submitted to the risks and the insecurity of the political economy in Latin America.

The last argument in our analysis of the intensified distributive conflict at the social foundations of the Brazilian society, characterizing what we call the current "circularity" of the social issue (Ivo 2004), concerns the sociopolitical level. How can we conceive the link of the new social policies and the socio-political conditions of their implementation and success?

There are three variables that should be pointed out. First, these policies are based on the decentralization of the activity of the State by commissions operating at the municipal level. In 2007, for example, there were 2,706 Social Assistance Municipal Councils set up in order to control the assistance programs. There also existed 2,310 municipal commissions in charge of the Family Sponsoring Program (IPEA 2007: 92). These centers have required the participation of civil society (civil associations and NGOs) in decisions taken together with state agents.[7] There is thus a strong emphasis on the participation of local social networks (family or community); they are considered important in order to mobilize social capital and the local capacity to improve the effectiveness of these bureaucratic policies. It is assumed that individual responsibility has an important role in promoting local activism and that this is necessary for self-sustained organizational and economic actions integrated into local networks. This would then facilitate their usefulness in local development programs and bring out adequate conditions in order to improve the effectiveness of compensatory social programs. Local civil society and actor empowerment constitute the framework of the socio-political environment at the local level in this new approach of social assistance. Nevertheless, the capability of civil society and local social networks to achieve positive outcomes depends on the politico-administrative situation of local power systems and local agents.

Second, the current social policies in Brazil take into account that the implementation of such programs will benefit from local political capacities, and that local actors seem to be well organized, what is not really the case. Often local governments—municipalities—do not have the institutional and operational capability to manage complex, multiple, and extended social programs; they are often poor and depend on resources provided by the national State (mainly by the Fund for the Participation of Municipalities (FPM), which disposes of mechanisms of tax-revenue transfers from the federal government to the local units). Often, they have difficulties in legally controlling administrative management. The enforcement of the recent Law of Fiscal Responsibility (Complementary Law no. 101 of 2000) stipulated that regional states and municipalities cannot spend more than they collect; the implementation of legal sanctions, according to this law, revealed that most of the Brazilian municipalities (approximately 3,425 of a total of 5,560 [2002]) were not capable of presenting a balanced budget in 2002 (*Folha de São Paulo* 2002). This makes a strong case against the alleged capability of local governments and agents to manage and implement targeted social assistance programs, because many of the expected benefits that would reduce family poverty are often neutralized by fiscal deficits of local governments and by debts that they have to re-imburse to the national government. In municipalities where social movements and municipal councils are well organized and exercise political pressure on the local government, this situation may be better. Thus, structural problems of income distribution and unemployment cannot be overcome by mitigating measures (such as compensatory social programs) or the efforts deployed by solidarity nets in local communities.

There is also the risk that the organizing capacity of actors in civil society, necessary for improving local social programs, is challenged by the local political system that may be characterized by traditionalism and patronage, and influenced by party politics and philanthropy. These would be severe impediments to what should be an efficient partnership between public and private sectors according to the strategy of governance asked for by international agencies (World Bank and International Monetary Fund). In general, many municipalities in Brazil encounter difficulties in implementing an integrated action of complex policies on different scales (national–local) due to the fact that quite frequently they face the opposition of socio-political forces and a State influenced by patronage.

Finally, the third variable related to the intensification of distributive conflicts at the social foundations of Brazilian society concerns the socio-economic agenda of the local development that new governmental policies have formulated. Community development, associations, and non-profit organizations—or better, a solidarity-based economy—are part of the core guideline model of self-sustained development in the context of a globalized economy and the shrinking employment market. Nevertheless, the solidarity-based economy seems to be a fragile alternative because it is currently overshadowed by the great importance of informal labor in Brazil.

According to Borges and Franco (1999), the specificities of the informal labor market in the metropolitan region of Salvador describe an organizational pattern of labor and production that does not benefit from the societal matrix based on solidarity and family organization networks, but instead is based on the individualization of labor activities. The main features of this informal labor market are: the predominance of self-employed workers, a very low degree of formal enterprises (e.g., absence of legal registry and tax payments) known in Brazil as *micro-business*, and the predominance of street vendor activities. These features do not portray work and production as part of a connected organic production chain. On the contrary, they participate in a survival strategy of precarious working conditions in an economy where only limited working positions within the formal economic market exist. In addition, Borges and Franco point out that the precarious situation of informal labor is aggravated by the more or less absence of social protection and social rights in this group of workers.

Despite the precarious conditions of the informal sector, an important link between informal labor and income-transfer programs can be identified. According to Asseburg and Gaiger (2007), and Dowbor (2008), these programs may have positive effects on a self-employment strategy when they reinforce this economic activity and form a virtuous micro-business. Eventually, they may stimulate the emergence of formal working positions for those who work in the informal sector.

CONCLUDING REMARKS: INDIVIDUALIZATION AND SEGMENTATION OF THE SOCIAL POLICY AND ITS IMPACT ON POLITICS

As we have pointed out at the beginning of this chapter, modernity was constructed on the principles of liberty and equality within a backdrop of justice and universality. It has built a complex institutional system of democratic relations and general solidarity schemes (reciprocity among generations) that has designed the framework of contemporary democracies, their norms, and institutions. These latter have been so important that they have permitted the linking of social, political, and economic exchanges—by including every political subject in citizenship—sustained by the regulations and distributions of the State. Civic, political, and social rights characterized the relationships between individuals, groups, social classes, and the State throughout the democratic achievements of the twentieth century. Their material elements have been welfare policies and the welfare State in developed countries and, *mutatis mutandis*, different degrees of welfare in the poorer countries. Therefore, justice as a universal principle and social justice as the historical manifestation of this principle became the fields of democratic struggles and negotiations, sanctioned by a system of political representations and the definition of policies related to interests, necessity, and equality.

Democracy in Latin America has evolved beside political contradictions and has displayed a deficit of social justice. It was based on social and political changes that crossed the Latin American continent in the 1980s and 1990s, transforming military dictatorships into democratic societies with important changes in the handling of the social issue. As mentioned earlier, these transformations were part of a dual historical logic that articulated the process of political democratization (liberties and participation) with the integration into the global market economy (deregulation and wealth concentration) and introduced a considerable change in the sphere of regulation and distribution. In most Latin American countries and in Brazil, in particular, universal welfare rights never became a distributive social contract in order to promote equity and social justice. High degrees of exclusion and inequality have developed simultaneously along economic growth and democratic institutional building throughout the twentieth century, and even after the re-democratization of the last two decades. Large segments of the poor have been characterized by a structural tendency that has influenced the development of citizenship, social integration, and the distribution of public goods on a minimum basis of equality and dignity.

Despite the development of a corporate system of social protection for professionals, wage workers, as well as civil servants, the growth of consistent social rights in Brazil has never reached all citizens. As already mentioned, rural workers achieved full social security rights (particularly the right to benefit from a full minimum wage retirement scheme) with the implementation of the Constitution of 1988, 22 years ago. In fact, this Constitution aimed at overcoming the normative barriers brought up to implement universal social rights; it defined the basic material and immaterial human needs and emphasized the importance of distribution in order to attain human dignity. Its main constitutional achievement has been to expand and to improve the conditions of citizenship (participation and distribution) and the usufruct of social rights. However, the 1990s faced neo-liberal economic changes and, despite constitutional advances and democratic politics, the globalized economy has reduced most positive effects that could have been achieved by enforcing the constitutional legal norms aimed at improving social justice.

In the past two decades, the deregulation of the economy and the labor market resulted in a vulnerability of wage earners and an increase in unemployment. In the urban sector, precarious and informal labor, exclusion from social rights, and compensatory public social programs have been part of the inconsistencies of recent social re-distribution in Brazil. The shift in State policy established by the new paradigm of the social issue—from social protection and collective solidarity to social assistance based on individual merit—has put emphasis on individualization and segmentation.

The impact of this pattern of social policies on politics is threefold: (1) it caused a rupture in the uncompleted process of developing and reaching a universal system of social protection based on reciprocity and increased the fragmentation of the social fabric; (2) it produced a new form of segmentation that touched the relationship between the political subjects (bearer of social rights) and the state by dividing citizenry into two blocks: those who have rights based on labor corporative organizations protected by the state and those who are clients of contingent and compensatory social policies promoted by the State at the discretion of governmental decisions that involve political negotiations and political exchanges; (3) it introduced, with the priority given to targeted social programs, the so-called "circularity of the social issue." (Ivo 2004) This means that the social issue as approached by these social policies is not understood as part of a larger structural problem of social distribution, but it becomes a self-contained political and social dynamic activity, where solutions destined to a large number of poor people are focused. As a general result of these threefold elements of analysis, it is possible to conclude that targeted social policies in Brazil have promoted income distribution from the waged strata to the poor strata of society, and not from the higher income strata to the bottom strata. The Gini index mentioned earlier is an efficient tool for illustrating this pattern of income re-distribution among different labor sectors.[8]

Income concentration can be found (Salm 2007) by observing labor income as compared to income from the distribution of assets based on the GDP.[9] In the case of Brazil and according to the Gini index, there is a tendency towards the re-distribution of labor incomes among those involved in labor activities. However, this tendency no longer exists if we observe the functional participation of the labor income in the GDP. Throughout the decade from 1993 to 2003, the labor income share in the GDP declined from approximately 56 percent to 45 percent, which represents a clear reduction of wealth distribution between labor and capital (DIEESE 2006).

These distribution patterns have introduced transformations in the way citizenship is related to the democratic binomial of rights and obligations, replacing it by scattered benefits conceived as individual assistance controlled by the local bureaucracy. Introducing individual assistance instead of improving social protection weakens the conditions of inclusion and social mobility. In the current historical conjuncture of the Brazilian democracy, the transformation of the social issue according to neo-liberal guidelines exposes a paradox, which makes it more difficult to find a solution to the democratic deficit in relation to social justice. Despite social policies for the poor, the country has not moved from the sphere of necessity to that of more liberty (Sen 2000).

NOTES

1. This chapter is the revised version of a paper presented at the First Forum of Sociology of the International Sociological Association: *Sociological Research and Public Debate*, Barcelona, Spain September 5–8, 2008; RC09—Research Committee on *Social Transformations and Sociology of Development*—Session 03.
2. The authors would like to thank for their support the following institutions: *Conselho Nacional de Desenvolvimento Científico e Tecnológico (CNPq), Fundação de Amparo à Pesquisa da Bahia (FAPESB)* and *Núcleo de Pós-Graduação em Administração/UFBA.*
3. Other emergent economies such as Russia, China, and India presented a Gini index of respectively 0.399 (2002), 0.469 (2004), and 0.368 (2004), which shows a less unequal distribution as compared to Brazil. Income inequality in Brazil is nearer to the Gini index of poor countries such as El Salvador (0.524, 2002), Panama (0.561, 2003), and South Africa (0.578, 2000) for the same period (see: World Bank 2007).
4. According to Castel (1995) the notion of *déffiliation* refers to the rupture of social bonds linked to the labor status as well as to social bonds in an actor's social life; this rupture characterizes a gradual change from the social condition of inclusion to that of risk and exclusion.
5. The difference between the categories *indigent poor* and *poor* is as follows: *indigent poor* income is up to one fourth of the minimum wage per capita per family; poor income is from one fourth to half of the minimum wage per capita per family. The Organic Law of Social Assistance (Law n° 8.742) of 1993 established these parameters.
6. In Brazil, data about income and poverty were as follows in 2005: 101.7 million people had a household *per capita* income of less than one minimum wage; 76 million people had a household *per capita* income above the minimum wage (IPEA 2007: 82). The minimum wage is R$ 415.00 (US$ 260 in July 2008; the exchange rate US$ to Real is the following in 2009: one US$ is R$ 1.59040).
7. These municipal councils and commissions face many technical and management difficulties due to their composition and the technical expertise often required to make decisions.
8. The National Household Survey data that measures inequality is based on inequalities of labor income. It does not include assets income. Therefore, it only gives limited information on the total income redistribution.
9. According to the Brazilian Institute of Geography and Statistics (National Accounts).

BIBLIOGRAPHY

Asseburg, Hans and Luis Gaiger (2007) "A economia solidária diante das desigualdades," *Dados* 50 (3): 499–533.
Barba, Carlos, Anete Ivo, Enrique Valencia, and Alica Ziccardi (2005) "Research Horizons: Poverty in Latin America," in Else Øyen *The Polyscopie Landscape of Poverty Research. State of Art in International Poverty Rresearch.* Bergen: CROP/ISSC. International Social Science Council, Norway: Research Council of Norway, www.crop.org, accessed on December 15, 2005.
Borges, Ângela and Angela Franco (1999) "Economia informal da RMS: verdades e mitos," *Bahia. Análise e Dados* 9 (3): 68–89.

Candia, José Miguel (1998) "Exclusión y pobreza. La focalización de las politicas sociales," *Nueva Sociedad* 156 (July/August): 116–126.

Castel, Robert (1995) *Les métamorphoses de la question sociale. Une chronique du salariat.* Paris: Fayard.

Castel, Robert (2003) *L'insécurité sociale. Qu'est-ce qu'être protégé?* Paris: Seuil.

DIEESE. Departamento Intersindical de Estatísticas e Estudos Socioconômicos (2006) "Os salários num contexto de baixa inflação," *Nota Técnica* 36 (October): 10.

Douglas, Mary (1995) "Justice sociale et sentiment de justice," in Joëlle Affichard and Jean-Baptiste Foucauld (eds) *Pluralisme et équité : la justice sociale dans les démocraties* , 123–149. Paris, Commisariat Général au Plan: Éditions Esprit.

Dowbor, Ladislau (2008) "Em defesa dos 'Territórios da Cidadania'," *Le Monde Diplomatique* [Brazil]. http://diplo.uol.com.br/2008–03,a2265, accessed on March 18, 2008.

Folha de São Paulo (2002) "Municípios com balanços atrasados chegam a 3.425," São Paulo, September 15.

Folha de São Paulo (2008) "Governo já estuda limitar benefício," São Paulo, May 25.

Fraser, Nancy (2000) "Rethinking Recognition," *New Left Review* 3 (May/June): 107–120.

IBGE (Instituto Brasileiro de Geografia e Estatística) (2008) *Indicadores IBGE 2008-Nova Série.*

IPEA. Instituto de Pesquisa Econômica Aplicada (2003) *Anexo Estatístico. Políticas Sociais: acompanhamento e análise* , 7, Brasília, DF, August.

IPEA. Instituto de Pesquisa Econômica Aplicada (2007) *Boletim de Política Social: acompanhamento e análise.* 13, Brasília, DF (Special edition).

Ivo, Anete Brito Leal (2001) *Metamorfoses da questão democrática: governabilidade e pobreza.* Buenos Aires: CLACSO/Asdi.

Ivo, Anete Brito Leal (2004) "A reconversão do social: dilemas da redistribuição no tratamento focalizado," *São Paulo em Perspectiva*, São Paulo, SEADE, 18 (2): 57–67.

Laniado, Ruthy Nadia (2001) "Troca e reciprocidade no campo da cultura política," *Sociedade e Estado* 16 (1–2): 222–244.

Laniado, Ruthy Nadia (2008) "As fronteiras da política democrática: a justiça social e as diferentes escalas da ação coletiva participativa," in Paulo Henrique Martins, Aécio Mattos, and Breno Fontes (eds) *Limites da democracia*, 109–124. Recife: Ed. da UFPE.

Lautier, Bruno (1999) "Les politiques sociales en Amérique Latine. Propositions de méthode pour analyser un éclatement en cours," *Cahiers des Amériques Latines* 30 (28/29): 19–44.

Milani, Carlos and Ruthy Nadia Laniado (2006) "Espaço mundial e ordem política contemporâneas: uma agenda de pesquisa para um novo sentido da internacionalização," *Caderno CRH* 19 (48): 479–498.

Miller, David (2001) *Principles of social justice.* Cambridge, Mass.: Harvard University Press.

PNAD (Pesquisa Nacional por Amostra de Domicílios) (2005) *Síntese de Indicatores.* Rio de Janeiro, IBGE. http://www.ibge.gov.br/home/estatistica/populacao/trabalhoerendimento/pnad2007/comentarios2007.pdf, accessed on August 4, 2009. http://www.ibge.gov.br/home/estatistica/populacao/trabalhoerendimento/pnad2007/comentarios2007.pdf, accessed on August 4, 2009.

PNAD (Pesquisa Nacional por Amostra de Domicílios) (2007) *Comentários,* Rio de Janeiro: IBGE.

Salm, Cláudio (2007) "Sobre a recente queda da desigualdade de renda no Brasil: uma leitura crítica," www.centrocelsofurtado.org.br/adm/enviadas/dez/17_20070512201723.pdf, accessed on March 17, 2008.

Schnapper, Dominique (2002) "Preface," in Serge Paugam *La disqualification sociale* , 9–11. Paris: Presses Universitaires de France (Essai).

Sen, Amartya (1999) *Development as Freedom*. Oxford University Press: Oxford.

Theodoro, Mário and Guilherme Delgado (2003) "Política Social: universalização ou focalização—subsídios para o debate," *Políticas Sociais: acompanhamento e análise* 7 (August): 122–126.

World Bank (2007) *World Development Indicators 2007*. World Bank: Washington, DC.

7 Limits to the Revitalization of Labor
Social Movement Unionism in Argentina

Ayse Serdar

INTRODUCTION

Since the late 1970s, social movement unionism (SMU) has emerged as a revitalizing alternative to the discredited unionism of the past. As such, the successful experiences of the Brazilian, South African, Filipino, and more recently the South Korean SMUs have been debated and analyzed by social scientists. Moreover, several SMU campaigns in North America appear as promising cases, in which labor unions collaborate with community-based non-union organizations. This chapter focuses on the Argentine experience of SMU. Although Argentine new social movements have attracted scholarly attention, recent developments in labor movements, in particular, union revitalization has been largely neglected as a topic of sociological inquiry. This chapter analyzes the Central of the Argentine Workers (CTA) as an SMU, and discusses the problems of labor revitalization. The case of Argentina is different from other well-known SMU experiences. The Argentine unionism engendered a powerful and militant labor movement solidly linked to a political party movement—Peronism. The Argentine SMU faces problems of building a new type of unionism due to the legacy of this former culture and of labor union institutions. I will first summarize the conditions of the labor movement and unions in Argentina before the foundation of the CTA. Then, I will discuss the case of the CTA as an example of SMU, and, finally, I will analyze the Argentine case in relation to other well-known experiences.

THE BACKGROUND

Although the history of labor movements in Argentina began with the rise of Juan Peron in 1945, it was the arrival of anarchist and communist workers in Argentina at the time of the European migrations of the late nineteenth century, which led to the emergence of a militant working class movement in the early twentieth century. Violent suppressions of workers' demands, such as the Tragic Week (*Semana Tragica*) in 1919 and massa-cres in Patagonia in 1921 and 1922 displayed laborers' lack of power. Yet, the anarchist and communist groups remained marginal and were not able to obtain the leadership of the labor union movement. Later, it was Juan Peron who seized the potential of the working class as a political agent. He formulated working class identity, extended workers' rights, and provided them with better living conditions.[1] Peron launched a massive program of re-distribution of wealth that henceforth caused the emergence of a strong anti-Peronist sentiment among upper classes. Juan Peron and his wife Eva Peron, thanks to their political discourse and pro-labor policies, became the leaders of the majority of the working class. During the presidency of Peron, the General Confederation of Work (CGT) was recognized as the only legal peak confederation; the 1945 Law of Professional Associa-tions and the 1953 law on collective bargaining established a centralized, hierarchical, and financially stronger labor union structure (Cook 2007: 67).[2] While workers obtained considerable economic benefits, dignity, and self-respect, the CGT became politicized and turned into an instrument of Peron's political project. However, it is argued that Peron never aimed at building a strong political party structure in order to maintain his personal rule, but rather sought to strengthen Peronism as a movement rather than a political party.[3] Peron himself declared that "(t)he Peronist movement is not a political party; it represents no political grouping (. . .). It is a national movement (. . .). We represent only national interests" (McGuire 1997: 64, cited in Carri 1967: 35). When Peron was overthrown by the armed forces in 1955 and sent away into exile, which lasted for 17 years, the loyalty of the working class to Peron remained intact. Labor unions, allied to him, struggled to bring him back. However, during this period, the left and the right wings of Peronism evolved into different poles that organized their own CGTs in the late 1960s, although none of them formally left or broke with the single peak federation. When Peron finally returned to Argentina in 1973, he discovered that a very militant left wing block of Peronism had emerged. It was composed of unionists, students, and intellectuals whom Peron found difficult to control. After his death in 1974, the subsequent president, his wife Isabel Peron, organized the Triple A (Argentine Anti-communist Alliance) in order to destroy the radical wing. Between 1976 and 1983, during Argentina's last and most brutal military dictatorship, more than 70 percent of the 30,000 people who disappeared were either workers or unionists. This military dictatorship sought to change the eco-nomic and social structure of Argentina and launched the first steps of structural adjustments. It weakened the Peronist labor movement by taking measures both to reduce unionization levels and to advance the precariza-tion and flexibilization of labor. Before the military coup, unions used to have internal commissions at factories and workplaces. As such, the orga-nizational power of unions, based on internal commissions and democratic representation of rank-and-file, was undermined during the six years of the military dictatorship.[4] Meanwhile, unions started to follow a model of business-like unionism whose leadership obtained considerable wealth and economic power.

The Peronist Party (*Partido Justicialista* or PJ) underwent an internal transformation in the 1980s and the 1990s that changed the party from a labor-based populist position into a party advocating neo-liberal reforms and appealing to middle class voters. The electoral failures of the 1980s led the PJ to find new ways to attract middle-class voters. The Menem administration established a multiclass and multisector coalition in which the role of unions had no longer its traditional meaning. The already mentioned institutional weakness of the party allowed the new leadership of Menem to re-orient the party and its base in the population (Ranis 1994: xii–xiii, Levitsky 2003). For example, within the CGT, the supporters of Menem tried to marginalize the more militant wing. The consequent split strengthened Menems's policy. Without any doubt, the new limited role assigned to the unions helped the PJ to realize its neo-liberal turn. The lack of bureaucratic autonomy within the state allowed cliental relationships to dominate the political arena ("La Decadencia del Poder Sindical," *Clarín*, October 6, 1991: 6). Menem's strategy of co-optation assigned a dependent role to the CGT. Selective incentives were provided to supporters and unions, and those who were not willing to cooperate were repressed (Manzetti 1993: 232–234). The government initiated measures that permitted many of the biggest industrial unions to possess shares in enterprises and to buy new assets. By means of cliental networks, the PJ also maintained its electoral coalition with urban poor. After the 1980s, the number of unionist politicians from the PJ in the Congress dropped significantly, highlighting the deunionization of the Peronist Party in the following years.[5] In the 1990s, the PJ became more comprehensively deunionized than other labor-based populist parties, including the Revolutionary Institutional Party (PRI) in Mexico and the Democratic Action (AD) in Venezuela. It is important to recognize the historical characteristics of the labor unions in Argentina in order to understand the significance of the neo-liberal turn of the Peronist Party in the 1990s and how remarkable the CTA's rupture from the CGT was. There are several critical legacies of Peronism at the legal and institutional levels as well as at the levels of identity and culture that until recently have affected the capacity and identity of the CTA. In the next section, I will discuss the lingering effects of traditional labor unionism.

THE EMERGENCE AND INITIAL SUCCESS OF THE CTA

The existence of one central union—peak confederation—since Peron's epoch aimed at strengthening not only the centralized union structure, but also the hegemony of the party. The vertical and non-democratic structure of the CGT[6] is a legacy of Peron's labor codes. Hence, the CTA was established not only against the Peronist Menem government but also against the CGT's hierarchical and undemocratic representation and its co-optation by various incentives, such as their participation in the privatization of state enterprises or the social security system. In the early 1990s, several big industrial unions agreed to negotiate with the government, whereas some others chose to stay neutral. The unions that established the CTA, such as ATE (Association of State Employees) and CTERA (Confederation of Teachers of the Republic of Argentina) were in opposition to the government ("Todos gestionan pero nadie saca el pie del acelerador," *Sur*, September 15, 1989: 2; "Realineamientos en el sindicalismo," *Clarín*, February 4, 1991: 12). Whereas they were not alone in their opposition to the government, only ATE, CTERA, some other small unions, and individual local branches took the initiative to organize a new union center ("Combativos crean su corriente," *Clarín*, December 19, 1991: 19).[7] These unions can be defined as the left wing of Peronist labor unions.[8] Some socialists, communists, and anarchists supported and joined the CTA, although they have always been a minority.[9] In late 1991, about 120 unionists organized a meeting to discuss a new center project; in 1992, they formed the Congress of Argentine Workers ("Fuerte Crítica de los gremios 'combativos'," *Clarin*, November 15, 1992).[10] The CTA sought to organize and to unite the new working class of Argentina. They believed that after the structural transformations, the neo-liberal policies of the military government, and the Menem government, the old type of unionism ended up representing only a minority of workers in the formal sector.[11] For that reason, the leadership of the CTA tried to organize a new model of unionism in which workers of the formal and informal sectors, unemployed and retired workers, as well as territorial organizations could come together. In its first congress, the CTA accepted direct affiliation and direct voting, opening up the movement to other organizations that used democratic and autonomous unionism as indispensable principles. It is obvious that what the CTA has aimed to introduce as new unionism, has been influenced by SMU. These progressive and democratic principles were strategies to compensate for its organizational weakness. In order to expand its union base as well as the non-union support, CTA introduced a structure in which formal, informal, and employed workers were affiliated. For five years, they formed a grouping of unions.

In 1996, the CTA was formally established as a labor peak confederation and changed its name to the Center of Argentine Workers. In the 1990s, the CTA also started seeking external allies in its struggle against the government and its policies. The CTA's allies varied from the dissident wing of the CGT, over the Movement of Argentine Workers (MTA),[12] to the small farmers' association, the Argentine Federation of Farmers (FAA). In addition to external allies, the CTA gradually initiated the creation of various organizations such as the Federation of Land, Housing, and Habitat (FTV); the National Liberation Movement (MTL); The Movement of Occupants

and Tenants (MOI); a number of NGOs, such as the Argentine Association of Sexual Workers (AMMAR), or the National Movement of People's
Children (*Movimiento Nacional de los Chicos del Pueblo*), an indigenous
people organization, *Tupac Amaru*, which had built up its strength on
worker cooperatives; and the National Association of Auto-gestion Workers (ANTA), whose members have been entitled to an equal representation
and legal rights in the CTA. Hence, the CTA displayed efforts to unite
distinct problems of the working class with a variety of actors. The CTA
provided legal protection, organizational support, and encouragement in
some cases ("Las prostutitas quieren tener su sindicato," *Clarín*, October,
26, 1996: 52). For example, the AMMAR was strongly encouraged and
supported by the leadership of the CTA. AMMAR members said that their
relation with the CTA began out of the necessity of an office; however, in
the meantime, they have become a part of the CTA's project of uniting the
working class and have created what can be named class-consciousness.[13]
The members of ANTA similarly stated that the CTA has provided legal
protection and their experience has helped them to advance their project.[14]
In the 1990s, the CTA in cooperation with other oppositional organizations carried on several protests and actions. During the first presidency of
Menem, it was the CTA-MTA alliance that organized two general strikes
to protest against the government ("Tuvo repercussion parcial el paro
general," *Clarin*, August, 3, 1994: 2–3). The CTA organized several big
marches to protest and to channel the claims of the victims of the neo-
liberal policies, in order to address unemployment and poverty. The FTV,
which includes territorial and *piquetero* organizations, became one of the
essential actors of these protests. *Piqueteros* emerged in the late 1980s in
the interior of the country, in provinces strongly hit by privatization and
massive unemployment. In the second half of the 1990s, *piqueteros* started
blocking highways in Buenos Aires. Soon, unemployed workers became the
main protagonists of social conflicts. Since the late 1990s, the CTA's focus
shifted to poverty and unemployment, while the participation of non-union
groups, such as *piqueteros*, in the CTA activities increased.

THE CTA'S BATTLE AGAINST POVERTY
AND UNEMPLOYMENT

One of the defining objectives of the CTA is bringing different working
class sectors together. For this reason, the informal sector, unemployed
workers, and *piqueteros* organizations have always been among the CTA's
principle supporters. In the period from 2000 to 2003, when Argentina
was suffering from extraordinary levels of unemployment and poverty,[15]
the CTA actively participated in protests and campaigns resisting poverty and unemployment. Moreover, it developed alternative proposals and
projects in order to solve these problems. In this section, I will focus on

what the CTA's remarkable campaign accomplished against poverty and unemployment.

The nucleus of the campaign against poverty emerged in 2000. In July–August 2000, the CTA carried out a two-week march, named "The Grand March for Work." CTA's pillars marched from the industrial city of Rosario to Buenos Aires crossing the former industrial belt of the country. They asked for work and protested against unemployment and poverty. This campaign included a collection of petitions in support of the CTA's proposal called "the security of employment." It proposed a subsidy of 380 pesos for the heads of unemployed families, an allowance of 60 pesos for every child under 18, and 150 pesos for those who were not retired but over 65 years old (CTA 2000). The CTA collected more than 400,000 petition signatures that were submitted to the Congress on the final day of the protest march ("Que no digan que no se puede," *Pagina/12 webonline*, August 10, 2000, accessed on April 19, 2009). The movement intended to force the Congress to organize a referendum on the proposal. When the government ignored it, the CTA established the National Front Against Poverty (FRENAPO) that carried out a campaign for the popular referendum.

With the aim of building a broader alliance against poverty and unemployment and implementing a clearly defined proposal for its solution, the CTA actively sustained the establishment of the FRENAPO. In December 2000, FRENAPO organized both national and local boards for the organization and promotion of this popular referendum. In addition to the CTA, the FRENAPO included the Assembly of Small and Medium Businessmen (APYME), the Mobilizing Institute of Cooperative Funds (IMFC), several human rights and religious organizations, university communities, and members of various leftist and center-left political parties. The FRENAPO defined unemployment as a problem of the whole community and a form of social exclusion. It was considered as a measure of social discipline, an overexploitation of the labor force, and a regressive income distribution. Thus, the solution of poverty was linked to that of unemployment (FRENAPO 2001). The proposal of the FRENAPO was similar to the original 'security of employment' campaign developed by the CTA. It should generate a 'distributive shock' by functioning as a minimum income, and should serve as a social salary, eliminating households living under the poverty line, and activating a productive national economy and social solidarity. In short, it was expected to promote consumption and to contribute to the recovery of the internal market via re-industrialization and productivity (FRENAPO 2001).

In September 2001, the FRENAPO carried out a march that lasted for ten days. The caravans of FRENAPO departed from the *Plaza de Congreso,* in Buenos Aires, heading to distinct parts of the country. They crossed more than one hundred towns, covered about 25,000 kilometers, and mobilized about 100,000 people in order to gather public support for the popular referendum. On the final day of the action, the caravans returned to Buenos

Aires and joined more than 60,000 people at the *Plaza de Mayo*. The last day, the CTA leaders defined their struggle as a fight against "poverty, hunger, unemployment, and injustice" ("Para que no haya ningun hogar pobre en Argentina," *Pagina/12 webonline*, September 22, 2001, accessed on April 19, 2009; lagaceta.com.ar, September 24, 2001). In December 2001, more than 3,000,000 people voted in favor of the referendum. Over three days, citizens voted in ballot boxes set up in 654 different localities (CTA 2002b: 12). The participation in the referendum exceeded the expectations of the organizers. This movement revealed that poverty and unemployment were considered some of the most urgent and structural problems of the Argentine society ("Dos millones de esperanzas por otro modelo economico," *Pagina/12 webonline*, December 17, 2001, accessed on April 19, 2009; "El 'urnazo' que nadie esperaba," *Pagina/12 webonline,* December 18, 2001, accessed on April 19, 2009). Although the voting ended a couple of days before the breakdown of the Argentine economy, it proved the gravity and legitimacy of the problems underlined by the campaign of the FRENAPO. Whereas the economic crisis diluted its impact and overshadowed its success, the FRENAPO accomplished a remarkable campaign. Not only was this march an efficient protest against poverty, it was also successful in mobilizing various sectors of the Argentine society.[16] The public consensus stimulated by the campaign was considered one of the most impressive mobilizations of laborers by unions in Argentina (Paredes 2008). As a basic actor of the FRENAPO, the CTA succeeded in merging distinct groups with a collective claim against poverty and unemployment.

PIQUETEROS AND LABOR UNIONS

Although the CTA had relationships with some of the *piquetero* organizations before and during the FRENAPO campaign, the alliance intensified after the 2001 economic crisis ("Ajuste pasado por agua," *Pagina/12 webonline*, July 20, 2001; "La protesta se hizo sentir en todo el pais," *Clarín webonline*, May 30, 2002, accessed on April 28, 2009; "La Protesta Opositora fue masivo," *Clarin*, July 12, 1997).[17] In particular, the alliance of the CTA with *piqueteros* was important, as protest by these unemployed workers was becoming the major source of conflict in Argentina.[18] Since the CTA sought to create a national movement and to unite the whole working class, it recruited some *piquetero* groups. In 1998, the CTA supported the establishment of one of the biggest *piquetero* groups, the FTV.[19] Until 2003, they waged campaigns and were successful in the cooperation of labor unions and territorial organizations. Unemployed workers and *piquetero* organizations have been defined as territorial, because they have emphasized the needs of the community, and have created organizations at the level of *barrios* (neighborhoods). The new slogan of the CTA "new factory is neighborhood" underlined the importance given to territorial issues. The movement supported the protests of FTV, and the Clasist and Combative Current (CCC), another *piquetero*-union alliance that emerged in Northern Argentina. They asked for food, work, health, and education by blocking the highways for days ("En la calle codo a codo," *Página/12 webonline,* January 29, 2002, accessed on April 29, 2009; "Una plaza muy dura con gremios y piqueteros," *Pagina/12 webonline,* March 21, 2001, accessed on April 19, 2009; "Levantaron el piquete en la Matanza," *Pagina/12 webonline,* November 5, 2000, accessed on April 19, 2009). The FTV interpreted its being part of the CTA as a unique opportunity, by which they could construct a national movement, unite the individual strength of territorial and union organizations, and broaden their vision (Rauber 2000: 93–96, 106–117). The alliance was beyond identifying common requests: the CTA and the FTV saw it as a process of building a common political movement (Massetti 2004: 77–78). At the 2002 National Congress of the CTA, the project of building a new political and social movement was discussed and proposed (CTA 2002a). It was interpreted as a project of building a political party similar to the PT of Brazil ("La CTA sesiona la busca del movimiento politico," *Pagina/12 webonline,* December 13, 2002; "Construyendo una esparanza," *Pagina/12 webonline,* December 14, 2002, accessed on April 19, 2009).[20] Nevertheless, when Nestor Kirchner was elected president, plans for a political opening up changed in the CTA. The neo-developmentalist and labor-friendly policies of the government of the Peronist Kirchner were different from the Menem and *Alianza* governments, which devalued the CTA project of constructing a workers' party (Armelino 2005: 307–308). In this sense, the government extended the poverty alleviation program, the Plan of Households.[21]

The return of the Peronist hegemony gradually demobilized social protests and opposition. In that sense, the government intended to "integrate, co-opt, discipline, or isolate" (Svampa and Pereyra 2003: 212) *piquetero* groups by successfully integrating some groups and isolating opponents. The FTV immediately allied with the government. The leader of the FTV was appointed as the Undersecretary of Land for Social Habitat and since that time the FTV base marched in order to advocate the policies of the government. The labor union base of the CTA was also divided on taking a position in the government.[22] Even if the dominant tendency had been to preserve autonomy, the CTA did not come to a firmly agreed upon conclusion.[23] On the other hand, there is some consensus that the open support of the FTV for the government has been a mistake. The government by providing material and political incentives co-opted the FTV leadership.[24] Today, the leadership of the FTV defines the origin of the conflict with the CTA as a political disagreement on the government and the organizational asymmetry between labor unions and territorial organizations.[25] Despite different organizational logics and the articulation of demands, territorial organizations and labor unions cooperated rather well for five to six years. The question is, then, why the alliance broke after 2003. A number of hypotheses can shed light on the fragmentation of the unity, hence the stagnation of SMU.

The suggestion of the government to the *piqueteros* revealed the contingency of the alliance between different working class segments and an under-lying conflict of interests: the dependency of *piqueteros* on external economic assistance undermined the principle of autonomy that was a fundamental principle in the foundation of the CTA. Hence, this change stimulated questions as to whether the political and organizational independence of the organizations of unemployed workers was sustainable while they were economically dependent and fragile. In the early 1990s, the founders of the CTA declared that their objective was to construct a "political-unionist current that would bring together and orient those who were opposed to the existing model" ("Un lugar bajo el sol," *Pagina/12*, September 27, 1992). What appears after 2003–2004 was the contingency of the once solid alliance that was formed in a context of recession, crisis, and growing social unrest. The alliance was built on the condition that it functioned as an opposition to the government. However, it was weakened after the emergence of a new political authority that had appeared as a nationalist, neo-developmentalist, and true Peronist ally to some segments of the CTA. Even if the CTA had agreed on the possibility of building a new worker's party in the 2002 congress—inspired by the success of PT in Brazil—the return of the Peronist Party with a *pro-labor* face weakened this project. The restoration of the alliance between the Peronist Party and the CGT narrowed the chances of the CTA to obtain full legal rights that would have threatened the influence of the CGT. The question is then how the new Peronist government blocked the autonomous political action of the CTA and divided its integrity by revealing the limits of the alliance of different working class segments. The analysis reveals the fragility of economically dependent movements in front of co-opting appeals of populist government. As one leader of the CTA noted, not only did the government change, but also the context. The proposal of the CTA and the strategy for waging resistance to a common opponent in a hostile political-economic environment were relatively successful and it was easier to support a common front. But while the economy was recovering and unemployment decreasing,[26] the CTA had to develop new strategies and to re-structure its alliance with territorial organizations. In this new context, legal obstacles to organizing the private and the informal sector have appeared to be the most urgent problems.[27] In short, on the one hand, the CTA has expanded its base, has taken positive steps to advance democratic participation,[28] and has developed national-level projects to call attention to the problems beyond formal workers' concerns.[29] On the other hand, it has been challenged by political fragmentation in territorial organizations composed of unemployed workers. Hence, the CTA is confronted with the challenge to unite the working class. In the next section, I will focus on the problems that the CTA faces in its attempts to organize formal sector workers, to expand its base, and to strengthen its legal and organizational structure.

LEGAL CHALLENGES AND THE PERSISTENT WEAKNESS OF THE CTA IN ORGANIZING NEW SECTORS

The existing legal structure is a serious obstacle to CTA's expansion and its project of "organizing the unorganized". Argentine governments have ignored the ILO Convention 86 that regulates the rights of workers to organize. Thus, at present in Argentina, due to Law 23.551, only one union, which represents many members, is allowed to function in each sphere of economic activity. Accordingly, new labor unions have to be recognized by the Ministry of Labor, a process that takes years. In Argentina, the current law defines two different forms of union organizations: those with simple union registration (*inscripcion gremial*) and those with state recognition as a legal entity (*personeria gremial*) (Cook 2007: 60). Currently, almost 2,000 unions exist in Argentina that are registered. Without legal entity status, unions cannot represent their members in conflicts, cannot collect affiliation fees, and employers can dismiss elected delegates of labor unions (CTA 2003).[30] The CTA, as the worker peak confederation, lacks *personeria gremial*, although its major and founding labor unions, such as ATE and CTERA, have all legal rights of a labor union. This means that it is extremely difficult for the CTA to organize new sectors and to establish unions because it cannot grant legal rights and protection to its members and delegates. Despite its relative success in organizing unemployed workers and militant public sector worker, the CTA is weak in the private sector. For that reason, when it sits at the negotiation table, the government often ignores demands of the CTA because it does not have significant power in the major service and industrial sector unions.[31]

Due to the labor codes that were established in 1943 by the then minister of labor Juan Peron, only one labor union is allowed to function in each branch of economic activity of the private sector. However, in the public sector—such as the unions of teachers and state employees—employees can be organized without any problem. In the private sector, only one union that represents more workers than the rest of the unions in its field of economic activity, has the right to declare its elected delegate immune so that the employer cannot dismiss him/her. When a delegate of the CTA is elected, the CTA cannot assure this protection, because it lacks *personeria gremial*. This prevents the CTA from increasing its membership, from establishing new unions, and therefore hinders workers from organizing without restriction ("Planteo de la OIT por la falta de libertad sindical,"*Pagina/12*, June 8, 2005, accessed on April 19, 2009; "Victor de Gennaro denunció de la falta de libertad sindical ante la OIT," *Pagina/12 webonline*, January 14, 2003, accessed on April 19, 2009; "Para Wal Mart la Constitucion Nacional es el papel higiénico," March 27, 2007, agenciacta.org.ar, accessed on April 19, 2009; "Las Empresas Disco y Molinos Violan derechos constitucionales," September 6, 2005, agenciacta.org.ar, accessed on April 19, 2009). The lack of representation in some strategic sectors, where the accumulation of capital occurs, still complicates the situation of the CTA.[32] In the 1990s, Menem's governments attempted to change labor codes and succeeded in advancing the flexibilization of the labor market and individual contracts. According to Cook, the reform process was a trade off between "individual flexibilization" and "collective resources." The CGT succeeded in protecting its organizational and collective rights. Cook argues that this shows the durability and the strength of the corporatist legacy by which unions in Argentina have managed to protect organizational and collective rights. However, the continuation of the corporatist union structure means the subordination of the CTA to a legal situation that restricts its rights as a syndicate. In that sense, the success of the CTA in maintaining its organizational rights complicates its legal situation. The juridical advisers of the CTA have underlined that even if the economic model that had supported the old legal structure had changed with neo-liberalization, the legal code has remained intact. It is no longer capable of satisfying the needs of the current situation.[33] In fact, the government has recognized the CTA as a peak confederation and has invited it to begin some decision-making processes and negotiations, such as those of the Commission of the Minimum Wage. Yet, the lack of legal entity status has prevented unionization by the CTA in the private sector. CTA leaders believe that big business, employers, and the CGT do not want the government to give CTA full legality.

The post-2003 economic recovery has triggered the stagnation of SMU in two ways in Argentina. First, the reduction of unemployment and the characteristics of newly growing sectors have forced the CTA to develop a strategy very different from that of the 1990s. While the informal and private sectors have been growing, the failure of the CTA in "organizing the unorganized"—considered one of the defining features of the SMU—has become more sensitive. Although only 12 percent of the private sector has been unionized in Argentina, CTA has not been able to increase its membership in sectors that are linked to the accumulation of capital. Impediments to unionizing activity have been maintained by a combination of forces: the interests of the business sector, the rival union CGT, and the unwillingness of the government that has prevented to foster an organization of unions without legal restrictions. The absence of the legal entity status despite its *de facto* functioning and the law on "one union per economic activity" have limited CTA's capacity to organize new sectors and enterprises. This fact shows that labor codes are very important in defining the limits of workers' organizations, which, in the case of Argentina, have also served the interests of the business sector as well as the rival CGT. The latter considers the organizational expansion of the CTA as a threat to its dominant position in Argentine unionism. Furthermore, the labor codes that used to empower Argentine unions in the past by creating centralized and financially strong unions, currently block the progress of independent unionism and its revitalization.

The axis of social protest and conflict shows a shift from *piquetero* type non-union conflicts to union-led conflicts. Since 2003, the number of union-led social conflicts has exceeded other types. In 2003, union-led conflicts were double non-union ones (Independent Social Research Consulting, cited in Etchemendy and Collier 2007: 371). Etchemendy and Collier's analysis has argued, that the recent revitalization of labor is based on the resurgence of the traditional Peronist CGT, which is a labor movement run top–down, scarcely pluralistic, and based on domination in some sectors, with few links to the informal sector or international social movements, rather than the SMU of the CTA (Etchemendy and Collier 2007: 368). The authors argue that the resurgence of the CGT instead of the CTA, in contrast to the theoretical expectations of SMU, can be explained by several factors: the tightening of the labor market in core CGT unions and the presence of a pro-labor government are obvious reasons. In addition, the long-term causes are related to the nature of neo-liberal transformations and the associational power of the CGT: in Argentina, already unionized sectors have benefited from the advantages of neo-liberal reforms and have experienced significant growth. Thus, the unions in question could revitalize and use their already existing collective bargaining practices and militancy. Finally, the CGT managed to preserve some forms of 'associational power'.[34] Etchemendy and Collier argue that thanks to these factors, the CGT affiliated unions have used militant mobilization. Hence, they have realized wage increases and numerical growth, whereas state sector employees and *piquetero* activism have been declining for the last years. The CGT achieved a reappearance of mobilization and neo-corporatist bargaining power without harming its alliance with the Peronist Kirchner government.[35] Even though Etchemendy and Collier do not focus on the emergence and stagnation of the CTA in their analysis, some of the variables that they have used can shed light on critical differences between the CTA and the CGT, and can explain the stagnation of the CTA: (1) the strengthening of the labor market that had worked as a form of structural bargaining power did not support the activities of CTA, given that the leading CTA affiliated unions are those of teachers and state employees; (2) the question of approaching or staying independent from the Kirchner government was a factor that divided the CTA and has weakened its unity; (3) because non-unionized sectors were not particularly developed, 'organizing the unorganized', as an opportunity to strengthen the CTA, has not become a viable option; (4) the associational power of the CTA has had to rely on building alliances with community organizations and informal sectors, because they lacked well-established access to the government. Hence, the CTA has been in a more disadvantageous condition in terms of associational and structural bargaining powers—as it is structurally rather weak—as well as regarding the relations with the government.

DISCUSSION AND CONCLUSION

In this concluding section, I will reconsider and assess possible challenges to SMU while comparing the Argentine SMU to other well-known cases. Beverly Silver, a critical scholar who utilizes the concept of "associational power," argues that the recent successful service sector–based new labor movements should develop their associational bargaining power,[36] because they lack both market and work place power. Her historical analysis shows that when workers in a particular sector do not have sufficient workplace or market place power, they attempt to compensate for it by relying on associational bargaining power. Silver writes "if the significance of associational bargaining power is growing, then the future trajectory of labor movements will be strongly conditioned by the broader political context of which they are a part" (Silver 2003: 173). Hence, the strength of the union, its relations with political parties and other alliances determine the power of the working class movement. When we consider the situation of the CTA, we find that it lacks market and workplace power. As noted above, legal problems and its sectoral characteristics weaken the structural power of the CTA. As Silver suggests, the CTA has to strengthen its associational power, and its political influence in parties, state, and its own organization. As the position of the CTA in front of the government and political parties is oscillating, it can be argued that building alliances with other working class segments, community-based organizations, and *piqueteros* is the backbone of its strength. Furthermore, its alliance with non-union groups and organizations reveals the CTA as an example of SMU. Interestingly, the government's success in co-opting several once independent and militant territorial organizations has weakened the associational power of the CTA.

SMU theorist Moody, in addition to his focus on essential and distinct aspects of SMU, such as union democracy and inclusion of communities, underlines that unions function as the leading partners in this relationship, and that they bring with them their organized groups and socio-economic power together with a broader political and class agenda. He adds:

> But it [trade union, AS] will be unable to do this if it neglects or bypasses the fundamental issues that affect the union's members. Necessarily, we always return to the first principle: the power the class possesses by virtue of its place at the heart of capitalist accumulation in the workplace or on-the-job. (Moody 2007: 237)

Moody's argument underlines the indispensable role of workplace power for unions. When SMUs are short in structural bargaining power, they depend on associational power that eventually forges vulnerability. The first successful experiences of South Africa and Brazil emerged in a period of late industrialization, in which SMU was based on core industrial sector workers.[37] Seidman's comparative study has shown that under particular historical conditions the combination of late authoritarian industrialization changed the production process and employment patterns. Furthermore, the social consequences of the racial inequality of an authoritarian regime, and the conflicts between business and state, produced militant working class movements in Brazil and South Africa, which reached out to neighborhood and community levels and asked for broader democratic and socio-economic justice (Seidman 1994). Accordingly, the structural change of late authoritarian industrialization, the emergence of business support for democratization, and the change in the relation between state and capital forged the political opportunity structure of the SMU in Brazil and South Africa.[38] Nevertheless, transformations of political and economic conditions have altered the later development of SMU. The political transformation was more radical in South Africa than in Brazil, hence, it stimulated a rich debate and analysis of the post-apartheid performance of the Congress of South African Trade Unions (COSATU) that indicated several problems SMUs may encounter: for example, the rise of the African National Congress (ANC) to a governing party changed the nature of the close alliance between the party and the COSATU. The alliance curbed the militancy and autonomy of the labor movement (Adler and Webster 1999, von Holdt 2002, Lier and Stokke 2006). In addition, it has been underlined that new economic conditions—such as neo-liberalism, the casualization of employment, and the fragmentation of collective bargaining—and the growing involvement of international financial institutions in the national economy left the COSATU in an ambivalent position (Barchiesi 2007: 59–65).[39] According to Barchiesi, the SMU was successful against the authoritarian and racist regime while the ANC was in opposition. Nevertheless, a similar sort of politics of resistance or union radicalism could endanger the current democratization process. The new conditions of democratization and liberalization introduced by the ANC government have limited the autonomy of the COSATU. The ambivalent situation of the COSATU has negatively affected its relation to the community organization and the rank-and-file. The deterioration of the alliance between unions and community organizations is considered an indicator of the decline of SMU. The case of South Africa shows the challenges that a successful SMU could be confronted with. For example, neo-liberal reforms change the structural bargaining power of the SMU; hence, it negatively affects its relation with the bottom at the factory and community levels. When the ANC became the ruling party while maintaining its hegemonic position in the South African society, the labor union–party alliance undermined the integrity of rank-and-file, and the leadership of the SMU limited its militancy and radical discourse. Hence, the COSATU has been confined between the demands of its base, its restraining historical alliance with the ANC, and the neo-liberal order. The recent trajectory of the South African SMU has shown that when the radical working class party of the past becomes a pro-labor governing party in power, it undermines the independence and militancy of the SMU.

The experience of the COSATU is quite illustrative in assessing the potentials and limits of SMU in neo-liberal regimes. In that sense, there are at least two critical similarities between the cases of South Africa and Argentina. The stagnation of SMU in South Africa indicates the very critical role of neo-liberal reforms and the economic context as factors that may undermine the power of laborers. Second, when the ANC became the ruling party, it curbed the autonomy and the militancy of the SMU. In Argentina, even if initially grievances caused by neo-liberal reforms led to the emergence of the SMU, the persistence of the same economic conditions later on prevented the group from moving forward. Thanks to its historical image as a populist–working class party, the Peronist Party took advantage of the leverage with the labor force in order to control its militancy.

As analyzed earlier, the post-crisis period was characterized by intense social protests, mobilizations, and conflicts, in which the CTA actively participated. However, after the election of Nestor Kirchner in 2003 and the consolidation of his political authority, social unrest softened. Unemployment and the number of people living under the poverty line gradually declined. The Program for Unemployed Household Heads, implemented by the government since 2002 co-opted some *piquetero* groups, including the CTA's ally FTV. The CTA has had a two-way relationship with poverty and unemployment. On the one hand, it works hard to resist poverty and unemployment and organizes campaigns to support unemployed workers and poor people. On the other hand, the capacity and preferences of the CTA are influenced by conditions of poverty and unemployment. The momentum of social unrest caused by the devastating consequences of neo-liberal transformations forced the CTA to develop measures and strategies to fight against them. The CTA learned how to mobilize unemployed workers against poverty and unemployment, and how to channel their demands and expectations. However, since 2003, the CTA has been confronted with a new economic and political situation, in which it was caught unprepared. Although these new conditions have pushed the CTA to change its strategy, a combination of global market forces and local political dynamics has hindered this possibility. The constraining effects of neo-liberal labor market conditions—linked to global forces—are further complicated by Argentina's peculiar history. The hegemony of Peronism and its strong ties with the working class confine not only the autonomous political action of SMU but also its renovation and expansion. The cases of the PT in Brazil and the ANC in South Africa indicate that pro-labor governments are likely to limit the autonomy and militancy of labor movements. Finally, the attempt of the Kirchner governments to give direct access to *piqueteros* and other community based organizations has played a role in cutting the link between the CTA and its allies. This is a critical point that can be looked at through the lenses of the neo-populism debate. In addition to that, a combination of the weak market place and workplace powers of the CTA-affiliated unions has negatively affected its associational power. The CTA has not been able to satisfactorily realize the defined and preferred objectives, such as wage increases, legal changes, retirement benefits, and the like. This in turn negatively affected the other factors distinctive of SMU, including the building of broader alliances, union democracy, and the claiming of a broader working class agenda, factors that have been vulnerable to structural economic and political constrains. Unless democratizing and innovative efforts of SMU are translated into associational and structural power, and thus economic and political power, SMU is likely to be faced by serious challenges and might fall short of bringing about labor revitalization.

NOTES

1. Daniel James attributes Peron's success in the working class to a rhetoric of citizenry, self-consciousness, and confidence in the process of working class incorporation into the system (James 2005).
2. In 1945, there were 529,000 union members whereas membership jumped to 2,257,000 in 1954 (McGuire 1997: 57).
3. See McGuire (1997). This analysis argues that Peron continued to prevent the routinization of the party after his exile. The lack of an efficient party structure complicated the democratic transition and civic participation in Argentina.
4. According to a CTA delegate interviewed by the author on February 6, 2008, Buenos Aires.
5. The proportion of unionist deputies came to 13.8 percent from 1983 to 1985. It dropped to 3.9 percent from 1993 to 1995 ("Se vienen los empresarios," *La Prensa*, December 14, 1994: 4).
6. In general, the CGT executive committee members have been steadily re-elected, including many secretary-generals who had appointments for more than two decades. The domination of a single list and the undemocratic delegate system did not allow radical changes in the structure of the CGT unions. Single lists run for more than 70 percent at the elections held in 1996 ("En los grandes sindicatos la reelección es una costumbre," *La Nación* January 29, 1997).
7. ATE and CTERA were also the two unions that had the highest proportion of conflicts in opposition to the government. They had a 21.1 percent and a 18.4 percent share of conflicts respectively from 1985 to 1991 ("La UOM protesta más con Menem," *La Nacion*, February 2, 1992: 4).
8. From 1968 to 1973, a wing of leftist Peronist unions that was called *CGT de los Argentinos* existed. In 1991, after the first meeting of a group of unionists, which were soon going to establish the CTA, this group declared that "we have just re-founded the *CGT de los Argentinos*" ("Hacia la otra verada," *Pagina/12*, April 28, 1991: 6–7). A unionist of the CTA also said that what they aimed at reviving was the unionism of the *CGT de los Argentinos*. (Personal interview by the author, February 6, 2008, Buenos Aires)
9. One of the voters of the CTA, the Villa Constitution branch of the UOM, was well known by its Marxist leadership since the 1970s ("Acusa a Piccinini el general Lopez Aufranc," *Clarín*, April 23, 1991: 2).

10. In 1997, the government recognized the CTA as the second peak federation ("El gobierno reconoció a la CTA," *Clarín*, May 28, 1997: 15). Today, the CTA has got more than 1,200,000 affiliates.

11. According to a personal interview with a CTA administrator on February 12, 2008, Buenos Aires.

12. In 1994, another dissident group of the CGT formed the Movement of Argentine Workers (MTA) ("Crearon otra central sindical," *Clarin*, February 2, 1994: 3). Yet, the MTA never separated from the CGT and did not go through a democratic re-structuring as the CTA did. Its opposition remained limited to protestations against the Menem government. The movement asked for a return to the original Peronism. When the leader of the MTA was elected president of the CGT in 2005, MTA terminated its mission and CGT united again ("Hugo Moyano llegó a la cima de la CGT," *Pagina/12 webonline*, July 7, 2005, accessed on April 19, 2009).

13. According to a personal interview with the secretary general of the AMMAR, Elena Reynaga, on February 18, 2008, Buenos Aires.

14. According to a personal interview with the secretary general of the ANTA, Mario Barrios, on April 7, 2008, Buenos Aires.

15. In May 2002, unemployment and under-employment levels reached respectively 21.5 percent and 14.9 percent of the economically active population. (See www.indec.org.ar, accessed on April 19, 2009.) Moreover, people living under the poverty line were estimated at 49.7 percent of the country's population in May 2002 (Rapaport 2005: 885).

16. Despite the popular support behind the proposal of the FRENAPO, the government implemented its own version of social assistance that is called the Heads of Family Plan. It is based on subsidizing unemployed households with 150 pesos in exchange for some activities in public services.

17. For an analysis of the CTA campaigns, see Armelino (2004).

18. According to the data of *Centro Estudio Nueva Mayoria*, the number of road blockings exceeded labor conflicts in 1997 (140 and 120 respectively), whereas the latter amounted to 949 in 1988: "Los cortes de rutas desplazaron a los paros," www.nuevamayoria.com, December 22, 2000, accessed on April 28, 2009.

19. The territorial group that was the nucleus of the FTV emerged in La Matanza district of Buenos Aires. It had substantial experience in organizing neighborhoods in struggles for land, housing, and public services since the late 1980s. They began to have contacts with the CTA in 1996 and agreed on uniting their potentials and forces by establishing the FTV (Svampa and Pereyra 2003: 41–42). It was expected to have about 90,000 affiliates in 2003 (Calvo 2008: 66).

20. The leader of the FTV even declared that Argentina had to build its own PT ("Decidimos construir nuestro PT," *Pagina/12 webonline*, April 8, 2003, accessed on April 19, 2009).

21. The number of beneficiaries attained more than two million in 2003 (Modolo 2005: 148).

22. The fragmentation has been displayed during the recent agrarian strike that blew up in April 2008. A coalition of big and small rural producers protested against the decision of the government to increase export taxes by blocking highways for weeks. In this crisis, while the FTV fiercely supported the national government, the founding president of the central supported the exclusion, whereas the then president supported the measures of the government ("Las heridas abiertas en la CTA," *Pagina/12 webonline*, April 29, 2008, accessed on April 19, 2009; "Las cicatrices de la CTA," *Pagina/12 webconline*, July 7, 2008, accessed on April 19, 2009).

23. According to Svampa, the CTA administration is currently more divided than at the beginning of 2000, in particular, on the question of supporting or not supporting the Kirchner government (Svampa 2007). Godio even writes that although the majority of the executive committee of the CTA is identified with the government, they do not publicly declare this, due to the leftist opposition (Godio 2006: 285–286).

24. In my interviews, several members of the executive committee of the CTA expressed their opinion that the FTV's position regarding the government is not shared by the CTA. Whereas some unionists are openly critical of the FTV, others say they still share the common project, even if the road to get there may vary. Yet, the leader of the FTV was not nominated in the 2006 election into the executive committee, which he used to hold during the prior period ("La CTA deja afuera D'elia," *Pagina/12 webonline*, September 22, 2006, accessed on April 19, 2009).

25. According to the secretary general of the FTV, Luis D'Elia, personal interview at February 27, 2008, Buenos Aires.

26. In May 2002, six months after the economic crisis, the unemployment rate reached the level of 21.5 percent, whereas it dropped to 7.5 percent in the last quarter of 2002, www.mecon.gov.ar, accessed on April 19, 2009.

27. According to CTA executive committee members, personal interview, Buenos Aires, on February 2, 2008.

28. More than 350,000 people voted in the elections of 2003, when the CTA had about 873,000 affiliates. In the elections of November 2007, more than 256,000 affiliates voted, whereas the confederation had about 1,127,000 affiliates. In 2007, a total of 14,571 persons in executive positions were elected by direct voting measures (CTA 2007: 6, 8).

29. In 2007–08, CTA began to discuss and to organize two projects at the national level: *Paritaria social*—to open up a debate on the re-distribution of wealth—and *constituyente social*—to create a new national project. The CTA still develops organizations in provinces with a broad dialogue and representatives of the popular camp that pursue this aim.

30. In Argentina, there are 1,792 unions without *personeria gremial* and 1,357 with *incripcion gremial* (CTA 2004: 22).

31. One interviewee said that the CTA has achieved a predominant representation in illegal and informal sectors in addition to the public sector. He added that "our principal objective is to organize the private sector, in which no one is dominant. In the Argentine private sector, only 12 percent have an elected union delegate." (Personal interview on February 12, 2008, Buenos Aires)

32. According to CTA executive committee members (personal interviews on February 12, 2008 and March 19, 2008, Buenos Aires).

33. According to a personal interview on March 19, 2008, Buenos Aires.

34. Eric Olin Wright developed the concepts of associational and structural bargaining power of the working class. Wright defined associational power of trade unions as the type based on the collective organization of workers, such as trade unions or political parties. Structural power is based on their place in the economic system, such as "tight labor markets or from the strategic location of a particular group of workers within a key industrial sector" (Wright 2000: 962). Beverly Silver has characterized the first form of structural power "marketplace bargaining power" including dimensions of tight labor market, low unemployment, skilled labor, and the second work place bargaining power that refers to the strategic location of a sector. (Silver 2003: 173)

35. Etchemendy and Collier have defined the current condition as "segmented neo-corporatism", meaning that it has covered and represented working class,

"post-reform unionism that emerged in Argentina as a particular kind of 'neo-corporatist' actor, which is neither demobilized, decentralized, nor on the defensive, as one might expect given the sweeping market reforms, nor populist according to the pre-reform model. Rather it is activated and quite centralized, achieving wage and institutional gains." (Etchemendy and Collier 2007: 382)

36. She writes "alliances with (and resources) from groups and strata in the community at large" to define associational power (Silver 2003: 173).

37. According to B. Silver (2003: 54–60), one of the protagonists of the SMU in Brazil and South Africa, the automobile sector workers, led militant strike waves counting on their strong work place bargaining power.

38. Social movement and collective action theories inspire social movement unionism theory. Political process theory, developed by various studies of Sydney Tarrow, Doug McAdam, and Charles Tilly, is rather influential. Political process theory argues that the emergence, the development, or the decline of collective actions—including social movements—are determined by three broad sets of factors: political opportunities, mobilizing structures, and framing processes (McAdam, McCarthy, and Zald 1996). Political opportunities and organizations can only function with shared meanings and definitions. Hence, social movement is defined "as a sustained campaign of claim making, using repeated performances that advertise the claim, based on organizations, networks, traditions, and solidarities that sustain these activities" (Tilly and Tarrow 2007: 8).

39. Barchiesi notes that "the public-sector unions, which in 1994 provided only 17% of COSATU members, soared to almost 41% in 2003" (Barchiesi 2007: 50).

BIBLIOGRAPHY

Adler, Glenn and Eddie Webster (1999) "The Labor Movement, Radical Reform and the Transition to Democracy in South Africa," in Ronaldo Munck and Peter Waterman (eds) *Labor Worldwide in the Era of Globalization: Alternative Union Models in the New World Order*, 133–157. London: MacMillan Press.

Armelino, Martin (2005) "Resistencia sin Integración," in Federico L. Schuster, Franciso S. Naishtat, and Gabriel Nardacchione (eds) *Tomar la Palabra: estudios sobre protesta social y acción colectiva en la Argentina contemporánea*, 275–311. Buenos Aires: Prometeo Libros.

Armelino, Martin (2004) "La Protesta Social en los anos 1990: El Caso de la CTA," *Estudios del Trabajo* 28: 3–27.

Barchiesi, Franco (2007) "Privatization and the Historical Trajectory of 'Social Movement Unionism': A Case Study of Municipal Workers in Johannesburg, South Africa," *International Labor and Working-Class History* 71 (1): 50–69.

Calvo, Dolores (2008) *Exclusión y Política: Estudio Sociológico sobre la Experiencia de la FTV (1998–2002)*. Buenos Aires: Mino and Davila.

Carri, Roberto (1967) *Sindicatos y Poder en la Argentina*. Buenos Aires: Sudestada.

Cook, Maria Lorena (2007) *The Politics of Labor Reform in Latin America: Between Flexibility and Rights*. University Park: Pennsylvania State University Press.

CTA (2007) *Memoria 2006–2007 en Palabras e Imágenes*. Buenos Aires: CTA.

CTA (2004) *La Lucha por la Libertad y Democracia Sindical, Denuncia Presentada abte la Comision Interamercana de Derechos Humanos de la OEA*. Buenos Aires: CTA .

CTA (2003) *Libertad Sindical y Criminalizacion de Protesta Social*, CTA Secretaria de Relaciones Internacionales, April. Buenos Aires: CTA.

CTA (2002a) *Construir la Unidad del Campo Popular, Hacia el IV Congreso de la CTA*, 9–10 December, 2002. Buenos Aires: CTA.

CTA (2002b), *Suplemente Especial Todo el Año 2001 fue Lucha*. Buenos Aires, CTA.

CTA (2000) *La Marcha Grande por el Trabajo, Material de Prensa*. Buenos Aires: CTA.

Etchemendy, Sebastian and Ruth Berins Collier (2007) "Down but not Out: Union Resurgence and Segmented Neocorporatism in Argentina 2003–2007," *Politics and Society* 35 (3): 363–401.

FRENAPO (2002) "Apuntes para el debate político del frente nacional contra la pobreza," *Presentación de Claudio Lozano en la Asamblea Nacional el 2 de Marzo 2002*. Buenos Aires: FRENAPO.

FRENAPO (2001) *Fundamentos, Propuestas y Estretegia del Movimiento por la Consulta Popular*. Buenos Aires: FRENAPO.

Godio, Julio (2006) *El Tiempo de Kirchner*. Buenos Aires: Letra Grifa.

James, Daniel (2005) *Resistencia e Integracion: El Peronismo y la Clase Trabajadora Argentina 1946–1976*. Buenos Aires: Siglo XXI.

Levitsky, Steven (2005) "Crisis and Innovation," in Steven Levitsky and María Victoria Murillo (eds) *Argentine Democracy: The Politics of Institutional Weakness*, 181–206. University Park: Pennsylvania State University Press.

Lier, David Christoffer and Kristian Stokke (2006) "Maximum Working Class Unity? Challenges to Local Social Movement Unionism in Cape Town," *Antipode* 38 (4): 802–824.

Manzetti, Luigi (1993) *Institutions, Parties and Coalitions in Argentine Politics*. Pittsburgh: University of Pittsburgh Press.

Massetti, Astor (2004) *Piqueteros: Protesta Social e Identidad Colectiva*. Buenos Aires: De las Ciencias.

McAdam, Dough, John D. McCarthy, and Mayer N. Zald (1996) "Introduction: Opportunities, Mobilizing Structures, and Framing Processes," in Doug McAdam, John D. McCarthy, and Mayer N. Zald (eds) *Comparative Perspectives on Social Movements: Political Opportunities, Mobilizing Structures and Cultural Framings*, 1–20. Cambridge: Cambridge University Press.

McGuire, James (1997) *Peronism without Peron: Unions, Parties and Democracy in Argentina*. Stanford: Stanford University Press.

Modolo, Cristian (2005) "Analisis del Caso Plan Jefes y Jefas de Hogar," in Mario Krieger (ed.) *Los Desafios de Transformar el Estado y la Gestion Publica Argentina*, 143–156. Fundacion Union.

Moody, Kim (2007) *US Labor in Trouble and Transition: The Failure of Reform Above, the Promise of Revival from Below*. London: Verso.

Paredes, Carmelo (2008) "La CTA Busca una Salida," *Revista Zoom*, July 30, 2008, www.revista-zoom.com.ar, accessed on April 28, 2009.

Ranis, Peter (1994) *Class, Democracy and Labor in Contemporary Argentina*. New Brunswick: Transaction Publishers.

Rapaport, Mario (2005) *Historia Económica, Política y Social de la Argentina (1880–2003)*. Buenos Aires: Emece.

Rauber, Isabel (2000) *Tiempos de Herejias*. Buenos Aires: CTA.

Seidman, Gay W. (1994) *Manufacturing Militancy, Workers' Movement in Brazil and South Africa, 1970–1985*. Berkeley: University of California Press.

Silver, Beverly J. (2003) *Forces of Labor: Workers' Movements and Globalization since 1870*. Cambridge, UK: Cambridge University Press.

Svampa, Maristella (2007) "Los avatares del sindicalismo argentino," *Le Monde Diplomatique*, January, Argentine edition. http://maristellasvampa.net/archivos/period17.pdf, accessed on April 28, 2009.

Svampa, Maristella and Sebastian Pereyra (2003) *Entre la Ruta y El Barrio: La Experiencia de las Organizacions Piqueteras*. Buenos Aires: Editorial Libros.

Tilly, Charles and Sydney Tarrow (2007) *Contentious Politics*. Boulder: Paradigm Publishers.

von Holdt, Karl (2002) "Social Movement Unionism: The Case of South Africa," *Work Employment Society* 16 (2): 283–304.

Wright, Eric Olin (2000) "Working Class Power, Capitalist Class Interests, and Class Compromise," *American Journal of Sociology* 105 (4): 957–1002.

Part IV
Regional Case Studies on Globalization and Social Inequality

8 *Communities*
A Lever for Mitigating Social Tensions in Urban China

Amandine Monteil

INTRODUCTION

Thirty years of economic reforms and opening-up resulted in a rise of global living standards in China, but also in a steady increase of social inequalities. Since 2000, the Gini coefficient has remained above the 0.4 *warning line* that is internationally considered as indicating a strong risk of social unrest.[1] The government has now identified development misbalances between coastal and inland provinces, and between urban and rural areas, as a pressing challenge to address. Since 2003, a new generation of leaders has demonstrated a strong commitment to reduce the gap between urban and rural *per capita* incomes, which constantly rose from 1985, and exceeded the ratio of three to one (UNDP China 2008: 14).

Intra-cities inequalities also exploded during the last decade as urbanization accelerated.[2] Since the 1990s, worsened social inequalities in the cities resulted in the new phenomenon of urban poverty, closely linked to job situations. Although the global economic crisis is presented since the end of 2008 as a major factor generating a rise of unemployment—in particular among the over 20 million rural migrants returning to the countryside because of the difficulties of export-oriented factories, tensions on the urban job markets are deeply rooted in the last decades of reforms. Public-sector restructuring, rural–urban migrations, and demographic growth are the three most crucial factors shaping the emerging urban labor market.

According to the National Commission in charge of Development and Reform during the 11th five-year plan (2005–10), China should annually create 20 million new jobs (half of which in urban centers) for newcomers in the job market, and should re-integrate four million unemployed workers and peasants left without land (Research Institute of State Development and Reform Committee 2007). With an annual growth rate of 8 to 9 percent, China can barely create 12 million jobs each year, which means that 12 million jobless people are left outside the job market each year. Furthermore, the plan does not take into consideration the estimated 120 million rural migrants, who are largely excluded from the formal job market.

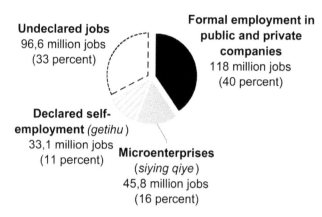

Figure 8.1   Urban Employment Structure in 2007.
Source: China Statistical Yearbook 2008.

Under these conditions, more and more workers are forced to earn their living in the informal sector. Nevertheless, this trend neither results in a strong increase of poverty (slums, begging, and homeless population), nor in urban violence or unrest.

In the twenty-first century, the Chinese government has become more and more aware of the threat to social stability that might stem from the expansion of an urban underclass of working poor. New slogans such as *building an harmonious society* (*hexie shehui jianshe*) or a *human-centered* approach (*yi ren wei ben*) have motivated the commitment of the Party-State to a more balanced vision of development, less centered solely on GDP growth and more focused on dealing with social issues. In urban centers, two sets of measures attempt to cope with the problems of the so-called vulnerable groups (*ruoshi qunti*): the revival of urban *residents' committees* (*chengshi jumin weiyuanhui*) within a larger project of *community building* (*shequ jianshe*), and the enacting of a panel of specific measures targeting jobless urbanites, put in motion by grassroots institutions.

This chapter questions the role of the new generation of residents' committees, commonly referred to as community (*shequ*), in the management of urban poverty and social inequalities. I argue that, based on an ambiguous status halfway between local administration and grassroots neighborhood association, residents' committees are becoming the main tool for implementing new methods of governance specially targeting vulnerable groups. I will first underline the close relationship between the deepening of social inequalities and the rise of informal employment, and the subsequent changed attitudes of the government towards the latter. The second part of the chapter addresses the role of urban residents' committees in the management of new forms of urban poverty linked to the rise of informal labor.

INFORMAL EMPLOYMENT: STABILIZING AN INCREASINGLY UNEQUAL SOCIETY

Economic Reforms and the Rise of Urban Inequality

Whereas the World Bank praises China as an example of rural poverty reduction, having lifted more than 500 million people out of poverty between 1981 and 2004, the country faces a new phenomenon of urban poverty. Its scope is difficult to measure, due to multiple reference lines: around 35 percent of the population would make a living on less than US$ 2 a day, and 15 percent (i.e., 130 million) on less than US$ 1.25 a day.[3] Estimates based on the official poverty line are much lower: even after an increase of this line, from 785 yuan/year (US$ 115) to 1,067 yuan/year (US$ 156), the number of poor reaches *only* 43.2 millions (3 percent of the population).[4] Chinese poverty estimates are also made difficult by strong gaps in living standards on the national territory: rural vs. urban, coastal vs. inland, and big cities vs. small towns. This situation can be translated into a variety of poverty standards pragmatically set by local authorities to define entitlements to social assistance (Hussain 2003: 5, Khan and Riskin 2001: 184). For example, the urban *Minimum Livelihood Guarantee* (*zuidi shenghuo baozhang*, commonly referred to as *dibao*) is set up at 350 yuan/month/person (US$ 51) in Beijing, 210 yuan (US$ 30) in Chengdu downtown, and 160 yuan (US$ 23) in Chengdu suburb.[5] In Chengdu, among a population of six million urbanites, this program benefits 150,000 persons (i.e., 2.5 percent of the total urban population).[6]

In three reform decades, Chinese cities have not only witnessed a sharp quantitative increase in poverty, but also a qualitative change in the nature of urban challenges. Whereas in pre-reform China the poverty incidence was mainly limited to the *Three-No* (*sanwu*: no work capacity, no source of income, and no family support), the new poverty phenomena largely impact people who have both the capacity and the willingness to work. The emergence of the label *vulnerable groups*, in the 2002 annual work report of the government, acknowledges the new trend. This unclear term is generally used to cover a variety of precarious situations, such as those faced by former employees of the public sector, rural migrants, peasants deprived from land, and other urban dwellers whose social characteristics (age, gender, job experience, education, and residential status) hinder their integration into the formal job market. As Wang Feng mentions, Chinese society is not only characterized by an emerging polarization of the rich and the poor, but also by structured inequalities that are based on individual group membership (Wang 2008: 9).

During the years of reform, the first group that had been officially identified as a legitimate target for social assistance was the one of *xiagang* (literally *down from the job*). Whereas the first steps of economic reforms had left the public employment system relatively untouched, the late 1990s witnessed a steady wave of job destruction in urban collectively owned and state-owned enterprises. Laid-off workers not only lost their salary but also the global social package once provided by their work unit (*danwei*), such as housing, schooling, medical protection, etc. To deal with this massive challenge, the status of *xiagang* was created, indicating that although they were no longer required to perform any work and did not receive any wages, the relationship linking workers to their *danwei* was not formally terminated. This situation has given laid-off workers the right to benefit from a range of measures: such as the creation of a monthly minimum allowance (*shenghuo fei*), the redefining of social security rights, and the access to free training and employment services. However, this set of social measures was only available to former workers of the biggest *danwei*, whose financial situation enabled them to set up *re-employment centers* (*zai jiuye zhongxin*). In a large number of smaller state-owned enterprises or collectives, as well as in bankrupted companies, less (or no) support was available to the workers (Solinger 2001: 684). Moreover, the formal status of *xiagang* was only temporary: as soon as a worker was *re-employed* (*zai jiuye*), either in a company or by himself (*zimou zhiye*), or at the end of a three-year period, the association of the worker and his former *danwei* came to an end. A decade after the *xiagang* wave, and in spite of the closure of most re-employment centers in 2005, the term is still deeply rooted in popular discourse and official rhetoric. But it took a looser definition, which now encompasses all former workers of the public sector who lost their jobs because of the economic reform process—whether or not they benefited from special compensation policies—and who became thus identified by the government and the public as legitimate recipients of social support.

At the same time, another social group emerged as a target of political concern. Rural migrants (*nong mingong*), whose flow steadily rose in the 1990s as a response to the need of laborers in the quickly growing cities, are still viewed as a temporary *floating* (*liudong*) population. Under the residential registration system (known as the *hukou* system), social rights are a consequence of the membership in an administratively defined local community and are reduced outside this territory. Although this system has evolved since the 1980s, a number of discriminations remained in the field of employment and social protection. For that reason, analysts consider that the dual system created under Mao, when urban and rural society were governed separately, gave birth in recent years to a dual urban labor market (*eryuan laodongli shichang*) and a dual social structure (*eryuan shehui jiegou*) (Cai 1998, Lu 1995). An estimated group of 200 million rural residents (one fourth of the total rural population) works outside of the agricultural sector, 80 percent of them outside their native district. Chinese cities counted around 120 million rural migrants in 2005 (UNDP China 2008: 95). Migrants should make up 40–50 percent of the total urban population in 2025 according to UNDP estimates (*The Financial Times* 2008). If some Chinese cities are depicted as fairly egalitarian compared to other Asian cities (UN-HABITAT 2008: 74),[7] this image is largely caused by the exclusion of rural migrants in the calculation of Gini indices, not only because bearers of non-local *hukou* have not been taken into account in most official reports on the urban situation, but also because they have been forced into lower informal jobs that are difficult to capture by statistics. However, recent evidence shows that even without an elimination of statutory *hukou*-based differences, some migrants have managed to integrate into the urban society, whereas inequality and poverty among urban *hukou* holders keeps worsening. Therefore, *hukou* can no longer be considered as the sole criterion to explain the rise in urban social inequalities.

Rising urbanization and industrialization are responsible for the creation of a new social group of *rural residents having lost land (shidi nongmin)*. The spatial extension of cities, the development of the traffic infrastructure, the building of dams, or the settlement of industrial development zones, all require the conversion of farmland to non-agricultural use. As a consequence of the Chinese collective land tenure system, this conversion is carried out by the state through land requisitioning. It is estimated that as many as 40 to 50 million farmers completely or partially lost land since 1987 (UNDP China 2008: 123). This process raises a number of social issues, as land is considered the main social security net for peasants in a weak rural social protection system. Deprived of their share in the collective ownership of land, *shidi nongmin* are often not fully integrated into the urban social welfare system (Lou 2007). According to the *Land Management Law (Tudi guanli fa)*, land requisition has to include financial compensations and resettlement subsidies. Depending on localities, *shidi nongmin* can get cash payment, sometimes assorted with a social protection package and job services. In some cases, former owners receive a local urban *hukou*. The inequality of compensations across places (partly worsened by corrupted local staff), added to the fact that *shidi nongmin* face an administrative decision without obtaining another option, has been nurturing social tensions. Furthermore, in numerous cases, low employability (due to age, job experience, or education), sometimes combined with inadequate policy implementation, forces *shidi nongmin* into the ranks of informal workers.

Finally, a fourth group considered being *vulnerable* is made up of holders of local urban *hukou* who had never enjoyed a status as workers in a *danwei*, either because they just worked as contract staff or because they were too young to have ever worked under the *danwei* system. They are referred to by Chinese social scientists as urban *outsiders (tizhiwai)*. In the first years of the reform, this group was mainly made up of millions of *young urban intellectuals (zhiqing)* who came back from the countryside where they had been sent in order to go through *re-education* during the Cultural Revolution. Back to the cities, most of them found no jobs in work units, and had to rely on self-employment in order to survive. Currently, more and more young people enter informal employment, due to a lack of suitable positions in the formal sector. Because of demographic growth, the urban formal job market is supposed to integrate each year 10 million new young urban workers, with a large and growing part of university graduates, whose number increased threefold from 2001 to 2006 (*Zhongguo Jingji Zhoukan* 2006).[8]

The Discovery of Informal Employment

In a country with weak formal social security networks, tensions in the formal job market result more from the expansion of the informal sector than from a worsening of inactivity. Informal activities are widespread, from street vending and petty jobs in the tertiary sector to household or construction work. According to official estimates, undeclared activities account for almost one third of all urban jobs.[9] If registered individual activities and even private micro-enterprises are added to this number, more than half of the urban jobs can be considered as informal.[10]

Migrant workers would still increase this estimation, as a large number of migrants are excluded from the formal job market. In 2008, migrants would have accounted for 46.5 percent of the urban workforce (Du 2009: 11).

The rise of informal employment is closely linked to the reform of the employment system and the emergence of a labor market. Since the early 1990s, undeclared activities have been the main motor of job expansion in urban areas, as an outcome of job destructions in the public sector, whose

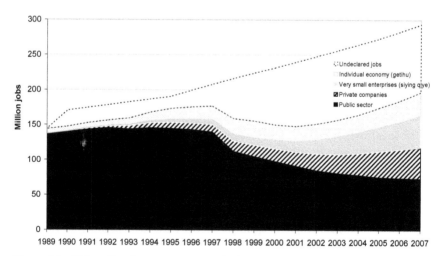

Figure 8.2   Urban Employment Structural Changes (1989–2007).
Source: China Statistical Yearbooks 2006 and 2008.

weight decreased from 82 percent to 26 percent of the urban workforce from 1990 to 2006. Over the same period, *registered self-employment* (*getihu*), gathering a variety of informal to semiformal job patterns, has been the second major channel for job creation. Private enterprises only started to have a significant influence on the widening of the labor market in the last years of this period.

The data given above highlight not only the wide spread of informal employment and its growing influence on the urban job market, but also the relative inability of traditional statistical tools to capture a large part of economic activities. In 2000, the government began to show a new willingness to better identify and measure small-scale sales and production activities. In 2004, one of the major innovations of the first national economic census was to adopt a new definition of individual activities, encompassing not only registered *getihu*, but also a number of unregistered activities, as long as they were performed at a fixed place and at least for three months. As a testimony of the high interest of the administration, the World Bank and the US Census Bureau were involved in the preparation and implementation of this survey, from the elaboration of indicators to the training of surveyors (US Census Bureau 2004).

In the late 1980s and early 1990s, small-scale economic activities and their resemblance to street vending in Southern countries did not fit the image of modernization that China attempted to display. Recently, in a context of growing under-employment, the capacity of these economic activities to generate incomes and social occupations for the destitute, as well as to provide affordable goods and services in urban neighborhoods, were re-discovered. This move explains the new willingness of political leaders to quantify informal employment and to take it into account when they develop strategies.

Currently, the focus lies on the contribution of these new forms of labor to the job market, rather than on activities such as law violations or fiscal evasion. The official terminology reflects this change: pejorative terms such as *unlicensed economy* (*wuzhao jingji*) or *under-ground economy* (*dixia jingji*) were progressively replaced in the mid-1990s by the more neutral *informal employment* (*fei zhenggui jiuye*), and since 2000, by positively connoted expressions such as *flexible employment* (*linghuo jiuye*) or even *community employment* (*shequ jiuye*) (Wang 2004: 276). This latter neologism applies to a variety of labor situations, ranging from household services to street surveillance or tiny activities of street restaurants. The distinction between real *community jobs* or *public interest jobs* (*gongyixing gangwei*) and mere informal activities is quite unclear, even in the eyes of public deciders (Dou 2005: 236). In principle, community workers are supposed to provide affordable goods or services to a given neighborhood, and to enjoy policy support. In fact, the difference between for-profit unlicensed activities and *community work* depends less on the nature of activities than on the status of the laborers who undertake them. *Xiagang* and *shidi nongmin* would be called *community workers*, whereas other urbanites or rural migrants pursuing similar activities would be considered as unlicensed merchants and could therefore be subjected to fines or other repressive measures.

COMMUNITIES AS LEVERS FOR MANAGING SOCIAL INEQUALITIES

Community: The Itinerary of a Localized Western Concept

The concept of community is central in recent urban social policies targeting the destitute. The support of community employment is only one of the multiple features of a larger project of *community building* (*shequ jianshe*) that is supposed to bring solutions to the new challenges stemming from increased social inequality in towns. The execution of this ambitious and transversal plan is entrusted to a network of grassroots institutions, the *community residents' committees* (*shequ jumin weiyuanhui*), which are commonly considered as communities (*shequ*) by officials and ordinary citizens. Therefore, it is a very specific meaning of community that is currently advertised in urban China. While officially located outside the urban administrative system, residents' committees are in charge of the grassroots implementation work for a wide range of policies on a given administratively defined neighborhood. Moreover, if residents' committees are presented as a masterpiece of the reform of urban governance, *de facto*, only the poorer part of the population is placed under their jurisdiction, as the richer part can access other channels to solve their daily problems and to interact with the administration (such as problems with the company they work for, the private residence they live in, or private associations and services).

The theme of community that has become recurrent in Chinese recent urban policies is rooted in Western sociology. The successive stages of its introduction in China and its re-discovery in the 1980s provide a good indication of the changing perspective of the administration in its way of dealing with social inequalities. Most Chinese scholars attribute the paternity of the concept to the German sociologist Ferdinand Tönnies, who, in the late nineteenth century, insisted on the opposition between community (*Gemeinschaft*, translated in Chinese as *shequ*) and society (*Gesellschaft*, translated in Chinese as *shehui*) (Chen 2006). The former would be characterized by tight organic links, shared values, and a sense of solidarity among community members. The latter would be an historical product of the former, and the result from conscious efforts to create new forms of associations, based on formal and impersonal relationships. However, the penetration of the concept of community in China was not directly based on Tönnies' research, but on the urban sociology of the School of Chicago. Robert E. Park, one of its founders, delivered several lectures on this topic at Yenching University (Peking University) in the early 1930s. He inspired the father of Chinese sociology, Fei Xiaotong, who was the first to suggest a Chinese translation of the concept. The term of *shequ* was formed on the association of *she*, representing in ancient China a place of worship of the patron deity, and *qu* that refers to the spatial dimension of a territory (Wang 2003: 13). Thus, this new word attempted to conciliate moral and organic dimensions of the community, as underlined by Tönnies, and its spatial anchorage. In the 1930s, the *shequ* concept was mainly applied to the study of rural villages and was then suppressed. Its comeback in the 1980s, after the rehabilitation of sociology as an academic discipline, took place in urban settings. Sociology was considered as an applied science and a toolbox that could provide guidance to political leaders in dealing with the new urban challenges. Indeed, some of the social challenges of the early twentieth century's Chicago present similarities with those faced by Reform-Era China: rapid social change due to urbanization and industrialization, social tensions linked to the integration of a non-native population (i.e., rural migrants), and risks of social disorder due to the loose social networks of city dwellers.

The re-appearance of the concept of community is closely related to new social challenges that cities were exposed to in the course of economic reforms, such as the re-insertion of former public employees, the integration of rural migrants and former peasants having lost their land into the urban society. As early as 1986, the Ministry of Civil Affairs had put forward the topic of *community services* (*shequ fuwu*) as a way to promote the access to affordable goods and services outside the public supply in neighborhoods. In 1989, a law set the basis for an extension of the role of urban residents' committees, an institution that was established in the 1950s but marginalized when the system of work units (*danwei*) gradually expanded inside urban social life. But only in the late 1990s, when the *danwei* system started to collapse, other institutions were interested in community matters. In 1998, the State Council identified *community services* (*shequ jumin fuwu ye*) as a main channel for the re-employment of laid-off workers from the public sector. Since 2000, at the instigation of Jiang Zemin and then supported by the Hu-Wen administration, the principle of community was put at the heart of a global reform of the structure of urban governance under the slogan of *community building* (*shequ jianshe*). From then on, residents' committees have been expected to become a node facilitating the interaction between the administrative structure and the urban population (Xu 2008: 146). Western principles of good governance inspired by the New Public Management School (*xin gonggong guanli xue*) and promoted by international agencies have also been mobilized to legitimate this project.

The pre-eminence of the concept of community in recent urban policies reveals some trends of the official approach intended to adapt the state-party/society relationship to a new urban social context that is exposed to rising social inequalities. The topic of community is inserted in a long tradition of local self-organizations charged to deal with daily issues. Under

Mao's guidance, work units were mobilized to pursue the quest of establishing *mini societies*, in which the urban social life should take place. The organization of residents' committees is rooted in the *baojia* system, established and improved by successive Chinese aristocratic dynasties that based the management of a number of local affairs on the gathering of families in a neighborhood. The contemporary *shequ building project* inherited from the *baojia* system the characteristics of tightly mixing self-help and mutual social control. The attempt to manage social tensions within each neighborhood and to contain their impact at the grassroots level is obviously at the heart of the *shequ* philosophy (Xu 2007: 35). Nevertheless, the community-building project cannot be reduced to the double logic of expense reduction (that replaces public investments by the mobilization of local social resources) and the re-deployment of social control (that transfers the lost political function of work units to residents' committees) in a supposedly submissive and amorphous post-socialist society (Lin 2003).

Beside concerns about economic efficiency and social order enhancement, the *shequ* building project is driven by the wish to re-inforce the Party's legitimacy among the disadvantaged in urban centers and to improve social cohesion in a context of rapidly growing inequalities that worsen the competition of social groups. The moral and cultural dimension of the community appears to be a particularly important part of the *shequ* building project. In an approach that shares many research aspects of the sociologists of the Chicago School, a community is viewed as a net of shared values and tight relationships among individuals (and, by extension, between ordinary citizens and party members) that resists social disaffiliation and strengthens *social harmony* (Xu 2007: 23). For this reason, strengthening interpersonal links within each neighborhood has emerged as a major stake for social stability.[11] Shaping a *community identity* (*shequ rentong*) becomes one of the major tasks of residents' committees, in order to counter-balance the lack of social links among residents coming from various geographic and social horizons. Whereas the spatial boundaries of urban communities are administratively defined, *shequ* are considered as *new social spaces* (*xin de shehui kongjian*), whose internal interpersonal relationships, economic activities, and cultural features need to be shaped.[12] The attention paid to socio-psychological factors and individual situations places the *shequ* building project in perfect line with the orientations of the Hu-Wen administration in promoting *human-centered* (*yi ren wei ben*) policies.

COMMUNITY, A TOOL FOR GOVERNING THE POOR?

The *shequ* building project aims at bringing administrative services and social support closer to citizens by establishing collaborations at the lowest level of the urban administrative system, the sub-district office (*jiedao banshichu*) and a number of residents' committees under its jurisdiction.

Various Chinese urban centers adopted slightly different models of task repartition. In Chengdu, residents' committees are deprived of any decision-making power. They have to follow policy guidelines and to achieve quantitative indicators fixed by the municipality, the district, or the sub-district. Nevertheless, they remain quite autonomous in the way they allocate resources and implement measures, so that there are sensible variations from one neighborhood to the other.

Regarding social assistance, the global amount to be distributed to the beneficiaries of the *dibao* is fixed at the district level. Each single allocation file has to be accepted at both the sub-district and the district level— the residents' committee provides only a recommendation on each case. Although the whole grassroots investigation process is in the hands of community teams, their effective power is much larger than their formal attributions. They not only help potential beneficiaries to gather necessary documents, but are also in charge of assessing their material situation by a variety of means including visiting flats and chatting with neighbors. The publication of the list of beneficiaries, with the monthly benefit amount, on the outside wall of some *shequ* offices makes denunciation a complementary anti-fraud tool.

The importance of personal agents' involvement is even more obvious in employment services. China has no unified national public job agency. Labor offices of municipalities and districts organize a number of job fairs. But the sub-district office and the *shequ* provide most of public job services to low-skilled jobseekers. Vocational and entrepreneurship training are usually sub-contracted to private agencies, community social agents being only in charge of informing, gathering, and registering participants. *Job presentation (gangwei jieshao)* services require a stronger involvement of community agents. The *shequ* is expected to play an intermediary role between local societies likely to hire new staff, local jobseekers, and other stakeholders such as private placement agencies. As these groups possess scarce financial and institutional resources, community agents are encouraged to mobilize their personal social networks to fulfill their individual re-employment objectives. *Community recommendation (tuijian)* is necessary if employers or newly re-employed workers want to benefit from some policies, such as tax deductions, social security allocations, micro-credit, etc. The *shequ* or the sub-district office manages some public interest jobs such as street surveillance, overseeing bike parking, or public toilet maintenance, possibly with some administrative subventions.

The social role of residents' committees lies in their ability to organize cultural activities, to facilitate the access to affordable leisure, and to improve the local environment. All these elements converge into the objective of diffusing new social norms among the poor, including individual responsibility, self-help (vs. dependence on public assistance), as well as harmonious and civilized behaviors (vs. disputes with neighbors, public disorder, and vandalism). In this context, self-employment and other petty jobs have to be accepted as a normal way of life, rooted in Chinese street culture and entrepreneurial traditions.

In dealing with local social affairs, community groups act as municipal agents. Although *shequ* are formally not part of the administration, community workers receive their assignments from, are paid by, and report to the administrative hierarchy. However, limited resources force them to acquire an in-depth knowledge of the grassroots social situation, to mobilize personal resources, and to build a cooperative relationship with various stakeholders in their area, including public and private companies, community management companies charged to take care of the property, owner committees, more or less governmental agencies such as Women Federations, foreign NGOs, and even informal interest groups. Community agents are also invited to *humanize (renxinghua)* the appearance of the party, by paying attention to individual situations on a case-by-case basis, and eventually circumvent a too strict implementation of technocratic criteria. Personalized social services facilitate patronage and conflicts of interest. Yet, limits between public and private motivations and methods remain unclear. The organization at the grassroots level out of the formal administrative reach of informal relationships between poor people and social agents is increasingly becoming a tool for governance.

If community organizations are far from enjoying a real autonomy from the Party-State and from providing a supportive framework to the development of a dynamic civil society, they cannot be analyzed as a mere neutral arm of an authoritarian government that would impose its power over a submissive society.[13] Instead, community agents are at the heart of community-based co-governance, characterized by a multitude of power relations. As Youmei Li puts it: "No actor in this structure may automatically gain authority through formal authorization. It will have to regenerate new power resources through strategic interactions. Thus, it is a structure where governance is always a process" (Li 2008: 139). The ambiguous nature of the *shequ* system, oscillating between grassroots activism and patronage, is characterized by Benjamin Read as a case of "grass-roots administrative engagement," in which "states create, sponsor and manage networks of organizations at the most local levels that facilitate governance and policing by building personal relationships with members of society" (Read 2003: 3). There is no opposition between an omnipotent state and a supposedly submissive and atomized civil society. Instead, there is a net of social interactions and power relations, in which the control of the party is based more on grassroots interpersonal relationships than on coercive methods.

The efforts of the regime to gain popular legitimacy by establishing new governance practices and the significance of the *shequ* building process demonstrate a new approach of social integration and citizenship. Social grassroots policies participate in reshaping local urban communities that were based on work units and were characterized by a strong social homogeneity some years ago. The coherence of communities is based on the exclusion of alien elements. The collapse of the *danwei* society, rural migrations, as well as rapid urbanization challenged former urban communities. In the 1990s, a restrictive conception of community was defended, characterized by pyramidal social rights: laid-off workers from the public sector were entitled to preferential policies, whereas rural migrants were rejected from the community and were subjected to various discriminations. By contrast, since 2003–04, under the new slogan of establishing a harmonious society, social policies implemented by *shequ* workers have tended to push back the frontiers of the community, without abolishing the formal status differences and with major local variations. In some localities, local peasants whose land had to be requisitioned in the urbanization process (*shidi nongmin*) were the first beneficiaries of this political softening, being officially granted local urban citizenship, and becoming entitled to a number of preferential job services. Although formally deprived of social rights attached to the possession of a local *hukou*, rural migrants have been exposed in recent years to lesser discriminations. For example, in Chengdu, a social security fund has been established for them, and additional school fees requested from non-local people can be circumvented by obtaining a certificate from the *shequ*. The *humanization* policy also makes the agents in charge of maintaining street order less severe in their fight against unlicensed street vendors. In the 1990s, these agents were renowned for their use of strong—and sometimes illegitimate—means of repressing street vending, frequently resorting to high fines (or hush-money), to the confiscation of goods, or even to violence. Nowadays, fines and physical abuses are less common. Migrant street vendors particularly benefit from this relative tolerance. Thus, by a variety of grassroots social and urban policies, the local sense of community is progressively broadened, and the various social groups that compose it enjoy an improvement of their conditions. At the same time, this reshaping of the community does not come with a redefinition or an equalization of social rights. On the contrary, the improvement of global living standards makes disparities of formal rights between social groups more acceptable. The middle class keeps growing rich, former employees from the public sector keep benefiting from preferential social policies, migrants keep suffering from limited social rights, but the work of grassroots municipal and community agents makes this situation acceptable (Tomba 2008). In short, community informal politics[14] and practices contribute to re-inforce the existing segmented social order.

In a context of rapid social change and strong increase in urban social heterogeneity, the attempt to build new grassroots institutions, in charge of supporting poorer social groups, confirms the purpose of the Party to adapt its system of social control, but also to re-inforce its legitimacy among the socially disaffiliated segments of the population. More importantly, community social policies contribute to avoid the emergence of a social problem that would gather heteroclite groups. By trying to improve life-standards and by adopting a case-by-case approach to solve individual social problems in their territory, community agents manage social issues and prevent the formulation of collective claims based on social comparisons.[15] Yet, such policies can only become sustainable if paired up with a global and centralized approach that would guarantee a balance between various communities and localities.

In the last decade, the Chinese government has progressively turned out to be aware of the emergence of a new social challenge: the rise of informal employment. Informal workers form a very heterogeneous group, whose sole common points are a relatively low level of income and a strong vulnerability due to a weak institutional integration (and especially a lack of access to the social protection system). Beyond humanitarian concerns social and political stability are at stake. Since the end of 2008, the impact of the global economic crisis on China has re-inforced the willingness of political leaders to address the multiple issues faced by informal workers, whose number has grown as a consequence of the difficulties that have faced formal enterprises. The opening-up, liberal reforms, and export-driven industrial strategies that nurtured the Chinese economic growth have also increased China's vulnerability to the global conjuncture. An extension of the social security system to informal workers, vocational and entrepreneurial training, micro-finance, and preferential tax policies are among the multiple measures aiming at encouraging unemployed rural migrants and young urban jobless people to set up their own small semiformal business in order to avoid falling into poverty and social exclusion.[16] The implementation and the financing of most of these policies are devolved to municipal authorities that largely rely on the work of the residents' committees. As grassroots para-public organizations, they not only apply higher-level directives, but also strengthen social cohesion by mobilizing interpersonal relationships. Recent Chinese urban social policies are thus at the cross between local life-worlds and globalization. Whereas the design of social policies increasingly involves a dialogue with international organizations and foreign agencies,[17] their implementation relies more and more on grassroots organizations with Chinese characteristics that deny possible divergences of interests between the administration, the Party, and the larger society, and thus contribute to re-inforce the existing social stratification.

NOTES

1. Prior to the economic transition, China was considered to have a fairly egalitarian income distribution, with a national Gini coefficient of approximately 0.3 related to a *per capita* income in 1978 on the eve of the reforms. In 2007, the Gini coefficient grew to an alarming 0.469. Today, China has among the highest level of consumption inequality in the Asia region (the Gini coefficient is only 0.368 for India, 0.417 for Cambodia, 0.42 for Thailand, and 0.249 for Japan) (UN-HABITAT 2008: 77–78 and UNDP 2008: 281–284).

2. The urbanization level almost doubled in only two decades, from 25 percent in 1987 to roughly 42 percent in 2007. If rural migrants are included, the urban population reaches 650 millions. It is estimated that by 2030, 60 percent of the population of the country will be urban (UN-HABITAT 2008: 78).

3. The number of people living with less than US$ 1.25/day was re-evaluated by the World Bank in 2008 in order to better take into account the purchasing power parity (Ravallion and Chen 2008: 2).

4. "New Poverty Line Raises Number of Poor," *China Daily*, December 23, 2008. 1 yuan represented US$ 0.15 in June 2009.

5. The *dibao* is supposed to guarantee that all urban households maintain a *per capita* income above a locally-set minimal threshold, by providing the poor with an allowance enabling them to reach this minimum income level. For a well-informed critical introduction to this plan, see: Solinger 2008, http://www.socsci.uci.edu/~dorjsoli/china_perspectives_2008.pdf, accessed on March 12, 2009.

6. In 2007, according to official statistics, over 11 million people lived in Chengdu with a *hukou* of Chengdu municipality. Among them, about six millions were administratively registered as *non agricultural (fei nongye)*.

7. This UN-Habitat report (2008: 74) states that "Beijing, the capital of China, is the most equal city in Asia; its Gini coefficient is not only the lowest among Asian cities (. . .)."

8. At the end of 2008, a survey by a government think-tank estimated that 1.5 million recent university graduates in China were unable to find work: "China's 20m unemployed raise risk of unrest," *The Financial Times*, February 2, 2009.

9. The possibility of an undeclared job is not an official statistical category, but can be deducted from the difference between the estimation of the urban workforce obtained by a sample survey and the sum of the declared employment in various forms of work units. This number is probably under-estimated because of the shortcomings in the counting of rural migrants.

10. Hu and Li (2006) adopted this indirect approach to estimate the scale of informal employment.

11. For an analysis of the recent changes of social relationships in urban neighborhoods, see Ray and Yip (2007).

12. Tian and Si (2005: 7). The authors refer to the book of a French sociologist, Lefebvre (2000).

13. For discussions about the eventual impact of community building on the emergence of a civil society and the development of a *third sector*, see Li (2008) and Guo (2004).

14. Lowell, Fukui, and Lee (2000: 342): "Informal politics" are defined by the authors as consisting in "the use of non-legitimate means (albeit not necessarily illegal) to pursue public ends," and a reliance on "conventions and codes of behavior," in contrast with explicit and definite rules and institutions.

15. Up to now, the worst *collective incidents (quntixing shijian)* mostly occur in the countryside, where conflicts tend to involve more people and take a more violent form. For detailed data, see Chung, Lai, and Xia (2006).

16. On the social consequences for China of the global economic crisis, see: "A great migration into the unknown," *The Economist*, January 29, 2009.

17. For example, the International Labor Organization established an office in China in 1985 and played a major role in the introduction of the *informal employment* concept in China in the late 1990s. The United Nations Development Program has been supporting micro-finance experiments in China

since 1996. The UK Department for International Development (DFID) has implemented cooperation projects on Chinese economic and social reforms since the late 1990s and has narrowed its focus on supporting China to reach the *Millennium Development Goals* in health, education, water, and sanitation since the opening of its Chinese office in 2003. The German Technical Cooperation agency (GTZ) has been working in China since 1982, with an initial focus on grassroots poverty alleviation initiatives (including micro-finance) that evolved towards policy advice to high-ranking decision-making institutions in order to promote sustainable development. The European Commission signed in 2005 a *Memorandum of Understanding* with China that provided a framework for cooperation in areas such as social protection, social cohesion, labor legislation, employment, labor relations, and social dialogue.

BIBLIOGRAPHY

Cai, Fang (1998) "Eryuan laodongli shichang tiaojian xia de jiuye tizhi zhuan-huan" (Changes of the employment system in a context of dual labor market), *Zhongguo Shehui Kexue* 2: 4–14.

Chen,Yunsong (2006) *Cong xingzheng shequ dao gongmin shequ: you zhong xi bijiao fenxi kan zhongguo chengshi shequ jianshe de zouxiang* (From Administrative Communities to Civil Communities: Analyzing Secular Trends in Chinese Urban Community Building using Comparative Methods). Hong Kong: Chinese University of Hong Kong.

China Daily (2008) "New Poverty Line Raises Number of Poor," December 23.

Chung, Jae Ho, Hongyi Lai, and Ming Xia (2006) "Mounting Challenges to Governance in China: Surveying Collective Protestors, Religious Sects and Criminal Organizations," *The China Journal* 56 (July): 1–31.

Dou, Zexiu (2005) "Shequ zhun minjian zuzhi" (Community quasi *minjian* organizations), in Min Wang and Peifeng Liu (eds) *Minjian zuzhi tonglun*, 222–238. Beijing: Shishi Chubanshe.

Du, Yang (2009) "Employment and Inequality Outcomes in China," paper presented at the conference *Employment and Inequality Outcomes. New Evidence, Links and Policy Responses in Brazil, China and India*. Paris: OECD, April 8.

Guo, Daojiu (2004) "Dujue 'xinren' huan 'laobing', goujian zhengfu yu disan bumen jian de jiankang guanxi" (Prevent the *new man* to catch the *old disease*: building healthy relationships between government and the third sector), *Zhanlüe yu guanli*, 3 (July).

Hu, Angang and Li Zhao (2006) "Wo guo zhuanxingqi chengzhen feizhenggui jiuye yu fei zhenggui jingji (1990–2004)" (Urban informal employment and informal economy in transitional China (1990–2004)), *Qinghua Daxue Xuebao (Zhexue shehui kexue ban)* 21 (3): 111–119.

Hussain, Athar (2003) *Urban Poverty in China: Measurement, Patterns and Policies*. Geneva: International Labor Organization.

Khan, Azizur Rahman and Carl Riskin (2001) *Inequality and Poverty in China in the Age of Globalization*. Oxford: Oxford University Press.

Lefebvre, Henri (2000 [1974]) *La production de l'espace*. Paris: Anthropos.

Li, Youmei (2008) "Community governance: the micro basis of civil society," *Social Sciences in China* 29 (1): 132–141.

Lin, Minggang (2003) *Fuli shequhua zhong de shequ ziyuan kaifa yu zhenghe tantao* (Discussion on exploiting and integrating community resources in the welfare communitization process). Report. Beijing: Chinese Academy of Social Sciences.

Lou, Peimin (2007) "A Case Study on the Settlement of Rural Women Affected by Land Requisitioning in China," *Journal of Contemporary China* 16 (50): 133–148.

Lowell, Dittmer, Hamhiiro Fukui, and Peter N. S. Lee (eds) (2000) *Informal Politics in East Asia*. Cambridge: Cambridge University Press.

Lu, Xueyi (1995) "21 shiji zhongguo de shehui jiegou—zhongguo de shehui jiegou zhuanxing" (Chinese Social Structure in the 21st Century—about the Chinese Social Transition), *Shehuixue Yanjiu* 2: 3–11.

National Bureau of Statistics of China (2006) *China Statistical Yearbook*. Beijing: section 5–2.

National Bureau of Statistics of China (2008) *China Statistical Yearbook*. Beijing: section 4–1 http://www.stats.gov.cn/tjsj/ndsj/2008/indexeh.htm, accessed on March 9, 2009.

Park, Robert E. (1921) "Sociology and the Social Sciences—the Group Concept and Social Research," *The American Journal of Sociology* 27 (2): 169–183.

Ravallion, Martin and Shaohua Chen (2008) *China is Poorer than we Thought, But No Less Successful in the Fight against Poverty*. Research working papers: World Bank.

Ray, Forrest and Ngai-Ming Yip (2007) "Neighbourhood and Neighbouring in Contemporary Guangzhou," *Journal of Contemporary China* 16 (50): 47–64.

Read, Benjamin (2003) *State, Social Networks, and Citizens in China's Urban Neighborhoods*. Unpublished PhD dissertation, Harvard University: Department of Government.

Research Institute of State Development and Reform Committee (2007) "2008 nian zhongguo jiuye xingshi yuce jiqi duice jianyi" (Forecast and policy recommandations about employment in China in 2008), December 19.

Solinger, Dorothy (2001) "Why We Cannot Count the 'Unemployed,'" *The China Quarterly* 167 (September): 671–688.

Solinger, Dorothy (2008) "The *Dibao* Recipients: Mollified Anti-Emblem of Urban Modernization," *China Perspectives*, 4. http://www.socsci.uci.edu/~dorjsoli/china_perspectives_2008.pdf, accessed on June 26, 2009.

The Economist (2009) "A Great Migration into the Unknown," January 29.

The Financial Times (2008) "China Braced for Wave of Urban Migrants," March 23. http://www.ft.com/cms/s/0/c11a84ca-f902–11dc-bcf3–000077b07658.html, accessed on March 28, 2008.

The Financial Times (2009) "China's 20m Unemployed Raise Risk of Unrest," February 2, 2009. http://www.ft.com/cms/s/0/19c25aea-f0f5–11dd-8790 –0000779fd2ac,dwp_uuid=0a8cf74c-6d6d-11da-a4df-0000779e2340.html, accessed on March 9, 2009.

Tian, Yipeng and Si Qi (2005) *Danwei shehui de zhongjie* (The termination of the "*work unit society*"). Jilin: Social Sciences Academic Press (China).

Tomba, Luigi (2008) "Fabriquer une communauté. Gestion des évolutions sociales dans les villes chinoises," *Perspectives Chinoises* 4 (105): 50–66.

US Census Bureau (2004) "Consultancy Report on First Economic Census of China," October 31, 2004. http://www.oecd.org/dataoecd/18/23/33969332.doc, accessed on March 14, 2005.

UNDP (2008) "2007/2008 Human Development Report," New York, 2008. http://hdr.undp.org/en/media/HDR_20072008_EN_Complete.pdf, accessed on November 14, 2008.

UNDP China (2008) "Access for All: Basic Public Services for 1.3 Billion People" (Human Development Report China) Beijing. http://www.undp.org.cn/downloads/nhdr2008/NHDR2008_en.pdf, accessed on January 18, 2009.

UN-HABITAT (2008) "State of the World's Cities 2008/2009: Harmonious Cities." http://www.unhabitat.org/pmss/getPage.asp?page=bookView&book=2562, accessed on December 16, 2008.

Wang, Di (2003) *Street Culture in Chengdu: Public Space, Urban Commoners, and Local Politics, 1870–1930*. Stanford: Stanford University Press.

Wang, Feng (2008) *Boundaries and Categories: Rising Inequality in Post-Socialist Urban China*. Stanford: Stanford University Press.

Wang, Fujun (2004) "Shequ jiuye cunzai de wenti yu duice de tantao" (Discussion on remaining issues and corrective policies about community employment), *Jingji Shi* 11: 276–277.

Wong, Christine (2005) *Can China Change Development Paradigm for the 21st Century. Fiscal Policy Options for Hu Jintao and Wen Jiabao after two Decades of Muggling through*. Working Paper, Berlin: German Institute for International and Security Affairs. http://www.swp-berlin.org/common/get_document. php?id=1248, accessed on May 4, 2005.

Xu, Feng (2007) "New Modes of Urban Governance: Building Community/*Shequ* in Post-*Danwei* China," in André Laliberté, and Marc Lanteigne (eds) *The Chinese Party-State in the 21st Century—Adaptation and the Reinvention of Legitimacy*, 22–38. London and New-York: Routledge.

Xu, Yongxiang (2008) "Division of Tasks and Cooperation between Government and the Community: An Essential Condition for the Reform and Innovation of China's Community-building System," *Social Sciences in China* 29 (1): 142–151.

Zhongguo Jingji Zhoukan (2006) "Di san ci jiuye gaofeng" (The third employment peak), June 19.

9 Rising Income Inequality in Central and Eastern Europe

The Influence of Economic Globalization and Other Social Forces

Nina Bandelj and Matthew Mahutga

INTRODUCTION

Socialism portrayed itself as a system that ensured social justice and equality. The Party-State would secure full employment and take care of the population's basic needs by providing universal education, health care, subsidized housing, and cultural goods (Kornai 1992). Whereas actual socialist systems did not erase inequalities (Szelényi 1978), scholars overwhelmingly agree that social inequality was substantially lower during socialism than inequality in other systems at comparable levels of industrial development (Boswell and Chase-Dunn 2000, Heyns 2005). Indeed, one of the very few quantitative cross-national studies of income inequality that includes socialist countries finds that the presence of a Marxist/Leninist regime significantly reduces inequality (Alderson and Nielsen 1999).

With the collapse of communist regimes, state-level efforts to reduce inequality were largely abandoned. After 1989, Central and East European states quickly embraced market exchange as the governing economic principle and capitalism as the preferred system of economic organization. They also began to integrate into the global economy, by opening up their borders to foreign direct investment, which was restricted during the socialist period.

Since the onset of these overarching transformations, social inequalities in Central and Eastern Europe (CEE) have, without exception, increased throughout the region (Heyns 2005). A common measure of social inequity within a population is the Gini coefficient of income inequality. The Gini coefficient ranges in value from 0 to 1, with zero indicating perfect equality (each member of the population has an equal share of the whole income pie, in case of income inequality) and one indicating perfect inequality (one member of the population has all the income). The rising income inequality trends in CEE are depicted in Figure 9.1, which shows levels of the Gini coefficient of income inequality from 1989 to 2001 for ten Central and East European countries. In 1989, the average Gini index was 22 across these

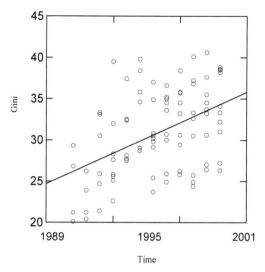

Figure 9.1   Rising Income Inequality in Post-socialist Europe (1989–2001).
Source: Gini coefficients come from the TransMONEE (2003) database.

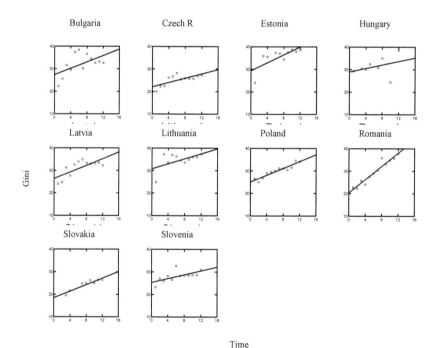

Time

Figure 9.2   Income Inequality Trends in Individual Central and East European Countries (1989–2001).

Source: Horizontal (X) axis is time, where 1989 = 1. Lines represent the linear relationship between the Gini coefficients and time. Gini coefficients come from the TransMONEE (2003) database.

countries, but increased to 34 only a dozen years later. The magnitude of this change becomes evident when we consider that the Gini index increased about two points in the US, from 40.4 to 41.7 and remained relatively constant in France (at 28) and Norway (at 31), and even slightly declined in the UK (from 33.5 to 33.1) and Australia (from 37.7 to 35.5) between 1990 and 2000 (World Income Inequality Database 2008).

Despite this general rising trend in CEE, Figure 9.2 shows that there is substantial variation in levels of inequality across these countries a dozen years into the transition: inequality remained comparatively low in some post-socialist states whereas it sky-rocketed in others. For example, Gini indices for Romania, Estonia, and Lithuania are close to the high levels we find in Anglo-Saxon countries by 2001. On the other hand, at the end of the millennium, inequality levels in the Czech Republic and Slovenia resemble those of archetypically equitable Scandinavian countries. How can we explain this cross-country variation? In particular, what is the role of globalization on the rising income inequality in the post-socialist world?

GLOBALIZATION AND ITS CONSEQUENCES

Whereas the concept of globalization is multifaceted and includes the intensification of cross-national flows of goods, services, people, technology, capital and the compression of time and space, a major indicator of economic globalization is the rapid increase in foreign direct investment. World FDI flows, which increased more than twenty-fold over the past 20 years, were valued at US$ 1.4 trillion in 2000 (UNCTAD 2002). The activities of multinational corporations (MNCs), most of which were US- and UK-based firms investing in other developed countries, started to make a significant impact on the international economy as early as the 1950s (Gereffi 2005: 164). A couple of early MNC studies examined these trends, highlighting the benefits of US FDI for host economies (Dunning 1958, Safarian 1966). Among the earliest attempts to extensively study MNCs was *The Multinational Enterprise Project*, started in 1965 by Raymond Vernon, an economist at the Harvard Graduate School of Public Administration. Vernon focused on the strategies of MNCs, highlighting the role of the product cycle in determining foreign investment decisions (Vernon 1971, 1999). Whether interested in macro international capital flows or micro-firm–level behavior, these first studies of MNCs were nevertheless grounded in neo-classical economic theory, analyzing corporate strategies as examples of rational profit maximization and believing transnational investment was beneficial to global welfare (Kindleberger 1970, Stopford and Wells 1972, Knickerbocker 1973, Hymer 1976).

New research approaches emerged in the 1970s that were skeptical of the claim that FDI naturally led to positive spillovers, emphasizing instead the uneven power relations between Western core nations that provided the source of FDI and underdeveloped peripheral countries that hosted it. Concerned with how the worldwide expansion of capitalism leads to situations of dependency in Third World countries, the dependency school argued that MNCs, as instantiations of the uneven link between developed and underdeveloped countries, create dependencies because they limit the ability of Southern countries to build domestic industries controlled by locally owned firms (Cardoso and Faletto 1969/1979, Gereffi 1978 and 1983, Evans 1979).[1] With a similar focus on the political economy of FDI, world system theorists have argued that foreign investment serves primarily the investors from developed core states and thus further halts the development of poor countries on the periphery (Wallerstein 1974, Chase-Dunn 1975, Bornschier and Chase-Dunn 1985). The deleterious effects of foreign investment, these researchers posit, result from the "disarticulation" of the domestic economy, which typically remains concentrated in low-wage sectors with unskilled labor producing goods at low levels of technological complexity. This creates few opportunities for beneficial "spill-over" effects across sectors, such as research and development activities, industrial services or differentiation, and has negative effects on economic growth (Galtung 1971, Bornschier and Ballmer-Cao 1979, Bornschier and Chase-Dunn 1985).

Furthermore, foreign capital penetration was thought to increase income inequality as well. Heavy dependence on foreign capital was thought to promote an uneven distribution of capital intensity across sectors and geographical regions in the host economy. This concentrates income in (typically more productive) outward oriented sectors, increasing overall income inequality (Frank 1967, Stack 1980). Scholars also argue that foreign capital penetration encourages inequality by influencing the distributive capacity of nation-states. Increases in global capital flows tend to produce a *race to the bottom* in which governments in developing nations seek to attract foreign investment by implementing policies that lower the bargaining power of labor, eliminate provisions that encourage full employment and wage enhancement, such as job training and local purchasing requirements, and thus remove institutional constraints on rising income inequality (McMichael 1996, DeMartino 1998, Ranney 1998, Beer and Boswell 2002).

Nonetheless, the proliferation of arguments about the positive effects of liberalization and foreign investment re-emerged in the 1980s as part of the Washington Consensus, advocated by international development agencies like the IMF and the World Bank (Gore 2000). John Williamson, who coined the name Washington Consensus, argued that its principles of stabilization, liberalization, privatization, and deregulation constitute "the common core of wisdom embraced by all serious economists" (Williamson 1993: 1334). Indeed, this Washington Consensus—also known as neo-liberalism—is closely related to the neo-classical development economics and a basic tenet that growth in the stock of capital is the primary driver of economic expansion (Solow 1956, Swan 1956, Barro and

Sala-i-Martin 1995). For *underdeveloped* countries with a dearth of domestic capital, it is the inflow of foreign investment that would increase the stock of capital and stimulate domestic economic growth (Balasubramanyam, Salisu, and Sapsford 1999). Next to propelling capital accumulation, the presence of MNCs would also have a variety of spillover effects, including the creation of new jobs, upgrading of skills, and the transfer of technological and managerial know-how to domestic firms (Markusen 1995, Blomstrom and Kokko 1997, Markusen and Venables 1999, Javorcik 2004). But how does this square with the empirical research that finds that FDI slows economic growth and increases inequality? It doesn't. In fact, there is very little consensus in the literature on the role of FDI in many of these outcomes. Scholars working in different theoretical/disciplinary traditions propose contradictory effects. But what does the recent empirical literature show?

Whereas much research in the world systems–dependency literature reports the deleterious effects of foreign capital penetration on economic growth and income equality or host nations, it underwent an extended period of critique. Firebaugh (1992) demonstrated that negative growth effects found for foreign investment stock were an artifact of introducing both foreign direct investment (FDI) flow (the yearly inflow) and FDI stock (the cumulated inflow) in the same equation, which resulted in spurious "denominator effects." Firebaugh showed that the correct interpretation for the findings from these studies was that the foreign investment rate (the ratio of flow/stock) *benefits* developing countries, but not as much as domestic investment. More recent studies that account for Firebaugh's critique continue to find that FDI slows growth in the long term and increases inequality (Dixon and Boswell 1996, Kentor 1998, Alderson and Nielsen 1999). In contrast, de Soysa and O'Neal (1999) find that contemporaneous flows of FDI promote growth and domestic capital formation.

PENETRATION OF FOREIGN DIRECT INVESTMENT INTO POST-SOCIALIST COUNTRIES

Private foreign investment was illegal under communism, after which the barriers to investment inflows were lifted (Bandelj 2008). Whereas some intra-regional investment activities did occur between members of the Council of Mutual Economic Assistance (CMEA) that resulted in the formation of a few joint enterprises and joint investment projects, such efforts did not involve direct equity investment of one COMECON state into another, and thus do not qualify as proper FDI (McMillan 1987: 4). Further, informal liberalization started before 1989 in Hungary, Poland, and former Yugoslavia, which put in place laws that allowed the formation of joint ventures with foreign firms after 1985 and legalized full foreign ownership of firms. This also happened in the Baltic states of Estonia, Latvia,

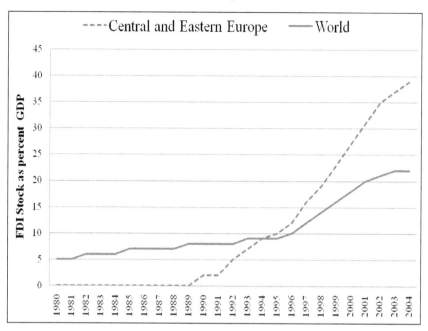

Figure 9.3   FDI Stock as a Share in GDP (1980–2006).
Source: compiled by the authors based on UNCTAD (2006).

and Lithuania as part of the perestroika in the Soviet Union by 1988. Nevertheless, as Figure 9.3 shows, real inflows of FDI were not really observable until 1989, when FDI flows started to penetrate Central and Eastern Europe. By 2000, the states received quite substantial amounts of FDI.

In evaluating the effect of FDI on income inequality in Central and Eastern Europe, we need to consider several factors that make these countries unique. First, the theory of foreign investment dependency was developed to explain why former colonies remained *underdeveloped* after formal independence. The argument was that FDI distorted the composition of the domestic economy in host countries, delimiting the spread of industrialization and disarticulating the economy over the very long term (Dixon and Boswell 1996). Contrarily, a major goal of the communist regimes was heavy industrialization in order to outpace the productivity of Western capitalist countries, resulting in a fairly rapid build-up of the productive capacity of these countries (Kornai 1992, Róna-Tas 1997). As a result, most post-socialist states were more industrialized than a prototypical *underdeveloped* former colony when communism collapsed and the opening up to economic liberalization and global integration began. Thus, whereas the foreign capital penetration effects were predicated on a long-term *disarticulation* of *peripheral* economies[2], foreign investment in the CEE can only change the income distribution in the very short term because of these countries immediate and rapid penetration of foreign capital.

Another point of contrast between these cases and the prototypical *under-developed* country was the low initial levels of inequality in the former. Prior to 1989, CEE countries embodied the socialist creed "from each according to his ability, to each according to his need" to varying degrees (Marx 1875). Whereas analyses show actual socialist systems did have some forms of inequality (Szelenyi 1978), scholars agree that income inequality was substantially lower than in other systems (Boswell and Chase-Dunn 2000, Heyns 2005). After 1989, CEE countries more or less quickly abandoned state-socialist ideals and replaced them with neo-liberal policy scripts as they embarked on market reform (Bockman and Eyal 2002). Uniquely socialist policies of full employment and the provision of basic needs such as universal education, health care, subsidized housing, and cultural goods became exposed to the logic of neo-liberalism, a major consequence of which was the opening up of CEE countries to FDI (Bandelj 2008).

The key question is whether foreign direct investment has significantly contributed to the rise of income inequality in Central and Eastern Europe. We argue that it has (Mahutga and Bandelj 2008). Figure 9.4 displays the scatterplot between income inequality and foreign capital penetration. As Figure 9.4 shows, there is a clear positive association between income inequality and foreign capital penetration. The Pearson correlation coefficient for these data is 0.421, indicating that levels of FDI penetration explain roughly 18 percent of the variation in the Gini coefficient across these cases.

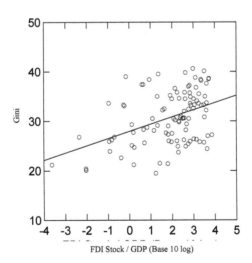

Figure 9.4 Relationship between Income Inequality and Foreign Capital Penetration in Post-socialist Europe (1989–2001).

Sources: Gini coefficients come from the TransMONEE (2003) database. FDI data come from the EBRD Transition Reports, 1999 and 2003. Gross domestic product data come from World Development Indicators online database: http://devdata.worldbank.org/dataonline, accessed on June 11, 2009.

We suggest three possible mechanisms. First, FDI can increase inequality through one of two possible types of dualism between the foreign and domestic sectors: firms in the foreign sector either pay less than those in the domestic sector or vice versa. The former is largely consistent with the FDI penetration literature, which suggests that, at the very least, foreign capital is *less productive* than domestic capital (Firebaugh 1992, Dixon and Boswell 1996). However, there is growing evidence for the latter type of sector dualism outside of Central and Eastern Europe (Aitken, Harrison, and Lipsey 1996, ILO 1998, Moran 2002). Exactly why foreign firms would tend to pay higher wages is open to debate, but a major culprit could be that foreign firms are more capital intensive and operate on a larger scale than domestic firms (Aitken, Harrison, and Lipsey 1996, Lipsey and Sjoholm 2001). This would increase the demand for skilled labor relative to unskilled and cause the two to diverge (Feenstra and Hanson 1997). Moreover, there is also evidence that CEE-based companies, which privatized with foreign capital, are, on average, more productive than domestically privatized firms (e.g., Smith, Cin, and Vodopivec 1997, for a review, see: Megginson and Netter 2001: 360). This latter type of dualism is not so different from early dependency hypotheses concerning the effect of FDI on income inequality (i.e., Frank 1967, Stack 1980). Given the findings from other geographical locations, firm-level studies in CEE and its similarity to the early dependency hypotheses, we suggest that either of these mechanisms is a plausible explanation for an inequality-boosting effect of foreign capital penetration in Central and Eastern Europe.

In addition to either of these forms of dualism, FDI could also increase the wage premium to management in the foreign sector, thus, increasing inequality between management and labor in this sector. First, FDI in post-socialist Europe is concentrated considerably in trade, business activities, and financial services (UNCTAD 2006), and comparatively high wages in these sectors accrue to the skilled managerial personnel that is a growing segment of high-wage employment (King 2001). Thus, regardless of whether or not FDI depresses labor wages, management premiums in foreign-owned firms would contribute to inequality in the distribution of wages within the foreign sector (Milanovic 1999). To summarize, we suggest that FDI can increase inequality by fostering one of two types of dualism between the foreign and domestic sectors, and by increasing wage inequality between management and labor within the foreign sector.[3]

OTHER FORCES THAT INFLUENCE INCOME INEQUALITY IN CEE

We have to acknowledge that globalization is not the only force that drives income inequality trends in post-socialist Central and Eastern Europe. In fact, the classic argument proposed by Kuznets (1953, 1955) posits a

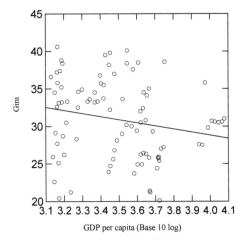

Figure 9.5 Relationship between Income Inequality and Economic Development in Post-socialist Europe (1989–2001).

Sources: Gini coefficients come from the TransMONEE (2003) database. Gross domestic product per capita data come from World Development Indicators online database: http://devdata.worldbank.org/dataonline, accessed on June 11, 2009.

relationship between economic development and inequality, suggesting an inverted U-shape. However, when we examine these trends for Central and Eastern Europe (Figure 9.5), we see that whereas inequality has risen, the relationship between GDP per capita and inequality is actually negative. Thus, we cannot claim that the rising inequality is due to the increases in *per capita* income.

There are, however, other factors that researchers have proposed to matter for determining the levels of inequality in a country. We want to discuss potential influences of most of these factors, specifically, the size of the agricultural sector and sector dualism, demographic trends, educational trends, labor market institutions, and discrimination of minority populations.

Size of the Agricultural Sector and Sector Dualism

According to the internal development model proposed by Alderson and Nielsen (1999, 2002), differences between agricultural and non-agricultural sectors in the course of development should matter for overall levels of inequality. At an early development stage, most of the labor force is in agriculture. With development, an increasing proportion of the labor force shifts to the higher-income industrial sectors, and in high stages of development, the agricultural sector should be very small. Moreover, differences between households in agriculture are relatively weak, so inequality in the agricultural sector is typically low (Alderson and Nielsen 1999,

2002). Therefore, rising income inequality could be explained by the contraction of the agricultural sector, causing an expanding difference in average income between agricultural and non-agricultural sectors, or "sector dualism" (cf. Nielsen 1994).

What are the agricultural sector and dualism trends in post-socialist Europe? In fact, none of these countries experienced major shifts in the agricultural sector during the transition period (in most countries, this share remains relatively stable over time). However, the contribution of the agricultural sector to overall GDP contracted. This could happen on account of the absolute decline in the agricultural sector or because of the relative decreased productivity of the agricultural sector compared to the non-agricultural sector. We propose that in post-socialist Europe the effect is due to both of these mechanisms. Some other studies provide evidence of struggling agricultural sectors in absolute terms. For instance, Greif (1998) reports that the Eastern European agriculture is in dire conditions. Maddock (1995), and Hristova and Maddock (1993) provide evidence of this fact for Lithuania and Bulgaria. Moreover, scholars examining poverty in Hungary, Bulgaria, and Romania report either that poverty is higher in villages than in towns (Szalai 1999) or that poverty is widespread among the farmers (Todorova 1999). All this is consistent with the image of a struggling agricultural sector that increased dualism would imply.

Demographic Trends

According to Kuznets, demographic trends also influence income inequality. In particular, increases in population growth in developing countries create an influx of young workers into the labor market that increases the supply of young and rather unskilled labor. This tends to drive wages down and increase inequality between the working poor and other strata of society. Empirical analyses following Kuznets substantiated the positive relationship between population growth and inequality (Ahluwalia 1976, Bollen and Jackman 1985, Simpson 1990, Alderson and Nielsen 1999).

The conjecture that population growth widens the income gap by depressing the relative position of the low-income strata provides a straightforward labor market explanation of the effect of the demographic transition. Adopting a broader perspective, Nielsen (1994: 662–664) argues that the negative effect of the demographic transition on inequality is also based on socio-cultural mechanisms. For Nielsen, population growth is also "a proxy for the heterogeneity, and resulting inequality, generated by many other processes of uneven diffusion of industrial technology in a traditional social system which stems from the uneven diffusion of modern technology throughout the population" (662). To capture the combined effect of the broader socio-cultural transformations related to industrialization, Nielsen coined a term "generalized socio(-)cultural dualism, to distinguish these effects from strictly economic (sector) dualism as associated with labor force movements away from agriculture" (664). Hence, based on both the labor market and the socio-cultural mechanisms, extant theory would expect a positive relationship between population growth and income inequality.

What is peculiar in CEE, however, is that the population is declining. From 1990 to 2001, all countries except Poland experienced population decline (Fig. 9.6). Hence, the real question is how population *decline* may have affected inequality. Kuznets did not stipulate about population decline but our data show that these relationships may not be symmetrical. That is, while influxes of young and unskilled workers into the labor market (due to population growth in the early stages of development) may *increase* inequality, the reverse process, i.e., the aging and contraction of the active labor force, does not *decrease* inequality. In fact, we propose that the impact of population decline on inequality is not due as much to the labor market mechanism as to demographic changes.

Demographic trends that we see in post-socialist Europe are consistent with those in many Western European countries undergoing "the second demographic transition" (van de Kaa 1987, Lesthaeghe and Surkyn 1988, Raley 2001, Lesthaeghe 1995, Lesthaeghe and Neels 2002). This transition is principally characterized by the decline in fertility to a level "well

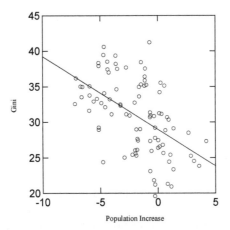

Figure 9.6 Demographic Trends in Post-socialist European Countries (1989–2001).

Sources: Gini coefficients come from the TransMONEE (2003) database. Population data (percent increase) come from World Development Indicators online database: http://devdata.worldbank.org/dataonline, accessed on June 11, 2009.

below replacement" (van de Kaa 1987: 4) as well as changes in family for-mation and living arrangements. The analysts link these shifts in demo-graphic behavior to "ideational and cultural change" (Sobotka, Zeman, and Kantorová 2003: 251, van de Kaa 1987: 6–7, Lesthaeghe 1995: 2–22). Similarly, Nielsen (1994) proposed that population growth in the internal development model captures not only the workings of the labor market but also serves as a proxy for broader socio-cultural changes that are hard to directly measure in regression models. We follow Nielsen and the "sec-ond demographic transition" literature to suggest that the effect of popu-lation decline in Central and Eastern Europe also points to the influence of social and cultural forces on rising income inequality trends. Certainly, the economic conditions, in particular, the economic crises that accom-panied the collapse of communism, had an effect on these demographic changes. But decisions such as to have fewer children, to postpone the first birth, or to remain childless are also linked to changes in people's cultural understandings accompanying the large-scale societal transfor-mations in Central and Eastern Europe (Lestheaghe and Surkyn 2002; Sobotka, Zeman, and Kantorová 2003). Transition from socialism to capitalism has entailed an increased focus away from collective interests and traditional family arrangements promoted by socialism to individual autonomy and self-fulfillment, spearheaded by the creation of democratic space for individual choice and lifestyle (Rabusic 2001). This manifests itself, for example, in the rising opinions that women do not need children for life fulfillment and that marriage would be an outdated institution (Lestheage and Surkyn 2002). Changes in demographic trends in Central and Eastern Europe become particularly pronounced after 1989, but this period is *not* marked by either secularization, the spread of reproductive technology,[4] or the increased participation of women in the labor force, all of which happened already during the socialist period. In addition, the patterns of population decline do not reverse once economic growth in post-socialism resumes (Lestheage and Surkyn 2002; Sobotka, Zeman, and Kantorová 2003), so economic factors cannot solely explain fertility behavior. Based on this, we believe that a cultural shift from a collectiv-ist to a more individualistic orientation shapes the population declines in post-socialist Europe. These cultural changes manifest themselves in the rise of new forms of living arrangements, including single-people house-holds, dual-earner professional couples who delay childbirth, or childless couples. Because fertility varies by educational and class status of parents (Bollen *et al.* 2001), we suggest that poor families continue to live in tra-ditional households and have more children so that wealth concentrates in the segment of households with more educated individuals from middle and upper class backgrounds who adopt new forms of living arrange-ments. Therefore, in cases where population declines are higher (with, consequently, fewer traditional multi-children households), the levels of inequality are greater.

Education Trends

An integral part of the internal development model is also the influence of the spread of education on inequality. According to a standard economic argument, education increases the overall human capital of the labor force and thus contributes to a more skilled labor supply. A higher aggregate skill level reduces the skilled wage premium, which lowers overall inequality between households (Tinbergen 1975, Lecaillon *et al.* 1984, Simpson 1990, Williamson 1991, Nielsen 1994, Gottschalk and Smeeding 1997, Alderson and Nielsen 1999 and 2002).

Consistent with their focus on social equality, socialist authorities made several provisions to equalize access to education (Ganzeboom and Nieuwbeerta 1999, Kreidl 2004). Although these efforts were often imperfect (Gerber and Hout 1995), they led to relatively high secondary school enrollments in socialist Europe (Ganzeboom and Nieuwbeerta 1999, Boswell and Chase-Dunn 2000, Heyns 2005). Hence, it is questionable whether differences in enrollment levels could strongly contribute to the explanation of the income inequality differences within and across these countries after the collapse of communist regimes. Indeed, as the trend line shown in Figure 9.7 indicates, the relationship between secondary school enrollment and Gini index is negative but it is not as strong as for foreign investment penetration or population growth.

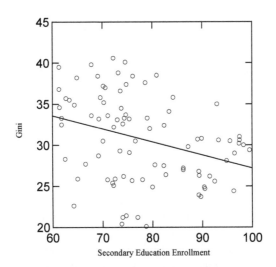

Figure 9.7   Education Levels in Post-socialist European Countries (1989–2001).

Sources: Gini coefficients come from the TransMONEE (2003) database. Education data (percent enrolled in secondary education) come from World Development Indicators online database: http://devdata.worldbank.org/dataonline, accessed on June 11, 2009.

Labor Market Institutions

Scholars have also paid attention to the influence of domestic institutions on income inequalities. In particular, labor market institutions play a key role in mediating social outcomes (Western 1997). The institutions that encourage an equitable distribution of income include corporatist arrangements, social-democratic parties, and other facets of what has generally been termed the welfare state (Esping-Andersen 1990). Labor unions also play a large role in the maintenance of equality by intervening in the productive relationship between workers and owners of plants to ensure that a larger income share ends up with workers. The presence of unions also represents an institutional constraint on widening wage differentials between blue- and white-collar workers. However, because of the precarious character of labor in the global economy, most advanced industrial countries have experienced "de-unionization" in recent years (Western 1997) and several authors have linked this trend to rising inequality. Studying the case of the US, for example, Freeman (1994) attributes a substantial inequality upswing to declining unionization and the declining bargaining power of labor. Likewise, Alderson and Nielsen (2002) find that countries with weak labor market institutions (i.e., where wage setting coordination is absent, and union density and de-commodification of labor are low) have significantly higher income inequality.

Unions during the socialist times did not have quite the same function as in capitalist societies because, rather than being essentially adversarial, they were generally part of the communist party structure. This changed with the transition to market but the neo-liberal reforms more or less embraced by communist governments posed great challenges to organized labor. The few studies on post-socialist unionization report low levels of coverage by collective agreements and the overall weak influence of unions on policy-making (Kubicek 1999, Ost 2000, Crowley 2001). Despite these general trends, cross-national differences in labor market organization within the post-socialist region do exist (Cox and Mason 2000, Avdagic 2005) and in some countries labor has more bargaining power than in others.

We would expect that post-socialist countries with stronger organized labor would, on average, show lower income inequality levels. Indeed, as Figure 9.8 shows, CEE countries with comparatively higher levels of unionization have average Gini coefficients that are roughly four points (13 percent) lower than countries with lower levels of unionization. A case in point may be Slovenia, where labor has quite a strong position, possibly the strongest in the post-socialist region. In contrast the embracing of neo-liberal policies after the Dzurinda government took power in 1998 in Slovakia weakened labor organization (O'Dwyer and Kovalcik 2007). We have also observed recently an increase in income inequality levels in Slovakia.

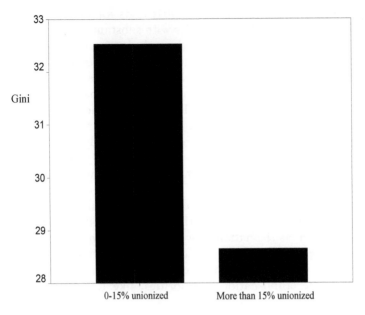

Figure 9.8 Average Gini Coefficient across Levels of Unionization in Post-socialist Europe (1989–2001).

Sources: Gini coefficients come from the TransMONEE (2003) database. Unionization data comes from Lado (2002).

Discrimination of Minority Groups

The world witnessed a proliferation of national movements and national sentiments in post-socialist Europe after the end of the Communist Party rule (Calhoun 1993, Cohen 1999). Competing parties used nationalism as a tool for political mobilization and support so that in a number of countries, "the rhetoric and symbols with the greatest electoral appeal were national(ist) ones" (Verdery 1998: 294). Nation-oriented idioms had a prominent place in the cultural repertoires of actors making sense of post-communist transformations. In short, they were "widely available and resonant as a category of social vision and division" (Brubaker 1996: 21) in post-communist Europe.

Such cultural differentiation may increase the likelihood of social exclusion and thus inequality. Indeed, as Figure 9.9 shows, countries with more sizable ethnic minority populations have significantly higher Gini coefficients than do those with smaller ethnic minority populations. Such exclusion leads to greater discrimination in schools and on the job market, especially when the general population is relatively intolerant of cultural diversity, which (Smooha 2001) finds for Central and Eastern Europe. This suggests that countries with substantial ethno-national minority populations, i.e., those of ethnicities/nationalities other than nominal nationals, will have larger segments of their populations subject to some form of discrimination and therefore social exclusion. In fact, as researchers report, Roma in Eastern Europe are particularly disadvantaged, and constitute an "underclass" (Emigh and Szélenyi 2001). There is also evidence of employment disadvantages among ethnic Russians in Estonia because employment requires knowledge of the national language, Estonian, but many elderly Russians never had to learn the language because in the former Soviet Union, the knowledge of Russian was enough (Budryte 2005). Instances like these lead us to believe that, on average, members of ethno-national minorities will be more disadvantaged on the labor market than the nationals, and will lag behind economically, whereas the nationals would benefit from more differentiated opportunities on the job market, compared to socialist employment structures. This would lead to higher levels of inequality in countries with more sizable ethno-national minorities, like Romania, Bulgaria, Estonia, and Latvia.

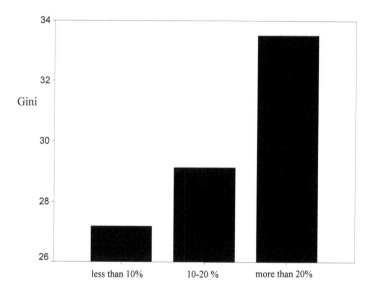

Size of Ethnic Minority Population in a Country

Figure 9.9 Relationship between the Size of Ethnic Minority Population and Income Inequality in Post-socialist Europe (1989–2001).

Sources: Gini coefficients come from the TransMONEE (2003) database. Ethnic minority population size comes from Freedomhouse Transition Reports: http://www.freedomhouse.org/template.cfm?page=1, accessed on June 11, 2009.

CONCLUSION

Communist regimes that prioritized social equality and industrialization produced an "anomalous" case that cannot be easily subsumed under the general economic theory of the inverted-U–shaped relationship between economic development and social inequality (Kuznets 1953). Socialist Central and East European states represented relatively egalitarian and economically developed societies that, when communist regimes collapsed, were suddenly exposed to the pressure of market order and globalization. Since 1989, income inequality in post-socialism rose significantly.

We reviewed several factors responsible for this increase, including (1) the extent of foreign capital penetration, (2) the contraction and impoverishment of the agricultural sector, (3) socio-cultural changes that induce population decline, (4) weak labor organizations, and (5) discrimination of ethno-national minorities that keeps them at the bottom of the income distribution. Our review therefore suggests that these inequality trends are related to social and cultural changes that accompany the institutionalization of a market-based order, rather than arise as normal byproducts of economic development.

This review should prompt us to rethink the dominant explanations of income inequality based on the market supply and demand mechanism proposed by classical theorists who linked income inequality to a "natural path" of economic development. Indeed, economic development is negatively related to income inequality in Central and Eastern Europe after 1989. Yet, inequality is increasing in all of these countries over time. In the first part of this chapter, we scrutinized the possible contribution of rising FDI to rising income inequality in Central and Eastern Europe. Many observers focused on the beneficial role of FDI as a catalyst in the transition process (IMF 1997, UNCTAD 1998). In contrast, we propose three possible mechanisms for the positive association between FDI and income inequality, including two forms of dualism between the foreign and domestic sectors, and one that increases the wage gap between management and labor in the foreign sector.

In the second part of the chapter, we examined other factors that reflect the overall trends in individualization, privatization, and marketization that accompany market transition, such as sector dualism, weakened labor power, population declines, and ethnic discrimination. All these processes can lead to greater social differentiation. In particular, the agricultural sector hardly benefited from market transition as farmers and agricultural laborers had less political and social capital to convert into an economic advantage. Ethno-national minorities, in particular the Roma, who were relatively well integrated during socialism (Magyari *et al.* 2001), have also been pushed to the underclass in post-socialism.

Overall, these effects point to social explanations of income inequality trends. The role of the foreign and domestic investment in post-socialist economies is strongly linked to the privatization process, which was not a natural byproduct of economic development. Rather, as research on post-socialist transformations shows, privatization strategies were largely a matter of political choice and were influenced by the paths of extrication from communism (Stark 1992, Stark and Bruszt 1998). In addition, the decisions to sell state-owned property to foreigners after 1989 were dependent on socialist institutions and concerns about foreign capital infringing on national sovereignty in the newly established states (Bandelj 2008). Ultimately, then, income inequality trends can be traced to social, cultural, and political forces that structure economic processes. The major implication of this finding is that rising inequality in post-socialist Europe is not a *natural*, and thus unavoidable, feature of the transition from socialism to capitalism. Post-socialist states that made political choices to support domestic rather than foreign sources of capital with which to privatize, and those that kept individualist orientations in check with institutional provisions that generated social protection and labor bargaining power, experienced less income inequality after the collapse of communism than did their counterparts.

NOTES

1. The dependency school does not characterize MNCs' impacts as unilaterally negative for the development of countries in the *periphery*. Cardoso and Faletto (1969/1979) argue that the interaction of local social classes and the multinational enterprises can explain growth in peripheral economies. According to Evans (1979), the state can mediate the negative role of foreign capital if it effectively takes part in a "triple alliance" together with the local bourgeoisie and MNCs. Gereffi (1978, 1983) emphasizes that supportive state policies are the key. Without those, MNCs are more likely to contribute to national development than local corporations, but with right policies, local corporations can contribute more.
2. This does not refer to the countries of East Asia, which were able to use their developmental states to advance economically.
3. Unfortunately, data on earnings that differentiates between employment in the foreign and domestic sector, and within the foreign sector, is not available to directly test these hypotheses.
4. The only exception is Romania where abortion was illegal and contraception was unavailable due to Ceausescu's pronatalist policy (Kligman 1992).

BIBLIOGRAPHY

Ahluwalia, Montek (1976) "Income Distribution and Development: Some Stylized Facts," *American Economic Review* 66 (2): 128–135.

Aitken, Brian, Ann Harrison and Robert E. Lipsey (1996) "Wages and Foreign Ownership: A Comparative Study of Mexico, Venezuela, and the United States," *Journal of International Economics* 40 (3–4): 345–71.

Alderson, Arthur (1997) *Globalization, Deindustrialization, and the Great U-Turn: The Growth of Direct Investment in 18 OECD Countries, 1967–*

1990. Unpublished PhD Dissertation. University of North Carolina, Chapel Hill: Department of Sociology.

Alderson, Arthur and François Nielsen (1999) "Income Inequality, Development, and Dependence: A Reconsideration," *American Sociological Review* 64 (4): 606–631.

Alderson, Arthur and François Nielsen (2002) "Globalization and the Great U-Turn: Income Inequality Trends in 16 OECD Countries," *American Journal of Sociology* 107 (5): 1244–1299.

Amemiya, Takeshi (1985) *Advanced Econometrics.* Cambridge, Mass.: Harvard University Press.

Antal-Mokos, Zoltán (1998) *Privatization, Politics and Economic Performance in Hungary.* Cambridge: Cambridge University Press.

Apter, David (1965) *The Politics of Modernization.* Chicago: University of Chicago Press.

Avdagic, Sabina (2005) "State-Labour Relations in East Central Europe: Explaining Variations in Union Effectiveness," *Socio-Economic Review* 3 (1): 25–53.

Balasubramanyam, V. N., M. Salisu, and David Sapsford (1999) "Foreign Direct Investment as an Engine of Growth," *Journal of International Trade and Economic Development* 8 (1): 27–40.

Bandelj, Nina (2008) *From Communists to Foreign Capitalists: The Social Foundations of Foreign Direct Investment in Post-socialist Europe.* Princeton: Princeton University Press.

Barro, Robert J., and Xavier Sala-i-Martin (1995) *Economic Growth.* Cambridge: MIT Press.

Beer, Linda and Terry Boswell (2002) "The Resilience of Dependency Effects in Explaining Income Inequality in the Global Economy: A Cross-National Analysis, 1975–1995," *Journal of World-Systems Research* 8 (1): 30–59.

Birdsall, Nancy, David Ross, and Richard Sabot (1997) "Education, Growth and Inequality," in Nancy Birdsall and Frederick Jaspersen (eds) *Pathways to Growth: Comparing East Asia and Latin America,* 93–130. Washington, DC: Inter-American Development Bank.

Blomstrom, Magnus and Ari Kokko (1997) *How Foreign Investment Affects Host Countries.* World Bank Policy Research Working Paper 1745.

Bockman, Johanna and Gil Eyal (2002) "Eastern Europe as a Laboratory for Economic Knowledge: The Transnational Roots of Neoliberalism," *American Journal of Sociology* 108(2): 310–352.

Bollen, Kenneth and Robert Jackman (1985) "Political Democracy and the Size Distribution of Income," *American Sociological Review* 50 (4): 438–457.

Bollen, Kenneth, Jennifer Glanville, and Guy Stecklov (2001) "Socioeconomic Status and Class in Studies of Fertility and Health in Developing Countries," *Annual Review of Sociology* 27: 153–185.

Bornschier, Volker and Ballmer-Cao Thanh-Huyen (1979) "Income Inequality: A Cross National Study of the Relationships between MNC-Penetration, Dimensions of the Power Structure and Income Distribution," *American Sociological Review* 44 (3): 487–506.

Bornschier, Volker and Christopher Chase-Dunn (1985) *Transnational Corporations and Underdevelopment.* New York: Praeger.

Boswell, Terry and Christopher Chase-Dunn (2000) *The Spiral of Capitalism and Socialism: Toward Global Democracy.* Boulder, CO: Lynne Rienner.

Brubaker, Rogers (1996) *Nationalism Reframed: Nationhood and the National Question in the New Europe.* New York: Cambridge University Press.

Budryte, Dovile (2005) *Taming Nationalism? Political Community Building in the Post-Soviet Baltic States.* Burlington, Vt.: Ashgate Publishing.

Calhoun, Craig (1993) "Nationalism and Ethnicity," *Annual Review of Sociology* 19: 211–239.

Cardoso, Femando Henrique and Enzo Faletto (1979) *Dependency and Development in Latin America*. Trans. Marjory Mattingly Urquidi. Berkeley and Los Angeles: University of California Press.

Carley, Mark (2002) "Industrial Relations in the EU Member States and Candidate Countries," *European Industrial Relations Observatory On-line*. http://www. eiro.eurofound.ie/2002/07/feature/tn0207104f.html, accessed on October 10, 2005.

Chase-Dunn, Christopher (1975) "The Effects of International Economic Dependence on Development and Inequality: A Cross-National Study," *American Sociological Review* 40: 720–738.

Cohen, Shari (1999) *Politics Without a Past: The Absence of History in Post-Communist Nationalism*. Durham: Duke University Press.

Cox, Terry M. and Bob Mason (2000) "Interest Groups and Development of Tripartism in East Central Europe," *European Journal of Industrial Relations* 6 (3): 325–347.

Crenshaw, Edward and Ansari Ameen (1994) "The Distribution of Income across National Populations: Testing Multiple Paradigms," *Social Science Research* 23 (1): 1–22.

Crowley, Stephen (2001) *Explaining Labor Quiescence in Post-Communist Europe: Historical Legacies and Comparative Perspective*. Central and Eastern Europe Working Paper no. 55, Center for European Studies, Harvard University.

Dallago, Bruno, Gianmaria Ajani, and Bruno Grancelli (1992) *Privatization and Entrepreneurship in Post-Socialist Countries: Economy, Law, and Society*. New York: St. Martin's Press.

De Soysa, Indra and John R. O'Neal (1999) "Boon or Bane? Reassessing the Effects of Foreign Capital on Economic Growth," *American Sociological Review* 64 (5): 766–782.

DeMartino, George (1998) "Foreign Direct Investment," *Foreign Policy in Focus* 3 (14): 1–4. http://www.fpif.org/briefs/vol3/v3n14fdi.html, accessed on April 24, 2005.

Dixon, William and Terry Boswell (1996) "Dependency, Disarticulation, and Denominator Effects: Another Look at Foreign Capital Penetration," *American Journal of Sociology* 102 (2): 543–562.

Dunning, John H. (1958) *American Investment in British Manufacturing Industry*. London: Allen and Unwin.

Earle, John S., Roman Frydman, and Andrzej Rapaczynski (1993) *Privatization in the Transition to a Market Economy: Studies of Preconditions and Policies in Eastern Europe*. New York: St. Martin's Press.

EBRD (1999, 2001, 2003) *Transition Report 1999, 2001, 2003*. London: European Bank for Restructuring and Development.

Emigh, Rebecca Jean and Iván Szelényi (eds) (2001) *Poverty, Ethnicity and Gender in Eastern Europe During the Market Transition*. Westport, Conn.: Greenwood Press.

Esping-Andersen, Gøsta (1990) *The Three Worlds of Welfare Capitalism*. Princeton: Princeton University Press.

Evans, Peter (1979) *Dependent Development: The Alliance of Multinational, State and Local Capital in Brazil*. Princeton: Princeton University Press.

Evans, Peter (1995) *Embedded Autonomy: States and Industrial Transformation*. Princeton: Princeton University Press.

Evans, Peter and Michael Timberlake (1980) "Dependence, Inequality, and the Growth of the Tertiary: A Comparative Analysis of Less Developed Countries," *American Sociological Review* 45 (4): 531–552.

Eyal, Gil, Ivan Szelenyi, and Eleanor Townsley (2001) *Making Capitalism without Capitalists: The New Ruling Elites in Eastern Europe.* London: Verso.

Feenstra, Robert C. and Gordon H. Hanson (1997) "Foreign Direct Investment and Relative Wages: Evidence from Mexico's Maquiladoras," *Journal of International Economics* 42 (3–4): 371–393.

Findley, Ronald and Stanislaw Wellisz (1993) *The Political Economy of Poverty, Equity, and Growth: Five Small Open Economies (A World Bank Comparative Study. The Political Economy of Poverty, Equity, and Growth).* Oxford: Oxford University Press.

Firebaugh, Glenn (1992) "Growth Effects of Foreign and Domestic Investment," *American Journal of Sociology* 98 (1): 105–130.

Firebaugh, Glenn (1996) "Does Foreign Capital Harm Poor Nations? New Estimates Based on Dixon and Boswell's Measure of Capital Penetration," *American Journal of Sociology* 102 (2): 563–575.

Firebaugh, Glenn (1999) "Empirics of World Income Inequality," *American Journal of Sociology* 104 (6): 1597–1630.

Firebaugh, Glenn (2003) *The New Geography of Global Income Inequality.* Cambridge, Mass.: Harvard University Press.

Firebaugh, Glenn and Brian Goesling (2004) "Accounting for the Recent Decline in Global Income Inequality," *American Journal of Sociology* 110 (2): 283–312.

Frank, Andre Gunder (1967) *Capitalism and Development in Latin America.* New York: Monthly Review Press.

Freeman, Richard (1994) "How Much Has Deunionisation Contributed to the Rise in Male Earnings Inequality?" in Sheldon Danziger and Peter Gottschalk (eds) *Uneven Tides: Rising Inequality in America*, 133–163. New York: Russell Sage Foundation.

Funk, Lothar and Hagen Lesch (2004) "Industrial Relations in Central and Eastern Europe: Organisational Characteristics, Co-determination, and Labour Disputes." Conference Paper. *The Industrial Relations in Europe Conference (IREC) 2004*, Utrecht, The Netherlands. http://www.usg.uu.nl/irec/papers/1_FunkLesch.doc, accessed on October 27, 2005.

Gagliani, Giorgio (1987) "Income Inequality and Economic Development," *Annual Review of Sociology* 13: 313–334.

Gal, Susan and Gail Kligman (2000) *The Politics of Gender after Socialism: A Comparative-Historical Essay.* Princeton: Princeton University Press.

Galtung, Johan (1971) "A Structural Theory of Imperialism," *Journal of Peace Research* 8 (2): 81–117.

Ganzeboom, Harry B. G. and Paul Nieuwbeerta (1999) "Access to Education in Six Eastern European Countries between 1940 and 1985. Results of a Cross-National Survey," *Communist and Post-Communist Studies* 32 (4): 339–357.

Gerber, Theodore P. (2002) "Structural Change and Post-socialist Stratification: Labor Market Transitions in Contemporary Russia," *American Sociological Review* 67 (5): 629–659.

Gerber, Theodore P. and Michael Hout (1995) "Educational Stratification in Russia during the Soviet Period," *American Journal of Sociology* 101 (3): 611–660.

Gerber, Theodore P. and Michael Hout (1998) "More Shock than Therapy: Market Transition, Employment, and Income in Russia, 1991–1995," *American Journal of Sociology* 104 (1): 1–50.

Gereffi, Gary (1978) "Drug Firms and Dependency in Mexico: The Case of the Steroid Hormone Industry," *International Organization.* 32 (1): 237–286.

Gereffi, Gary (1983) *The Pharmaceutical Industry and Dependency in the Third World.* Princeton: Princeton University Press.

Gereffi, Gary (2005) "The Global Economy: Organization, Governance, and Development," in Neil J. Smelser and Richard Swedberg (eds) *The Handbook of*

Economic Sociology, 160–182. 2nd ed. Princeton: Princeton University Press; New York: Russell Sage Foundation.

Gore, Charles (2000) "The Rise and Fall of the Washington Consensus as a Paradigm for Developing Countries," *World Development* 28 (5): 789–804.

Gottschalk, Peter and Timothy M. Smeeding (1997) "Cross National Comparisons of Earnings and Income Inequality," *Journal of Economic Literature* 35 (2): 633–687.

Greif, Franz (1998) "The End of the Traditional Agricultural Society—And What is to Follow? A Status Report of the So-called Agriculture Report," *Mitteilungen der Österreichischen Geographischen Gesellschaft* 140 (1): 25–52.

Gustafsson, Björn and Mats Johansson (1999) "In Search of the Smoking Guns: What Makes Income Inequality Vary over Time in Different Countries?" *American Sociological Review* 64 (4): 585–605.

Halaby, Charles (2004) "Panel Models in Sociological Research: Theory into Practice," *Annual Review of Sociology* 30: 507–544.

Hanley, Eric (2003) "A Party of Workers or a Party of Intellectuals? Recruitment into Eastern European Communist Parties, 1945–1988," *Social Forces* 81 (4): 1073–1105.

Hanousek, Jan and Eugene Kroch (1998) "The Two Waves of Voucher Privatization in the Czech Republic: A Model of Learning in Sequential Bidding," *Applied Economics* 30 (1): 133–143.

Hausman, Jerry A. (1978) "Specification Tests in Econometrics," *Econometrica* 46 (6): 1251–1271.

Heyns, Barbara (2005) "Emerging Inequalities in Central and Eastern Europe," *Annual Review of Sociology* 31: 163–197.

Hirschman, Albert O. [1945] (1980) *National Power and the Structure of Foreign Trade*. Berkeley: University of California Press.

Hristova, Monika and Nicholas Maddock (1993) "Private Agriculture in Eastern Europe," *Food Policy* 18 (6): 459–462.

Hymer, Stephen (1976) *The International Operations of National Firms: A Study of Direct Foreign Investment*. Cambridge: MIT Press.

Ingham, Geoffrey (1996) "The 'New Economic Sociology'," *Work, Employment and Society* 10 (3): 549–564.

International Labor Organization (1998) *Labor and Social Issues Relating to Export Processing Zones*. Geneva: ILO.

International Monetary Fund (1997) *World Economic Outlook*. Washington, D.C.: International Monetary Fund.

Jacobs, David (1985) "Unequal Organizations or Unequal Attainments? An Empirical Comparison of Sectoral and Individualistic Explanations for Aggregate Inequality," *American Sociological Review* 50 (2): 166–180.

Javorcik, Beata Smarzynska (2004) "Does Foreign Direct Investment Increase the Productivity of Domestic Firms? In Search of Spillovers through Backward Linkages," *American Economic Review* 94 (3): 605–627.

Karpov, Vyacheslav (1999) "Religiosity and Political Tolerance in Poland," *Sociology of Religion* 60 (4): 387–402.

Kentor, Jeffrey (1998) "The Long-Term Effects of Foreign Investment Dependence on Economic Growth, 1940–1990," *American Journal of Sociology* 103 (4): 1024–1046.

Kentor, Jeffrey (2001) "The Long Term Effects of Globalization on Income Inequality, Population Growth, and Economic Development," *Social Problems* 48 (4): 435–455.

Kindleberger, Charles P. (1970) *The International Corporation*. Cambridge: MIT.

King, Lawrence (2001) *The Basic Features of Postcommunist Capitalism in Eastern Europe: Firms in Hungary, The Czech Republic and Slovakia*. Westport, Conn.: Praeger.

Kligman, Gail (1992) "The Politics of Reproduction in Ceausescu's Romania: A Case Study in Political Culture," *East European Politics and Societies* 6 (3): 364–418.

Knickerbocker, Frederick (1973) *Oligopolistic Reaction and Multinational Enterprise.* Cambridge: Harvard University Press.

Kornai, János (1992) *The Socialist System: The Political Economy of Communism.* Princeton: Princeton University Press.

Kreidl, Martin (2004) "Politics and Secondary School Tracking in Socialist Czechoslovakia, 1948–1989," *European Sociological Review* 20 (2): 123–139.

Krueger, Anne O. (1997) "Trade Policy and Economic Development: How we Learn," *American Economic Review* 87 (1): 1–22.

Kubicek, Paul (1999) "Organized Labor in Postcommunist States: Will the Western Sun Set on it, Too?" *Comparative Politics* 32 (1): 83–102.

Kuznets, Simon (1953) *Shares of Upper Income Groups in Income and Savings.* New York: National Bureau of Economic Research.

Kuznets, Simon (1955) "Economic Growth and Income Inequality," *American Economic Review* 45 (1): 1–28.

Lado, Maria (2002) "Industrial Relations in the Candidate Countries," *European Industrial Relations Observatory On-line.* http://www.eurofound.europa.eu/eiro/2002/07/feature/tn0207102f.htm, accessed on May 27, 2009.

Lecaillon, Jacques, Felix Paukert, Christian Morrisson, and Dimitri Germidis (1984) *Income Distribution and Economic Development: Analytical Survey.* Geneva: International Labor Organization.

Lesthaeghe, Ron (1995) "The Second Demographic Transition in Western Countries: An Interpretation," in Karen Oppenheim Mason and An-Magritt Jensen (eds) *Gender and Family Change in Industrialized Countries,* 17–62. Oxford: Clarendon Press.

Lesthaeghe, Ron and Johan Surkyn (1988) "Cultural Dynamics and Economic Theories of Fertility Change," *Population and Development Review* 14 (1): 1–45.

Lesthaeghe, Ron and Johan Surkyn (2002) "New Forms of Household Formation in Central and Eastern Europe: Are They Related to Newly Emerging Value Orientations?" *UN ECE Economic Survey of Europe* 1: 197–216.

Lesthaeghe, Ron and Karel Neels (2002) "From the First to the Second Demographic Transition: An Interpretation of the Spatial Continuity of Demographic Innovation in France, Belgium and Switzerland." *European Journal of Population/Revue européenne de démographie* 18 (4): 225–260.

Lindert, Peter H. and Jeffrey G. Williamson (1985) "Growth, Equality, and History," *Explorations in Economic History* 22 (4): 341–377.

Lipsey, Robert E. and Fredrik Sjoholm (2001) *Foreign Direct Investment and Wages in Indonesian Manufacturing.* NBER Working Paper no. 8299. Cambridge, Mass.: National Bureau of Economic Research.

Lipton, David and Jeffrey Sachs (1990) "Privatization in Eastern Europe: The Case of Poland," *Brookings Papers on Economic Activity* (2): 293–341.

Maddock, Nicholas (1995) "Agriculture after Socialism—The Transformation and Development of Lithuanian Agriculture," *Food Policy* 20 (2): 129–137.

Magyari, Nandor L., Eniko Magyari-Vincze, Livia Popescu, and Troian Rotariu (2001) "The Social Construction of Romanian Poverty: The Impact of Ethnic and Gender Distinctions," in Rebecca Jean Emigh and Ivan Szelényi (eds) *Poverty, Ethnicity, and Gender in Eastern Europe During the Market Transition,* 123–156. Westport, Conn.: Praeger.

Mahutga, Matthew C. (2006) "The Persistence of Structural Inequality? A Network Analysis of International Trade, 1965–2000," *Social Forces* 84 (4): 1863–1889.

Mahutga, Matthew C. and Nina Bandelj (2008) "Foreign Investment and Income Inequality: The Natural Experiment of Central and Eastern Europe," *International Journal of Comparative Sociology* 49(6): 429–454.

Markusen, James R. and Anthony J. Venables (1999) "Foreign Direct Investment as a Catalyst for Industrial Development," *European Economic Review* 43 (2): 335–356.

Markusen, John (1995) "The Boundaries of Multinational Enterprises and the Theory of International Trade," *Journal of Economic Perspectives* 9 (2): 169–189.

Marx, Karl (1970) [1875] "Critique of the Gotha Programme," in *Marx / Engels Selected Works*. Volume Three, 13–30. Moscow: Progress Publishers.

McClelland, David (1964) "Business Drive and National Achievement," in Amitai Etzioni and Eva Etzioni (eds) *Social Change: Sources, Patterns, and Consequences*, 165–178. New York: Basic Books.

McMichael, Philip [1996] (2004) *Development and Social Change: A Global Perspective, 3rd ed*. Thousands Oaks, Calif.: Pine Forge Press.

McMillan, Carl (1987) *Multinationals from the Second World: Growth of Foreign Investment by Soviet and East European Enterprises*. London: MacMillan Press.

Megginson, William and Jeffrey Netter (2001) "From State to Market: A Survey of Empirical Studies on Privatization," *Journal of Economic Literature* 39 (2): 321–389.

Meyer, John W. and Michael T. Hannan (1979) *National Development, and the World System: Educational, Economic, and Political Change, 1950–1970*. Chicago: University of Chicago Press.

Milanovic, Branko (1999) "Explaining the Increase in Inequality during the Transition," *Economics of Transition* 7 (2): 299–341.

Moran, Theodore (2002) *Beyond Sweatshops: Foreign Direct Investment in Developing Countries*. Washington D.C.: Brookings Institution.

Mrak, Mojmir, Matija Rojec, and Carlos Silva-Jáuregui (2004) *Slovenia: From Yugoslavia to the European Union*. Washington, D.C.: The World Bank.

Nee, Victor (1989) "A Theory of Market Transition: From Redistribution to Markets in State Socialism," *American Sociological Review* 54 (5): 663–681.

Nielsen, François (1994) "Income Inequality and Industrial Development: Dualism Revisited," *American Sociological Review* 59 (5): 654–677.

Nielsen, François and Arthur Alderson (1995) "Income Inequality, Development, and Dualism: Results from an Unbalanced Cross-National Panel," *American Sociological Review* 60 (5): 674–701.

Nielsen, François and Arthur Alderson (1997) "The Kuznets Curve and the Great U-Turn: Income Inequality in U.S. Counties, 1970 to 1990," *American Sociological Review* 62 (1): 12–33.

O'Dwyer, Connor and Branislav Kovalcik (2007) "And the Last Shall be First: Party System Institutionalization and Second-Generation Economic Reform in Postcommunist Europe," *Studies in Comparative International Development* 41(4): 3–26.

Ost, David (2000) "Illusory Corporatism in Eastern Europe: Neo-liberal Tripartism and Postcommunist Class Identities," *Politics and Society* 28 (4): 503–530.

Rabusic, Ladislav (2001) "Value Change and Demographic Behavior in the Czech Republic," *Czech Sociological Review* 9 (1): 99–122.

Raley, R. Kelly (2001) "Increasing Fertility in Cohabiting Unions: Evidence for the Second Demographic Transition in the United States?" *Demography* 38 (1): 59–66.

Ranney, David (1998) "Investment Liberalization Agenda," *Foreign Policy in Focus* 3 (21): 1–4. http://www.fpif.org/briefs/vol3/v3n21trad.html, accessed on April 24, 2005.

Robinson, Sherman (1976) "A Note on the U-Hypothesis Relating Income Inequality and Economic Development," *American Economic Review* 66 (3): 437–440.

Robinson, William I. (2004) *A Theory of Global Capitalism: Production, Class, and State in a Transnational World*. Baltimore: Johns Hopkins University Press.

Róna-Tas, Ákos (1994) "The First Shall Be Last? Entrepreneurship and Communist Cadres in the Transition from Socialism," *American Journal of Sociology* 100 (1): 40–69.

Róna-Tas, Ákos (1997) *The Great Surprise of the Small Transformation: The Demise of Communism and the Rise of the Private Sector in Hungary*. Ann Arbor: Michigan University Press.

Rostow, Walt W. (1960) *The Stages of Economic Growth: A Non-Communist Manifesto*. Cambridge: Cambridge University Press.

Sachs, Jeffrey and David Lipton (1990) "Poland's Economic Reform," *Foreign Affairs* 69 (3): 47–66.

Sachs, Jeffrey (1989) "My Plan for Poland," *International Economy* 3 (6): 24–29.

Safarian, Edward (1966) *Foreign Ownership of Canadian Industry*. Toronto: McGraw-Hill.

Simpson, Miles (1990) "Political Rights and Income Inequality: A Cross-National Test," *American Sociological Review* 55 (5): 682–693.

Smelser, Neil and Richard Swedberg (2005) *The Handbook of Economic Sociology*, 2nd ed. Princeton: Princeton University Press.

Smith, Stephen C., Cin Beom-Cheol, and Milan Vodopivec (1997) "Privatization Incidence, Ownership Forms, and Firm Performance: Evidence from Slovenia," *Journal of Comparative Economics* 25 (1): 158–179.

Smooha, Sammy (2001) *The Model of Ethnic Democracy*. ECMI Working Paper 13. http://www.ecmi.de/download/working_paper_13.pdf, accessed on January 15, 2005.

Sobotka, Tomás, Kry tof Zeman, and Vladimíra Kantorová (2003) "Demographic Shifts in the Czech Republic after 1989: A Second Demographic Transition View," *European Journal of Population/Revue européenne de démographie* 19 (3): 249–277.

Solow, Robert M. (1956) "A Contribution to the Theory of Economic Growth," *Quarterly Journal of Economics* 70 (1): 65–94.

Stack, Steven (1980) "The Political Economy of Income Inequality: A Comparative Analysis," *Canadian Journal of Political Science* 13 (2): 273–286.

Standing, Guy (1996) "Social Protection in Central and Eastern Europe: A Tale of Slipping Anchors and Torn Safety Nets," in Gøsta Esping-Andersen (ed.) *Welfare States in Transition: National Adaptations in Global Economies*, 225–255. London: Sage Publications.

Staniszkis, Jadwiga (1991) *The Dynamics of Breakthrough in Eastern Europe: The Polish Experience*. Berkeley: University of California Press.

Stark, David (1992) "Path Dependence and Privatization Strategies in East Central Europe," *East European Societies and Politics* 6 (1): 17–54.

Stark, David and László Bruszt (1998) *Post-socialist Pathways: Transforming Politics and Property in East Central Europe*. Cambridge: Cambridge University Press.

Stopford, John and Luis Wells (1972) *Managing the Multinational Enterprise*. New York: Basic Books.

Swan, Trevor W. (1956) "Economic Growth and Capital Accumulation," *Economic Record* 32: 334–361.

Swedberg, Richard (2003) *Principles of Economic Sociology*. Princeton: Princeton University Press.

Szalai, Julia (1999) "Recent Trends in Poverty in Hungary," in Yogesh Atal (ed.) *Poverty in Transition and Transition in Poverty: Recent Developments in*

Hungary, Bulgaria, Romania, Georgia, Russia, Mongolia, 32–76. New York: Berghahn Books.

Szelenyi, Ivan (1978) "Social Inequalities in State Socialist Redistributive Economies," *International Journal of Comparative Sociology* 19 (1–2): 63–87.

Szelenyi, Ivan (1988) *Socialist Entrepreneurs: Embourgeoisement in Rural Hungary*. Madison: University of Wisconsin Press.

Szelenyi, Ivan and Eric Kostello (1996) "The Market Transition Debate: Toward a Synthesis?" *American Journal of Sociology* 101 (4): 1082–1096.

Tinbergen, Jan (1975) *Income Distribution: Analysis and Policies*. Amsterdam: North Holland.

Titma, Mikk, Liina Mai Tooding, and Nancy Brandon Tuma (2004) "Communist Party Members: Incentives and Gains," *International Journal of Sociology* 34 (2): 72–99.

Todorova, Sasha (1999) "Emerging Poverty in Bulgaria," in Yogesh Atal (ed.) *Poverty in Transition and Transition in Poverty: Recent Developments in Hungary, Bulgaria, Romania, Georgia, Russia, Mongolia*, 77–101. New York: Berghahn Books.

TransMONEE (2003) *Database*. Florence: UNICEF Innocenti Research Center.

Trif, Aurora (2005) *Collective Bargaining Practices in Eastern Europe: Case Study Evidence from Romania*. Cologne: Max Planck Institute for the Study of Societies, Working Paper 05/9.

Tsai, Pan-Long (1995) "Foreign Direct Investment and Income Inequality: Further Evidence," *World Development* 23 (3): 469–483.

Tuma, Nancy B. and Michael T. Hannan (1984) *Social Dynamics: Models and Methods*. Orlando: Academic Press.

UNCTAD (1998) *World Investment Report*. Washington, D.C.: United Nations Conference on Trade and Development.

UNCTAD (2002) *World Investment Report*. Washington, D.C.: United Nations Conference on Trade and Development.

UNCTAD (2006.)*World Investment Report: Search by Country/Economy*. http://www.unctad.org/Templates/Page.asp?intItemID=3198&lang=1, accessed on March 20, 2006.

United Nations University (2010) "World Income Inequality Database 2008." http://www.wider.unu.edu/research/Database/en_GB/satabase/, accessed on February 15, 2010.

van de Kaa, Dirk J. (1987) "Europe's Second Demographic Transition," *Population Bulletin* 42 (1): 1–59.

Verdery, Katherine (2003) *The Vanishing Hectare: Property and Value in Postsocialist Transylvania*. Ithaca: Cornell University Press.

Verdery, Katherine (1998) "Transnationalism, Nationalism, Citizenship, and Property: Eastern Europe since 1989," *American Ethnologist* 25 (2): 291–306.

Vernon, Raymond (1971) *Sovereignty at Bay: The Multinational Spread of U.S. Enterprises*. New York: Basic Books.

Vernon, Raymond (1999) "The Harvard Multinational Enterprise Project in Historical Perspective," *Transnational Corporations* 8 (2): 35–49.

Wallerstein, Immanuel (1974) *The Modern World System*. New York: Academic Press.

Western, Bruce (1997) *Between Class and Market: Postwar Unionization in the Capitalist Democracies*. Princeton: Princeton University Press.

Williamson, Geoffrey (1991) *Inequality, Poverty, and History: The Kuznets Memorial Lectures of the Economic Growth Center*. Cambridge, Mass.: Basil Blackwell.

Williamson, John (1993) "Democracy and the Washington Consensus," *World Development* 21(8): 1329–1336.

10 Indian Society and Globalization
Inequality and Change

Gérard Djallal Heuzé

India has been for a long time a symbol of inequality. Its global poverty reputation has its origin in the nineteenth century. Since the beginning of the British intrusion (1757), India (*The Indies*) was considered to be a place of wealthy people. It produced one fifth of the world income,[1] but this part fell under 4 percent at the end of the colonial period (1947), despite the development of a national industry.[2] Prior to European rule, there were numerous privileged groups living from rents. Yet, a large group of owners (or—more commonly—beneficiaries[3]) of land and craftsmen were at the center of the society.

In this chapter, inequality is measured according to the availability of food. To estimate the level of poverty, the Indian administration considers that the necessary income should permit one to get 2,400 calories a day. This perception has a dramatic importance: from 23 million babies born in a year, 8 million die before reaching adulthood. The infant mortality rate is as high as 67/100 and malnutrition is the main problem. By 2004, India occupied place 127 among 177 on the Human Development Index. Three years later, 79 percent of Indian children had nutrition problems and 75 percent of citizens had a weight inferior to the norm.[4] Thus, linking inequality and the level of food availability remains important.

The percentage of seriously under-fed populations is a very important concern for governments, NGOs, and economists.[5] The poverty rate was at about 55 percent of Indians during the 1970s. After this period, authorized sources claimed that it regularly decreased. The official rate is currently around 27 percent, a figure that hides very important regional (it amounts to almost 50 percent in Bihar) and class (marginal peasants, agricultural workers, and casual laborers are those who encounter most hunger[6]) disparities.

SYMBOLIC FRAMEWORKS OF INEQUALITY

Within most of India, material inequality and class differentiations are deeply combined with status differentiations. In the framework of Hindu religion—80.5 percent of the populations are Hindu—we find large social sub-divisions. They are associated with a religiously justified hierarchy that includes the four *varna*.[7] Moreover, many communities organize marriages inside their group, that shape their identity. They are *jati* (birth groups with a specific status). These communities have been conditioning wealth distribution. Lower status *jatis* (*Dalit*, 16 percent of the Indian population) include a majority of agricultural workers, casual workers, and service workers who are poor. Higher status *jatis* (about 12 percent of the population comprising the two highest *varnas*) are well positioned regarding capital, wages, education, and housing. Probably the traders of the third *varna* form the richest group. Intermediary castes[8] (*jatis*) of a *middle* rank make up the large majority. This is the group of petty-landowners. These social segments form the bottom of a system where material inequality is combined with an unequal dispersion of pride. A symbolic mark created of religious beliefs and attitudes of scorn still aggravates the existing conditions of deprivation.

Caste hierarchy is associated with clientelism. It is a fabric of inequality that puts *inferior* groups under the control of the higher and more powerful *jatis* and notables. Clientelism protects weak people but has an exploitative potential as it is characterized by debt bondage.[9] For two centuries, money-lenders used to alienate millions of people, especially peasants and artisans, and employed their workforce free of charge. In South Asia, strong gender inequalities have associated status considerations to strong symbolic contents. Women have been considered as inferior and polluting, so that they could be exploited sexually and at work.

1989: UNDERDEVELOPMENT AND STATE INTERVENTIONISM

India has become a strong democracy in a federal state. According to the Constitution of 1950, building a "united and fraternal country" is a "central aim." The document insists on "equality, justice, and freedom" (articles 14 to 18) that are parts of the "basic principles."

Since 1947 and the birth of the post-colonial India, several kinds of action against poverty were undertaken. Land reform was the most important measure that imposed agricultural property ceilings (10 to 25 acres). Associated with a low level of taxation, it gave a steady basis to middle castes and petty-land-owners.

This change came together with the emergence of an embryonic provident welfare state. The state imposed regulations on the prices of essential items and on markets, creating a network of storage facilities. The aim was to provide minimal rations for the poor. A network of *Fair Price Shops*, selling basic items at a subsidized rate, was created in 1973.[10] However, the Congress Party that dominated the political life for about 40 years after independence never tried to promote equality. This party was an association of conservative notables and modernist elites who wanted to satisfy basic needs while promoting very cautious social transformations with usually very insufficient means.

I will focus here on four periods. From 1950 to 1964, infrastructures and industries were built in an optimistic ambiance. The development of roads, railways, and thus, the communication network brought some betterment to the conditions of poor men and women. From 1965 to 1977, a state populism arose that favored a socialistic rhetoric but that did not succeed in changing the situation. Authoritarian excesses, exacerbated socialistic rhetoric, and technocratic changes characterized the period from 1975 to 1977. Between 1977 and 1990, well-organized social groups, the *jatis,* who had political influence and an educated elite, *fought for grasping the spoils of the state.*[11]

In these four periods, Indian society could not achieve equality. The attempts at creating cooperatives and other alternative production systems failed. The state had neither the means nor the will to change the situation but occupied a central position without being able to become a provident welfare state. On the one hand, the English-educated higher caste groups who ignored the aspirations of the masses controlled the state. On the other, the notables persisted in their age-old patronage. The state was often scornful with common people, an attitude inherited from the colonial period and the British colonizers.

In 1985, new liberal policies began to influence Indian society. The first transformation was linked to the textile policy of 1985 that could not be considered a move towards equality. The failure of the educational policy, the reduction of already miserable public health budgets, the rise of unemployment, the multiplication of slums, the growing difference between the *organized* (formal) sector economy and the *unorganized* (informal) sector aggravated the situation. The society became increasingly city-based and characterized by regional disparities. The conditions of women, threatened by the demands of *dowry* (that is considered in India a kind of a groom-price), and selective abortion practices targeting unborn female descendants, had worsened. The assertion of reservation systems for the lower castes (*dalit*) and the *tribes* (*adivasi*), the promulgation of laws prohibiting untouchability practices had however bettered the position of the lower *jatis.* Parts of *symbolic inequality* slightly receded. Democracy, despite its association with clientelism, was acclaimed for this move.

TWENTY YEARS OF PRO-MARKET AND PRO-RICH POLICIES

Changes in economic policy were important so that the year 1991 was the main demarcation line. Policy measures imposed the cutting down of customs duties. The country was now open to foreign investment. There was a liberalization of monetary, commercial, and industrial policies. In the private sector, there were many closures and modifications in industries. Let us analyze here the social consequences of these events.

Assistance Systems

The state did not try to change assistance systems that were established after 1973. They gave work or assets to the poor in order to alleviate poverty or to promote development. Systems of ration cards had been established in 1973 and continued to function. When the Congress party came to run the Progressive Democratic Front coalition in 2004, the National Rural Employment Program (NREP) was intensified. Its aim was to provide three months of employment every year to 100 million people.[12] Pushed forward by the fragile character of its government coalition,[13] the Congress party tried to go further in 2005–06. Afterwards, under pressure from the communist parties,[14] it was decided to create a system of retirement allowances and a social security scheme for the workers of the *unorganized* (informal) sector (90 percent of the population).

These progressive ventures have persistently been associated to their opposites: a pervasive relationship of inequality between the state and the poor. Clientelist systems have continued to deliver as a gift or an onerous service what should be considered a right, so that state assistance has steadily been misappropriated by smaller but richer social groups.

Health and Education

The situation of public health and education systems has continued to worsen. Budgetary allowances have been weak. Regarding health, there was a recrudescence of tuberculosis, an explosion of AIDS, and the persistence of curable diseases such as measles and leprosy that are ailments of the poor. Beside, a large and profitable system of private clinics has expanded. It has focused on medical problems of high-status groups, especially heart diseases. There has been a similar development in education. Primary education organized by the state has regressed while private colleges have multiplied. Using computers for the pupils' education, even in a limited way, did not bring great changes. This practice has benefited limited groups familiar with the English language, a major element of cultural inequality. Yet, computers without electronic access (as in 30 percent of the villages), and/or even with one, are very problematic because of the frequent breakdowns of the electrical system. Less than 3 percent of the population that belong to the richer and urban groups could thus afford to buy a computer.

Liberal Policies and Employment

The new policy measures failed to provide massive employment but developed the services so that India became the world's *office system*, which is divided according to a three-tier structure. At the center, one can find jobs of engineers and executive staff in the software industry. These job opportunities (1 million anticipated for 2010) are well paid and associated with good working conditions. Then, there are poorly paid but well-organized jobs for other workers. These people toil in call centers and other kinds of services. Finally, large groups of peons, dispatchers, drivers, guards, and cleaners exist in the *world-office*. There are employment possibilities for poor people in the service sector, as well as in the new and numerous five-star hotels, private colleges, and hospitals. These laborers get better salaries than others working in street-vending or as home service workers. In the service sector, the income distribution is rather unequal so that an engineer's salary is 20 to 50 times what the cleaner gets.

The Development of Construction and Small Enterprises

In India, there is a lack of 30 million houses. The new policy, inciting rich people to invest, was implemented by an important growth of this sector. Manpower in the construction industry has more than doubled from 15 to 31 million workers between 1991 and 2006.[15] These new laborers are most often casual workers that labor contractors have frequently recruited.[16] Nine out of ten jobs in this category are insufficient for sustaining a family. Enslaving debt systems, child labor, and economic activities of pregnant women are generalized. *Freedom* prophesized by the partisans of the market does not apply to these people. Even bonded laborers often prefer to stay bonded, because the *free market* seems to be too harsh for them.[17]

Casual workers are also concerned by the recruitment in industry. The pool of permanent jobs in the *organized* sector only rose by 800,000 people from 1991 to 2006. The percentage of manpower in this sector decreased from 9.8 to 9.4 percent.[18] The growth of employment in the *organized* sector concerns small enterprises that moved to the countryside in order to avoid trade unions and flout labor laws. Indeed, a large majority of the new industrial workers remained in the *unorganized* sector. Informal employment possibilities include street-vending and home-based work. As there seems to be a trend that the state considers street-vendors as criminals, the conditions of the urban poor get even worse. There has been a twofold increase of the manpower from 20 to 40 millions in the last 20 years. Yet, the life conditions of these workers are difficult. They don't benefit from any social laws, and they can only get low earnings. Working hours are long and working conditions are dangerous. In India, there are now more industrial workers but they are getting poorer and poorer, and are unable to help their families. A worker in the *organized* sector can normally feed five persons. A worker in the *unorganized* sector feeds only one and a half persons if he/she lives in a slum or in a cheap location. Poverty having previously characterized the non-irrigated countryside is now concentrated in the periphery of the metropolitan areas. It is also located in the industrialized countryside of regions such as Gujarat and Tamil Nadu.

The Rise of Housing Inequalities

The life conditions of the poor in cities have changed from bad to worse. Steady attacks against the slums had begun with the Asian Games in 1981 when the state had tried to display a positive image of towns. In 1989, a steady offensive against slums[19] was launched. Yet, no viable alternative solutions existed. For example, 1.5 million people were displaced in the last 20 years in the metropolis of Mumbai. They were pushed away from public facilities, jobs, and commercial stores. The percentage of the population living in shanty-towns is stable or even growing but these places are exposed to frequent attacks. The policy of poor cleansing[20] that was aggravated by the pro-market reforms has been a powerful element raising inequality. For a long time, it was possible to be poorly housed but to benefit from the opportunities and the facilities of the urban areas by staying in the center or in well-situated locations. The move of industrial plants to distant suburbs and Special Economic Zones (SEZ) has aggravated the situation of the poor. They have been forced to live in shanty-towns far away from the center so that they have to travel long distances between their place of employment and their home. The housing conditions of state employees and workers in the *organized* sector also tend to worsen in large cities. The huge rise of rents (rents in Mumbai are as expensive as in London, but wages are about eight times lower), the abolition of the legal protection of the tenants still accentuated by liberal policies, and the unsafe conditions of some districts have made their lives difficult.[21] The period from 1989 to 2009 has been characterized by the appropriation of urban areas by a minority of about 20 percent of the population. These are rich owners, who struggle in order to control still more space. There has been a multiplication of five-star hotels and housing for wealthy people including *gated communities* (closed estates where the richer population lives), which is a buoyant activity so that a noticeable percentage of the new owners have numerous apartments.[22]

Inequality and Development in the Countryside

Pro-market economists have often considered the countryside and especially subsistence agriculture as useless.[23] Land property ceilings and other land reforms have not been abolished but have become targets of a growing criticism. Although under-investment in the rural landscape is an old tradition, pro-market thinkers wanted to sack subsidies. They aimed at abolishing non–profit-making farms, and, in particular, the small ones that represent a majority. A growing group of small farmers had thus to accept wage migrant labor, handicrafts, or home-based work in order to survive and in addition to their agricultural revenue. Yet, people did not massively quit the countryside because of the fact that opportunities have been too scarce in the urban areas.

Malnutrition is still prevalent among the rural population. Educational facilities are not of a high quality and health facilities are scarce. The abolition of market regulations in agricultural productions (e.g., subsidized prices) has provoked the suicide of ten thousands of farmers. The privatization of common land that was intensified during the period that interests us here had negative consequences for the poorest of them. Marginal farmers and agricultural laborers lost one of their opportunities to obtain revenue. Some craftsmen such as rope-makers have entered a deep crisis. Great dams, for example the Narmada Sardar Sarovar that was completed in 2006, displaced hundreds of thousands of people. The problem appeared in the 1960s but the new administration continued to be particularly tough with the *oustees* (evicted people). The financial compensation of sharecroppers (*baitidars*) and marginal farmers has been very low. Large industrial, export-oriented farms have been promoted by the new policies. Several states, such as Gujarat and Maharashtra, which are the most industrialized regions, have promulgated new laws facilitating the eviction of farmers for industrial purposes.

However, a certain quantity of wealth trickles down to the countryside. The spreading of new seeds and irrigation, the bettering of the infrastructure (roads), the partial mechanization of agriculture, and the wages in the construction industry have given many rural people a sort of confidence. New items such as small motorcycles have been introduced. The upper third among the farmers that is able to produce for the market benefits from this sort of prosperity.

Inequalities and the Environmental Scene

The past period of 20 years showed signs of a rather moderate development of the productive forces. In the meantime, there was a growing impact of better-off people on the natural environment. This process had tremendous results. For example, one tenth of the villages (55,000 out of 550,000) lost their access to drinking water.[24] The pumping of deep water by rich peasants depleted the water resources. Six hundred golf courses have been created for tourists and expatriates. Their lawns are particularly appreciated when they appear in the middle of the desert (*Rajasthan*). The watering of these lawns corresponds to the missing water of the villages.[25] Moreover, rich people are beginning to eat a lot of shrimps, which originate from farms that endanger the environment. However, ten million sea and river fishermen have to fight a desperate battle to protect their resources that are sold to multinational corporations or destroyed by pollution.[26] While hundreds of thousands agricultural workers get ill[27] by spreading pesticides with their hands, engineers and officers living in the metropolis are busy with "environmental concerns." They target these "ugly slums" and their "antisocial elements" (quotations). Dozens of millions of peasant women look for wood at far away distances[28] (up to 60 km) while the upper classes demand more and more electronic power for air-conditioned facilities.

Middle Class Farce and Tragedy

The reform decades were again and again presented as the years of the *middle class*. There was an affirmation of rich or petty rich urbanized groups and higher caste tax-payers. These strata had existed prior to pro-market policies but, after the changes in commercial and economic rules, they started to live in a new environment. Goods that were missing or bought through illegal channels overflew the market. Consumption was fashionable. As media professionals belong to this group, the *reforms* were interpreted as an important change. The *middle class* rose from 12 percent to 18 percent of the Indian population. Yet, these figures are probably an overestimation. Even if this is a major transformation, the *middle class* remains only a numerous minority.

The *middle class* is not one but multiple. There are *middle classes*: there are differences of community (e.g., the emergence of a *dalit middle class*), region, and occupation in India. What are the links between a state employee of grade II, dwelling in a poorly maintained tenement, and a rich clinic owner, living in a posh area, despite their common higher-caste family name and their quest for *Americanization*, features which are common among the *middle class*? Probably there are very few! The *upper middle class* (6 percent of the Indian population), a privileged part of the *middle class* influences the image of the new globalized society. The development of this *upper middle class*, that is urban, professional, qualified, educated, and polluting, has nothing to do with a process of equalization. A middle class constituting the majority of the population, illustrating a way of life considered to be good and moral, has been an essential part of the class mythology of the United States of America and Great Britain.[29] In *liberalized* India, the case is different. The *middle class* is neither central nor a majority. Present-day frequent incomes amount to approximately ten euros a day (including non-market services). This implies that people who have got a car (less than 2 percent of the population[30]), people who have got air-conditioned facilities, and the minority, who can spend holidays in two to five-star hotels, are not a *middle class* but a high or wealthy group, with different degrees of *Americanization*—for example, speaking English with a US accent, listening to American music, and eating fast food—introducing numerous nuances. The rise of a stratum of IT engineers and other professionals introduces a strong group of wage earners among these wealthier people who remain privileged. Finally, the very rich, those who have most benefited from globalization, industrial magnates and big merchants, but also the new group of finance specialists, mafia-type *nouveaux riches*, and engineers, all of them enjoy some privileges so that they may be considered as members of the *middle class*.[31]

However, the Indian society is living a stressful situation. The *middle class* has grown sufficiently to be the most important beneficiary of the *reforms* but not enough to become a massive reality. At the same time, its characteristics have changed. The frugal postures of the Nehru era have been abandoned. Nowadays, it is impossible for a large majority of Indians to think of emulating it. The so-called *middle class* has no sociological cohesion. Yet, it has acquired particular symbolic and imaginary dimensions so that it claims to be the only future of India. This group provokes the wrath of the *have-nots*, but also of educated individuals. This *middle class*, more exactly the *upper middle class*, has been able to get the attention and the money of the state. Many investments in airports, roads, universities, and the sophisticated railway system are for its specific use. However, this group discards and vilifies the state.

The globalization process and pro-market reforms have thus brought to prominence a new group of rich people who have found new ways to function: television programs (*Bollywood*) are the most efficient ways to impose a life and consumption style that imitates affluent Western populations.

Caste Inequality

Caste inequality is a field where inequality has receded the most. These changes are the result of several factors. The practice of reservation has finally produced results. Jobs have been reserved for the lower castes and tribal groups since 1950. Elites emerged among many *jatis* of former untouchables and *Other Backward Classes*.[32] The growth of the group of skilled workers and employees has also been noticeable. Elites of the lower castes are primarily associated to state employment. But the rise of other categories of elites, such as labor contractors and petty entrepreneurs, can also be found. The state support of lower castes was several times opposed to movements of the higher and dominant castes (in 1981, 1985, and 1990).[33] The failure of these attempts was linked to the disaffection from the state of elites belonging to higher castes, a tendency that has provoked peevish criticism of the *bureaucracy*. Ideas associated with globalization have been the perfect idiom for this offensive. Indeed, higher castes have been the main actors of the New Economy. These groups have also continued to migrate to the US.

A majority of the *scheduled castes* and *tribes* are still poor. One half of the population living under the poverty line belongs to these groups. They are among the less educated and the most poorly housed Indians but the setting is changing. Parts of the self-depreciation of the lower castes have disappeared. Their *symbolic inequality* is less visible. There are numerous processes of self-assertion and pride recovery. Their spatial marginalization is receding. The most important changes have been occurring in places where political movements of the lower castes have existed, such as in Maharashtra and Uttar Pradesh. Political mediation has thus played an important role in the transformation process.

Gender

Gender inequalities are more resilient. They exist in all castes. New professions are open to women, rich actresses mobilize the media; affirmative actions for women have been introduced at the local level,[34] and B. Mayavati, a Dalit Chamar[35], has tried to concretize the political progress of poor women. Yet, inequality remains the norm. In numerous circumstances, it is even increasing. This issue has never been a priority for the Indian pro-market *globalizers*.

The system of *groom-price* (the so-called *dowry*) has continued to expand. Its prohibition, in 1961 and then in 1976, has not been a high priority for enforcement. The growth of consumption and the fascination for the rich people's lifestyle has fueled this system among poor communities. Among the better-off strata, the young brides are exposed to very strong pressures, culminating in a series of selective abortion practices against female fruits of womb. The result is that, in India, there are now 115 men for 100 women.

In the aggravated conditions of poverty and marginalization of the slums, the lives of women are particularly difficult. They are forced to work outside but they have to do the house chores alone, men being unconcerned by them.[36] Two trends improve this rather bleak scene of gender inequality. Women are less educated than men but some changes are happening in several regions, especially in the South and in the West of India. Education helps women to master their fertility. In half of the national territory, the birth rate is strongly decreasing. Moreover, a growing number of women has the courage to think about their own health. In 2007, the Hindu family code was changed in order to give inheritance rights to women. However, women rights seem to regress among Muslims (13.4 percent of the population).

THE FUTURE OF INEQUALITY

The *free market* ideology valorizes individual consumers and consumption, and denies the importance of rules favoring the community. Most often, the downsizing of inequality is not considered important because inequality is thought to be a normal fact of a society functioning according to the economic rules of the market. In fact, the Indian Union, with its 1.15 billion inhabitants supported for 30 years an *aborted* socialism. Its pro-market policy was deeply mitigated by the resilience of state interventionism and the importance of the public sector.[37]

The first period of economic liberalism during the nineteenth century caused a free circulation of people that has continued to exist in 2010. This principle does not explain the advent of unmanageable cities, because these have derived from the long absence of an urban policy. Major social and economic trends existed before the New Economic Policy. They have only been aggravated, which is the case, for example, for the casualization of labor and housing, the development of the *informal* sector, the rising differentiation of the formal and *informal* sectors, the agricultural mechanization, and the marginalization of more than one half of the farms. Caste and gender inequalities have even older origins.

The weak industrialization of the country is a dominant feature. Sixteen percent of the population works in the secondary sector; they were 11 percent in 1971. Recruitments in the construction industry and in smaller industrial sectors were unable to seriously better the level of income of the majority of the population. Meanwhile, the worsening aspects, such as the housing crisis, concern most of them. For more than one half of Indians, the situation in the educational and health sectors went from bad to worse. Budgetary allocations decreased from 3.1 percent to 2.7 percent of the global budget in the period from 1991 to 2001. Beside sophisticated clinics with all facilities, that nowadays cure the entire world, the situation is pitiable for state-promoted hospitals where self-styled practitioners *cure* the masses of the *informal* sector. In this situation, the community-based organizations (caste, region, and religion) and family solidarity have become more important than ever. Local associations are spreading, such as temple committees and community welfare associations. Despite their involvement in social services, these organizations are primarily refuges. Yet, they are threatened by the impact of the commercial television that induces new desires and consumption styles. The globalizing aspects of their programs let on the one hand people identify with local dimensions, such as caste and kin, but on the other, they contribute to a significant change in the understanding of these same institutions.

Rich Predatories

Wealth accumulation is currently a major problem. Parts of the better-off groups create employment, but a large part of the present prosperity has become predatory so that it triggers social and environmental tensions. The appropriation of urban areas by the upper middle class and the wealthiest groups and their recent interest in important rural zones[38] mean threat and discomfort for the majority of the population. The consumption habits[39] of the more affluent, their practices regarding industrialization, and the recruitment of labor are directed against the poor and the working classes, particularly in the *informal* sector. Their behavior in front of the natural environment is a practice relating to the whole society. The conditions of this environment are important for millions of poor who live from the earth and its produces. The prosperous car industry provides thousands of jobs but the multiplication of enormous sport-utility vehicles and the proliferation of Special Economic Zones[40] where parts of labor laws are not enforced, concretize a sort of inequality growth that is characteristic of India's recent global period.

The State

State intervention against inequality remains pertinent. It is very difficult to predict the future of recent laws on retirement allowances and social security in the *informal* sector, and thus among 90 percent of the population. They could be treated as the numerous laws abolishing debt bondage, which were flouted regularly since 1843 and the first Bonded Labor Abolition Act. The policies intended to help the poorest of the poor who are old and have never been abandoned during the reform period are a field where the Indian state has continuously reacted. However, assistance programs of the state never tried to eradicate poverty. They wanted to "give a chance to the poor," as it is promoted by and in US ideology, or to prevent the poor from starving, a preoccupation inherited from the colonial state. However, a large part of the assistance programs of the state was diverted towards the middle-income groups. It is doubtful whether assistance structures, such as the Integrated Rural Employment Program (IREP), which has intended to bring assets and training to poor families, will become more efficient or will remain at the present low level of competence. Whatever the case, assistance programs will be more and more solicited, a massive industrialization of the country being out of question for the near future (Boillot 2006).

The Organized Sector

The dichotomy *organized* sector and *unorganized* sector is central to the problem of inequality. The trend towards a growing differentiation of the better-protected part of the *organized* sector was not altered by global pro-market policies. IT engineers and other well-paid employees of the new economy belong to the *best* parts of the *organized* sector. Pro-market publicists[41] support the new rich professional classes, their *alter ego*. Besides, they criticize the privileges of the *organized* sector, mainly targeting trade unions and industrial workers. Indeed, policy makers have not even dared to change the complicated labor laws. The numerical expansion of the *informal* sector, associated with a process of a rather slow and incomplete industrialization, and the growing differences between wages of the different sectors and sub-sectors, have continued to be dominant trends.

NGOs and the Fight against Inequality

During the last 20 years, NGOs were often considered an alternative to state intervention. There are hundreds of thousands of associations, which benefited from a worldwide wave of popularity and a local favorable status. NGOs do not fight against the state. They benefit from its money, staff, and cooperation. It is very difficult to evaluate the impact of the NGOs on inequality. As far as I know and could investigate, it is rather limited in

India.[42] The interventions of the NGOs are efficient if they are associated to a state program. Ready-made fashionable recipes such as micro-credit do not seem to work very well.[43] According to several researchers (Guérin *et al.* 2004), money-lenders, labor contractors, and politicians make a mockery of many ventures of micro-credit.

Social Insurgents for Equality

Leftist guerillas are getting greater importance in Central India, between Andhra Pradesh and the Nepalese border. Their position is radical on the topic of inequality: fair wages are demanded at gunpoint, land-owners possessing large territories are killed, the guerillas try to redistribute land and fight against the state. These movements are primarily agrarian and focus on poor regions. They are supported by the landless, the scheduled castes, and tribes. By targeting the land-owners who prevent land reforms and by demanding a rise of agricultural wages, these guerillas have been more efficient than many laws and a lot of NGOs, in particular, in certain parts of Bihar, Telengana, or Jharkhand. Nevertheless, the improvements are fragile and the beneficiaries pay rapidly, because of violence, and *revolutionary taxes*, but the consecutive decay of infrastructures reduces the benefits they have been able to grasp. However, the leftist armed groups have been able to change the mentalities of the lower castes and to destroy a part of the *symbolic inequality*. These groups have also tried to change women's conditions. They have introduced, for example, primary education and military training for women.

CONCLUSION: A COMPLICATED SCENE

Indian society has changed but has not been overturned, as the existence of more and more social tensions has proven. Large parts of the urban bourgeoisie—the middle class—remain aloof from social preoccupations. The state is often the last recourse, despite its doubtful efficiency and uncertain commitment. Present-day India has become as much unequal as the US, China, or colonial India. There is much more wealth than in the 1980s but it has been concentrated among a few groups, and there are social strata and regions that have witnessed a degenerating situation. Policy changes in the field of inequality are unthinkable without an empowerment of common people: it seems as if important parts of the legislation deserve changes or even eradication.[44] An improvement of state interventions that would necessitate the recruitment[45] of numerous and motivated civil servants seems to be necessary. Political measures on the *organized–unorganized* social and economic divides that should regulate and improve the *unorganized* sector and not the reverse should be a further condition of the future development of the sub-continent.

NOTES

1. This percentage can be found in the book of Boillot (2006).
2. Created in the second part of the nineteenth century, the economy was mainly based on cotton and textile (Chandra 1980).
3. There were various rights on land, water, and their produces.
4. *Times of India*, January 16, 2009.
5. See Heuzé (2007).
6. There are also widows and people without family members.
7. See Dumont (1966) who has underlined a structuralist point of view.
8. The meaning of the word *caste* comprises *jati* and *varna*, and seems thus inadequate to understand Indian society. The *jati* notion includes an equalitarian content (Gupta 2000).
9. See the publications of Breman (1999 and 2008) and Heuzé (2008).
10. In several provinces, specific programs existed that delivered rice or kerosene to local people before elections.
11. This expression is very common in India and means that people try to obtain privileges from the state and its administration.
12. This figure gives a clue about the size of rural unemployment. In 1995, the ILO estimated at 20 percent the percentage of "severely under-employed" people in India (special correspondent in 1995).
13. The National Democratic Alliance (the opposition led by the rightist Bharatiya Janata Party (BJP) associates 18 parties. The PDF (Progressive Democratic Front) is made up of 24 parties. The Congress Party controlled a minority of parliamentary seats in 2005. This minority was enlarged in 2009.
14. There are two larger communist parties and several smaller ones. The most powerful Communist Party in India (Marxist) has obtained a regional base in West Bengal and Kerala.
15. The data on manpower in the construction industry are dubious and can only be taken as a landmark.
16. Intermediaries get a part of the wages because patronage relationships exist. See Heuzé, Jagga, and Zins (1993).
17. Guérin, Bukuth, and Venkatasubrahmaniam Parthasarthy (2007). This article explains why Indian laborers prefer bondage to a competition that would make them even more miserable.
18. The working population is traditionally under-estimated in India. Nevertheless, the number of workers in the *organized* sector is well known. Yet, the importance of this sector may be inferior to the official figures by about 8 percent.
19. There are wealthy people in the slums, but they form a minority. Moreover, commercial companies and industries exist in slums.
20. See Heuzé (2003).
21. See Dupont and Heuzé (2007). This book presents some global approaches of large cities, some articles on slums, and gives information on urban policies. From 1989 until today, the proportion of *urban* people rose from 24 percent to 30–31 percent.
22. This is not a new phenomenon. At the end of the nineteenth century, a few dozens of owners possessed in Bombay (Mumbai) one half of the buildings.
23. See, for example, Vyas (1993).
24. There is a strong involvement of international agencies aiming at assisting India, and, in particular, waterless villages.
25. The strange proposal to build a golf course in Dharavi, a large slum of Mumbai, was considered very seriously despite the legal and protected character

of the slum. One may even say that India has a long tradition of cruelty to the poor.

26. The Mumbai metropolis destroys sea life within a radius of 100 km. There is no effluent treatment station for 19 million inhabitants.
27. NGOs speak of 30,000 dead or seriously sick people a year.
28. This is a common reason for suicides. The forest management (forests are most often state-owned) is hostile to local tribal people and peasants even if a recent policy measure (2008) wanted to provide some rights to local people. However, India holds large stocks of coal so that these problems should not exist.
29. This myth was elaborated in Europe, especially in British Victorian society.
30. There are 2.5 cars for 100 people. This rate is growing but a noticeable number of the vehicles belongs to enterprises, political parties, and NGOs.
31. In 2007, India had the largest progression of dollar millionaires in the world. They were officially 123,000 but a huge share of their revenue is not traceable. (*Dépêche du Midi*, September 16, 2008)
32. *Other Backward Classes* is a category with more than 4,000 *jatis*.
33. See Heuzé (1992). This publication focuses on the 1990 movement against the extension of reservations for other backward classes.
34. 30 percent in *gram panchayat* (village councils and municipal councils).
35. Dalits are the politicized version of the former untouchables. The Chamar are the largest *jatis* (caste) of North India.
36. This corresponds to the sexual division of labor observed in Europe. Young men of the poorer groups participate much in the caring for children.
37. According to Polanyi, a *free* and self-regulated market never existed anywhere (Polanyi 1983).
38. Around the urban capital of Delhi, within a radius of 60 km (about 40 miles) better-off people have some sorts of holiday farms, resembling to US ranches. Is it necessary to underline that this happens in a country that does not feed its population? This tradition has been emulated elsewhere in India while the consumption level of cereals has fallen for the last ten years.
39. In 1996, 60,000 persons were invited to a marriage in the Hinduja family who is made up of prominent businessmen.
40. There has been for 10 years an enthusiasm of better-off people about SEZ so that a law has organized these areas (2005). These areas take over the best agricultural lands, occupy immense spaces, and benefit from the particular attention of engineers and the state. In 2007, in West Bengal and Orissa, the police killed 20 persons opposed to the capture of their lands (13 in Orissa and 7 in West Bengal). Yet, hundreds of thousands of farmers resist quietly.
41. There is a constant interference of advertisement, propaganda, and biased theory in the pro-market rhetoric in India, which claims to "abolish ideologies."
42. Based on field observations in Varanasi, Mumbai, Singrauli, and Raipur during this period. They lasted about six years and allowed me to approach many NGOs.
43. See Guérin *et al.* 2004.
44. For example, laws against street-vending, slum development, or prostitution.
45. During the 1990s in Bihar, only 30 percent of the development budgets, although low, were utilized because of the absence of qualified staff. The wages in the administration are ten times less attractive than in the private sector.

BIBLIOGRAPHY

Aseem, P. (2007) *Towards Understanding the Nature of Labour Markets in Brick Kilns*. Paper presented at the Debt-Bondage Issues and Perspectives Workshop, New Delhi, April 19–20.

Bales, K. (2004) *New Slavery: A Reference Handbook*. Santa Barbara: University of California Press.

Banaji, J. (2003) "The fictions of Free Labour: Contract, Coercion and So-called Unfree Labour," *Historical Materialism* 9 (3): 69–95.

Bhalla, G. S. (2008) "Globalisation and Employment Trends in India," *The Indian Journal of Labour Economics* 51 (1): 1–24.

Bhimal, S. (1993) "Reluctant Reforms," *India Today* 15 (9): 78–79.

Boillot, J. J. (2006) *L'économie de l'Inde*. Paris: La Découverte.

Breman, J. (1999) *The Labouring Poor in India. Patterns of Exploitation, Subordination and Exclusion*. New Delhi and Oxford: Oxford University Press.

Breman, J. (2008) "On Labour Bondage, Old and New," *The Indian Journal of Labour Economics* 51 (1): 546–608.

Byres, T., J. Kapadia and J. Lerche (eds) (1999) *Rural Relations in India*, Special Issue, *Journal of Peasant Studies* 26 (2–3).

Chakraborthy, B. (2004) *Gender Issues in Bonded Labour*. Geneva: International Labor Organization.

Chandra, B. (1980) *The Rise and Growth of Economic Nationalism*. New Delhi: People's Publishing House.

Chengappa, R. and S. Rekhi (1995) "The Price of Populism," *India Today* 15 (2): 92–101.

Chopra, R. (1995) "Meet Alerts Women on Trade Policies," *The Pioneer* 8 (2): 10.

D. N. (2004) "Low Employment Growth," *Economic and Political Weekly* 39 (23): 2192–2194.

De Neve, G. (2005) *The Everyday Politics of Labour*. Delhi: Social Science Press.

D'Monte, D. (1996) "There are Lies, Damned Lies and Statistics," *Mid-Day*, February 15: 4.

Dupont, V. and G. Heuzé (2007) *La ville en Asie du Sud*. Paris: Éditions de l'École des Hautes Études en Sciences Sociales.

Dumont, L. (1966) *Homo hierarchicus*. Paris: Gallimard.

Guérin, I., A. Bukuth, K. Marius-Gnagnou, J. M. Servet and G. Venkatasubrahmaniam Parthasarthy (2004) *Indebtness, Vulnerability to Bondage and Microfinance*. Geneva: International Labor Organization.

Guérin, I., A. Bukuth, and G. Venkatasubrahmaniam Parthasarthy (2007) "Labour in Brick Kilns: A Case Study from Chennai," *Economic and Political Weekly* 42 (7): 599–606.

Guhan, S. (1995) "Social Expenditure in the Union Budget," *Economic and Political Weekly* 30 (18–19): 1095–1101.

Gupta, D. (2000) *Interrogating Caste*. New Delhi: Penguin Books.

Heuzé, G. (1992) "Les anthropologues dans la tourmente, la controverse sur les quotas d'embauche en Inde," *Journal des anthropologues* 43–44: 167–178.

Heuzé, G., L. R. Jagga, and M. J. Zins (1993) *Les conflits du travail en Inde et au Sri Lanka*. Paris: Karthala.

Heuzé, D. G. (2003) "Logement des pauvres, médiation politique et contrôle urbain à Mumbai," *Revue Autrepart* 25: 153–168.

Heuzé, D. (2007) "Anthropologues et économistes face à la poussée séculaire des forces du libre-échange" in E. Baumann, L. Bazin, P. Ouldahled, P. Phélinas,

M. Sélim, and R. Sobel *Anthropologues et économistes face à la mondialisation*, 205–228. Paris: L'Harmattan.

Heuzé, D. (2008) "Il bondage in India, raffigurazione de la società o eccezione?" in P. G. Salinas *La vita en Prestito*, 105–152. Lecce: Argo.

Iyer, K. G. (2004) *Distressed Migrant Labour in India*. New Delhi: Kanishka Publishers.

Joshi, S. (2006) "Impact of Economic Reforms on Social Expenditure in India," *Economic and Political Weekly* 41 (4): 358–365.

Kaplinsky, R. (2005) *Globalisation, Poverty, and Inequality*. Cambridge: Polity Press.

Kiely, R. (2007) *The New Political Economy of Development*. London: Macmillan.

Munck, R. (ed.) (2004) *Labour and Globalisation, Results and Prospects*. Liverpool: Liverpool University Press.

Nagaraj, R. (1997) "What has happened since 1991? Assessment of India's Economic Reforms," *Economic and Political Weekly* 32 (44–45): 2869–2879.

National Commission for Enterprises in the Unorganized Sector (2007) *Draft Report on Conditions of Work and Promotion of Livelihoods in the Unorganized Sector*. New Delhi: Government of India. Accessed at nceus.gov/in on July 25, 2007.

Noorbasha, A. (1996) "Handlooms in Distress," *Economic and Political Weekly* 31 (23): 1384–1387.

Polanyi, K. (1983) *La grande transformation*. Paris: Gallimard.

Rajalakshmi, T. K. (2006) "Asian Lessons," *Frontline* 20 (10): 47–48.

Shiva, V. (1996) "Creating a Space for the Smallest of Ourselves," *The Times of India* 11: 2.

Singh, A. K. (1993) "Social Consequences of New Economic Policy," *Economic and Political Weekly* 28 (7): 279–285.

Subramaniam, D. (2005) "Deregulation and Labour Policies in a Public Sector Firm," *Economic and Political Weekly* 40 (22–23): 5233–5245.

Sundaram, K. and S. Tendulkar (2003) "Poverty among Social and Economic Groups in India in 1990s," *Economic and Political Weekly* 38 (50): 5263–5277.

Thakore, D. (1995) "Conspiracy of the Mediocrity," *Sunday*, February 19–25: 58–60.

11 Economic Globalization and the Empowerment of Local Entrepreneurs in Nigeria[1]

Adeyinka Oladayo Bankole

INTRODUCTION

There is scarcely any country in the contemporary world where improvement in the living conditions of the population is not a desirable goal for both the rulers and the ruled. However, with the increasing global economic interdependence and interconnectedness, there has been growing scholarly and public debates on what should be the appropriate response of *underdeveloped* societies towards preserving local production activities. Globalization as a phenomenon is a process that manifests itself in different forms. Africa's incorporation into it dated back to the fifteenth century (Jegede, Bankole, and Adejumo 2003: 29). As an economic phenomenon, Andre Gunder Frank noted that "the economy has been global since 1492" (Frank 2004: 607). Interactions between some Africans south of the Sahara and the Europeans began in the early fourteenth century with voyages sponsored by the Portuguese Prince Henry the Navigator, who set himself the task of bypassing the Arabs that controlled North Africa and of establishing direct trade, in particular with the great kingdoms of West Africa (Keim 1995: 115). Trading ships had arrived at Cape Verde by 1460, then reached the Gold Coast (1471), Kongo (1483), and the Cape of Good Hope (1488). In 1497, Vasco da Gama reached the Indian Ocean and the Swahili towns of East Africa, and sailed onward to southern India (Keim 1995: 116).

The situation changed dramatically in the late sixteenth century with the emergence of sugar plantations in South America and the Caribbean. The cultivation of sugar, tobacco, coffee, and cotton required large groups of laborers that the plantation owners could not find among native American workers. This set the stage for the triangular trade between European traders and African middlemen who delivered slaves, captured in the interior regions of Africa. The implications of the slave trade in Africa disrupted Africa's internal agricultural production and commerce (Keim 1995: 123). The abolition of slavery three centuries later—in the second half of the nineteenth century—was followed by decades of colonization, and a system of political, economic, and cultural domination imposed by Europe. This system justified itself by an ideology that asserted the superiority of the colonizer and the inferiority of the colonized (Gellar 1995: 140). In this circumstance, Africa assumed the status of the supplier of cheaply priced raw materials, such as palm and peanut oils, rubber, beeswax, ivory, gum, and coffee to support the Industrial Revolution in Western Europe and to receive in return costly European manufactures. Colonial policies were designed to bind African people more closely to the metropolitan economy and interests. In Nigeria, for instance, colonial policies disrupted the developmental role entrepreneurs had been playing since the pre-colonial period (Olutayo 1999:147). In the pre-colonial period, there were local entrepreneurs who engaged in peasant production, crafts, and trading. They could not favorably compete with the colonially-established expatriate trading firms which had superior capital and possessed monopoly control of banking and shipping facilities. On the one hand, the financial institutions that came with colonialism discriminated against Nigerian businessmen; and on the other, whenever these local entrepreneurs found a profitable new line of business, the European companies, such as the Royal Niger Company, John Holt, and United Africa Company, would move quickly to drive them out of business (Forrest 1995: 16). The top-to-bottom approach to development that was entrenched then negatively affected the ordinary people "who possess the energy required for mobilizing development efforts" (Olutayo 1999: 148). Many Africans began to migrate from rural areas to urban centers where they got poorly paid urban jobs, thus setting the stage for the "de-entrepreneuring" of the African peoples. The post-colonial regimes in Nigeria in the 1960s and 1970s continued in this trend by establishing state-owned enterprises (SOEs) in all sectors of the economy, the volume of which was estimated at more than 1,800 SOEs (Alayande 1999: 1). The economic recession of the 1980s, the burden of managing these SOEs, the entrenched corruption, and the external pressure from the international financial institutions eventually prompted governments and policy-makers in Nigeria and the Sub-Saharan African (SSA) countries to adopt policies aimed at curtailing the economic role of the state and empowering the private sector.

Entrepreneurs constitute critical elements in the private sector, as they are the social actors that make calculated decisions and accept risks on the use and coordination of scarce resources. The overt preference of Nigerian governments for the private sector–led economy makes it imperative to examine entrepreneurship in Nigeria in the twenty-first century within this historical context. Widespread poverty and unemployment that characterize Nigeria and the SSA region seem to be outcomes of the past that brought about an alteration in Africa's economic products and defined the role of the African entrepreneurs within the global economic system. This process stimulated a fundamental shift in the organization of business and ensured the emergence of a class of political elites who exploit governance for private gains. The question is in what ways the quest for a private sector–led economy has impacted on local entrepreneurship and resource utilization in Nigeria. This chapter assesses the situation of entrepreneurship in present day Nigeria and its empowerment needs in the increasingly competitive global economy.

WHY THE NEED FOR EMPOWERING ENTREPRENEURS IN NIGERIA?

The United Nations through her Millennium Development Goals (MDGs) has designated 2015 as the target year for halving absolute poverty globally. As the world approaches this year, available records have singled out Africa as the only region that would not meet the fixed goals, as the continent continues to show a steady increase in absolute poverty (Jerome 2006: 15, Chen and Ravallion 2007, UNCTAD 2007: 1). This fact constitutes a paradox in view of the high economic growth rates in some countries of the region linked mainly to their primary commodities. Nigeria's economic growth is tied to the oscillating price of its main export commodity, petroleum. So far, the capital-intensive nature of the petroleum industry offers limited prospect for employment generation and no guarantee of economic diversification. The situation is so critical that only "in few countries of the world has the gap between actual and potential economic and political performance been wider than in Nigeria" (Herbst and Olukoshi 1994: 453).

With regard to employment, whereas one third of the world's labor force is either unemployed, under-employed, or belongs to the working poor, Nigeria experiences one of the highest urban unemployment situations in Africa (ILO 2008: 2). Her economic situation not only constitutes a national problem but has implications for the whole of Africa, as Nigeria constitutes more than 50 percent of the West African population and is the most populous nation in Africa. As the successive Nigerian governments have taken measures on employment generation, job preservation, and economic transformation, the role of the local entrepreneurs as job creators and as a special class in the production process is incontestable.

Lying in between the expansive world of artisans in the informal sector and the foreign-owned transnational corporations or SOEs in Africa are modern entrepreneurs who are concentrated mainly within the small and medium-scale enterprises (SMEs) in the formal sector. Although these entrepreneurs were found to have possessed the capacity to exhibit good judgment and sound business sense when making investments for expansion, modernization, or diversification of projects (Marsden 1990), there is no doubt of the need to strengthen them as a major strategy towards local resource mobilization and development. Empirical research conducted in Botswana, Côte d'Ivoire, Ghana, Kenya, Malawi, Tanzania, and Nigeria, representative of modern entrepreneurs has shown that they run their enterprises with hired labor and set up businesses in fields with which they were familiar either through family upbringing or work experience (Olutayo 1999: 149). Their strength and relevance in contemporary African economies would depend on how much is invested into human capital development and how supportive basic social infrastructures and other economic institutions are, in particular, financial institutions.

Development actions have not been well directed insofar as there have not been any concerted efforts to harness resources from the large and vibrant informal sector in Nigeria (UNCTAD 2007: 2). Most efforts of the government since the 1960s have not yielded a significant change or caused a substantial shift in its economic output structure as policies and policy-makers have overlooked some essential facts (Egbon 1995: 27). For instance, in the pre-structural adjustment policy era, when government policies were designed to encourage public ownership of heavy industries through protection and subsidies, no particular attention was paid to the large sector of small-scale manufacturing that employed about 875,000 persons in 1987 as against modern manufacturing that employed then about 48,000 persons (Egbon 1995: 4). Two decades after embracing these neo-liberal policies, not much has been achieved in transforming and strengthening local capacities and entrepreneurship (Bankole 2006). This research therefore provides empirical analysis of the situation of local entrepreneurs in Nigeria *vis-à-vis* the contemporary global economic order and highlights some ways of empowering them.

METHODOLOGY AND THEORETICAL FRAMEWORK

In attempting to understand the contemporary situation of entrepreneurship in Nigeria, empirical data were obtained in Ibadan in 2006 by using structured and in-depth interview techniques from 58 purposively selected entrepreneurs in the manufacturing and service sectors of the economy. Both quantitative and qualitative data analysis methods were combined to present the data and to draw out their sociological meaning. Ibadan was chosen based on its historical significance in the colonial period, the development attention it has received as the capital city of the former Government of the Western Region of Nigeria, its socio-political and economic significance in the post-colonial era, and for its character as a melting pot of *traditional* and *modern* economic practices, a place with visible interplay of local entrepreneurial actions and global economic processes.

In this context, the psychological version of modernization theory can be explored that emphasizes motives as an essential factor to stimulate economic growth and development. However, observations suggest that psychological motives alone do not constitute sufficient explanation for entrepreneurial actions as the economic environment can either facilitate or hinder economic actions. One of the pioneer proponents of this theory, McClelland (1963) did not deny the impact of external factors that could influence human motivations. For him, the values and motives that people have are important factors that can lead them to exploit opportunities, to take advantage of favorable trade conditions, and to shape their own destiny (McClelland 1963: 74, Larrain 1989: 94).

McClelland (1963: 76) isolated the "need-for-achievement" that he defined as the "desire to do well, not so much for the sake of social recognition, or prestige, but to attain inner feelings of personal accomplishment." This desire to do well correlates with Max Weber's much criticized postulation of the "Spirit of Capitalism" where he argued that business entrepreneurs in Europe must have had a high level of "n" achievement that led to Europe's rapid economic development. McClelland (1963: 79) defined "business entrepreneur" as anyone who exercises control over the means of production and produces more than he can consume in order to sell it and to improve individual or household income; someone who is prepared to take moderate risks and to innovate although not behaving as a gambler as his/her decisions are well informed and rationally taken. McClelland explained the reason why "n" achievement has existed in some societies and not in others as based on the motivation to do well that was not hereditary or innate but acquired early in life, as children are educated for self-reliance and achievement. Nevertheless, authoritarian and interfering parents may produce the opposite result. In other words, a country can cultivate "n" achievement among its population by means of education and related opportunities so that more people can acquire "entrepreneurial drive." Thus, in societies with authoritarian regimes and an *underdeveloped* economy, where external pressure relating to globalization is strong, local entrepreneurship would be negatively affected.

MAJOR FINDINGS AND DISCUSSIONS

Some of the variables analyzed in this section include: the socio-demographic characteristics of the entrepreneurs (sex, age, level of educational qualification, and primary occupational training); variables relating to the respondents' enterprises such as date of establishment, rationale for the organization, particularities of the start-up capital, and ownership structure; and the character of government economic policies and how these affect entrepreneurship. These data were analyzed descriptively using pie charts, frequency distributions, and content analysis of the qualitative responses.

Gender and Entrepreneurship

A gender gap features prominently in the composition of the respondents, as it reflects patriarchy and dominance of men in the formal economic sector in Africa. The data show that the world of entrepreneurship within the formal sector employment in Nigeria is skewed almost exclusively in favor of the male population (Fig. 11.1).

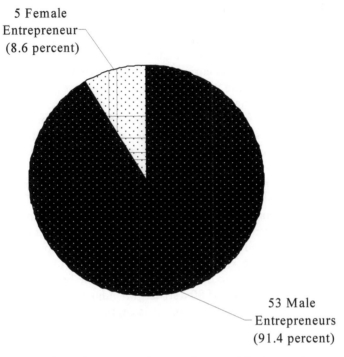

5 Female
Entrepreneur
(8.6 percent)

53 Male
Entrepreneurs
(91.4 percent)

Figure 11.1 Pie Chart Showing Gender Distribution of the Respondents.
Source: Author's field survey in Ibadan.

The chart shows that gender is a major factor that must be considered in any empowerment of entrepreneurship in Nigeria. Despite women's large participation in the informal sector of the Nigerian and African economy, their involvement as entrepreneurs in the formal sector is still insignificant, as women constitute just 8.6 percent of the entrepreneurs surveyed and men 91.4 percent. Being an entrepreneur thus remains largely an activity in the "men's world." This finding is consistent with Katepa-Kalala's (1999: 5) assertion that much of women's burden of work and poverty remains hidden to official policies, resources, and strategies for reducing poverty. This structural problem dates back to the colonial period when land and labor policies of the colonial government resulted in women's loss of land ownership and property rights (Bankole and Eboiyehi 2003: 102). The *status quo* of differential access to valued resources based on gender was maintained in the development programs of post-colonial regimes, resulting in women's lack of independent access to capital, education, and skills. The employment statistics even show that few women relative to men do secure jobs in the Federal civil service that can make them earn cash income and that lots of them are confined to low paying jobs (Olusi 1998, Bankole and Eboiyehi 2003: 103).

Age and Entrepreneurship

Entrepreneurial skills and functions are linked to age and to experience acquired over time in a particular field. Figure 11.2 reveals a youthful age composition of the entrepreneurs who were interviewed: 70.7 percent of them were 39 years old and younger.

Figure 11.2 reveals that 22.4 percent of the interviewees were less than 30 years old, whereas further analysis shows 69.2 percent of this group as entrepreneurs in the service sector. On the other hand, five entrepreneurs (71.4 percent) of the seven entrepreneurs aged 50 years and above were found in the manufacturing sector. This observation reflects recent economic trends that increase investment opportunities in the service sector and favor young professionals with minimal financial capital. That 41 (70.7 percent) of the 58 entrepreneurs interviewed were not more than 39 years old was also consistent with the fact that the majority of the enterprises came into being in the 1990s (Table 11.1). Most of the respondents linked the infant status of the enterprises to the slow pace of entrepreneurial response to global economic dynamics as well as the high unemployment rates arising from the mid-1980s structural adjustment programs. The respondents also attested to this opinion as captured by an entrepreneur in the in-depth interview below:

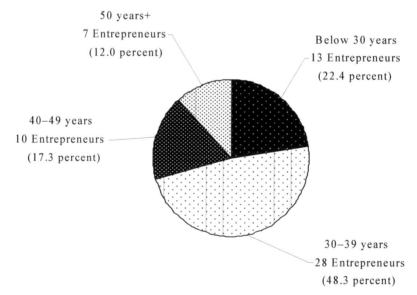

Figure 11.2   Pie Chart Showing Age Distribution of the Respondents.
Source: Author's field survey in Ibadan.

The life span of most indigenous organizations in Nigeria and here in Ibadan, except the multinationals, is short as many organizations die with the owners. Second, several organizations folded up in the recent past due to difficult economic conditions. This situation and rapid changes in the business environment today gives very limited space for the survival of organizations run in a traditional way but more to individuals with an adequate understanding of the contemporary business field and fresh ideas. (In-depth interview with an entrepreneur in Ibadan, March 2006)

What kind of knowledge is required to withstand the challenges of the contemporary economic environment? To find an answer to this question, we examine in the following section respondents' educational qualifications and specific training obtained in the course of their working experience.

Education and Entrepreneurship

As much as 72.5 percent of the respondents possess Nigeria's Polytechnic Higher National Diploma (HND) or university degrees; 15.5 percent with Ordinary National Diploma and National Certificate of Education (OND/NCE) are just above an average level of education.[2] Whereas 10.4 percent have only what is necessary to facilitate basic economic transactions, it was

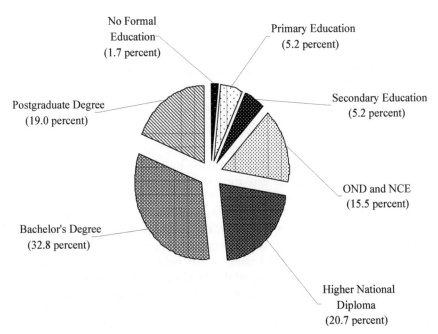

Figure 11.3 Pie Chart Showing Respondents' Level of Educational Attainment.
Source: Author's field survey in Ibadan.

found that most of the respondents have no formal educational training in business management and entrepreneurship. However, many in the younger age groups claimed to have had the opportunity to attend recently some vocational trainings and workshops where basics of business management were taught. As much as 39.1 percent of the entrepreneurs have no plans to acquire additional professional training as they are no longer driven either by the need for promotion at work or the search for another paid employment where such training may be an advantage. In addition, the resources needed to acquire such training do not seem to be available as the respondents claimed to be pre-occupied with the pressure for organizational survival. However, formal education is essential to entrepreneurship in the formal sector. Two actions are therefore inevitable if entrepreneurship is to be enhanced in the region: (1) the need to motivate today's entrepreneurs to seek cutting-edge knowledge in business management; and, (2) the need to convert the wealth of knowledge of the elder generation of entrepreneurs into a resource that could nurture and mentor upcoming generations.

All the entrepreneurs interviewed had previous work experience in formal organizations; 76.2 percent of them worked mostly in the technical, production, and administration departments before creating their enterprises. The nature of their previous work experiences was found to correlate with the type of enterprises they eventually established as the majority of those who worked in the technical units and had acquired capabilities in manufacturing ended up investing in the manufacturing sector. Even though "the Nigerian capital market is still underdeveloped and emerging" (Adelegan 2006: 47), a significant proportion of the respondents did not limit investment to their enterprises alone as most of them take advantage of buying shares in other profitable medium- and large-scale organizations all around Nigeria.

Operational Characteristics of the Respondents' Organizations

Entrepreneurship flourishes with easily accessible capital, a distinct middle class, and favorable business environment. For Nigeria, research has shown the almost complete absence of the middle class with its negative effect on wealth creation; the situation worsened by unfavorable economic policies and the Structural Adjustment Programs (SAP) implemented in the mid-1980s (Mabogunje 1998: 5, Ade-Ajayi 2001: 2). SAP and other institutional conditions negatively affected the prospect of enterprise survival. Some basic characteristics of the respondent's enterprises are examined in Tables 11.1 and 11.2.[3] These entrepreneurs belong to two categories: the *owner-managers* (47.3 percent) and the *employee-managers* (52.7 percent). As Olutayo (1999: 149–50) noted on these groups, they are the class of people that "accept risks which are usually calculated rather than gambling; they are motivated by personal gain and the need for personal achievement and self-expression; they are individualists, open to new ideas; they are continually searching for self-improvement through contacts with suppliers,

Table 11.1　Selected Characteristics of the Respondents' Organizations

Responses	Manufacturing Organizations		Service Organizations		Total	
	No.	Percent	No.	Percent	No.	Percent
Time of Joining/Establishing the Organization						
Less than 10 years ago	10	45.4	22	71.0	32	60.4
11 to 15 years ago	7	31.8	4	12.9	11	20.8
16 to 20 years ago	3	13.6	2	6.5	5	9.4
21 years and above	2	9.1	3	9.7	5	9.4
Formal Registration of the Organization						
Yes	17	85.0	32	94.1	49	90.7
No	3	15.0	2	5.9	5	9.3
Form of Ownership						
Sole proprietorship	12	54.5	16	45.7	28	49.1
Partnership	1	4.5	7	20.0	8	14.0
Family business	1	4.5	-	-	1	1.8
Private limited company	6	27.3	11	31.4	17	29.8
Public limited company	2	9.1	1	2.9	3	5.3
Time of Establishing/Starting the Plant in Ibadan						
Less than 10 years ago	11	55.0	15	55.6	26	55.3
11 to 15 years ago	4	20.0	4	14.8	8	17.0
1 to 20 years ago	3	15.0	5	18.5	8	17.0
21 years and above	2	10.0	3	11.1	5	10.6

Source: author's field survey in Ibadan.

customers, and other entrepreneurs in the field; they live and breathe their businesses, day and night, and build upon success."

The majority of the enterprises are young: 60.4 percent of the entrepreneurs established or joined the organizations as the owner-managers or employee-managers respectively less than ten years ago. This is further corroborated by 55.3 percent of the entrepreneurs dating their enterprises to less than ten years ago. In other words, the entrepreneurial history of the respondents matches with the active years of the enterprises. The most widespread forms of ownership have been sole proprietorship (49.1 percent), private limited company (29.8 percent), and partnership (14.0 percent). The majority of the organizations have not been one-unit–based firms as 43.1 percent have branches in other parts of Nigeria; 19.0 percent

Table 11.2 Operational Characteristics of the Respondents' Organizations

Responses	Manufacturing Organizations		Service Organizations		Total	
	No.	Percent	No.	Percent	No.	Percent
Factors Considered When Locating the Organization in Ibadan						
Market	11	73.3	15	68.2	26	70.3
Favorable business environment	1	6.7	1	4.5	2	5.4
Presence of industrial estate	1	6.7	2	9.1	3	8.1
Availability of land	1	6.7	2	9.1	3	8.1
Others	1	6.7	2	9.1	3	8.1
Sources of Start-up Capital						
Personal savings	9	52.9	6	27.3	15	38.5
Banks	2	11.8	2	9.1	4	10.3
Personal savings and banks	2	11.8	4	18.2	6	15.4
Combination of 3 or more sources	1	5.9	-	-	1	2.6
From abroad	2	11.8	2	9.1	4	10.3
Inheritance/family assets	-	-	2	9.1	2	5.1
Within the country and abroad	1	5.9	3	13.6	4	10.3
Others	-	-	3	13.6	3	7.7
Current Monetary Value of the Organization (in Naira)						
Less than N 1 million	4	30.8	2	11.1	6	19.4
N 1 million to N 10 million	5	38.5	10	55.6	15	48.4
N 10,000,001 to N 500 million	3	23.1	5	27.8	8	25.8
Personal/private/don't know	1	7.7	1	5.6	2	6.5
Proportion of Output Sold in Ibadan and Its Region						
£25 percent	3	15.0	3	10.0	6	12.0
26 to 50 percent	3	15.0	4	13.3	7	14.0
51 to 75 percent	7	35.0	4	13.3	11	22.0
76 to 100 percent	7	35.0	19	63.3	26	52.0
Any Major Retrenchment Exercise in Your Establishment Recently?						
Yes	4	19.0	9	28.1	13	24.5
No	16	76.2	22	68.8	38	71.7
Don't know	1	4.8	1	3.1	2	3.8

Source: author's field survey in Ibadan.

have branches in other parts of Oyo State of which Ibadan is the capital; 32.8 percent have organized their operations only in Ibadan; whereas the remaining 5.2 percent maintained some forms of partnership with similar enterprises abroad.

Just as the modernization perspective identifies profit as the foremost motivation of a rational economic being, 70.3 percent of the respondents indicated the market as the major factor when locating their organizations in Ibadan.

The distributions of the entrepreneurs based on the sources of their start-up capital show personal savings (38.5 percent), personal savings and bank loans (15.4 percent), and 20.6 percent funds from abroad, or within and abroad. This distribution attests to the dominance of household savings in enterprise ownership in Africa as alluded to by UNCTAD (2007: 10, 15). Our findings on those who raise their capital from abroad reveal the increasing importance of monetary and non-monetary remittances from abroad that recent publications have identified as the second largest source of capital flows to the developing countries behind FDI but ahead of Official Development Assistance (ODA) (UNCTAD, 2007: 25–26). Whereas UNCTAD noted that household savings were not always channeled into productive use in the SSA region, this was not the case in Ibadan where the majority of the respondents depends on personal savings as the source of their start-up capital. The difficulties and unattractiveness of accessing bank loans made this trend inevitable. The overall effect of this is that the firms are frequently small- or medium-scale and their monetary value is low. On the question of where outputs are sold, 74 percent of the respondents offer for sale more than 50 percent of their outputs in Ibadan and its surroundings. In response to the unfavorable economic environment and the global economic crisis, a quarter of the entrepreneurs has recently had to carry out major retrenchment exercises in their enterprises.

Economic Policy and Entrepreneurship in Nigeria within the Global Economic Order

The successive governments of the post-colonial Nigerian state have packaged several economic policies. These are official plans enacted to improve people's wellbeing and to reduce their socio-economic vulnerability. Yet, the policy-making arena in Nigeria has been problematic and characterized by an exclusivity that leaves out the vast majority of the people, entrepreneurs included, from making inputs to the policy-formulation process. The lack of adequate attention to the entrepreneurial associational platforms and entrepreneurs as potential development agents turned them into a major vulnerable group in Nigeria's transformation process. The respondents were unanimous on this as represented in this response:

> Entrepreneurs are a highly vulnerable group in present day Nigerian economy. There are all kinds of uncertainty emanating from the

volatility of the policy environment. The situation demands that even when we sleep, we must keep our eyes widely open (. . .). I think we need much psychological support and encouragement from the government. (In-depth interview with an entrepreneur in Ibadan, March 2006)

One major obstacle faced by African entrepreneurs has been the nonavailability of investment funds. This has greatly limited their capacity to function as job creators. The majority of the respondents strongly advised that government policies on the role of the banking sector in promoting and supporting local businesses should be firm and enforced. They identified high lending rates and the conditions attached to loan facilities as major disincentives to asking the Nigerian banking sector for loans. Yesufu (2002: 9) noted this prevailing unfavorable condition in Nigeria and affirmed "at the lending rate range of 28 to 38 percent, there are very few businesses that can profitably produce and/or export." As an economy operating within the global economic order, he drew his prescription for tackling this problem from the financial practice in the developed world:

Every time any developed country is in depression, or wishes to stimulate its economy and/or to raise the employment level, the foremost, most expeditious, most effective, and most famous first line of approach, is to reduce the prevailing interest rates. This is the case in Western European countries, Japan, and the USA. (Yesufu 2002: 9)[4]

Another Nigerian professor of economics shared a similar view on this approach:

If mature economies of America, the United Kingdom, the European Union and others keep their interest rates well below 5 percent (and inflation rate at about 2 percent) what justifies high interest rates in Nigeria all in the name of liberalization? On Thursday August 4, 2005, the Bank of England's Monetary Policy Commission (MPC) reduced its lending rate from 4.7 percent to 4.5 percent to boost the economy by encouraging manufacturing and reduce unemployment. The manufacturing sector in Nigeria has virtually ceased to exist except for the producers of beer, soft drinks, and fake drugs. The contribution of the sector to GDP has declined from 9.9 percent between 1975 and 1981 to about 4.2 percent in 2003. Is there any wonder why the economy is stagnant? (Ekpeyong 2005: 12)

The respondents in this study expressed their disappointment that not much has been achieved despite the suggestion of the Federal Government to the local financial institutions to reduce the interest rates in order to make bank loans attractive to the prospective investors.

Factors contributing to the weakness of the Nigerian state and its inability to evolve as a developmental state can be found in its faulty post-colonial political system that promotes fragmentation, rivalry, and corruption (Gellar 1995: 146). These aspects have impacted negatively on the contest for political power and the probability of using government machinery as a tool for social transformations. The peak of the political fraud was perfected in the 2007 general elections where, rather than competence, brazen *handpicking* of public office holders by the ruling elites replaced all democratic principles, thereby denying the population of any input into governance. The overbearing influence of the more or less corrupt political structures by which these political office holders emerged invariably turned them into surrogates of predatory political interests whereas many others were impeached by the same forces that installed them, as witnessed in some states of the federation in the current democratic dispensation that succeeded the military regimes since 1999. Therefore policy statements have become mere political rhetoric and instruments for political propaganda.[5] The dysfunction of the political system was thus identified as a major disincentive to local entrepreneurship whereas the reward system is skewed against them in favor of the political office holders.

The major strategy Nigerian governments used to initiate development programs since political independence on October 1, 1960, up until the 1980s had been economic planning. For instance, in the Second and Third Development Plans (1970–74 and 1975–80, respectively), plans to aid small-scale industrial enterprises and by extension entrepreneurship were initiated in three categories: technical and managerial assistance projects, credit projects, and, infrastructural and promotional projects. The first category encompasses such initiatives as the Industrial Development Centers (IDCs) located in Owerri (Eastern Nigeria), Zaria (Northern Nigeria), and Western Nigeria; Vocational Improvement Centers (VICs), which began as Business Apprenticeship Training Center in Kaduna, Northern Nigeria, and other initiatives. Industrial Development Centers were designed to promote small-scale private ventures in woodwork, metalwork, automobile repair, textiles, and leatherwork through technical, management, and accounting assistance. Moreover, they organized demonstrations, trainings, and seminars at the enterprise level employing at least ten workers. The problem IDCs faced was inadequate support facilities during implementation. The credit projects were dispensed through the Small Industry Credit/Loan Scheme (SIC), the Small Industries Development Bank (SIDB), the Small Industry Bank Window (SIBW), and the National Industrial Development Bank. Most prominent in the infrastructural and promotional projects was the establishment of the Industrial Estates as well as National Export Promotion Councils. The Industrial Estates that have survived till today were initiated as nurseries for the development of entrepreneurial talents in small-scale enterprises and for economies of scale in providing common services, in particular, infrastructural amenities, such as water supply, electricity, road networks, among others. Disappointingly, the observations of this survey at the Oluyole Industrial Estate in Ibadan reveal the failure of the government to follow this idea at implementation. One of the entrepreneurs in manufacturing interviewed at the estate narrated the suffering of his organization as follows:

> Electricity supply in this area is grossly unreliable. We spend an average of N1.5 million on diesel every month to remain in operation while our turnover per month is about N8 million. That notwithstanding, we pay about N300,000.00 as NEPA bill and another N100,000.00 as kickback to them. Bank charges about 35 percent interest rate on loans obtained from them. Now I'm thinking of how I will pay about N2.6 million salaries to my staff by the 26th of this month. Each time that I am paying so much on diesel, I always feel bad because this is a land that flows with milk and honey. We import much of our inputs. We cannot be in this mess and be talking of foreign investment (. . .). Foreign investment: Forget it! Foreign investors are only interested in such sectors as the petroleum and telecommunication that yields huge profits. Just as the family, apart from caring financially for the children, we also have to train the children rather than throw them to teachers. We must first put our house in order. (In-depth interview with an entrepreneur in Ibadan, March 2006)[6]

Another entrepreneur in the manufacturing sector highlighted the problem further: "In the 1970s, we had more than 125 viable foreign owned companies all around Ibadan such as Leventis, CFAO, Kingsway, UAC, and many other indigenous firms. But today, most of them have gone because they were killed by taxes and poor infrastructure." Respondents were unanimous in saying that the operating environment in Nigeria at present was not supportive of entrepreneurship. An entrepreneur in the glass-making industry compared the performance of his organization with a similar one in Egypt:

> A glass making industry that started in Egypt about five years after ours is doing ten times better today than ours, not because they have a better management structure, but because of series of problems in our environment that limits our performance. There are peculiar problems and general problems. Electricity and other infrastructures are general problems faced by most Nigerian organizations whereas peculiar problems are those that directly affect our organization within the glass making industry. (In-depth interview with an entrepreneur in Ibadan, March 2006)

As these organizations struggle for survival and have got domestic problems, they are faced with the impact of globalization in the form of a continuous influx of imported products. This fact is described in another respondent's answer:

Just walk through the streets and you will see numerous imported products competing side by side quite unfairly with our local products. This importation sends out of business local investors in the real sectors, especially those in the manufacturing. Many domestic firms have closed down because they don't have the muscle to compete. (In-depth interview with an entrepreneur, March 2006)

The possibility of addressing this condition is also limited due to the lack of democratic space within the Nigerian polity. Entrepreneurs cannot influence policy-making by using their associational platforms. For instance, the Manufacturers Association of Nigeria (MAN) was established in May 1971 as a medium of communication and consultation between the industry on the one hand, and the government and the general public on the other hand (Bankole 2003: 159–160). However, the association has over the years not been so effective to significantly influence policy-making. In defense of their members' competence, MAN is however confident that "if Nigerian manufacturers are provided friendly manufacturing environment, they will be able to benchmark themselves against global standards and give Nigerian consumers world-class quality products" (MAN 2002: 16). Yet most respondent's disappointment with the economic policies of the government was vivid and captured in the following responses:

Everything we have been hearing is rhetoric. Power supply has not improved. The same situation goes for other infrastructural facilities. The business environment generally has not improved. Those of us in the manufacturing are hard hit; it is as if there is no end in sight to the problems. I think the government should involve entrepreneurs in policy formulation and should not only be dishing out theories without knowing the practical implications of their ideas. (In-depth interview with a 47-year-old entrepreneur in Ibadan, February 2006)

A brief insight into the critical situation of the social infrastructure in Nigeria, particularly electric power generation, will suffice here. As Iwayemi (1998: 1) had noted: "There is a strong feedback relationship between the energy sector and the national economy." Reliable electricity supply has been the foremost infrastructure problem Nigerians have always identified for urgent attention in the nation's quest for development. The situation is so critical that as at July 2008, only about 900 megawatts of electricity was generated for over 140 million Nigerians (*The Punch* 2008b). This poor performance becomes more vivid if we compare Nigeria's data with that of South Africa that generates 45,000 megawatts for its 45 million people and Nigeria's electricity consumption of about 2 kilowatts per capita compared to 3,000 in South Africa and 456 for Sub-Saharan Africa (Okonjo-Iweala 2007: 5 and 33; Bankole, Odia-Ndongo, and Tegnerowicz 2007).[7] As critical as the building of infrastructure is to local development, the outcomes of government actions to improve infrastructure delivery have remained at the level of speculations and projections. Underlining this failure is corruption in government circles and the failure to execute budgets as planned. For instance, the National Automotive Council (NAC) recently accused President Olusegun Obasanjo's government (1999–2007) of diverting financial allocations meant to rejuvenate the ailing automobile industry into the agricultural sector.[8] In the NAC report submitted in July 2008 to the Minister of State for Commerce and Industry, President Obasanjo's regime was alleged to have diverted the sum of N 3.72 billion (about US$ 31 million) from the Automotive Development Fund (ADF) to the defunct National Fertilizer Company of Nigeria (NAFCON) (*The Punch* 2008a).[9]

A combination of internal and external factors explains thus the weakness and the inability of the vast majority of Nigerian entrepreneurs to be locally and globally competitive. These entrepreneurs have suffered a decline in their economic status as imported manufactured goods have replaced their own products (Gellar 1995: 140). In addition, the relative absence of viable platforms through which they could engage the policymakers contributed to the resurgence of crafts associations that were characteristic of pre-colonial Nigeria, so that to enter into the local domain of entrepreneurship requires an associational membership as a device for individual and enterprise survival.

GLOBALIZATION, THE STATE, AND ENTERPRISE SURVIVAL IN THE TWENTY-FIRST CENTURY AFRICA

Beyond the neo-liberal thoughts, sociological research does have a crucial role to play in mediating public debates on critical issues such as entrepreneurship and economic transformations in Africa. Although there are divergent views on the implications of economic globalization on African societies, the results of this investigation point at a combination of factors that are internal and external to Nigeria's social system that predisposes entrepreneurs and enterprises to vulnerability and failures. Contrary to most analyses that prevailed at the close of the twentieth century, this chapter attests to the need to widen intellectual space for inputs from the sociological community in regions of the geographic South into the debate on global processes. The Nigerian situation within the global economic order mirrors distinctive realities of other African countries south of the Sahara.

As a mono-economy, Nigeria's dependence on the petroleum industry and the neglect of other sectors is a major factor limiting its transformational potential and increasing the vulnerability of the entrepreneurs as major economic stakeholders.[10] The prevailing unfavorable economic conditions could be traced to a discontinuity in the internal development process due largely to historical factors and the nature of the inherited post-colonial Nigerian state. Writing on *The Colonial Era*, Gellar (1995: 152) added another factor and explained how non-indigenous groups such as the Lebanese and the Asians function as middlemen in West and East Africa respectively at the expense of African nationals. This legacy endures so far as Lebanese people constitute a very prominent entrepreneurial diaspora within the Central Business District (CBD) and Oluyole Industrial Estate in Ibadan, whereas the Lebanon Street remains a highly visible part of the CBD.[11]

Nigeria's economic and political structure obviously constitutes a major impediment to the realization of its vast potential in human and material resources. The overdependence of political actors on huge money amounts from the petroleum sector can be translated into political disputes that have characterized the post-colonial Nigerian state, politics of social exclusion, and the absence of an official framework for policy dialogue and co-operation among major stakeholders in the development process. As such, local entrepreneurs suffer the negative consequences of the domestic and international political structures: policies are formulated to serve narrow interests. In the quest for empowerment, most of the respondents in this survey emphasized that entrepreneurs who possess practical knowledge of the situation of local entrepreneurship have not been given a voice in the policy-making process.

Therefore, the explanations for the low performance of local enterprises transcend the dominant assumptions of modernization theory, especially psychological propositions of the need-for-achievement motivation. Whereas the role of the educational system at inculcating business and entrepreneurial culture into individuals is indisputable, the respondents' rational thinking was found to be consistent with the requirements of the overall business environment. There are two issues with significant implications for the success or failure of entrepreneurs and their enterprises in Nigeria: the capability of the state to provide enabling environments for their operations and the capacity to withstand pressures emanating from the global economic system. To achieve these, the respondents affirmed the urgent need that the state should evolve as a development actor with the capacity to mobilize resources for development purposes, to involve and to empower local entrepreneurs, and to commit to the implementation of economic policies that trigger positive development outcomes.

The broadening of the space destined to entrepreneurship is crucial in view of the current global financial crisis and the challenges it posed to people's wellbeing in poor countries that depend exclusively on a limited range of primary products whose prices at the international market are dollar denominated. The crisis has largely compounded the situation of several sectors in Nigeria, particularly the few domestic industries, that have experienced significant downturn and job losses since the SAP era of the mid-1980s (Bankole 1996 and 2006). The Governor of the Central Bank of Nigeria, Professor Charles Soludo, on January 21, 2009, admitted the collapse of commodity prices (especially petroleum), revenue contraction, declining capital inflows, deaccumulation of foreign reserves and pressure on exchange rate, and capital market downturn and divestment by foreign investors (Soludo 2009a). This has been the trend across Africa where the effects of the global financial crisis have been larger than expected on African currencies and investment flows (*The Guardian* 2009).[12] In response, the incumbent Minister of Finance in Nigeria, Mansur Muhktar, announced that the Federal Government is planning to use external borrowing as a measure to bridge the emergent financing gap (*The Punch* 2009a). Similarly, the Nigerian government on January 16, 2009 inaugurated the Presidential Steering Committee on Global Economic Crisis. These scenarios have shown that the Nigerian economy is not immune from the global economy, and in fact, Nigeria is one of the countries "at greatest risk" (IMF 2009: 4). The local entrepreneurs constitute a major vulnerable group as this crisis deepens and a critical assessment of the Government's action on the crisis may reveal that it has not differed from the previous rhetorical, reactionary, and haphazard responses as the domestic investors have continued to record significant losses. For instance, the current crash in the stock market resulted in an average investor losing about 70 percent of his or her investment (Eso 2009).[13] The emerging challenges therefore make imperative a rethinking of social policy beyond the dogma of the received knowledge and neo-liberal prescriptions. The governments of the major industrial countries are already following this path with the release of stimulus packages of trillions of dollars as a measure against the crisis and as a mark of commitment to the wellbeing of their citizens (Soludo 2009b: 3). It is thus important that their African counterparts also implement policy instruments in the best interest of their citizens.

CONCLUSION

Global economic interconnectedness constitutes one of the major characteristics of the modern world and offers different outcomes for different people. The experience of each society depends on its level of participation and control, and the extent to which development initiatives place priority on people as the ultimate beneficiaries. For a developing region such as Africa, the role of governments in creating enabling environments for local entrepreneurs cannot be overemphasized. The benefits of expanding the socio-economic space for entrepreneurship are diverse, including openness to innovation, economic diversification, higher economic performance associated with competition, creation of a higher stock of jobs in the long run, and social empowerment. These are features that have eluded Nigerian society and its economy as globalization intensified.

What then should be the appropriate policy response? Whereas globalization has been advanced by neo-liberal thinking and has favored the pursuit of a growth-centered market economy, *underdeveloped* economies such as Nigeria that share MDGs' ambition of halving poverty by 2015 cannot under-play the strategic role of state policies that promote social inclusiveness at the local level. The current global financial crisis and the response of the leading economies have given further credence to the need to strengthen the economic boundaries of developing countries and harness globalization to the benefit of the governed. The transformations of the Asian Tigers followed this path of an inward-looking development agenda that is socially responsive to the needs of local entrepreneurs and other vulnerable groups.

For most of the entrepreneurs, urgent solutions must be found to the problem of inefficient infrastructure that contributes to the high cost of doing business in Nigeria. As the reports of the recent probe panels instituted by the Nigerian National Assembly reveal, the absence of functional infrastructure is not due to the lack of budgetary allocations but more to a lack of transparency in governance.[14] Whereas there was no viable institutional framework to challenge *misappropriation* of public funds during the years of the military rule in Nigeria, the current democratic structure provides the Nigerian people with the opportunity to engage political office holders. Although the present government of Shehu Musa Yar'Adua at the inauguration on May 29, 2007, promised to declare a state of emergency in the energy sector, this was more or less rhetoric, as electricity generation in Nigeria by the end of 2008 stood at the record low mark of 900 megawatts. Public investment in infrastructure as well as transparency in project execution would certainly be crucial factors in enhancing the performance of the private sector in Nigeria.

Similarly, the lack of access to capital was a major limitation to entrepreneurial aspirations in Nigeria. The country's fragmented financial sector has over the years played a marginal role in real sector development and has hardly supported long-term entrepreneurial initiatives. Notwithstanding the recent reform in the sector facilitated by the Central Bank of Nigeria,[15] commercial banks still need to provide enterprise-friendly rules and procedures relating to collateral requirements, interest rates, access to bank loans, and other investment facilities. Such initiatives as *Entrepreneurship Development Funds* may be considered and administered in such a way that they would enable entrepreneurs with a low capital base to realize their business aspirations. Such facilities may be aimed at procuring basic equipment to support entrepreneurs in specific sectors identified as being vital to national development, particularly the manufacturing sector. The procedure for administering this must be different from the widespread micro-finance system that often supports short-term investments.

Finally, to sustain the industrial estates strategy, the option of business incubator designed to provide management assistance, finance, and other technical supports such as flexible leases of space and shared access to equipment may help highly vulnerable entrepreneurs. Such incubators could be designed to support the transformation of selected early-stage enterprises that manifest high potentials into self-sufficient, growing, and profitable businesses. The period of incubation may last three to five years during which the viability of the plants could be determined. By reducing the risks during such early stages of business formation, business incubators may provide the context to sustain new enterprises that may otherwise have failed due to lack of support associated with doing business in such a volatile economic environment as Nigeria.

NOTES

1. An earlier version of this chapter was presented at the *First Forum of Sociology* of the International Sociological Association, Barcelona, 5–8 September 2008.
2. HND and OND are *Higher National Diploma* and *Ordinary National Diploma* awarded by Nigerian Polytechnics; NCE is the *National Certificate of Education* awarded by Colleges of Education.
3. The exchange rate of naira to dollar has not been stable. In 2006, when the fieldwork was conducted, it was approximately N 138 to US$ 1; by December 2008, it was N 120 to US$ 1; and as at May 7th, 2009, it was N 147.250 to US$ 1. This weakness becomes more obvious when the current monetary value of the organizations as shown in Table 11.2. is converted to its dollar equivalent. The exchange rate of naira to dollar has been unstable, hovering from approximately N 138 to US$ 1 in 2006; N 120 to US$ 1 in December 2008; and N 147.250 to US$ 1 as at May 2009. A number of these entrepreneurs indicated that they would have sought for recapitalization, especially through the banking sector, but underlined the unattractiveness of bank loans due to high interest rates and the difficulty in securing such facilities.
4. This disposition is observable in the *bailout* plan for the prevailing economic recession in the United States of America by the government of President Barack Obama, who assumed office on January 20, 2009.
5. This explains the credibility problem being suffered by the *Seven Point Agenda* of President Umaru Musa Yar'Adua's government (2008).
6. NEPA is the acronym for the National Electric Power Authority.
7. Dr. Ngozi Okonjo-Iweala was Nigeria's Finance Minister from 2003 to 2006. Although she estimated the level of energy generation in Nigeria in 2007 as high as 4,500 megawatts, the wide gap between this figure and that of 2008 was due to further deterioration in power generation in the year that followed her submission.
8. President Obasanjo, as a practicing farmer, has got large farm holdings in his hometown (Ota) and substantial agricultural investment interests all around Nigeria.
9. This fund was already lost as NAFCON was privatized by President Obasanjo's regime in the current privatization program (2009).
10. About 95 percent of Nigeria's foreign revenue is earned from petroleum.
11. The poor conditions of service offered to the local staff by these Lebanese firms were observed in another study I recently conducted (unpublished). However, the Chief Executive of one of these firms when he discovered that questionnaires had been adminsitered to his staff, decided to seize all the completed questionnaires for fear of possible results of the survey on issues such as conditions of employment, working environment, working hours, and job security of local employees.
12. This observation was pronounced by the President of the African Development Bank, Donald Kaberuka, to Reuters reporters at the International Monetary Fund/World Bank Spring Meeting in 2009.

13. Justice Kayode Eso is a retired judge of the Supreme Court of Nigeria; he is a distinguished jurist and holder of the national award *Commander of the Order of the Niger.*
14. The investigations led by the Nigerian National Assembly have shown that the previous government of President Olusegun Obasanjo (1999–2007) spent about US$ 16 billion for the energy sector without improving energy generation; rather, there was a decline in electricity supply when compared to the situation in 1999. Other public utilities (roads, health, water supply, etc.) are also in a deplorable situation.
15. In 2005, Nigeria had about 90 banks. After the restructuring and merger enforced by the Central Bank of Nigeria with Professor Charles Soludo as Governor, the number was reduced to 25 banks, each with a minimum capital base of no less than N 25 billion (US$ 215 million in December 2008).

BIBLIOGRAPHY

Ade-Ajayi, Jacob F. (2001) "Paths to the sustainability of higher education in Nigeria," *Proceedings of the 12th General Assembly of the Social Science Academy of Nigeria,* July 3–7. Abuja: Social Science Academy of Nigeria, 1–11.

Adelegan, Olatundun Janet (2006) "Market Reactions to Dividend Initiations and Omissions on the Nigerian Stock Market," *Ibadan Journal of the Social Sciences* 4 (1): 47–59.

Alayande, Tunde (1999) *Privatisation of Public Utilities in Nigeria: Policy Issues for Consideration.* Working Paper 22. Ibadan: Development Policy Center.

Bankole, Adeyinka O. (1996) "Socio-Psychological Implications of the Period of Prolonged Economic Recession on Nigerian Workers," *African Journal for the Psychological Study of Social Issues, (AJPSSI)* 3 (2): 187–202.

Bankole, Adeyinka O. (2003) "Non-Governmental Organisations and the Industrial Sector in Nigeria," in Elżbieta Puchnarewicz (ed.) *Non-Governmental Organizations in Developing Countries and Eastern Europe,* 156–173. Warsaw: University of Warsaw Press.

Bankole, Adeyinka O. (2006) *Industrialization and Development: A Sociological Investigation of the Manufacturing Activities in Ibadan, Nigeria.* Unpublished PhD Thesis Submitted to the Department of Sociology, University of Ibadan, Nigeria.

Bankole, Adeyinka O. and Friday A. Eboiyehi (2003) "Formal Education, Women Employment and Poverty," *Gender and Behaviour* 1 (1): 94–114.

Bankole, Adeyinka O., Yves F. Odia-Ndongo, and Joanna Tegnerowicz (2007) "Globalization and the Challenges of Industrial Development in Sub-Saharan African Countries: A Study of Nigeria and Cameroon." Paper presented at the First Congress of the African Sociological Association, Rhodes University, Grahamstown-iRhini, South Africa, July 15–18.

Chen, Shaohua and Martin Ravallion (2007) *Absolute Poverty Measures for the Developing World, 1981–2004.* World Bank Working Paper 4211, Development Research Group. Washington, D.C.: World Bank.

Egbon, P. C. (1995) *Industrial Policy and Manufacturing Performance in Nigeria,* Monograph Series No. 7. Ibadan: National Center for Economic Management and Administration, NCEMA.

Ekpenyong, David B. (2005) "The Nigerian Financial System, Unholy Trinity, Original Sin and the Interface between Theory and Practice: The Tragedy of Our Experience." Valedictory Lecture Delivered at the University of Ibadan, September 27.

Eso, Kayode (2009) *World Economic Meltdown and the Implication for Nigeria.* A Lecture presented at the 9th Convocation Ceremony of the Ladoke Akintola University of Technology, Ogbomoso, Oyo State, Nigeria, April 24.

Forrest, Tom (1995) *The Makers and Making of Nigerian Private Enterprise.* Ibadan: Spectrum Books.

Frank, Andre Gunder (2004) "Globalizing 'Might is Right': Spaghetti Western Law of the West is No Solution," *Development and Change* 35(3): 607–612.

Gellar, Sheldon (1995) "The Colonial Era," in Phyllis M. Martin and Patrick O'Meara (eds) *Africa,* 3rd ed., 135–155. Bloomington: Indiana University Press.

Herbst, Jeffrey and Adebayo Olukoshi (1994) "Nigeria: Economic and Political Reforms at Cross Purposes," in Stephen Haggard and Steven B. Webb (eds) *Voting for Reform: Democracy, Political Liberalization, and Economic Adjustment,* 453–502. Washington, D.C.: The World Bank.

Ikpeze, Nnaemeka (1991) "New Industrial Policies and Perspective for Manufacturing in Nigeria," quoted in P. C. Egbon (1995) *Industrial Policy and Manufacturing Performance in Nigeria.* Monograph Series No. 7. Ibadan: National Center for Economic Management and Administration, NCEMA.

International Labor Organization (2006) *Implementing the Global Employment Agenda: Employment Strategies in Support of Decent Work, 'Vision' Document.* Geneva: ILO.

International Monetary Fund (2009) *Impact of the Global Financial Crisis on Sub-Saharan Africa.* http://www.imf.org/external/pubs/ft/books/2009/afrglobfin/ssaglobalfin.pdf, accessed on May 11, 2009.

Iwayemi, Akin (1998) "Energy Sector Development in Africa." Background Paper prepared for the African Development Report 1998. http://www.afdb.org/fileadmin/uploads/afdb/Documents/Publications/00157620-EN-ERP-43.PDF, accessed on May 7, 2009.

Jegede, Ayodele S., Adeyinka O. Bankole, and Olabisi P. Adejumo (2003) "Globalization and HIV/AIDS: Implications for National Development in Africa," *Journal of National Development* 16 (1): 29–48.

Jerome, Afeikhena (2006) "Infrastructure Reform in Africa: What Has Happened and What to Be Done?" *Ibadan Journal of the Social Sciences* 4 (1): 15–32.

Katepa-Kalala, Perpetua (1999) "Assessment Report on: Women and Poverty, and the Economic Empowerment of Women." Paper presented at the Economic Commission for Africa Sixth African Regional Conference on Women, Addis Ababa, Ethiopia: *Mid-Decade Review of the Implementation of the Dakar and Beijing Platforms for Action in the African Region,* November 22–26.

Keim, Curtis A. (1995) "Africa and Europe before 1900," in Phyllis M. Martin and Patrick O'Meara (eds) *Africa,* 3rd ed., 115–134. Indiana: Indiana University Press

Larrain, Jorge (1989) *Theories of Development: Capitalism, Colonialism and Dependency.* Cambridge: Polity Press.

Mabogunje, Akin L. (1998) *A Critique of the Nigerian Economy.* Working Paper 99/1, August 13. Ibadan: Development Policy Center.

Manufacturers Association of Nigeria (2002) *MAN Economic Review 2001–2002.* Lagos: Manufacturers Association of Nigeria.

Marsden, Keith (1990) *African Entrepreneurs: Pioneers of Development.* International Finance Corporation Discussion Paper No. 9. Washington, D.C.: The World Bank.

McClelland, David (1963) "The Achievement Motive in Economic Growth," in Bert F. Hoselitz and Wilbert E. Moore (eds) *Industrialization and Society,* 74–95. UNESCO: Mouton.

Okonjo-Iweala, Ngozi (2007) "The State of Nigeria's Economic Reforms," featured speaker, The Brookings Institution, Washington, D.C., Friday, March 23.

http://www3.brookings.edu/comm/events/20070323.pdf, accessed on April 20, 2007.

Olusi, Janet O. (1998) "Socio-Cultural, Economic and Environmental Determinants of African Women's Poverty and Disempowerment: The Nigerian Example," in Mary E. M. Kolawole (ed.) *Gender Perceptions and Development in Africa: A Socio-Cultural Approach*, 261–288. Lagos: Arrabon Academic Publishers.

Olutayo, Olanrewaju Akinpelu (1999) "The Igbo Entrepreneur in the Political Economy of Nigeria," *African Study Monograph* 20 (3): 147–174.

Soludo, Chukwuma Charles (2009a) *Global Financial and Economic Crisis: How Vulnerable is Nigeria?* January (Abuja: Central Bank of Nigeria). www.cenbank.org/OUT/SPEECHES/2009/GOVADD-21-1-09.PDF, accessed on May 5, 2009.

Soludo, Chukwuma Charles (2009b) *Banking in Nigeria at a Time of Global Financial Crisis*. Presentation at the Special Interactive Session on the Banking System at the Eko Hotel and Suites, Victoria Island, Lagos, March 30.

The Guardian (2009) "Meltdown Hits Africa Faster than Anticipated, Says ADB," April 27.

The Punch (2008a) "How Obasanjo's Government Killed Automotive Industry—Report," July 3, Nigeria

The Punch (2008b) "Power Generation Drops to 900 MW," July 3, Nigeria.

The Punch (2009) "Meltdown: Nigeria May Resort to External Borrowing—FG," April 29, Nigeria.

United Nations Conference on Trade and Development (2007) *Economic Development in Africa: Reclaiming Policy Space, Domestic Resource Mobilization and Developmental States*. Geneva: UNCTAD.

Yesufu, Tijani M. (2002) "Nigerian Economy on the Brink: The Way Out." Paper presented at the Development Policy Center, Ibadan, August 25.

12 Poverty in Senegal
Theoretical Approaches and the Manifestation of Poverty in People's Living Conditions

François-Xavier de Perthuis de Laillevault and Ulrike Schuerkens

INTRODUCTION

What appeals to the researcher when he/she examines the literature on poverty is the lack of definitions, despite an abundance of research and publications. Indeed, whatever social science is considered, none is able to provide an explicit definition of poverty. Definitions abound and differ according to their authors, institutions, or the political discourse on poverty alleviation.

Furthermore, the scientific literature dealing with different conceptual approaches on poverty is characterized by the crossing of many subjects of the social sciences. Much research efforts address the subject by emphasizing economic, political, philosophical, sociological, or anthropological issues. These publications are too numerous to be listed here. Despite their diversity, it is interesting to highlight two predominant approaches in the literature on the empirical understanding of poverty: the monetary or utilitarian[1] approach and the non-monetary one that continue to lead research in this field since the 1970s.

Theories and the discourse on poverty in international institutions remain characterized by a parallel but not linear change. Although the concept of poverty invested the international political arena in the late 1960s, early writings tackling the issue of poverty and its social and economic aspects in the late nineteenth century and at the beginning of the twentieth century can be found in the publications of Booth (1889) and Rowntree (1901, 1913, 1941) that describe the situation of poor households in London. Despite the empirical dimensions of poverty highlighted by this research, a theoretical approach on poverty continued to dominate the theory of economic growth. Poverty alleviation was apprehended by including the macro-economic indicator of gross domestic product (GDP) as a means of poverty measurement on a national scale. In the 1960s, the discourse on poverty was still influenced by the liberal economic model: economic growth was correlated with poverty reduction, the benchmark being the GDP per capita.

The late 1970s heralded the appearance of a discourse that was opposed to the liberal economic doctrine fuelled by the debt crisis, which questioned the solvency of African states. Despite some criticism of the emerging liberal doctrine, the discourse on poverty created by international institutions continued to be characterized by the desire to promote the stabilization of the economy through the implementation of Structural Adjustment Programs (PAS) based on both the reduction of public expenditure and the integration of national economies in a global economy characterized by free trade. It was not until the late 1980s that the problem of poverty became the focal point of development policies implemented by international institutions. This re-orientation revealed a rupture in the political discourse: the notion of targets for poverty alleviation replaced the notion of economic growth objectives (Lautier 2002, Emmerij 2006, Bertin 2007). In 2009, the objective of institutional policies was no longer limited to the economic development of African nations but emphasized poverty reduction as its primary aim so that the problem of poverty was detached from economic growth.

Despite this important change, it was not until the 1990s that poverty reduction became a major economic policy, developed and implemented by international institutions. This change has been initiated by the close collaboration of Amartya Sen with the United Nations Development Program (UNDP). In 1990, this partnership culminated in the publication of the first report on human development. The report re-iterated the theoretical work conducted by A. Sen since the early 1980s and reflected a major change in the apprehension of poverty: it was no longer reduced to a state of deprivation in monetary terms but referred to economic and social opportunities that could be claimed by poor individuals. In 1997, UNDP published a Human Development Report devoted to the eradication of poverty and introduced the concept of human poverty based on basic dimensions of deprivation such as a short life expectancy, lack of basic education, and lack of access to public and private resources.

The declaration of the Millennium Development Goals (MDGs) adopted by 189 United Nations Member States at the 8th plenary meeting of the United Nations General Assembly held on September 8th, 2000, marked a renewal by emphasizing poverty alleviation as essential to development and making it a development priority.[2] With the adoption of the Poverty Reduction Strategy Papers (PRSP), the reduction of poverty became the central concern of international institutions. The MDGs made poverty alleviation a universal concern to be accepted by civil society. These goals have then been listed on the agenda of charitable, intergovernmental, and non-governmental organizations and in policy strategies. These latter are supported by a multitude of projects that have to promote and to strengthen the socio-economic conditions of individuals and families.

This chapter proposes to underline the characteristics of poverty in Senegal by emphasizing predominant approaches to the understanding of poverty, available statistical data, and the coping behavior developed by poor people.

THEORETICAL APPROACHES ON POVERTY IN SENEGAL

The Utilitarian Approach and Multidimensional Aspects of Poverty

Supporters of welfare developed the monetary approach whereas its critics developed the non-monetary approach, citing the other for overlooking the non-material aspects of poverty. In addition to the methodologies and indicators worked out, these two approaches have characterized the empirical understanding of the phenomenon of poverty but they differ in their definitions of poverty. The utilitarian approach places its focal point on income and consumption as opposed to the non-monetary approach, that focuses on the social environment of the actor, and, in particular, on social goods. Despite an abundance of research efforts, these approaches still contain much ambiguity in the understanding and empirical analysis of poverty if the researcher chooses an anthropological approach that consists in the empirical observation of poverty such as the study of people's living conditions.

Whatever the approach, research involves the conceptualization of a coherent analytical framework. The two dominant approaches on poverty are based respectively on the concepts of welfare and utility, concepts that have been empirically implemented by the notions of basic needs and *capabilities* (Sen). Despite their apparent differences, both theoretical approaches converge and define poverty by a gap. The conceptual discussion of poverty comes to the conclusion that *something is missing*. Yet, the discourse on the nature and the level of poverty should not invest in a unique social aspect but should refer to the opportunities of each and should determine a monetary threshold that permits characterization of an actor as poor or not poor.

More comprehensively, theoretical approaches on poverty in Africa invest the political sciences corpus through the design of development policies elaborated and implemented by international institutions and governments. Therefore, the empirical understanding of poverty focuses on statistical tools as a means of evaluating and analyzing it in order to identify the members of a given society that should be considered being poor.

The Poverty Issue in Senegal

The scientific literature on poverty in Senegal is abundant. However, most research on measuring and analyzing poverty has favored the monetary approach. The World Bank (1995), the Ministry of Economy and Finance[3] (1997, 2000, 2001), Ndiaye (1999), Cissé (1997, 2003), Badji and Daffé (2003), de Ki *et al.* (2005), and Azam and Dia (2004) have developed the most important studies. The limitations outlined earlier, linked to the different approaches, show that the poverty profiles highlighted remain very sensitive to changes in the respective poverty lines used.[4] Nevertheless, there is a consensus that poverty is widespread in Senegal.

As part of its program of poverty alleviation, Senegal has undertaken a number of surveys and studies to improve the system of monitoring household living conditions, to increase the knowledge of poverty, and to provide information that may support decision-makers in the selection and implementation of socio-economic policies. The scientific literature on the empirical understanding of poverty corresponds to the political discourse of international institutions. The research results of the Senegalese administration show that the understanding and empirical conceptualization of poverty is linked to the analysis of development processes. This understanding of poverty in Senegalese political programs on poverty alleviation began in the 1980s. Therefore, it is necessary to return to the implementation of policies on poverty alleviation in Senegal.

Senegal was the first African country south of the Sahara that introduced structural adjustment policies. In the late 1970s, the government was on the verge of bankruptcy as a result of falling revenues from exports of groundnuts, the increased costs of agricultural development, and the augmentation of external debts. In 1983, the Senegalese government signed a credit adjustment with the IMF. The New Agricultural Policy (NAP), established in 1984, provided for the reduction of state interventionism. The implementation of the NAP has resulted: (a) in the dismantling of companies that are partly or wholly owned by the government and that focus on regional development, (b) the reduction of the supply of public services, (c) price liberalization, (d) the removal of subsidies on imports, and (e) the reduction of debts. Market liberalization has been the focus of structural adjustment programs implemented in all Sub-Saharan African countries. The reforms implemented did not take into account the lack of organization and the low development of the private sector, a feature obvious in most countries of the region and in particular in Senegal. Failing to contribute to poverty reduction, the economic liberalization of Sub-Saharan African countries has been reflected in a process of impoverishment of the population, a phenomenon still exacerbated by structural adjustment reforms whose main purpose was to reduce the costs of social policy by budget cuts in public expenditures.

In the late 1990s, the debt burden was the major concern on the international political agenda.[5] In 1999, the Jubilee 2000 campaign put pressure on the G8 Summit in Cologne, Germany. The negotiations resulted in the adoption of the initiative for Heavily Indebted Poor Countries (HIPC) so that debt relief became the new strategy of poverty alleviation policies. In 2002, Senegal adopted the Strategic Document for Poverty Reduction (SDPR), a new policy as part of its strategy for the alleviation of poverty. Nevertheless, despite the theoretical approach developed by A. Sen, strategies of poverty alleviation have still been influenced by the discourse of the World Bank based on two principles of the utilitarian approach: to increase the incomes of the poor through economic growth and to promote trade liberalization.

At the national level, surveys were realized such as the Consumer Budget Survey Priorities (ESP 1991–92), the first Senegalese Household Survey (ESAM I 1994–95) and the Survey of Household Expenditure of the Capital (EDMC 1996). These surveys permitted the collection of quantitative information on income, assets, household consumption expenditure, and prices. By focusing on the monetary aspects of poverty, these surveys helped to define poverty profiles that permitted the identification of the population groups most in need according to the monetary approach. However, these investigations had limitations and needed to be supplemented by more detailed knowledge on different dimensions of poverty.

The understanding of poverty as an economic and social manifestation of a complex and heterogeneous reality appeared rather late in the political discourse. Since 2001, due to the survey on Perceptions of Poverty in Senegal[6] (EPPS 2001), research conducted by the Ministry of Finance favored a participation by poor households in order to connect the perception of poverty to the interviewed people. This research led to the emergence of a new approach, the so-called "subjective"[7] approach in the analysis and understanding of poverty in Senegal. The focus on the wellbeing of each individual took into consideration the individual's subjective relation to his/her economic and social situation. The various investigations mentioned earlier identified a profile of poverty at the national level and made it possible to isolate determinants of poverty in Senegal.

DETERMINANTS OF POVERTY IN SENEGAL

The National Trend

At the national level, the phenomenon of poverty is characterized by a very high incidence. According to the surveys ESAM I and ESAM II, the share of poor decreased from 67.9 percent in 1994–95 to 57.1 percent in 2001–02. Similarly, the share of households in poverty decreased from 61.4 percent to 48.5 percent, a decrease of 16 percent in terms of poverty incidence. In 2001–02, about 1,063,325 households were found in Senegal, from which 515,238 (48.5 percent) lived below the national poverty line estimated at FCFA 143,080 per year, or 392 FCFA per day, while GDP *per capita* was estimated at 343,360 FCFA[8] in the year 2000–01. When we consider spatial concentrations, the area of residence highlights the disparity in the geographical distribution of poverty in Senegal. Thus, the incidence of poverty includes most households in rural areas where 57.5 percent are poor, against 33.3 percent in the urban area of the capital and around 43.3 percent in other towns. Rural areas accounted for the largest share of poverty with almost two in three poor households, or 65 percent of poor households, while 54.7 percent of national households are rural. The Dakar region that concentrates over a quarter of Senegalese households (25.9 percent) accounts for 17.8 percent[9] of the poor. Urban centers outside the capital city contribute less to the phenomenon of poverty: they comprise 19.4 percent of the households and 17.3 percent of poor households. At the national level, urban Dakar contributes most to poverty comprising 18.4 percent of all poor households. The statistics highlight the uneven geographical distribution of poverty that the rates of poverty support when different geographical areas are considered.

A disparity between rural and urban areas characterizes the urban centers and the administrative regions (absence of banks, corporations, and infrastructure). Indeed, the lack of infrastructure, and economic and social assistance limit the access of the population to products and services, a feature resulting from the isolation of certain regions (such as Kolda[10] in the South, near the border of the Republic of Guinea-Bissau, and Louga[11] in the North, near the city of Saint-Louis in Senegal). The opposition of rural and urban areas is also reflected in the inequality of income opportunities, and the access to basic care, consumer products, and food supplies.

The Poverty Profile in Senegal

The analytical approach of the Senegalese administration relying on the concept of objective poverty helps to establish a profile of poverty in Senegal by referring to socio-economic parameters that can be compared to global characteristics of poverty.

The results of the ESAM II survey confirmed a strong correlation between the level of household consumption[12] and the educational level of the head of household. Households whose head of household had no formal education experienced the highest poverty rate (54.2 percent). This rate was at the level of 45.9 percent when the head of household had attended primary school and decreased by more than a half when he attained a secondary school level. Only 12.5 percent of household heads that had reached the level of higher education were characterized by a situation of poverty. The number of poor households whose head had no formal education rose to 415,484, what means that more than 80 percent of poor households are in this situation. Statistics highlight a strong correlation between poverty incidence and level of education. In addition to access to employment opportunities, education remains an important factor that may allow the improvement of the conditions of poor households. Indeed, when indicators such as education, income, and social status are correlated, the result is that education seems to be the element that most affects the status of individuals. The higher the educational level of social actors, the more they can improve their opportunities.

In addition to the educational status of the head of household, the activity rate of the latter is a determinant of household poverty in Senegal. Households whose head is employed have a lower poverty incidence (44.5 percent) than households whose head is unemployed (59.9 percent) or inactive[13] (63 percent). The incidence of poverty is more widespread among households whose head performs an activity within the informal sector (49.2 percent), while it is lowest among households whose head works in an administrative office (18.9 percent); households whose head works for a private company are characterized by an intermediate position (32 percent). These figures are meaningful because small individual companies make up the bulk of the informal sector, which can be distinguished by the weakness of its means of production and working conditions that leave households in a situation of vulnerability and instability associated with economic weakness and the irregularity of incomes. This category of poor households contributes with 85 percent to poverty. In contrast to anticipated outcomes, households headed by women accounted for 14.8 percent of the phenomenon of poverty at the national level. Women remain less affected by the phenomenon of poverty compared to households headed by men: 37 percent of households headed by women are living in poverty conditions whereas the figure reaches 50 percent when the head of household is a man. This result is probably linked to the fact that many female-headed households receive remittances from husbands settled in France, other Western countries, or in further African countries. According to the International Monetary Fund, Senegalese workers residing abroad repatriated via official channels nearly 60 billion FCFA (US$ 92.5 million) in 1997 (Tall 2002).[14] This amount increased to FCFA 242 billion in 2003, FCFA 250 billion in 2004, FCFA 285 billion in 2005, and FCFA 410 billion in 2006,[15] an increase supported by money transfer systems such as Western Union and MoneyGram. However, several studies agree that these approximations under-estimate the extent of these financial operations because an important part of the transfers of emigrants uses non-official mechanisms (Ghosh 2000, Babou 2002). Tall (2005) estimates that 50 percent of the transfers pass through informal channels.

Emigrants' transfers of funds passing through official channels rose in 2007 to nearly 460 billion FCFA (nearly 10 percent of the GDP).[16] Approximately 11.5 percent of the income of Senegalese households stem from such transfers. Several studies show that, on the one hand, these transfers contribute significantly to an increase in the expenditure *per capita* (+60 percent of increase on average), especially in Dakar (+95 percent) and in other cities (+63 percent); but, on the other hand, their impact is rather small on spending in rural areas (+6 percent). Yet, transfers have a strong impact on the reduction of the incidence (–31 percent)[17] and the depth (–6 percent) of poverty, but also tend to increase the severity of poverty (+41 percent) because they widen the income gap between the poor and the less poor, the latter profiting mainly from the transfers (MEF/DPEE 2008). Transfers are often used for everyday consumption needs. In some villages in the region of Louga, transfers represent 90 percent of the household income (Tall 2001). Thus, they constitute an important component of poverty alleviation (PNUD 2008).

The EPPS[18] conducted during the years 2001–02 revealed that nearly two thirds of the households surveyed (67 percent) were poor. The part of people living in poverty was higher than the share obtained by the *objective* analysis of poverty that determined the proportion of the population able to assure basic needs. The statistical difference resulting from the comparison of both studies displays the subjective nature of poverty in Senegal. Indeed, a significant proportion of the households classified as poor according to their consumption level is perceived as non-poor, whereas in contrast, a significant share of households considered, according to the monetary approach, as non-poor based on their consumption, judge themselves as being poor. The study revealed that the primary determinant of poverty acknowledged by the groups surveyed referred to a situation that does not guarantee the family's basic needs. Other indicators referred to were the inability to work or to afford medical expenses for family members, or the fact of being deprived of a decent home.

Although the region of Dakar is one where the smallest part of Senegalese poor live, the population of the region was still characterized by a poverty rate of 33.6 percent of the households[19] in 2001. In Dakar, the groups characterized by poverty are composed of families with low and episodic incomes. Households whose head is employed display a lower incidence of poverty (44.5 percent) than households where the head of household is unemployed (59.9 percent), inactive, or retired (63.0 percent). It is therefore obvious that the vast majority of heads of households interviewed in Dakar complained first of all about the high food prices. In the *Point E* and *HLM*[20] neighborhoods respectively 82 percent and 87 percent of the heads of households consider that their food expenditures have risen and claim almost their entire income.

Moreover, the place of residence affects the incidence of poverty and gives rise to a mapping of poverty in the town. In Senegal, most urbanized areas are characterized by a high population density per square meter that concentrates the bulk of poor households in specific neighborhoods. In Dakar, poverty is concentrated in disadvantaged and peripheral neighborhoods such as *Grand Yoff* or *Colobane*, and downtown areas such as the *Medina* and the *Gueule Tapée*. Therefore, within the urban area of Dakar, the poor are concentrated in disadvantaged neighborhoods, both in terms of individual characteristics (the average income is lower) and in terms of public facilities access (low access to water, electricity, etc.).[21]

In 2006, the poverty situation in rural areas was analyzed by SENA-GROSOL. The study showed that depending on regional assets (rainfalls, transfers of financial resources by oversea migrants, diversity of natural resources, etc.), poverty has regressed, stagnated, or prospered for the last ten years. In the countryside, savings associations and groups can be found as in urban areas. They are considered one of the best ways of reducing poverty. The study underlined that the number of poor households has remained unchanged over the last ten years even if there are people who have fallen back in poverty and others who have escaped poverty.

What are the welfare indicators of households according to this study? The first characteristic is the possibility of meeting basic needs: food, health, clothes, and housing. If these basic needs are fulfilled, households seek stable incomes (business) and invest in real estates. Upwardly mobile households diversify their activities and sources of income, develop pieces of land, and pay a part of their workforce. Diversification of incomes means to accept part-time jobs in the town, to invest in additional activities, and/or to save money.

In rural areas, very poor are those households which exclusively depend on agriculture. Poor are those who depend on agriculture but who carry out selling activities. Middle classes in rural areas are those groups whose main activity is agriculture but who develop secondary activities, such as a sustainable business. The rich as a category include those who rely on agricultural activities but who also have access to production factors and loans. Among the very rich are those whose children have a job by which they contribute to the household expenses. Often, these people have a prosperous business and large lands for agriculture.

To fall back into poverty can be caused by a loss of working loads, an increase of competing shops in the community (Chinese shops), mismanagement, poor health conditions, or the return of migrants. There is thus no one way of getting into poverty or staying in it. Senegalese people think that inequality has *divine causes*: God has decided "to set the difference between poor and rich people" (SENAGROSOL 2009: 37). There are educational, social, and economic inequalities according to the interviewees. Moreover, there are huge gender differences in Senegal because men control almost all the income-generating activities so that their position in the household is predominant.

People believe generally that intervention of the government and of NGOs would help in fighting back poverty. But what are the aspirations of the poor? A great part of those who are better off than they were ten years ago show some confidence in the future. They think that the conditions in their households would be better in ten years time. Among the priorities of rural communities but also of individual actors are promotions of income-generating activities, the development of basic social services, and better market opportunities for agricultural produce. Poverty is thus no static category but people try hard to change their situation. They have agency and are not left alone to face the consequences of globalization and the neo-liberal market ideology. However, a description of poverty would be incomplete without a report on the manifestations of poverty revealed by the observation of living conditions in a context of poverty.

THE MANIFESTATION OF POVERTY IN PEOPLE'S LIVING CONDITIONS

It is necessary for poor people to develop strategies that ensure the satisfaction of daily family needs. The main concerns of poor households in Senegal are not very different from other poor people living in African, Asian, or South-American countries. However, their strategies demonstrate the diversity and originality of the behavior observed in Senegal.

Poor Households Comprise Two Geographical Areas: Urban and Rural Regions

In Senegal, the history of poverty refers to rural poverty that has caused low agricultural productivity coupled with adverse weather conditions, an exhaustion of soils, and the fluctuation of raw material prices on international markets. Nevertheless, an opposition between urban and rural areas on poverty lines is controversial in this country but also in other West African countries.

The phenomenon of seasonal migrations from rural to urban areas and the importance of money transfers made by the diaspora contribute to transform the mapping of poverty. Seasonal migration to urban centers is one of the major responses to rural poverty. This observation is not only confined to Senegal but extends to the whole region of West Africa. The rural economy of Senegal depends on large urban centers such as Dakar and Saint-Louis, but also on the capacities of the coastal regions to absorb rural people's seasonal or permanent migrations. Each year, hundreds of thousands of migrants migrate to these coastal towns. Thus, the level of rural poverty does not only depend on conditions in rural areas, but also on the income obtained through the solicitation of social networks and employment in urban regions.

The rural economy of the regions situated at 60 to 120 miles from Dakar is made sustainable with remittances provided by seasonal workers who leave their villages during the dry season (Ba 1996). Localities situated in the region of the Djoloff (e.g., Diourbel and Louga) depend on the revenues of seasonal or permanent migrations. Most of the families are dependent on the remittances sent by their relatives working in Dakar. For instance, young girls from the Sereer communities from the Sine and Saloum region (Kaolack) work in households in Dakar and send at least 50 percent of their monthly incomes to their parents. The same situation prevails in the Joola communities in the south of Senegal as well as in the south-east with the Peulhs of the Fouladou (Kolda). In Senegal oriental (Tambacounda, Bakel, and Kedougou), the situation is different, because rural households depend on the diaspora living abroad (in France, Spain, and Italy). The Soninke people of the region are well known for providing ongoing financial assistance to their family, relatives, and the community.[22]

Seasonal migrations in Senegal play an important role in times of chronic food shortages. Employed migrants in the urban areas use most of their revenues to secure alimentation (rice, millet, sugar, salt, and dried fish). Insofar as they are able, they help their rural relatives to escape famine in times of drought.[23] Poor rural families depend thus on several geographical areas that permit them to ensure their subsistence. Migrating to urban centers is a strategy that allows the diversification of household incomes. In urban centers, the informal sector enables rural people to find jobs that permit some financial returns.

The Social Network at the Heart of Adaptation Strategies in Situations of Poverty

Social networks are built on alliances that underline the principle of reciprocity. In the past, social relations were based on social networks that referred to ethnic alliances and family links. Since the European colonization, and more recently linked to the phenomenon of globalization, these logics are in perpetual transformation and give an increasing role to the elaboration of behaviors of a clientelist type: rules that govern the network of social relations are now determined by alliances: (a) according to rules governed by both the system of family links and membership in an ethnic group, and (b) focusing on behaviors privileging individual socio-economic opportunities such as clientelism.

Modern behavior emphasizes socio-economic opportunities and seems to neglect family and ethnic networks. For example, during our investigations in Senegal, a carpenter informed us of the importance of opening up his social network to other individuals with privileged social positions and a higher social prestige, sometimes at the expense of family members. These networks of solidarity permit the shaping of alliances that go far beyond the boundaries established by belonging to an ethnic community. The solicitation and maintenance of social networks is then thought of as a means of livelihood that permits creation of socio-economic opportunities and resistance every day to precariousness.

Nowadays, individual actors depend on the effectiveness and the quality of their social networks that should offer daily opportunities. During our field surveys conducted in Senegal and Niger, the characteristic often mentioned was the trust between the actors and the social position of the members who made up this relationship. Trust is dependent on the reciprocity exercised *vis-à-vis* the demands of the network. Reciprocity can be defined as the cost of maintenance of the network. The amount and the frequency of fees are not determined in advance but depend on the opportunities and difficulties encountered in everyday life: the network assists when one is in need. The cost supported by a member is equivalent to a charge while it is a resource for the applicant. It seems inconceivable not to satisfy a request if the individual actor has asked for a minimum of means, even if this means seems to be very low. Thus, the construction, use, and preservation of social networks appear actually as a means of subsistence in order to create commercial opportunities.

The perception of poverty is influenced by social appreciations: "We are poor, when we do not have social relationships," answered one interviewee to the authors' question "What is poverty?" In the urban area of Dakar, poverty can be left behind because of social capacities that permit a change in the individual position in a given social network. This feature determines the perception of poverty. Being poor does not mean being able to build networks or to be alone, but to have no social recognition. The idea of poverty is thus linked to the absence of social relationships and refers to social exclusion.

In the borough called *Gueule Tapée*, research on homeless people was undertaken. At the start of our inquiry, it was possible to begin a dialogue, not directly with the homeless, but with local residents. The reactions and comments of the residents displayed the sensitivity and taboos that have characterized this topic. At the beginning of our study, the residents did not allow the taking of pictures of the homeless so that it was difficult to interact with them. This behavior was surprising because of the existing close links with the neighborhood. Initial reactions of the residents were to deny the presence of the homeless while claiming that they were occasionally present but that they did not form a recognized population at this place. Being embarrassed, they did not answer questions about this category of homeless people. Yet, some time afterwards, people became more talkative. The residents' notion frequently used to designate this population was *fools*. In fact, the word *fool* refers to people in situations of social exclusion resulting from the absence of family links and social networks: a socially lost person.

Adaptation strategies in poverty situations depend thus on efficient social networks. The value of these strategies is linked to satisfactory solicitations originating from the members of social networks. The arrangements following this solicitation can take various forms (e.g., services, consumer goods, and money). The pressure exerted is such that families include the costs linked to reciprocity in the family budget: economic resources are used in order to preserve the social network. To maintain the quality of the relationship is considered a short-term benefit. This primacy underlines the fact that strategies consist of trade opportunities and that the immediate economic profit is not the only purpose. The concept of wealth cannot be reduced to an accumulation of economic capital that would correspond to an accumulation of cash income, but includes the quality of social relationships. The societal environment is considered an important capital that may be more important than economic resources. Thus, the concept of wealth refers more to social status and future opportunities for upward mobility than to the accumulation of an immediate cash income. Social networks motivate cultural processes at the origin of this behavior that exhibits strategies favoring the rule of reciprocity. The direct economic benefit is not the primary purpose. An individual, a family, or a household is rich when they are inserted into powerful social networks consisting of many opportunities even if the individual actor does not obtain great cash benefits.

Reciprocity is regarded as being important. Members of extended family clans and clusters that cover up the urban and rural society develop social links. Due to powerful relationships with influential individuals, actors included in major social networks are themselves influent persons. These social actors become thus popular partners because they are seen as re-distributors of goods and favors. Social networks are hierarchical: some partners are more important and more desirable than others. As already underlined, the purpose is not only cash, but the social status of the person, which may or may not be proportional to his/her monetary wealth. Moreover, the preferred relationship with a man/woman owning major economic assets is not necessarily synonymous with trading at discount: sometimes a price higher than that generally practiced is even asked for. This amount depends more on influence than on real purchasing power. What is taken into account is social capital building. The latter takes precedence over the economic price. Even if it is essential for individuals, the diversity of support made possible by the solicitation of a solidarity network does not always resolve the difficulties of the household, particularly when the difficulties encountered cannot be resolved by a request to the social network due to the lack of members and consequently the weakness of opportunities.

The Daily Management of Expenses in Poverty Situations

A family has to handle two kinds of expenses: predictable and unpredictable expenses. Anticipated expenditures are associated with everyday life (housing, clothing, and food in the normal life course) and religious expenditures (e.g., the religious events *Korité* and *Tabaski*). These outflows correspond to particular items in a family budget that can be divided into different categories such as food, debts, personal items, gifts given at the occasion of religious events, and miscellaneous expenses. The unpredictable costs are much more diverse than the previously described costs. They may occur in case of disease and death. These expenditures may even result from inflationist tendencies. When these costs occur in a poverty situation, they can threaten the survival of the entire household.

Tabaski is celebrated two months and ten days after Ramadan. It is one of the most important religious events in Senegal. Traditionally, the family head buys a sheep for relatives. In Thiès, the second urban area[24] of Senegal, prices increased sharply on *Tabaski* in 2005. In mid-January 2005, it was necessary to spend from 50,000 FCFA[25] to 80,000 FCFA to buy a sheep. In Dakar during the year 2008, the medium price was approximately 70,000 FCFA for a sheep, corresponding to double the monthly minimum wage in Senegal. The prices of a bigger sheep can sometimes reach 500,000 FCFA, or even one million FCFA.

In Senegal, these sums are excessive and are at the origin of debts and family discord. For the urban populations, the size of the sheep characterizes the membership in a certain social class. The sheep is a symbolic expenditure: the larger the animal is, the more important the social status of the family. Nowadays, the recognition acquired through the size of the animal constitutes a social phenomenon, which pushes Senegalese households to spend more than their budgets allow.

To fulfill his/her duties, the family head does not hesitate to spend huge amounts of money in order to buy the animal. The purchase price of the animal will then be communicated to the immediate surroundings and will contribute to the prestige of the whole family. The higher the purchase price is, the higher the status of the family. Often, populations in rural areas do not have the financial resources to buy a sheep for their families, so they may ask their social network to contribute to the purchase of the latter. Moreover, *Tabaski* requires the purchase of new clothing for all household members. The practice of owing money thus causes difficult situations for the household heads. When possible, parts of the debt are refunded by the input of members of social networks.

Religious events ask for huge expenditures of family and friends. The practice of fasting during the Ramadan has a particular cost. During Ramadan, the breaking of fasting consists in eating special or festive meals with meat and pasta. Although this practice is widespread in families with adequate resources, meals are usually made up of imported food products. Traditional produce such as millet and cowpeas are replaced with products such as pasta. The period of Ramadan is marked by an inflationary tendency of the prices of foodstuffs in all West African countries. In Senegal and particularly in urban areas, the period of Ramadan is associated with the observation of the practice of *sukaru koor* that consists in offering sugar and date palm fruits (the quantity of sugar offered can be up to three packs of five kilograms) to in-laws in order to strengthen family ties. In its traditional form, the *sukaru koor*[26] consisted in offering a gift to the husband or the wife to ensure the esteem of and to strengthen the relationship with in-laws.

Since the time of decolonization, this practice was influenced by modern behaviors of the market economy. Indeed, sugar and date palm fruits, formerly customary gifts, are increasingly replaced by money, food, and other kinds of market economy products such as clothes or jewelry. The economic crisis of 2008–09 has exposed families to difficult economic conditions. Nevertheless, social pressure is so important that the poorest women are forced to go into debt to fulfill this obligation in order to be appreciated by their in-laws. It seems that *sukaru koor* has become a practice that contributes to the destabilization and the weakening of women. The *sukaru koor* practice has thus become more a moral obligation than a customary way of recognition.

Senegalese households have to envisage budget items for ceremonial services such as weddings, baptisms, religious events, funerals, and family gatherings. These expenditures have a symbolic character. The amount of the expenditure associated with ceremonial events varies and depends on the extent of the social network and the number of children in the family. It is not uncommon for several consecutive years that a family head uses his relationships to contribute to the financing of one or more ceremonial celebrations (baptisms, marriages, or funerals). There are also female groups that collect money within *tontines*, amounts that are often only spent for these particular events.

In Senegal, women participate more than men in *tontines*: the average participation by women is as high as 1.75 *tontines* while men participate in only 1.38 *tontines* (Dromain 1990). The activities of women's groups are part of a vast network made up by *tontines*, neighborly relations, and Muslim brotherhoods based on a permanent circulation of small monetary contributions. Contributions, services provided, and permanent exchange give an insurance to alleviate risks caused by precariousness. Rotating associations of saving and credit, or *tontines*, are informal groupings that respond to the desire of a group to satisfy the saving needs of its members, whose behaviors not only have economic motivations but also aim at raising social status. As highlighted by Ndione (1994: 31), associations of mutual assistance, in particular *mbotaye*, perpetuate a type of social management that intends to assure a better integration of its members in an urban environment. The purpose of *mbotaye* is thus less economic than social.

The *mbotaye* is a group formed for mutual and social aid by women from the same district, and to which women are admitted by co-optation. This form of re-grouping is very common in poor families established in Dakar. The origin of *mbotaye* consisted in ensuring its members' food safety. A *mbotaye* counted soon about 30 women living in the same district. The principle of this organization was simple and consisted of delivering monthly, or according to the possibilities of each participant, food products necessary to guarantee the food security of the family members. These food products generally consisted of oil, tomatoes, and rice. Thus, each member was certain to ensure, at least for a month, the complete food intake of her family. In contemporary Senegalese society, the proposed services of *mbotaye* are much wider than at the beginning of this form of association. Often, the monetary input has replaced the collected and re-distributed food products. *Mbotaye* signifies a means of managing food insecurity but also urgent expenditures such as ceremonial, religious, or health expenses. Women contribute with a predefined monetary sum[27] in order to support those members whose lives are difficult. These participants may receive the entire sum of the collected contributions.

CONCLUSION

In the 1980s and 1990s, the development paradigm was influenced by the hegemony of economic growth based on the stabilization of the macroeconomic framework, itself guaranteed by the implementation of structural economic reforms. In fact, development policies were based on a conception of development resulting from political stabilization and the liberalization of the economy. However, the 1990s witnessed an important change in the analysis of development: the multidimensional nature of poverty was officially acknowledged. The debate on the multidimensional nature of poverty suggests that the factors mentioned in this chapter were not considered in the classical approach to poverty. Yet, monetary variables cannot only account for the dynamics of poverty and the redistribution of wealth among the poor themselves.

Despite the various criteria of poverty, it is undeniable that poverty is strongly influenced by social networks. Whereas poverty also refers to material conditions, monetary aspects are only one part of the phenomenon. Beyond statistics and low monetary incomes, poor people develop strategies to ensure their families' daily needs. Coping strategies underline the diversity and originality of this behavior in a poverty situation.

The economic and ethnological approach developed in this chapter underlines the important role of social networks as part of coping strategies developed by poor households in Senegal. Nevertheless, the assistance provided by social networks exerts a high economic pressure on the poorest. Indeed, reciprocity rules restrain the opportunities that are available to the poor. In Senegal, we have seen small entrepreneurs trying to develop businesses through access to micro-credits, a practice that is possible with the help of local associations. Solicitations of members of social networks have forced them to re-distribute parts of the credit granted by relatives. This may then result in the failure of the initiative.

There are recent voices, which underline that "poverty is a condition, not a characteristic" (Narayan 2009: 23). This chapter has shown that poor people pursue activities with each other to cope with poverty. Big movements of households up or down the poverty lines have characterized some countries during the last 30 years (e.g., China and India). It seems as if mobility from poverty is an individual or country specific phenomenon so that it is better for poor people to live in a prosperous region than in a poor one. National governments can implant solutions in order to provide communication networks and markets, and can work with organizations of the poor at the local level. Participatory approaches may reinforce people's personal agency even if there are limited economic choices. In Senegal, youths have dreams of doing better than their parents (SENAGROSOL 2009) so that responsive local political actors should implant programs to improve the situation of these poor youths. A better access to schools and health facilities may help communities to change their conditions. As this chapter has displayed, poor women and men do not lack the drive to improve their lives; they aspire to better lives and work hard to seize opportunities. Only small parts of them are unable to help themselves. It is thus important to make them utilize their agency so that they become important players who decide how to influence their conditions. Growing new crops, starting a business, or migrating for employment are initiatives based on agency and empowerment that show the potential to succeed. Future research efforts should then focus on opportunities at the local level that may influence the movement out of poverty. Powerful political groups can create these opportunities so that economic success may follow that permits innovation that can influence the poor.

NOTES

1. In the text, the term *utilitarian* refers to the monetary approach.
2. The first target of the Millennium Development Goals has been to diminish the number of people living on less than one dollar per day (purchasing power parity) from 1990 to 2015.
3. *Ministère de l'Économie et des Finances* (1997, 2000, 2001).
4. In Senegal, most current research takes into account the calculation of poverty lines made from data collected as part of ESAM I (1994–95) and ESAM II (2001–02) carried out jointly by the *Direction de la Prévision et de la Statistique* (DPS) and the World Bank. The food poverty lines that were chosen rose to FCFA 342,40 (Dakar), 317,80 FCFA (other urban centers), and FCFA 290,90 (rural regions), whereas the global poverty lines (including auto-consumption) rose to FCFA 879 (Dakar), FCFA 712,80 (other urban centers) and FCFA 497,90 (rural regions). FCFA means *Franc de la Communauté Financière d'Afrique*.
5. In 1991, the World Bank, the United Nations Development Program, and the African Development Bank launched a series of programs to address the consequences of Structural Adjustment Programs (SAP). These programs underlined the social dimensions of adjustments in Africa. Within the World Bank, the social dimension of SAP led to the creation of a division responsible of poverty observation and the classification of poverty in three layers: the chronically and traditionally poor, the *new poor*, and lower socio-economic vulnerability.
6. *Ministère de l'Économie et des Finances* (2001).
7. Ibid.
8. This amount corresponds to US$ 464. One dollar is the equivalent of FCFA 740 (2009).
9. *Ministère de l'Économie et des Finances* (2004).
10. According to the survey ESAM II, the Kolda region belongs to regions where poverty is most prevalent in households, with an incidence of 60 percent in 2001.
11. According to the survey ESAM II, the region of Louga is one of the areas where poverty is fairly widespread in households, with an incidence of 40 percent in 2001.
12. The consumption level corresponds to the level of household poverty.
13. The *Direction de la Prévision et de la Statistique* defined several development indicators (Quid (*Questionnaire Unifié des Indicateurs de Développement*) 2001): unemployment is reported when people have not worked in the past four weeks preceding the survey and will not work for the same period in the next four weeks.
14. International Monetary Fund (2000).
15. Daffé *et al.* (2008).
16. Statistics on the transfers of migrants strongly vary from one source to another. The BCEAO (2009) indicated a net value of 469 billion FCFA received in 2007 electronically, including 530 billion FCFA received by transfers and 61 billion FCFA emitted as outside flows. However, these statis-

tics do not incorporate the transfers passing through informal ways, which should increase very much the full amount.

17. One third of households receiving transfers would have passed under the poverty line if they had not received them. (MEF 2008)
18. *Ministère de l'Economie et des Finances* (2001).
19. 94,714 households.
20. *HLM* is a popular neighborhood in Dakar.
21. Herrera and Roubaud (2003).
22. Amadou Papa Sarr (2009) gave this information from his ongoing PhD research at the EHESS on migrant remittances from France in Senegal.
23. Idem.
24. The population in Thiès consists of 1,654,141 inhabitants (*Ministère de l'Economie et des Finances* (MEF) (2007).
25. US$ 107.34 (FCFA 1000 corresponded to US$ 2.14 in 2009).
26. Similar practices of the *Sukaru Koor* can be observed in other West African countries such as the Niger. In the Niger, at the beginning of the month of Ramadan, it is customary to provide families a quantity of sugar of the brand *Saint Louis*, equivalent to the consumption of one month. This sugar is also subject to speculation: the price increases by nearly 50 percent of the purchase price during the month preceding Ramadan. In the Zinder region (Niger), inflation can sometimes reach 50 percent of the price of certain products. These foodstuffs are subject to rising prices on the part of traders selling their goods in urban and rural areas. During these periods, inflation increases the daily expenses of families and the vulnerability of the poorest families.
27. The monthly amount is usually around 5,000 FCFA.

BIBLIOGRAPHY

Azam, J.-P. and M. Dia (2004) *Pro-Poor Growth in Senegal*. Institut d'Économie Industrielle (IDEI), Toulouse, Working Paper 325. http://idei.fr/doc/wp/2004/propoor_senegal.pdf, accessed on May 10, 2009.
Ba, Cheikh Oumar (1996) *Dynamiques migratoires et changements sociaux au sein des relations de genre et des rapports jeunes—vieux des originaires de la moyenne vallée du Fleuve Sénégal*. PhD thesis, Université Cheikh Anta Diop, Dakar.
Babou, C. (2002) "Brotherhood Solidarity, Education and Migration: the Role of the Dahiras Among the Murid Muslim Community of New York," *African Affairs* 101 (403): 151–170.
Badji, M. S. and G. Daffé (2003) *Le profil de pauvreté féminine au Sénégal*, Rapport de recherche MIMAP/Senegal-CREA. http://cres-ucad.org/file/mimap006.pdf, accessed on April 12, 2009.
Bahri, A. (2004) "Sur la définition de la pauvreté," *African Population Studies Supplement A to vol. 19, Étude de la population africaine*, 1–12, Union for African Population Studies.
Bensaâd, A. (2003) "Agadez, carrefour migratoire sahélo-maghrébin," *Revue européenne des migrations internationales* 19 (1): 7–28. http://remi.revues.org/index336.html, accessed on April 12, 2009.
Bertin, A. (2007) *Pauvreté monétaire, pauvreté non monétaire: une analyse des interactions appliquée à la Guinée*. PhD in Economic Sciences, Université Montesquieu—Bordeaux IV. http://tel.archives-ouvertes.fr/docs/00/15/53/64/PDF/TheseBERTIN.pdf, accessed on March 14, 2009.
Booth, C. (1889) *Labour and Life of the People*. Volume 1: *East London*. London: Macmillan.

Booth, C. (1902) *Life and Labour of the People in London.* Vol. 1. London: Macmillan.

Chossudovsky, M. (2003) *The Globalization of Poverty and the New World.* 2nd ed., Oro, Ontario: Global Outlook, Center for Research on Globalization.

Cissé, F. (1997) *La pauvreté rurale au Sénégal: profils et determinants.* DEA thesis, Faseg- Université Cheikh Anta Diop, Dakar.

Cissé, F. (2003) *Profil de pauvreté au Sénégal: une approche monétaire.* Rapport MIMAP-Sénégal, CREA, UCAD, Dakar. http://cres-ucad.org/file/mimap002. pdf, accessed on December 12, 2008.

Cling, J.-P., M. Razafindrakoto, and F. Roubaud (2001) *La Banque mondiale et la lutte contre la pauvreté: tout changer pour que tout reste pareil?* DIAL, Document de travail, n° 9. http://www.dial.prd.fr/dial_publications/PDF/Doc_ travail/2002–09.pdf, accessed on December 10, 2008.

Daffé, G., M.-C. Diop, B. Riccio, and I. Barro (2008) *Le Sénégal des migrations: Mobilités, identités et sociétés.* Paris: Édtions Karthala.

Diane, O. D., O. Faye, and S. Faye (2007) *Le noyau dur la pauvreté au Sénégal.* Cahier de recherché PMMA 2007–17, Politiques économiques et pauvreté (PEP). http://www.pep-net.org/new-pep/Group/papers/papers/PMMA-2007-17.pdf, accessed on April 4, 2009.

Dromain, M. (1990) *L'épargne ignorée et négligée: les résultats d'une enquête sur les tontines au Sénégal.* Éditions John Libbey Eurotext: Paris. http://www.bibliotheque.refer.org/livre17/l1709.pdf, accessed on April 10, 2009.

Emmerij, L. (2006) *Turning Points in Development Thinking and Practice.* United Nation University—World Institute for Development Economic Research, Research Paper n° 2006/08. http://www.rrojasdatabank.info/widerconf/ emmerij1.pdf, accessed on December 12, 2008.

Ghosh, B. (2000a) "Introduction: Towards a New International Regime for Orderly Movements of People," B. Ghosh (ed.) *Managing Migration—Time for a New International Regime?* 6–26. Oxford: Oxford University Press.

Ghosh, B. (200b) "Return Migration: Reshaping Policy Approaches," B. Ghosh (ed.) *Return Migration, Journey of Hope or Despair?* 181–226. Geneva: IOM/UN.

Herrera, J. and F. Roubaud (2003) *Dynamique de la pauvreté urbaine au Pérou et à Madagascar 1997–1999: Une analyse sur données de panel,* DIAL-Unité de Recherche CIPRÉ. http://www.dial.prd.fr/dial_publications/PDF/Doc_ travail/2003–03.pdf, accessed on February 12, 2009.

Ki, Bosco J., B. Faye, and S. Faye (2005) *Pauvreté multidimensionnelle au Sénégal: approche non monétaire fondée sur les besoins de base.* Cahier de recherches PMMA 2005–05, Politiques économiques et pauvreté. http://www.pep-net.org/new-pep/ Group/papers/papers/PMMA-2005-05.pdf, accessed on September 10, 2008.

Kohl, R. (ed.) (2003) *Mondialisation, pauvreté et inégalité.* Paris: Séminaire du Centre de Développement, OCDE.

Lautier, B. (2002) "Pourquoi faut-il aider les pauvres ? Une étude critique du discours de la Banque mondiale sur la pauvreté," *Revue Tiers Monde* 43 (169): 137–165. http://matisse.univ-paris1.fr/doc2/ID0118b.PDF, accessed on February 15, 2009.

Minvielle, J.-P., A. Diop, and A. Niang (2005) *La pauvreté au Sénégal. Des statistiques à la réalité.* Paris: Éditions Karthala.

Narayan, D., L. Pritchett, and S. Kapoor (2009) *Moving Out of Poverty: Success from the Bottom-Up,* vol. 2, Basingstoke, Hampshire: Palgrave Macmillan and World Bank.

Ndiaye, A. (1999) *Essai de quantification et d'identification des déterminants de la pauvreté à Dakar. Des concepts aux réalités.* Thèse de doctorat d'État, Université Panthéon-Assas, Paris II.

Ndione, E. S. (1993 [1st ed. 1987]) *Dakar, une société en grappe.* Paris: Éditions Karthala and Dakar: Enda Graf.

Ndione, E. S. (1994) *L'économie urbaine en Afrique—Le don et le recours*. Paris: Éditions Karthala–Dakar : Enda Graf Sahel.

Razafindrakoto, M. and F. Roubaud (2005) *Gouvernance, démocratie et lutte contre la pauvreté en Afrique: Expérience et point de vue de la population de huit métropoles. Enquêtes 1-2-3, Premiers résultats.* Développement, institutions et analyse de long terme. http://www.dial.prd.fr/dial_publications/PDF/Doc_travail/2005-18.pdf, accessed on November 11, 2008.

Reis, E. P. and M. Moore (2005) *Elite Perceptions of Poverty and Inequality.* London: Zed Books.

Rowntree, B. S. (1901) *Poverty: A Study in Town Life.* London: Macmillan.

Rowntree, B. S. and M. Kendall (1913) *How the Labourer Lives: A Study of the Rural Labour Problem.* London: Nelson.

Rowntree, B. S. (1941) *Poverty and Progress: A Second Social Survey of York.* London: Longman's.

Rowntree, B. S. and G. R. Lavers (1951) *Poverty and the Welfare State: A Third Social Survey of York Dealing Only with Economic Questions.* London: Longman's, Green, and Co.

Rutherford, S. (2002) *Comment les pauvres gèrent leur argent.* Paris: Éditions Gret-Karthala.

Sarr, A. P. (2009) "Transferts de fonds des migrants et développement en Afrique: Une étude de cas sur le Sénégal," *Techniques Financières et Développement* 95 (2): 15–27. http://www.oecd.org/dataoecd/30/49/43912387.pdf, accessed on October 25, 2009.

Schuerkens, U. (2003) "The Sociological and Anthropological Study of Globalization and Localization," *Current Sociology* 51 (3–4, 1/2): 209–222.

Schuerkens, U. (ed.) (2008). *Globalization and Transformations of Local Socioeconomic Practices.* New York and London: Routledge.

Sen, A. (2003) *Un nouveau modèle économique.* Paris: Odile Jacob.

Silla, O. (1968) *Structure familiale et mentalité religieuse des Lébou du Sénégal.* Notes Africaines, 119, Dakar: IFAN.

Simmel, G. (1998 [1907]) *Les pauvres.* Paris: PUF-Quadrige.

Sylla, A. (1992) *Le peuple Lébou de la presqu'île du Cap-Vert.* Dakar: Les Nouvelles Editions Africaines du Sénégal–NEAS (NEA).

Tall, S. M. (2002) "L'émigration internationale sénégalaise d'hier à demain," in M. C. Diop (ed.) *La société sénégalaise. Entre le local et le global,* 549–578. Paris: Khartala.

Tall, S. M. (2005) "The Remittances of Senegalese Migrants: A Tool for Development?" in T. Manuh (ed.) *At Home in the Worlds? International Migration and Development in Contemporary Ghana and West Africa,* 153–170. Accra: Sub-Saharan Publishers.

Other Studies

Banque Centrale des États de l'Afrique de l'Ouest (BCEAO) (2009) *Balance des Paiements et Position Extérieure Globale du Sénégal au titre de l'année 2007.* Dakar.

Direction de la Prévision et de la Statistique (DPS) and Programme des Nations Unies pour le Développement (PNUD), Département des Affaires Économiques et Sociales (DAES), (2001) *La perception de la pauvreté au Sénégal: volet statistique.* Preliminary version, November 2001. Project SEN/99/003. http://www.ansd.sn/publications/DSRP/Perception.pdf, accessed on April 10, 2009.

Ministère de l'Économie et des Finances (MEF) (1997) *Rapport de synthèse de l'enquête sénégalaise auprès des ménages.* Dakar.

Ministère de l'Économie et des Finances (MEF) (2000) *Ciblages des communautés rurales selon le niveau d'accès aux services sociaux de base.* Dakar.

Ministère de l'Économie et des Finances (MEF) (2000) *Rapport de synthèse de l'enquête sénégalaise auprès des ménages.* Dakar.

Ministère de l'Économie et des Finances (MEF) (2001) *Document de Stratégie de Réduction de la Pauvreté.* Dakar.

Ministère de l'Économie et des Finances (MEF) (2004) *La pauvreté au Sénégal: de la dévaluation de 1994 à 2001–2002.* Preliminary version, January 2004. http://www.ansd.sn/publications/DSRP/Pauvrete4.pdf, accessed on January 10, 2009.

Ministère de l'Économie et des Finances (MEF) (2007) *Situation économique et sociale de la région de DAKAR—Année 2006.* Dakar. http://www.ansd.sn/publications/annuelles/SES_Region/SES_Dakar_2006.pdf, accessed on February 14, 2009.

Ministère de l'Économie et des Finances (MEF) (2008) *Impacts des transferts des migrants sur la pauvreté au Sénégal.* Report prepared by Y. S. Diagne and F. Diane. Document d'Étude n° 7, Dakar. http://www.dpee.sn/pages/resume.php?id=73, accessed on January 11, 2009.

SENAGROSOL (*Cabinet d'études spécialisé en développement rural, urbanisme et génie civil*). (2009) *Senegal Survey National Synthetic Report.* http://web.worldbank.org/WBSITE/EXTERNAL/TOPICS/EXTPOVERTY/EXTMOVO UTPOV/0,,contentMDK:21449189~menuPK:5902056~pagePK:148956~piPK:216618~theSitePK:2104396,00.html, accessed on July 30, 2009.

United Nations Development Program (UNDP) (2007) *Human Development Report 2007/2008: Fighting Climate Change: Human Solidarity in a Divided World.* New York: Palgrave Macmillan.

United Nations Development Program (UNDP) (2008) *Migration au Sénégal— Dynamique et Orientations Stratégiques.* Report prepared by O. Ndoye and L. J. Grégoire, 2/2008. Unité de Politiques et d'Analyses Stratégiques, Dakar.

United Nations Development Program (UNDP) (2009) *Human Development Report 2009: Overcoming Barriers: Human Mobility and Development.* New York: Palgrave Macmillan.

World Bank (2000) *World Development Report 2000/2001. Attacking Poverty.* Oxford and New York: Oxford University Press.

Contributors

Nina Bandelj is associate professor of sociology and faculty associate at the Center for the Study of Democracy, University of California, Irvine. Her research in economic and comparative sociology, social change, political economy, and culture has been published in *Social Forces, Current Sociology, Sociological Forum,* and *East European Politics and Societies,* among others. She is the author of *From Communists to Foreign Capitalists: The Social Foundations of Foreign Direct Investment in Post-socialist Europe* (Princeton, Princeton University Press, 2008) and *Economic Sociology of Work* (ed.) (West Yorkshire, Emerald Publishing, 2009). E-mail address: nbandelj@uci.edu.

Adeyinka Oladayo Bankole obtained a PhD in sociology at the University of Ibadan, Nigeria. He is currently senior lecturer in sociology at the Redeemer's University, Department of Behavioral Studies, College of Management Sciences, Nigeria. His areas of research include sociology of development, organizational sociology, entrepreneurship, and social policy with focus on Nigeria. He was a UNESCO Fellow and MacArthur Foundation–University of Ibadan Scholar at the University of Warsaw, Poland. Some of his publications include: "Privatization Policy and Social Security in Africa" in I. Łęcka (ed.) *Społeczne Skutki Globalizacji—Globalizacja a Bezpieczeństwo i Zdrowie Publiczne* (IKR-WGiSR, Uniwersytet Warszawskiego, 2005); "What Hope for Africa's Development in the 21st Century? Some Comments by an African Sociologist," *Africana Bulletin* (2007, 55); and, with E. Puchnarewicz, *NGOs, International Aid and Development in the South* (Warsaw, University of Warsaw Press, 2008). E-mail address: adebanks@yahoo.com.

Djallal Gérard Heuzé is *directeur de recherche* at the CNRS, *Centre d'anthropologie* of Toulouse (LISST). He published recently: *D'intouchable à Dalit* (Paris: Aux lieux d'être, 2006); (with V. Dupont) *La ville en Asie du Sud* (Paris: Editions de l'École des Hautes Études en Sciences Sociales, 2007); *Les mots de l'Inde* (Toulouse: Presses universitaires du Mirail, 2008). E-mail address: djallal.heuze@wanadoo.fr.

Anete Brito Leal Ivo holds a PhD in Sociology (Federal University of Pernambuco, Brazil). She is associate professor (Federal University of Bahia, Brazil), professor (Catholic University of Salvador), and research fellow at the *Centro de Recursos Humanos*. She was visiting professor of the Simon Bolivar Chair, University of Paris III and at the University of Paris XII. She is the editor of the social sciences review *Caderno CRH* (Brazil). Her research fields include the social issue, poverty, inequalities in Brazil/Latin America, and democracy. Main publications: *Metamorfose da Questão democrática* (Buenos Aires: CLACSO, 2001); "A urban governance e as políticas sociais," in A. Ziccardi (ed.) *Participación Ciudadana y Políticas Sociales.* (Mexico: UNAM/COMECSO, 2004); "The Redefinition of the Social Issue and the Rhetoric on Poverty," in A. Cimadamore, H. Dean, J. Siqueira (eds) *The Poverty of the State* (Buenos Aires: CLASCO/CROP, 2005); "La destitución de lo social," *Estudios Sociológicos* (23, 2005); *Viver por um fio: pobreza e política social* (São Paulo: Annablume, 2008). E-mail address: anetivo@hotmail.com.

Ruthy Nadia Laniado holds a PhD in Political Science (University of Essex, UK), is associate professor (Federal University of Bahia, Brazil) and research fellow of the World Politics Studies Laboratory (Bahia, Brazil). She was a visiting fellow at the Center of Latin American Studies (University of Cambridge, UK). Her research interests are social movements, social justice, human rights, political culture, and democracy. Her main publications include: "As fronteiras da política democrática," in P. H. Martins, A. Mattos, B. Fontes (ed.) *Limites da democracia* (Recife, UFPE, 2008); (with C. Milani) "Solidarités environnementales, contestation transnationale et renouvellement de la politique mondiale," *Lien social et politiques* (Montréal: Saint-Martin, 2007); (with C. Milani) "Transnational social movements and the globalization agenda," *Brazilian Political Science Review* (1, 2, 2007); (with C. Milani) "Espaço mundial e ordem política contemporânea," *Cadernos do CRH* (19, 2006); "Troca e reciprocidade no campo da cultura política," *Revista Sociedade e Estado*, Brasília (16, 1–2, 2001). E-mail address: ruthy.laniado@gmail.com.

Ilse Lenz is professor for social structure and gender at the Faculty of Social Science and co-opted Professor at the Faculty for East-Asian Studies at Ruhr-University Bochum, Germany. Her research interests include globalization, gender and work, labor markets, and gender relations in Japan and Germany, the new women's movement in Germany and Japan, and complex inequalities of gender, class, and migration. Among her recent English publications are (with Ch. Ullrich and B. Fersch) *Gender Orders Unbound. Globalisation, Restructuring and Reciprocity* (Opladen, Budrich, 2007); "Globalization, Varieties of Gender Regimes, and Regulations for Gender Equality at Work," in H. Gottfried *et al.*

(eds) *Gendering the Knowledge Economy: Comparative Perspectives* (London: Palgrave 2007); "Global Gender Policy: Differences and Convergence in Transnational Women's Networks," in U. Ruppert *et al.* (eds) *Beyond the Merely Possible. International Women's Movements.* (London, Zed Press, 2009); "Transnational Social Movement Networks and Transnational Public Spaces: Glocalizing Gender Justice," in L. Pries (ed.) *Rethinking Transnationalism. The Meso-link of Organisations* (London and New York: Routledge, 2008). E-mail address: ilse.lenz@ruhr-uni-bochum.de.

Matthew Mahutga is assistant professor of sociology and associate director of the Institute for Research on the World-System at the University of California, Riverside. His research interests include quantitative macro-comparative sociology, economic development, global political economy, and requisite quantitative methods. Past research includes studies of the relationship between globalization and changes to the international division of labor, the effect of foreign direct investment on income inequality and pollution, and advances in macro-comparative social network methods. Current projects examine the emergence of global production networks and their contribution to economic growth and labor market inequalities cross-nationally. His research has been published in the *International Journal of Comparative Sociology, Social Forces, Social Problems* and elsewhere. E-mail address: matthew.mahutga@ucr.edu.

Katharina Manderscheid holds a PhD in Sociology and is currently working as a lecturer and researcher at the Department of Sociology in Luzerne, Switzerland. She is also affiliated to the Center for Mobilities Research, Department of Sociology at Lancaster University, UK. Her present research focuses on the links and inter-relations between social inequality, mobilities, and space against the background of climate change and implications of the sustainability paradigm. In particular, she is working on the theoretical integration of these three strands, on an empirical comparison of socio-spatial inequalities and mobility patterns in different countries, as well as on the discursive production of socio-spatial inequalities within the field of policy and planning. Recent publications in English: "Integrating Space and Mobilities into the Analysis of Social Inequality," *Distinktion* (18, 2009); "Unequal Mobilities," in H. Maksim, T. Ohnmacht, and M. M. Bergman (eds) *Mobilities and Inequality* (Aldershot, Ashgate, 2008). E-mail address: k.manderscheid@lancaster.ac.uk.

Susana Melo is an ESRC-funded PhD candidate at the Center for Globalization, Education, and Societies, University of Bristol, UK. Her on-going research project focuses on the Bologna Process and the efforts made to create a European dimension in education, comparing the role of two different actors: the Council of Europe and the European Union. She has got teaching experience in European Union–sponsored adult education programs in Budapest, Lisbon, and Barcelona. E-mail address: edsjdm@ bristol.ac.uk.

Eva Militaru is an economist and PhD candidate in Economics, senior researcher (3rd rank) at the National Research Institute for Labor and Social Protection, Romania. She obtained a diploma in policy analysis skills for transition economies at the Institute of Social Studies, The Hague. Her main research interests are social protection, welfare regimes, inequalities, migration, labor market participation, and vulnerable groups. Her recent research focuses on the macro- and micro-quantitative analysis of the relationship between the welfare system and labor market participation in Romania. Recent publications include: (with C. Ghinararu *et al.*) "System of Indicators for Social Protection in Romania," (*Romanian Review of Statistics*, Bucharest, 2007); (with C. Mocanu and A. M. Zamfir) "Tackling Migration for Employment in an Emergent Medium-sized Open Market Economy," in *National Human Development Report—Romania* (UNDP, Bucharest, 2007); (with C. Radu *et al.*) *Main Elements for Evaluating the Degree of Social Integration and Participation of People with Disabilities* (University Publishing House, Bucharest, 2008). E-mail address: militaru@insmps.ro.

Amandine Monteil is a PhD student at the Center for Modern and Contemporary Chinese Studies, École des Hautes Études en Sciences Sociales (EHESS), Paris. She holds a master diploma in political sciences from Sciences Po, Paris, and a master diploma in comparative development research, EHESS, Paris. Her research has been published in the journals *Outre-Terre, Monde en développement* and *Monde Chinois*. She has done field research in Chengdu (China) from 2006 to 2008. E-mail address: monteil@ehess.fr.

Cristina Mocanu is a sociologist, PhD candidate in political sciences, and senior researcher (3rd rank) at the National Research Institute for Labor and Welfare in Romania. Her recent research endeavors focus on the links between discrimination and discouraging on the labor market, multiple discriminations, labor shortages and skill needs, migration and gender issues. Main publications are: *Discriminarea Multipla in Romania* (ed., Agora Publishing House, Calarasi, Romania, 2007); (with E. Militaru, A. M. Zamfir) "Tackling Migration for Employment in an Emergent Medium-sized Open Market Economy," in *National Human Development Report—Romania* (UNDP Publishing House, Bucharest, 2007); "Romania," in (I. Kogan, M. Gebel, and C. Noelke, eds) *Europe Enlarged. A Handbook of Education, Labour and Welfare Regimes in Central and Eastern Europe* (Policy Press, Bristol, UK, 2008). E-mail address: mocanu@incsmps.ro.

Thomas Muhr is a post-doctoral fellow in socio-legal studies, School of Law, University of Bristol (UK). He completed his PhD *Venezuela: Global Counter-hegemony, Geographies of Regional Development, and Higher Education For All* in the Center for Globalization, Education, and Societies, University of Bristol, in 2008. He has worked in secondary and tertiary, formal and non-formal educational institutions in diverse socio-economic settings in Europe and Latin America and the Caribbean, especially in Nicaragua, Venezuela, and Guyana. He publishes and presents his inter-disciplinary work in several languages in academic environments as well as alternative forums worldwide. He is on the International Academic Board of the *Poetics of Resistance* network (http://poeticsofresistance. com/gl/), a reviewer for the journals *Globalisation, Societies and Education* and *In-Spire: Journal of Law, Politics and Societies*, and a contributor to the *GlobalHigherEd* blog (http://globalhighered.wordpress.com/). E-mail address: Thomas.Muhr@bristol.ac.uk.

François-Xavier de Perthuis de Laillevault is a PhD candidate associated to the Center of African Studies (CEAf) at the École des Hautes Études en Sciences Sociales, Paris, and preparing his thesis in the PhD program *Sociétés, Territoires, Développement*. He has been a consultant in the following regions: Niger: region of Zinder; Ethiopia: region of Diré Dawa; Laos: Province of Savannakhet, a border region with Vietnam and Thailand; and Indonesia, Province of Banda Aceh. The title of his doctoral thesis is *La perception de la pauvreté à Dakar (Sénégal) dans une ère de glocalisation*. His main publications are: *Zinder*, "Illustration de la crise alimentaire au Niger en 2005"; several articles published in *Panoptique*, 2007, Montreal, on the food crisis in Niger in 2005; "Poverty and visual materials" published by Ethnoweb, the Internet website of French ethnological studies, 2007 (http://www.ethno-web.com/articles.php?action=show&numart=128). Paris. E-mail address: fxperth@yahoo.fr.

Speranta Pirciog is an economist and holds a PhD in labor economy, senior researcher (1st rank), and scientific manager at the National Research Institute for Labor and Welfare in Romania. She has worked on poverty and social exclusion, income inequalities, regional development, transition from school to work, and the link between skill needs and migration for employment. Recent publications as both editor and co-author are: *Evolution of Occupations on Romanian Labour Market on 2010 Perspective* (Agora Publishing House, Calarasi, Romania, 2006); and *Decalaje Regionale privind inovarea si dezvoltarea capitalului uman in Romania* (Agora Publishing House, Calarasi, Romania, 2008). E-mail address: pirciog@incsmps.ro.

Ulrike Schuerkens has doctorates in both sociology, and social anthropology and ethnology, from the École des Hautes Études en Sciences

Sociales in Paris. She received the diploma 'Habilitation à diriger des recherches' from the University Paris V—René Descartes. Currently, she is senior lecturer at the École des Hautes Études en Sciences Sociales, Paris, France. She has published extensively on globalization, development, social change, migration, multiculturalism, and colonialism. Her latest monographs are *Globalization and Transformations of Local Socio-Economic Practices* (ed., London and New York, Routledge, 2008); *Transnational Migrations and Social Transformations (*ed., *Current Sociology, 53, 4, 2, 2005); Global Forces and Local Life-Worlds: Social Transformations* (ed., London, Thousands Oaks, New Delhi, Sage, 2004); *Changement social sous régime colonial: Du Togo allemand aux Togo et Ghana indépendants* (Paris, L'Harmattan, 2001); *Transformationsprozesse in der Elfenbeinkueste und in Ghana* (Muenster, Lit, 2001). E-mail address: Ulrike.Schuerkens@ehess.fr.

Ayse Serdar obtained a PhD degree in Sociology in 2009 at the State University of New York, Binghamton. She is a faculty member at Istanbul Technical University, Turkey. Her research interests include political economy and social movements. E-mail address: ayseserdar@yahoo.com.

Ana Maria Zamfir is a sociologist and PhD candidate in sociology and senior researcher (3rd rank) at the National Research Institute for Labor and Social Protection from Romania. Her main research topics are transitions from school to work, migration and development, social stratification, and labor market segmentation. Main publications are: (with E. Militaru and C. Mocanu) "Tackling Migration for Employment in an Emergent Medium-sized Open Market Economy," in *National Human Development Report—Romania* (UNDP Publishing House, Bucharest, 2007); (with V. Ciuca and S. Pirciog) "Tendinte si prognoze privind fenomenul migratiei pentru munca la nivel international si national," in *Migratia Fortei de Munca* (University of Bucharest Publishing House, Bucharest, Romania, 2008); (with C. Gheorghe and C. Mocanu) *Sindicatele la intersectia dintre gen si etnie* (AMM Publishing House, Cluj-Napoca, Romania, 2009). E-mail address: anazamfir@incsmps.ro.

Index